W9-CTW-760

Rhetoric and Argumentation

David L. Vancil
Colorado State University

Allyn and Bacon
Boston   London   Toronto   Sydney   Tokyo   Singapore

To Gayle

Series Editor: *Steve Hull*
Production Administrator: *Annette Joseph*
Production Coordinator: *Susan Freese*
Editorial-Production Service: *TKM Productions*
Photo Researcher: *Lynda Griffiths*
Manufacturing Buyer: *Louise Richardson*
Cover Administrator: *Linda K. Dickinson*
Cover Designer: *Suzanne Harbison*

Copyright © 1993 by Allyn and Bacon
A Division of Simon & Schuster, Inc.
160 Gould Street
Needham Heights, MA 02194

All rights reserved. No part of the material protected by this copyright notice may be reproduced or utilized in any form or by any means, electronic or mechanical, including photocopying, recording, or by any information storage and retrieval system, without the written permission of the copyright owner.

Library of Congress Cataloging-in-Publication Data

Vancil, David L.
    Rhetoric and argumentation/David L. Vancil.
        p.   cm.
    Includes bibliographical references and index.
    ISBN 0-205-13592-7
    1. Debates and debating. 2. Persuasion (Rhetoric). 3. Rhetoric.
I. Title.
PN4181.V36   1993   93-9839
808.53—dc20   CIP

Printed in the United States of America

10 9 8 7 6 5 4 3 2 1   97 96 95 94 93 92

Photo credits: Pages 8 and 245: North Wind Picture Archives; pages 240 and 241: The Bettmann Archive.

Contents

Preface   ix

1   ***The Study of Rhetoric and Argumentation***   **1**

The Nature of Conflict   2

Responses to Conflict   4

The Nature of Rhetoric   5
The Study of Persuasion   7
A Power of Discerning   7

Elements of Rhetoric: The Modes of Proof   9
Ethos: Proof Based on the Speaker   9
Pathos: Proof Based on the Audience   13
Logos: Proof Based on the Message   16

The Focus of Rhetoric and Argumentation   19

Summary   20

Exercises   21

Endnotes   22

2   ***The Anatomy of Controversy***   **23**

Central Questions   25

Types of Central Questions   26
Questions of Fact   26
Questions of Value   30
Questions of Policy   33
Ways of Expressing Central Questions   34
Principles for Phrasing Central Questions   35

Issues   38
Relationship of Issues and Central Questions   38
Elements of Issues   38

Arguments, Premises, and Evidence   41
Arguments   42
Premises   45

Evidence   48

Summary   49

Exercises   50

Endnotes   51

3   *Methods for Analyzing Controversies*   53

Models for Discovering Issues   54

Stasis Model   55
Four Stasis Issues   55
Applying the Stasis Model   59

Stock Issues Model   62
The Principal Stock Issues   63
Understanding the Logos of the Model   64
Subordinate Stock Issues   67
Three Categories of Issues: Potential, Contested,
and Admitted   69
Using the Stock Issues   70

The Relationship of Stock Issues and Stasis Models   73

Summary   74

Exercises   75

Endnotes   76

4   *The Research Process*   79

The Focus of Research   80
Issues Focus Research   81
Key Elements in the Context of a Controversy   82

How to Find Research Materials   86

Reading and Recording Research Material   90
Efficient Reading   90
Recording Evidence   91

Summary   92

Exercises   94

**5   *Rhetorical Argument: The Logic of*
Good Reasons   95**

The Nature of Rhetorical Argument   97
The Claim   98
Good Reasons   99

The Structure of Rhetorical Argument   101
   General Tests of Argument   102
   Inductive Reasoning   104
   Deductive Reasoning   112
   Toulmin's Critique of Induction and Deduction   120
Summary   125
Exercises   128
Endnotes   129

6 *Analysis of Forms of Argument* 131

Argument by Example   133
   The Form of Argument by Example   134
   Tests for Argument by Example   136
Argument by Analogy   138
   The Form of Argument by Analogy   138
   Tests for Argument by Analogy   141
Argument by Causal Correlation   143
   The Form of Argument by Causal Correlation   143
   Tests for Argument by Causal Correlation   147
Argument by Sign   149
   The Form of Argument by Sign   149
   Tests for Argument by Sign   152
Argument by Causal Application   154
   The Form of Argument by Causal Application   154
   Tests for Argument by Causal Application   157
Argument by Applied Generalization   158
   The Form of Argument by Applied Generalization   158
   Tests for Argument by Applied Generalization   160
Summary   161
Exercises   165
Endnotes   167

7 *Testing Evidence and Premises* 169

Tests of Value Premises   170
   The So What? Test   171
   The Value Comparison Test   174
   The Value Application or Interpretation Test   176
Testing Evidence and Factual Premises   177
Tests of the Evidence-Claim Relationship   178

Test of Assertion   179
Test of Relevance   180
Test of Recency   182
Test of Sufficiency   183
Tests of the Evidence Source   184
Test of Identification   185
Test of Expertise   187
Test of Bias   190
Tests of the Evidence Substance   192
Test of Integrity   192
Test of Context   193
Test of Consistency   193
Tests of Statistical Evidence   195
Summary   201
Exercises   203
Endnotes   204

8 *Organizing the Analysis: The Brief*   **207**

Developing the Brief   208
Rules for Constructing a Brief   211
Illustrative Brief   214
Summary   221
Exercises   222

9 *Procedural Rules in Advocacy*   **223**

Constitutive and Regulative Rules   224
Constitutive Rules Define Elements   225
Regulative Rules Govern Behavior   227
Presumption and Burden of Proof   229
Presumption   230
Burden of Proof   232
Applying Rules of Presumption and Burden of Proof   235
Rules for Debate   239
*Debate Should Provide Light Rather Than
    Merely Heat*   242
*Debate Should Focus Disagreement Over a
    Central Question*   242
Debate Rules Should Be Perceived as Fair   243
Time Available for Debate Is Always Limited   244

Rules for the Presentation of Evidence and Argument Should
Be Adapted to the Purpose of the Debate   246
Debate Formats Should Foster a Productive Clash   247
Summary   248
Exercises   250
Endnotes   250

10   *Building Affirmative Cases in Debate*   **251**

Criteria for Affirmative Cases   252
Persuasion and Time Criteria   252
Burden of Proof and Persuasion   253
Affirmative Cases for Policy Questions   254
Traditional Needs Case   254
The Comparative Advantages Case   258
Affirmative Cases for Fact and Value Questions   263
The Conjectural Case   264
The Definitional Case   265
Using Audience Beliefs in Fact and Value Cases   267
Summary   268
Exercises   269
Endnotes   270

11   *Building Negative Cases in Debate*   **271**

Principles for Negative Case Construction   272
The Negative Has the Advantage of Presumption   273
Negative Argumentation Is a Response to an
Affirmative Attack   274
The Negative Can Prevail by Winning One Issue   275
Four Negative Case Strategies for Policy Questions   277
Defense of the Present System   277
Repair of the Present System   281
Straight Refutation   284
Counterproposal   286
Negative Case Strategies for Questions of Fact
and Value   290
The Conjectural Case Strategy   291
The Definitional Case Strategy   292
Summary   295
Exercises   296
Endnote   296

**12   Rhetoric and Argumentation in
      Social Conflict   297**

The Nature of Conflict   299
   Issue Conflict   299
   Hostility Conflict   300
   Two Differences Between Issue and Hostility Conflict   303
   Kinds of Conflict versus Harmfulness of Conflict   307
Methods of Conflict Termination   308
   Avoidance   309
   Conquest   311
   Reconciliation   314
   Compromise   316
   Award   318
   Chance Mechanisms   320
Termination Methods and Kinds of Conflict   322
   Useful Termination Methods for Issue Conflict   322
   Useful Termination Methods for Hostility Conflict   322
   *Uses and Limitations of Debate in
      Terminating Conflict*   323
Summary   325
Exercises   327
Endnotes   328

Appendix A   Sample Bibliography   331

Appendix B   Correct Rebuttal Form   332

**Appendix C   Debate Format and
   Speaker Responsibilities   337**

**Appendix D   A Public Policy Debate: Should the
   Equal Rights Amendment Be Ratified?   348**

**Appendix E   Argument and Evidence Brief
   by James H. Joy, III   371**

Index   381

Preface ━━━━━━━━━━━━━━

One of the most gratifying developments in the current ferment over core curricula in higher education is the broad consensus that every student needs to be competent in argumentation and critical thinking. As the dean of my college stated, *"All* students should be able to draw upon their education and argue persuasively; they should be able to analyze complex public controversies, distinguish sound from unsound arguments, and evaluate evidence. In other words, all students need to master the principles and skills of a good argumentation class."

Rhetoric and Argumentation is intended for undergraduate students in introductory courses in argumentation and debate. The aim is to present the essential principles and methods of argumentation as simply and clearly as possible. I am especially interested in reaching the vast majority of students who need to develop competency as advocates but have never seen a debate before taking an argumentation class. Such students often feel some anxieties about the very idea of submitting their arguments to scrutiny and refutation. But the text is also aimed at deepening the understanding of students who have a practical debate background yet never got around to examining the theory underlying their practices (and mistakes). With both groups, my aim is to awaken their interest and to build confidence in their abilities to understand and apply the core principles of argumentation. Wherever possible, I have tried to write in an engaging style and to provide examples that are clear and interesting to students.

The title *Rhetoric and Argumentation* is an expression of my central theme, and it is also a way of calling attention to five central premises that inform its development. My first premise is that argumentation is inherently rhetorical; it has a dynamic relationship to dialectic, politics, and law, but the aim of argument is always to influence an audience. Chapter 1 examines the general connections between rhetoric and argumentation and explicates the Aristotelian definition of rhetoric as the unifying perspective for the central concepts of argumentation.

My second premise is that the functions of persuasive argumentation and the place of debate in society become clear when we examine their relationships to the principal kinds of conflict and the primary modes of conflict termination. This relationship is introduced in Chapter 1 and explored in depth in Chapter 12, but it is important throughout—especially in the discussions of central questions and issues in Chapter 2 and the analysis of the "good reasons" concept of argument in Chapter 5.

Third, I believe that students must learn to evaluate the substantive elements in issue conflicts in order to master the art of argumentation. Chapters 2 and 3 develop principles for evaluating central questions and issues. Chapter 4 outlines the process of research and examines six elements in the context of controversy over central questions. Chapter 5 explains Karl Wallace's "good reasons" concept of rhetorical argument and explores the traditional concepts of inductive and deductive reasoning, the Toulmin model, and Aristotle's enthymeme. Chapter 6 analyzes six common forms of argument and provides students with criteria for testing them. Chapter 7 examines tests for value premises and evidence as the "good reasons" substance of argument support. Chapter 8 explains the argument brief as a primary means of synthesizing the substance of research and analysis.

My fourth premise is that the process of advocacy is governed by formal and informal rules that spring from the situation and audience. Rules of presumption and burden of proof, for example, are potentially important in any issue conflict, but their effect varies profoundly as we move from the courtroom to the family dispute. Procedural rules in advocacy, the topic of Chapter 9, provide a way of analyzing the process of advocacy. This discussion provides the foundation of Chapter 10, on affirmative cases, and Chapter 11, on negative case strategies.

Finally, in common with everyone I know in the argumentation community, I am committed to the process of argumentation and advocacy as the foundation of citizenship and a free society. It undergirds our most precious freedoms and it fosters the improvement of the human society. If argumentation professionals seem to have an almost evangelistic zeal for its principles, it is because we believe that they enable students to find unity and purpose in a liberal education.

In addition to the illustrations and case studies presented in the text, each chapter begins with an initial outline of central ideas and concludes with a numbered summary of chapter contents to assist student review. Individual and class exercises help students to apply the principles and methods.

Acknowledgments

I owe my thanks to a rather large number of colleagues, former teachers, students, and many others who helped make this book possible. First, I wish to acknowledge the assistance of my reviewers for their many helpful suggestions: Michael Allen, University of Wisconsin, Milwaukee; Richard Crable, Purdue University and Lafayette University; John Gossett, North Texas State University; Carl Heidel, Michigan State University; Robert Kully, California State University, Los Angeles; Bruce Landis, University of Akron; Ronald Matlon, Towson State University; and Gene Yahrmatter, Eastern Michigan University. Their perceptive comments and questions were most helpful, and I appreciate their support.

At Allyn and Bacon, I am especially grateful for the patience and support of my editor, Steve Hull. He and his assistants, Amy Capute and Brenda Conaway, were consistently helpful and congenial, and I deeply appreciate their encouragement.

At Colorado State University, several of my colleagues read the manuscript in its early stages and provided perceptive comments. Carl Burgchardt, Karen Whedbee, and Brenda Kuseski were especially generous with their suggestions and their willingness to teach from a text in progress. James Irvine, Jack Gravlee, and Ann Gill provided cheerful emotional support throughout this project. In addition, a large number of former students and debaters have contributed to my thinking over the years, and they have always encouraged me by their intuitive understanding of academic community.

Finally, I am deeply grateful to former teachers: Jimmie Trent, Karl Wallace, and George Ziegelmueller.

1

The Study of Rhetoric and Argumentation

Central Ideas in This Chapter

1. Persuasive argumentation is a response to conflict.
2. Conflict is an intrinsic feature of human society.
   - We are uncertain about what is real.
   - We disagree about what is good.
   - We dispute about what should be done.
3. Persuasive argument is the preferred response to conflict in democratic societies.
4. Many people have misconceptions about rhetoric.
   - Rhetoric is the study of persuasion.
   - Rhetoric is a power of discerning.
5. The elements of rhetoric are modes of proof.
   - Ethos is proof based on the speaker.
   - Pathos is proof based on the audience.
   - Logos is proof based on the message.
6. To master the skills of argumentation is to understand the kinds of conflict, the crucial elements in a dispute, and the nature of persuasive argument.

Rhetoric and Argumentation is a book about the rational elements of persuasion and conflict. In any situation where there is *conflict* among competing beliefs or actions and where there is also perceived *choice,* all of us need to be able to make sense of the rational elements of persuasion—that is, the arguments that are presented as "good reasons" why we should believe something is true, or good, or a wise course of action. As Aristotle noted more than 2,000 years ago in ancient Greece, we do not try to persuade with argument where there is no sense of choice. Argument serves no purpose if only one course of action is possible. Likewise, if everyone agrees that something is true, there is no role for persuasive argument. Rather, we argue and attempt to persuade others when we disagree about what is true or false, good or bad, or the best course of action.

Does this seem rather abstract? Probably. But we can readily understand Aristotle's point if we examine some of the primary situations where people use argument to persuade others. Attorneys in the courtroom furnish us with one familiar arena where there is a great deal of persuasive argument and disagreement over a central question in dispute. Suppose the central question is whether the defendant, John Hinckley, Jr., is guilty of attempting to assassinate former President Reagan. If the defense attorney were to agree with the prosecuting attorney that Hinckley is guilty of the crime as charged, there would be no need for argument. The trial would be over. Likewise, if the prosecution agreed with the defense that Hinckley is not guilty (agreeing, say, that he was clearly insane when he shot Reagan), there would be no dispute over the central question, and persuasive argument would serve no purpose.

The Nature of Conflict

Uncertainty, a perception of choice, and conflict are clearly preconditions for using argument to persuade. But what are we uncertain about, and what do we mean by *conflict?* For many people, the general notions of conflict and argument seem to be associated with the unpleasant things in life, like having fights with family members and friends. Because most of us want peace and harmony in our lives, conflict is generally thought of as something we want to avoid. It is easy to see evidence of this tendency in almost any social setting. Family members, for example, often choose to avoid the discussion of topics that touch a nerve, disrupting the otherwise harmonious relationships everyone prefers. Taboo topics vary from family to family, of course. In some families, the problem topics may concern religious or moral issues. Other families may avoid political topics or even such mundane matters as the clothing or hairstyles of their younger members. Similarly, when they are in the workplace, employees often feel pressure to avoid controversial topics—except for those that may be considered safe, such as who will win the Super Bowl.

In a vague sort of way, many people think of conflict as an abnormal as well as unpleasant phenomenon and believe it results only when the normal and preferred ways of getting along in a group or community break down. According to this way of thinking, conflict is a sort of illness, and an ideal, healthy society or family would not be troubled with it. Apparently, an ideal human society would utilize something called *good communication* to prevent conflict from ever occurring, sort of like the notion that a sufficient intake of vitamin C will prevent the common cold. Thus, as this way of thinking would have it, parents and children in an ideal family would never disagree on the importance of school, the value of a clean room, going to bed on time, and what is the best (and worst) sort of music. In a perfect society, people would never argue about tax increases, land use, gun control, or the elections of officials. And if we could be so perfect, not even diplomats would argue. The nations of the world would never disagree over territory or trade.

As you may have guessed, I do not share this view. Apart from my intuition that a world or community without differences of opinion would be unbearably boring, I agree with the noted conflict theorist, Lewis Coser, that conflict is an inherent feature of human society—*any* human society.[1] We can easily find convincing evidence for this position by examining our own experience. All of us have experienced internal conflict as we try to decide (1) what is actually real, (2) what is good or bad, and (3) what actions we should take or reject as we try to attain the good or avoid what is evil or harmful.

The first sort of question that inevitably provokes conflict within us is the question What is really *real* or *true?* None of us can escape the problem of trying to decide what is true or false on a wide range of questions where the facts always seem to be uncertain or incomplete. For some students, the most bothersome questions are concerned with uncertainty about what is true on a very personal level: Can I pass this course? Is my boyfriend (or girlfriend) faithful to me? Will I be able to pay my tuition if I buy this car? These are important questions to anyone who is troubled by them, but our uncertainties are not confined merely to questions about what is true on the personal level. Consider, for example, some of the controversial questions about what is true in the medical arena: Can the dreaded disease AIDS be transmitted by kissing? Does the sugar substitute aspartame cause cancer? Does marijuana use lead to loss of memory? Can the use of steroids cause sterility?

Clearly, if we experience conflict over questions about what is actually real or true, we are even more likely to experience conflict over questions about what is good or bad, what is desirable or undesirable, or what we should do. Such internal conflict is universal among all normal, thinking humans.

There are, of course, different kinds of conflict, and we will explore its varieties in later chapters. Here, it is enough to understand that even if conflict is construed narrowly, as any sense of disagreement or uncertainty about alternative choices, it is an intrinsic feature of the human condition.

Responses to Conflict

Notice that my use of the term *conflict* here does not necessarily include the idea of violence. Unfortunately, violence is always a possible response to conflict, and it seems to be the preferred option for the participants in some conflicts. Witness, for example, the terrible violence between Catholic and Protestant groups in Northern Ireland or the battles among various branches of the Islamic faith, such as the Sunni and the Shiite Muslim groups. Over the centuries, participants in many religious disagreements seemingly have preferred to kill each other in response to their theological conflicts. As Mark Twain put it, the people involved in some of these religious disputes have evidently decided to carry their quarrels to a higher court! But a nonviolent option is always available if the participants really want one.

Although we do not always have a choice as to whether we will have conflict, we usually can choose how we will respond to it. There are at least three ways of responding to a conflict:

1. We can try to *avoid* it (or perhaps ignore it).
2. We can attempt to *force* our position, perhaps in the style of the Old West, by shooting it out with our opponent (or by some other kind of force).
3. We may discuss our differences and try to manage or resolve conflict through the use of *persuasion.*

Avoidance, of course, is not always possible or desirable. Likewise, violence or force may seem to be the easy way of responding to conflict, but it is a risky option. Moreover, the use of force is often accompanied by the questionable assumption that might equals right or that the side with superior power really knows what is best.

The difference between totalitarian and democratic societies is perhaps nowhere more apparent and important than in their response to disagreement. Nations with totalitarian governments generally rely on force as a primary way to settle disputes: The governments merely impose their decision, and there is little tolerance for disagreement. Totalitarian rulers typically assume that they know what is true and good and therefore should make all of the important decisions for society. Opposing arguments are not permitted.

Democratic societies, however, are fundamentally opposed to the idea that any group has a monopoly on truth. If a degree of uncertainty about what is true or good is obvious in many cases, as I have argued, then no one can honestly claim certain knowledge of all controversial questions. Even our foremost experts cannot claim certainty in their predictions about what will happen in the future. Therefore, how should we decide when there is disagreement over what course of action will solve our problems?

The preferred response in democratic societies is that all viewpoints should be heard. Especially in our courts and legislative bodies, we believe we are more likely to discover what is true or wise by listening to a clash of opposing arguments. If a defendant is guilty, the prosecutor should be able to convince a jury with good reasons, despite the best efforts of the defense to argue otherwise. If a proposed law is wise, its supporters will be able to demonstrate its wisdom and convince other lawmakers with persuasive arguments.

However, despite its importance in democratic society, the use of persuasive argument is for most people an uncertain business. We realize that we need to support our claims, but most of us know very little about the principles of persuasive argument. As a result, efforts to present a persuasive case are frequently an exercise in trial and error, and the errors can be costly. Fortunately, there is an art that is especially concerned with the principles and methods of persuasion: the art of rhetoric.

The Nature of Rhetoric

The term *rhetoric* conjures up a variety of images these days, and most of these images are somewhat negative in a vague sort of way. Politicians, using rather self-righteous tones, refer to the "empty rhetoric" of their opponents. Journalists (who ought to know better) oppose the idea of "mere rhetoric" to action. And the stereotypical sophomore uses rhetoric as a kind of heavy artillery to fire against the ideas or arguments of any available opponent!

You may have noticed that the meaning of *rhetoric* in each of these instances is hardly clear. It seems to serve merely as a simplistic term of disapproval or as a way to give the user an air of

RHETORICA

sophistication or an aura of moral superiority. We can find no fault
with the position that all of us should oppose sham arguments and
pretense. But such pejorative uses of the term *rhetoric* are objection-
able because they misuse a valuable word and are uninformative.
They seem comparable to the empty bombast of some politicians
who profess to be in favor of "truth and the American way"—that is,
they seem to mean something profound only to the uneducated.

If rhetoric really signified nothing more than empty talk or fallacious reasoning, someone might reasonably ask (as someone did
ask me at a social gathering): Why would *anyone* want to study *that*?
This is a fair question except that it springs from a pervasive mis-
conception of the meaning of rhetoric. So we must begin our answer
by gently informing the questioner of his or her ignorance. (I say
"gently" because we should always keep in mind Will Rogers' observation that "we are all ignorant—just on different subjects.")

The Study of Persuasion

For more than 2,000 years, rhetoric has been the study of persuasive communication, and especially the sort of persuasion that is based on argumentation and debate. The fascination with effective argumentation runs deep in the ancient Greek world. Homer's *Iliad*, for example, which dates from the eighth century B.C. contains dramatic examples of advocates arguing persuasively in the deliberative councils of warriors. In order to achieve heroic status, according to the Homeric ideal, a warrior had to be "a speaker of words" as well as a "doer of deeds." Even the hero Achilles was required to learn the skills of argumentation in order to participate in "debate, where men are made preeminent." Thus, it is not surprising that the first treatise on rhetoric, written by Corax in the fifth century B.C., was designed to teach a systematic method of persuasive argument for advocates in the courtroom. Even ordinary citizens were expected to speak in their own behalf in the courtroom, whether they were prosecuting or defending.

Notice that the focus of this long-term study is not manipulative or unethical persuasion, as some of the misinformed usages of rhetoric suggest—but *all* persuasive communication that is initiated in response to conflict or the need to make a decision. Of course, someone might claim that we are conceding at least some of the negative connotations of rhetoric since "all persuasion" necessarily includes unethical tactics, but that is a rather silly complaint. Would anyone seriously maintain that we do not need to be able to recognize deceitful persuasion or to develop defenses against it? An analysis of unethical methods of persuasion neither promotes nor encourages their use. On the contrary, we are more likely to fall victim to corrupt advocates if we are ignorant of the tricks they have in their arsenals. A comprehensive study of persuasive communication, which is the chief focus of rhetoric, can only enhance our critical abilities. Rhetoric fosters self-defense; it enables us to recognize fallacious reasoning and to see ways of defending ourselves against unethical methods of persuasion.

A Power of Discerning

Initially, the most important thing to understand about rhetoric is that it shares an important feature with all the arts: It helps us to *see* things we did not see before. It is an art of perceiving and understanding persuasive discourse. If it seems strange to think of rhetoric as an art of seeing, we need only to consider how other arts increase our perception in relation to their special provinces. A friend of mine, who is a painter, maintains that anyone can paint

Aristotle

landscapes or portraits if he or she learns how to really *see* the world around him or her. The principles of perspective, form, color, and texture enable a painter to execute on a canvas what is perceived in his or her mind's eye. The core of the painter's art is a way of seeing the world.

All knowledge, when it is applied, becomes an art of seeing the world around us in a more perceptive way. Have you ever had the experience of walking in the fragile world of the tundra, the land above the tree line in the high mountains, with a knowledgeable botanist? During the brief summer of the high country, the tundra transforms itself from a rather dull-appearing lawn into a magnificent carpet of diminutive flowers. Anyone ignorant of botany, like me, might notice lots of little yellow and white flowers as one walks the trails through the tundra. But my botanist friend *sees* and can identify literally hundreds of distinct species. His knowledge enables him to see the condition of the tundra and dozens of other things that are functionally invisible to me.

From the earliest efforts of the ancient Greeks to articulate the principles of rhetoric, rhetoricians have understood that an art of rhetoric enables its practitioners to see things about persuasion that are functionally invisible to others. Notice the emphasis on seeing things in the definition of *rhetoric* proposed by Aristotle in 336 B.C. Rhetoric is "the faculty of discerning in every case the available means of persuasion."[2] The term *faculty* means the ability or power to do something. The term *discerning* means to perceive, or to see in an intellectual sense, by recognizing with the mind.

Aristotle thought of rhetoric as an art that enables its user to discern the possible means for persuading another person or audience in any situation. Just as my botanist friend can recognize all of the tiny plants on the tundra and can inform me of their wonderful abilities to endure extreme drought and harsh sunlight, the rhetorician should be able to recognize persuasive tactics and arguments in a variety of settings, no matter how subtle, even though such tactics or arguments might be invisible to others. Moreover, the capacity to do all of this should be based on principles that can be explained and learned by others in a systematic way.

Elements of Rhetoric: The Modes of Proof

Aristotle's concept of rhetoric is especially useful for our focus on persuasive argument because it is based on the central idea that ethical persuasion should be construed as a kind of proof. This idea is so central, in fact, that Aristotle sometimes used the Greek terms for *persuasion* and *proof* (*pithe* and *pistis*) almost interchangeably. According to this view, an advocate persuades a listener by proving that his or her position is true, or worthy of acceptance, and the proof consists of arguments that provide good reasons for an audience to accept the ideas of the speaker. But how does an advocate find such arguments? What are the sources of proof in persuasion?

For Aristotle, the ability to find persuasive arguments requires mastery of three modes of proof, or ways of convincing an audience. In a fascinating way, these modes of proof roughly correspond to the foundation elements of our modern communication model: (1) the speaker, (2) the audience, and (3) the message. Each of these elements is crucial in the persuasive process, and each provides a powerful way of seeing and understanding persuasive argument. Let us examine each element, beginning with the mode of proof that is based on the speaker.

Ethos: Proof Based on the Speaker

We know, from our own experience, that the success of a persuasive argument depends largely on who is presenting it, or, more precisely, what an audience thinks of the person who is trying to persuade them. When an audience trusts a speaker, the reasons for trusting constitute a powerful kind of proof, which Aristotle called *ethos*. Thus, ethos refers collectively to all of the persuasive qualities an audience can perceive in a speaker, and especially those qualities that seem to prove that a speaker should be trusted and believed. The meaning of ethos is therefore fairly close to our modern idea of credibility.

In some situations, as Aristotle observed, a speaker's ethos is "the most effective means of persuasion he possesses," and especially when "exact certainty is impossible and opinions are divided."[3] Suppose George has been suffering from severe pain in his hip joints, and his physicians disagree about the best treatment for his condition. Some of them advocate immediate surgery; others say he should delay surgery as long as possible and use other methods to control his pain. What should George do? The arguments and evidence for each treatment may seem equally strong: Expert opinions are clearly divided, and George knows there is no certainty in his case. In this situation, George will find that he must assess the advocates, and his decision will probably be to accept the advice of the physician he trusts the most.

George's reasons for trusting one physician more than another could, of course, be based on irrational factors that would not be considered proof. Ethos is a kind of proof only when the perception of trustworthiness is based on good reasons. Thus, when speakers try to persuade listeners that they are trustworthy, or more trustworthy than their opponents, they offer proof in three more or less separable categories: (1) good sense, (2) goodwill, and (3) good moral character.

Good Sense

Good sense simply means that we are more likely to believe the speaker who knows the truth about the subject, or, as some put it, the speaker who knows what he or she is talking about. If there are opposing speakers, we try to determine which one knows the truth, or has the best judgment on the matter in dispute.

The concept of good sense subsumes a number of intellectual qualities: knowledge, intelligence, good judgment, experience, education, expert credentials, and what Aristotle called *practical wisdom*. You may notice that such a list of intellectual qualities constitutes, in a sense, a set of standards or criteria listeners may use to determine whether a speaker's statements can be relied on as true or wise. When we believe that speakers have such qualities, we are inclined to accept their arguments and assertions. Conversely, we tend to dismiss the statements of speakers we perceive to be lacking in such qualities.

It is easy to test this idea. Notice, for example, how we trust those with *experience* (one manifestation of good sense) and distrust those we regard as inexperienced. Consider the difference in our response to surgeons when they are perceived to be experienced or inexperienced. A friend of mine, who had decided to have her vision corrected through a procedure that involved reshaping the lens of the eye by making tiny incisions at precise points, was understandably very careful to seek out an eye surgeon with extensive experience in that particular operation. In a similar way, most of us look to the experience of an attorney, financial planner, or teacher as we try to determine whether such people know the truth or have good judgment about their subject. We tend to believe the experienced professional—especially if there is disagreement between experienced and inexperienced individuals.

Goodwill

Goodwill is the audience's perception of the extent to which a speaker cares about them or is interested in promoting their welfare. This dimension of ethos is perhaps clearest when we examine the grounds for our trust in family members and friends and why we are inclined to believe them. Generally, our perceptions of goodwill are more or less automatic when the persuasive arguments come from the people who love us. Because we believe they want only what is best for us, we do not put up our guard or erect defenses against their arguments. In fact, it is not unusual for us to seek out the advice of friends when we face an important decision, in effect, asking them to persuade us in one direction or another. However, there is one exception to this principle: We do not grant persuasive powers to friends or family members if we think they are hopelessly deficient in good sense (which is why parents sometimes have difficulty in persuading their teenagers).

Goodwill is most easily understood in relation to family members and friends, but we must also assess the goodwill of speakers with whom we have no personal relationship. When the speaker is a stranger to us, or at least not a friend or family member, it becomes more important to assess the grounds or reasons for deciding whether he or she is interested in our welfare. In some cases, our reasons for perceiving goodwill or its opposite may be based on a stereotype of the persuader's role. Thus, we may readily perceive goodwill in our attorney, physician, or religious leader because such people have a professional obligation to promote our welfare. On the other hand, we are usually on guard if the persuader is a salesperson or politician.

Interestingly, the goodwill concept helps to explain why persuaders use "common ground" appeals to listeners, pointing out their similarities in group membership ("We're all Americans") or shared beliefs ("All of us agree that something needs to be done to help the homeless"). We tend to assume that people who share membership in our group or believe as we do are more likely to have our interests at heart.

Good Moral Character

Good moral character seems to be the most difficult component of ethos for contemporary Americans to grasp, perhaps because of a deemphasis in the direct teaching of virtue and ethics in our schools. Good moral character refers to our assessment of a speaker's moral code and the qualities of character that are thought to indicate either truth or deception. What do we look for in making such an assessment? Virtues such as honesty, courage, fairness, a sense of justice, and a reverence for truth are thought to enhance the trustworthiness of the speaker. They indicate, at least, a desire to be truthful and to influence in an ethical way. Conversely, we distrust a speaker we perceive to be dishonest or otherwise corrupt.

The most important perceptions of good moral character, according to Aristotle, are those that are based on our direct observations and responses to a speaker's discourse. As we listen, we accumulate direct evidence of a speaker's moral choices from the claims he or she advocates and the kinds of arguments a speaker is willing to use. We use this direct evidence to infer that he or she is courageous and honest or lacking in these virtues. Thus, when Pope John Paul II traveled to the Philippines, his reputation as a man of splendid moral character preceded him. But his statements on the Philippines' national television network, condemning the actions of then-President Marcos, provided dramatic and immediate evidence of his courage and honesty for the national audience. The persuasive potential of perceived good moral character is exceptionally powerful when the evidence is so direct.

Normally, our perceptions of goodwill and good moral character in a speaker will coincide, but sometimes they are opposed. We know, for example, that our friends generally will tell us the truth, but sometimes they tell "little white lies" when they think that telling us the truth might make us angry or feel hurt. Risking the anger of a friend is unpleasant, so truth telling sometimes requires the virtues of courage and honesty as well as a friendly attitude of goodwill.

The three components of ethos—good sense, goodwill, and good moral character—help us to see why some speakers are successful in their persuasive efforts. But they are equally valuable in helping us to understand why some speakers fail or may have difficulties before particular audiences or with particular topics. And sometimes we can learn a great deal about how ethos works by looking to examples of speakers with weaknesses in one or more of the components.

In the 1976 presidential campaign, for example, former President Ford's advisers were fully aware that many Americans were attracted to Ford's evident traits of honesty, courage, and decency (the good moral character dimension). But many of these same people doubted Ford's intellectual abilities as a chief executive (the good sense dimension). The former president had the unfortunate tendency to stumble on stairways, hit spectators with his golfballs, fall down on ski slopes, and bump into furniture—all under the unforgiving glare of television lights. In Western culture, rightly or wrongly, physical clumsiness tends to be equated with mental clumsiness or deficiency. So, Ford's campaign staff was very much concerned about what they called the "dummy issue" in the campaign, and they tried to devise a persuasive strategy to reverse public perceptions that Ford lacked good sense.

Pathos: Proof Based on the Audience

The second mode of proof, which Aristotle called *pathos*, is concerned with those materials of argument that can put the audience into a receptive frame of mind. "Persuasion comes through the hearers," Aristotle said, "when the speech stirs their emotions. Our judgments when we are pleased and friendly are not the same as when we are pained and hostile."[4] The term *pathos*, like ethos, has been carried into modern English, but its contemporary use seems restricted primarily to feelings such as sadness, sympathy, and pity. It is important to realize that Aristotle intended to include all of the emotions that can effect our response either to the advocates or their arguments.

When emotions such as anger, pity, friendship, or their opposites are directed toward a speaker, his or her opponent, or the topic, they can affect judgment and possibly determine the audience's decision on the question at issue. Thus, if members of a jury feel anger toward the prosecutor, he or she will find it difficult to be successful, even though the jury might otherwise find the arguments in support of the prosecutor's case quite compelling. Unless the prosecutor does something to dispel the jury's anger or redirect it toward a more desirable target—such as the defense attorney or the defendant—the jury is likely to resist anything the prosecutor says.

Understanding Pathos as Proof

Most people understand that emotional appeals can be effective in persuasion. Even children understand that the mood of parents can very much affect their receptiveness to a request or a persuasive argument. But the idea of pathos as proof can be difficult to understand for two reasons.

First, if emotions can be manipulated and possibly prevent a listener from accepting an otherwise sound argument, then is the use of emotional appeals an unethical method of persuasion? This is an important question. Unscrupulous persuaders do try to manipulate our feelings, and they may deliberately attempt to confuse or stampede our judgment with emotional distractions. But the mere potential for abuse does not mean there is anything wrong with emotional arousal per se. It is possible for any of the modes of proof to be misused by unethical persuaders. Moreover, ethical persuaders also arouse feelings, as they must in order to move people to take action against suffering or injustice. Human beings need to care about a problem if they are to take action, and to care is to be emotionally aroused.

But there is a second problem: The idea of emotional proof may seem almost contradictory if we think of emotions as being outside the province of rational argument, or reason. Here, the concern is more complex. Clearly, our emotions are not entirely rational, and they do not always respond to good reasons. At the same time, however, our emotions are partly a reaction to what we perceive to be true or real about the world and other people, and perceptions of reality can be altered by argument. Think of it this way: If emotional responses were completely irrational, we could not make sense of the idea that anger is sometimes justified and sometimes unjustified.

Most people understand that anger can be warranted or justified in circumstances where we would say, "She has good reasons to be angry." In this respect, an emotion like anger is quite different from a pure sensation, like an itch. We can neither produce nor eliminate an itch with arguments. Anger, however, can be produced if a speaker shows that it is warranted, and it can be dispelled by showing that it is wrong, mistaken, or unjustified.

Kinds of Knowledge Needed for Pathos

Pathos is a kind of proof that provides good reasons for a listener to feel a particular emotion toward the speaker, the speaker's opponent, or the speaker's persuasive claim. Aristotle maintained that we need to master three kinds of knowledge in order to find such good reasons, or to see the possibilities for proof by pathos: (1) the kinds of emotions that can affect the judgments of an audience, (2) toward whom such emotions are directed or felt, and (3) how such emotions are aroused or dispelled.

How would an advocate use this knowledge to develop persuasive argument? Let's consider a practical case. Suppose that a prosecuting attorney believes that the jury will convict the defendant only if they feel anger toward his actions. If the anger is to be justified by argument, the attorney will need to find good reasons for the jury to feel it. How can this be done? If the principles of pathos are correct, anger may be aroused with proof if the prosecutor can show that the defendant has done those kinds of things that the community regards as sufficient causes of anger. Among the ancient Greeks, Aristotle reports that anger was caused by the perception of insult, or the idea that we have been slighted by someone:

> *Now slighting is the actively entertained opinion of something as obviously of no importance. . . . There are three kinds of slighting—contempt, spite, and insolence. Contempt is one kind of slighting: you feel contempt for what you consider unimportant. . . . Spite . . . is thwarting another man's wishes, not to get something yourself but to prevent his getting it. . . . Insolence . . . consists in doing and saying things that cause shame to the victim . . . simply for the pleasure involved.*[5]

If such manifestations of slighting are really the causes of anger, the attorney can justify anger by showing that the defendant's actions or words express contempt, spite, or insolence toward the victim, the jury, or the society they represent.

Modern Extensions of Pathos

Aristotle's original concept of pathos has been extended over the centuries as rhetoricians and scholars in other fields have identified other features of the audience that seem to affect the success or failure of persuasive messages. Especially in the twentieth century, a great deal of research has been devoted to audience analysis and the identification of factors that govern whether listeners will be difficult or easy to persuade. Studies on the knowledge level of audiences, for example, suggest that more knowledgeable audiences are able to understand complex arguments but may be less inclined to yield to them. In general, people are more easily persuaded when they do not know much about the topic under discussion or when they do not have any opinions, beliefs, or attitudes in relation to the topic. It is simply easier to persuade people to accept a new belief than it is to change their minds when they already believe something else to be true or correct.

The study of persuasion in relation to the audience has received contributions from many disciplines in the humanities and social sciences during the twentieth century, and rhetoricians have borrowed freely from the contributions of scholars in other fields. The contributions of psychology and sociology, especially, help us to understand how audiences respond to persuasive arguments.

Logos: Proof Based on the Message

Like so many Greek words, *logos* has an extraordinary range of possible meanings. In its largest sense, logos refers to our general ideas of order and rationality in the universe and to the principles of order that enable us to make sense of the world around us. In a more limited sense, logos can mean "word" or "speech," or those parts of a speech that we would call the speaker's arguments or reasons. Notice, however, that there is a basic unity in this range of meanings—namely, the core notion that we make sense of the world around us by talking about it, by reasoning with each other, and by argument. This core notion of making sense is reflected in the way logos is incorporated into some English words that have Greek roots. Thus, for example, when logos becomes the suffix *-logy*, it means "the study of," as in *biology* (the study of living things) and *pathology* (the study of disease or suffering).

While ethos furnishes reasons for agreeing with a speaker, and pathos provides materials that can have a powerful effect on the receptiveness of listeners, it is logos that enables us to make sense of a disagreement and provides us with good reasons for our judgments. As a mode of persuasive proof, logos thus refers to all of the arguments that directly support or oppose claims in relation to a central question in dispute.

Relationship of Logos to Ethos and Pathos

Although each of the three modes of proof furnishes persuasive materials of argument, only logos provides reasons that directly support the position advocated by the speaker. Recall our courtroom example. If we were on a jury, the ethos of witnesses and attorneys could have powerful influence on whom we decide to trust and believe. Likewise, elements of pathos could determine whether we feel sympathetic or hostile toward the defendant. But no conscientious juror could be satisfied merely with ethos and pathos. Wouldn't we also want to consider the central question of the trial? If the defendant was charged with burglary, wouldn't we want the prosecution to support its claim with convincing arguments? And surely we would want to consider the evidence and examine closely the reasoning of both prosecution and defense in deciding whether the evidence was strong enough to support a conviction. Whenever we consider arguments of this sort, which either support or oppose a position that is in dispute, we are examining logos.

Knowledge Needed for Logos

What do we need to know in order to discern persuasive proof in the logos? How do we find effective arguments in relation to the central question in dispute? The ancient Greeks were quite pragmatic about this task; their approach initially was to identify and to imitate whatever arguments seemed to work in relation to disputes of a particular kind. Thus, Corax, the rhetorician we mentioned earlier, analyzed the kinds of arguments that seemed to work in courtroom persuasion. Corax found that arguments based on probability were quite effective and that jurors were likely to convict or acquit a defendant on the basis of what they thought was *likely* to be true. Therefore, if a small man were accused of violent assault on a big man, Corax said he should use the juror's ideas about what is probable and argue that a small man does not attack a larger and stronger man.

Succeeding generations continued the study of what worked and extended the analysis of logos to the jurors' grounds for decision, or the kinds of reasons that seem to be crucial when a jury decides a defendant is guilty or innocent. Aristotle synthesized these studies and outlined five major kinds of knowledge an advocate needs in order to develop persuasive arguments in the courts. Since the central question in the courts is always whether an injustice has been done, an advocate needs to know (1) the community's concepts of justice and injustice, (2) the community's definition of *wrongdoing*, (3) the causes of all actions, (4) the state of mind of wrongdoers, and (5) the kind of persons wronged.

Each of these types of knowledge can suggest arguments or a useful approach to finding arguments because they reflect the persistent patterns of arguments that were found to be persuasive in previous trials. In addition, they make sense to us. Consider the potential importance of arguments based on knowledge of the causes of our actions. Ordinarily, an action is not considered criminal if its cause is beyond the control of the person who does it. Therefore, if a defendant cannot deny that she participated in a bank robbery, she may nevertheless argue that she is not guilty because the cause of her action was compulsion—and therefore beyond her control. This was essentially the argument that F. Lee Bailey used in defending Patricia Hearst. Bailey argued that Hearst was not guilty of bank robbery because her abductors forced her to participate in the robbery.

In addition to the forensic, or courtroom, persuasion, Aristotle also outlined the kinds of knowledge needed to find arguments for two other kinds of persuasion: the deliberative and the epideictic. Since *deliberative persuasion* consists of arguments for and against a proposed course of action, Aristotle maintained that advocates need to understand, first, the ends or goals that we try to reach with our actions. On a general level, these goals are happiness and the good. An advocate cannot argue persuasively for an action without knowing what goals are considered most important by the society, or at least worth reaching.

Second, an advocate must be knowledgeable about the major subjects we debate. For example, if the question is whether Congress should authorize the president to go to war with another country, anyone who wants to persuade others should first become as knowledgeable as possible about the military strength of each country, the past wars each nation has waged, how it has waged them, and with what effect. Without such knowledge, the advocate will seem uninformed.

Epideictic persuasion, which is sometimes dismissed merely as ceremonial speaking, is concerned with the evaluation of individuals, institutions, groups, or even the nation as a whole. When we evaluate, we engage in praise and blame, and we therefore need to know the grounds or bases for these. Aristotle thought the primary knowledge needed was the important virtues and their opposites, the vices. If a persuader has a deep understanding of such virtues as justice, courage, and wisdom, it becomes possible to examine the condition of society, finding persuasive reasons for deploring its shortcomings or praising its better impulses and actions. Martin Luther King, Jr.'s speech, "I Have a Dream," is a superb example of modern epideictic.

Logos and Argument Form

To this point, we have focused our attention primarily on the *materials* of argument, or the substance of the reasons that an advocate might use in relation to each arena of persuasion. But an argument does not consist solely of material, or content, no more than a house consists merely of its building materials. Both houses and arguments must have *form* as well as content, and their form or structure can be crucial in both cases to their appeal as well as their strength. But how do we make sense of argument form?

You may have noticed that the term *logos* is closely related to our modern term *logic*. This is a useful connection to keep in mind because rhetoric and logic complement and complete each other in the analysis of argument form. Traditionally, the rules and principles of logic are applied to the forms of argument to determine whether they are valid or invalid, which is to say that an argument either does or does not conform to rules of correct inference. Such analysis is very important for rhetoric because persuasive arguments should be trustworthy and reliable, and an invalid argument is neither.

As ethical persuaders, we do not want our arguments to be flawed, nor do we want to fall prey to the fallacious arguments of others. At the same time, however, we should not focus solely on the ways that reasoning can go wrong. The forms or shapes of arguments, as well as that of houses, can have persuasive appeal. For the rhetorician, an argument is a persuasive unit; it provides an audience with good reasons for accepting the ideas of the speaker, and part of its appeal may be in the form it takes.

To understand the principles of argument form is not merely to understand its logical structure but also the typical ways in which argument is expressed in the courtroom, in the marketplace, and with friends and others. To understand its use in persuasion, we need more than just a notion of form for an individual argument. Persuasive discourse in the real world typically consists of a number of arguments, assembled in an order that is likely to meet the needs of an audience or a situation. Audiences always have expectations about what must be presented or what would be considered tedious or unnecessary in relation to the issues. Hence, as Aristotle noted, we need a rhetorical perspective on the form of argument in persuasion.

Logos and Argumentation

When the term *logos* is understood as comprising all of the rational persuasive elements in a central question that is in dispute, it corresponds exactly to what is meant in this book by the term *argumentation*. Thus, following Aristotle's scheme, *rhetoric* is the faculty of discerning (or seeing) all of the persuasive elements in a speaker, audience, and message; *argumentation* is a subordinate art of rhetoric, more or less equivalent to Aristotle's notion of the scope and function of logos. A clear grasp of the principles of logos means that a speaker can make sense of a dispute by discerning what it is about, by seeing clearly the crucial elements of the dispute, including all of the possible arguments for both the pro and the con sides. The principles of logos, or argumentation, should enable us to see the potential strengths and weaknesses in arguments and help us to develop critical thinking abilities in relation to arguments and evidence. And finally, the principles should help us to develop persuasive cases for either side of the central questions we deliberate in a democratic society.

The Focus of Rhetoric and Argumentation

Because the scope of rhetorical studies in persuasion is very broad, over the years a more or less general division of the material has developed into two kinds of courses. The first, which typically includes the term *persuasion* in its course title, emphasizes the relationships between rhetoric and psychology, and tends to survey experimental and empirical studies of persuasion variables in relation to audiences, or receivers, with relatively less attention, respectively, on the speaker and the message. In general, the speaker and the message components tend to be examined as collections of variables that may or may not effect persuasive change in audiences.

The second type of course, which is frequently called *argumentation* or *debate*, is primarily concerned with the substance, or the message element, of the persuasive process, and spends relatively little time with audience analysis or with the speaker. Such courses emphasize the relationships between rhetoric, logic, and that portion of jurisprudence that is concerned with standards of rational analysis and proof.

This book falls primarily into this second type; its purpose is to enable students to make sense of the persuasive elements of argument and conflict. Audience response certainly is important in a course in rhetoric and argumentation, but our principal focus is on the rational elements in persuasion, such as issues, arguments, evidence, and message strategies. We are now prepared to survey and identify the rational elements of persuasion—the topic of Chapter 2.

Summary

1. This book is designed to develop three skills: (a) to make sense of conflicts by seeing clearly their nature and their crucial elements; (b) to become effective critics of persuasive argument and its support; and (c) to become proficient in developing and responding to persuasive cases.

2. Because we cannot avoid uncertainties about what is really real, or good, or the best course of action, conflict is an intrinsic feature of the human condition. Therefore, we do not usually have a choice about whether we will have conflict and controversy.

3. We do, however, have choices about what to do in response to conflict. Generally, our major choices are to avoid a conflict, to use some form of force or superior power in dictating a solution, or to use persuasion. Totalitarian societies are characterized in part by their reliance on force. Democratic societies opt for persuasion as the preferred method of responding to conflict.

4. Rhetoric, which is the study of persuasive communication, has a rich history dating from ancient Greece. However, it is easy to become confused by misinformed uses of the term *rhetoric* unless we understand its principal focus as an art. Like all arts, rhetoric is a way of seeing or discerning. As Aristotle defined it, rhetoric is a faculty of discerning the available means of persuasion in any case.

5. The Aristotelian perspective on rhetoric is especially useful for our focus on persuasive argumentation because he construes persuasion as a kind of proof. The modes of proof, which correspond roughly with the elements of the communication model, are *ethos*, *logos*, and *pathos*. Each of these modes suggests ways of seeing the possible materials of argument for any central question that is in dispute.

6. Since arguments have *form* as well as content, logic and rhetoric complement and complete each other as we examine the strengths and weaknesses of persuasive argumentation. Logic enables us to recognize reliable and trustworthy forms of argument and to see why some arguments are fallacious.

Exercises

1. We explored a few of the controversies over what is real in the medical arena. Identify three controversies about what was really real, or true, in relation to the so-called Persian Gulf conflict of 1990–91.

2. Although a speaker's ethos can be one of the most powerful modes of persuasion, Aristotle's components of ethos also enable us to see why some speakers have major persuasive problems. Discuss the following speakers, and see if you can identify their strengths and weaknesses in relation to the components of ethos.
   a. Senator Edward Kennedy, in his efforts to persuade voters that he should be president
   b. Former President Ronald Reagan, in his efforts to explain the so-called Iran-Contra scandal of his administration (What is the implication of Reagan's testimony in court that he could not remember many of the important details about what he authorized or encouraged?)
   c. The Reverend Jesse Jackson, in his campaign for the presidential nomination in 1984 (What is the implication of Jackson's alleged reference to the Jews in New York in a derogatory way?)

3. If New York Jews were angry with the Reverend Jesse Jackson because of his alleged insulting statement about them in 1984, how might Jackson use the principles of pathos to dispel or lessen their anger?

4. Aristotle suggests that a speaker in the legislative arena needs to have knowledge on the major subjects of debate. He identified five major topic areas: war and peace, ways and means, national defense, imports and exports, and laws. How does Aristotle's list compare with the subject areas reflected in a current listing of the committees of Congress?

5. What sorts of conflicts or controversies do we respond to with avoidance (or by trying to ignore them) on our college campus?

6. As a class discussion project, list the uses of the term *rhetoric* that you have either heard or have seen in newspapers and magazines.

Endnotes

1. Lewis Coser, *The Functions of Social Conflict* (New York: Free Press, 1956).
2. Richard C. Jebb, trans., *The Rhetoric of Aristotle* (Cambridge: Cambridge University Press, 1909), p. 5. I use Jebb's translation of Aristotle's definition because it seems the clearest, even though some would argue that it is not the most literal translation. You might find it interesting to compare Jebb's use of "discerning" to the choices of other translators. See John H. Freese, trans., "The 'Art' of Rhetoric," *Aristotle*, 23 vols. (Cambridge, MA: Loeb-Harvard University Press, 1975), vol. 22, p. 15; and W. Rhys Roberts, trans., "Rhetoric," *Aristotle: Rhetoric and Poetics* (New York: Modern Library-Random House, 1954), p. 24.
3. Roberts, "Rhetoric," p. 25.
4. Ibid.
5. Ibid., pp. 92–93.

2

The Anatomy of Controversy

Central Ideas in This Chapter

1. The ability to make sense of argument and controversy yields two benefits.
   - It develops the capacity for self-defense.
   - It enhances our ability to use persuasive argument.
2. We can understand a controversy by examining its anatomy.
   - Anatomy refers to the whole-part relationships of a dispute and its critical elements.
   - Rational controversies have four critical elements: (1) central questions, (2) issues, (3) arguments, and (4) premises and evidence.
3. Three kinds of central questions express the essential nature of disputes.
   - Factual questions focus disputes over what is real or true.
   - Value questions focus disputes over what is good or bad.
   - Policy questions focus disagreement over a proposed course of action.
4. Principles for phrasing questions help to prevent confusion about the focus of a dispute.
5. Central questions are analyzed by discovering their critical components, called *issues*.
6. Arguments provide good reasons in support of the pro and con responses to the issues.
7. Premises and evidence are the materials that support argument claims.

How many times have you felt frustrated during an argument with a friend, knowing that you will think of a brilliant response to your friend's insane arguments an hour or so after your friend has departed? What makes the frustration almost unbearable is that you know, during the argument, that there is a serious flaw in your friend's reasoning, and you could demolish it if you had just a little time to sort out the elements of the dispute between you. The problem, however, is not simply a problem of timing—that is, your thinking of the argument too late. If you were to confront your friendly foe with the new argument, you might be dismayed to discover that he or she has a ready response, easily regaining the upper hand. The problem is that most people argue in a rather miscellaneous way. They have little or no idea of what is relevant in their arguments with others or what each side needs to prove in order to provide complete support for the claims made in a dispute. It is rather like driving off in an automobile, hoping to arrive at a party, but without any knowledge of the roads, or a road map, or even the address of our destination. Should we be surprised that we get lost in our arguments when we do not know where they are going?

A related problem is our vulnerability to the manipulative, and even fallacious, persuasive arguments of others. Some of us may have been victimized by a manipulative sales pitch at a used-car lot or at a home jewelry party; others may have been tormented by persuasive arguments of someone we thought to be a friend. We hate to admit it, but most of us have been manipulated by an amazing assortment of persuaders, and the result is that we find ourselves in possession of unwanted subscriptions to magazines, insurance policies, Girl Scout cookies, and a host of other products. Once again, the vulnerability to manipulative persuasion stems, in part, from an inability to sort out and analyze persuasive arguments, at least at the moment when such analysis could be helpful.

The ability to make sense out of argument and controversy yields dual benefits: It helps us to defend ourselves against manipulative persuasion and it enhances our ability to develop our own persuasive arguments. As we noted in Chapter 1, all persuasion involves controversy (or opposition) at one level or another. Thus, as we learn to sort out the complex components of controversy, we begin to understand what a reasonable persuasive argument should look like—and unreasonable arguments, from unethical persuaders, start to become obvious to us. At the same time, the ability to see clearly the important elements in a dispute helps us to see the possible arguments available to our side. To develop this ability, we need to begin by examining the anatomy of rational controversy.

The term *anatomy* derives from a Greek word that means to cut up an organism in order to determine its *structure* and the *relation-*

ship of its parts. Thus, for our purposes, the "anatomy of controversy" is the simplification of a complex dispute by breaking it down into its simpler components, which are easier to understand. We can make sense of a dispute when we can see clearly its critical parts and their relationships to each other. The process of doing this is called *analysis.*

So, what do we need to analyze? Students are often surprised to discover that the critical parts of all rational controversies are fairly few in number, regardless of what the controversy is about. In this chapter, we shall examine four critical elements in the anatomy of all rational disputes: (1) the *central questions* in dispute, (2) the *issues* that are inherent in the central questions, (3) the *arguments* used to support pro and con responses to the issues, and (4) the *premises* and *evidence* cited as support for argument claims.

Central Questions

The first step in the process of analysis is to determine what the particular controversy is about—the critical element called the *central question* in dispute. Central questions express the essence of a controversy, and their duty is to pinpoint the nature of the disagreement between opposing sides. Since the idea of expressing the essence of a controversy is an unfamiliar notion to most people, let's examine central questions in two well-defined arenas of controversy: law courts and legislative assemblies.

In criminal law courts, central questions express the essence of the disagreement between prosecution and defense on the guilt or innocence of a person accused of a crime. For example, if a student, say Abner Fratperson, has been accused of mail fraud in the recruitment of pledges for his fraternity, the central question would be: Is Abner Fratperson guilty of mail fraud? Notice how this central question focuses the dispute between prosecution and defense, indicating precisely *what must be decided* by a judge or jury. Properly phrased, such central questions encompass all of the elements of a particular court dispute. This means that when the central question is decided, the dispute as a whole has been decided.

In a legislative or policy-making body, such as the United States Senate or a state legislature, central questions focus the disagreement between opposing sides in relation to a particular bill, resolution, or proposed course of action. In 1986 and 1987, for example, several states considered and passed bills that mandate seatbelt usage for automobile passengers. When these bills were being considered, the debates over them could have been phrased as a central question: Should the state of Colorado (or whatever state) adopt a mandatory seat-belt law?

Notice that the question on the topic of mandatory seat belts is the same for both the pro and con sides. Observe, also, in our discussion of criminal courts, that the central question is the same for prosecution and defense. The opposition between the two sides is revealed in their *responses* to the central question. Those in favor of the change (the pro side) say yes to the question, and those opposed (the con side) say no. If the two sides were to agree in their response to the central question (both saying either yes or no), we could conclude one of two things: (1) either there is no dispute between the two sides or (2) the central question has not been phrased correctly in expressing their disagreement.

Types of Central Questions

The possible number of controversial subjects is perhaps unlimited, but happily, we do not need to worry about an infinite variety of central questions. Although there is some variation in what they are called in various textbooks, central questions are generally classified into three basic types: *fact, value,* and *policy*.[1] When you understand these three archetypal kinds of central questions, you will have made a major step in eliminating some of the confusion and frustration you have experienced in past arguments. A clear understanding of each of the three central questions enables us to make some sense of almost any public controversy. We can at least say what the dispute is about.

Questions of Fact

Questions of fact are concerned with disputes over alleged events, relationships, properties, or facts—whether in the past, present, or future. They are not concerned with whether something is good or bad; they are concerned solely with *what is* or *has been* or *will be true* or *false* in the real world. In other words, questions of fact are concerned with disputes over what is actually real about the world around us and the universe we inhabit.

Before we consider the varieties of factual questions, however, we need to clarify the distinction between *facts*, which are quite obviously true and easily verified, and *questions of fact*, where the best we can do is to arrive at sound judgments about what is probably true or probably false.

Fortunately, not everything requires argument. People usually do not argue about facts that are clearly true and that nobody doubts, unless they are trying to be tiresome. Communities in any culture enjoy a surprisingly broad consensus about the existential world—a kind of practical certainty that some things are certainly true or false, and they will be regarded as such by any sane adult who has been properly educated. As Aristotle observed, if someone wants to question whether snow is white, he or she needs perception, not argument. Likewise, my tennis friends have a practical certainty that I will not be invited to become a member of the U.S. Davis Cup team, and they would be surprised if I wanted to argue the matter (at least seriously).

But we do need argument when uncertainty about our factual questions is inescapable. Factual controversies tend to be confined to matters that are important, at least to the participants in a dispute, and about which a judgment must be made. Thus, when we refer to "questions of fact," we have in mind those disputes that are about what is really real. The best we can achieve with such questions is a high level of *probability* that our judgments will be correct.

Past Fact

Some of our disagreements are focused on questions about what is alleged to have been true or false about matters in the past. For example, historians argue questions such as whether John Wilkes Booth really shot President Lincoln or whether the Japanese government signaled its willingness to surrender before the United States dropped the second atomic bomb on the city of Nagasaki. If you were to observe our trial courts, as they handle civil and criminal cases, you would observe that much of the argument involves disputes over what happened in the past: Did the general manager of the professional football team promise the running back a coaching position if he signed his contract? Was the deceased about to divorce the defendant, the present widow, just prior to his demise?

The range of subject matter for disputes over past fact is, of course, almost infinitely varied, but all share a common focus: In each case, the dispute is about *what was true or false* in a time past. Consider the range of disputes in the following central questions of past fact:

> Did the Soviets warn the pilots of Korean Airlines Flight 007 that they must land or be shot down?
>
> Did Francis Bacon write some of the plays attributed to Shakespeare?
>
> Was the decline in out-of-state student enrollment at State University the result of tuition increases?

Did former President Reagan encourage his national security aides, Poindexter and North, to divert profits from the sale of arms to the Iranians to the so-called Contras in Nicaragua?

Did human beings evolve from an orangutan-like creature (called Sivapithecus) in Africa?

Notice in these examples that all of the questions are concerned solely with factual matters. We may, of course, have strong feelings about one or more of these questions and we may strongly prefer an answer of either yes or no for one or another of them, but the questions themselves are not concerned with such feelings. The important judgment dimension for all questions of fact is "true" or "false" rather than "good" or "bad," "desirable" or "undesirable." This means that the question of whether human beings evolved from Sivapithecus is a factual matter that may be true or false regardless of how we feel about it.

Present Fact

The second type of factual question is concerned with disputes over alleged present facts. A dispute is about present fact whenever we argue about what is true or false about any facet of our world or our lives at the present time. Public opinion polls, for example, provide quantities of data on what the public thinks on a large number of issues, candidates, products, and so on, but the evidence from national polls merely focuses the extraordinary range of controversies over present public opinion. Does the public prefer candidate X more than candidate Y? Do people believe that Democrats in the White House are more likely than Republicans to get the country into wars? Do people fear public speaking more than unemployment? Do people believe that world stocks of oil are being rapidly depleted?

Opinion polls provide a kind of evidence for what the public thinks about such questions, but the polling data do not provide us with certainty and often do not end controversy. As all politicians know, and will announce whenever the polls show their opponent as being in the lead, the polls have been wrong in the past.

Disputes over present fact are not limited to public opinion, of course. Economists argue over the present status of the economy; nutritionists argue about the effect of vitamin C in the body; broadcasters and public interest groups argue about the effects of the recision of the fairness doctrine. Even in the so-called hard sciences, much of the effort of researchers is concerned with disputes over present fact. Is the world heading toward an overheated condition, called the *greenhouse effect?* Are chemicals from refrigerants, called *chlorofluorocarbons*, destroying the protective ozone around the earth? Does chewing tobacco cause cancer of the mouth?

On a more personal front, all of us must make factual judgments when we make decisions about the probable effects of consuming drugs such as aspirin or drinking apparently "clean" water from a mountain stream. Likewise, arguments we have with friends concern questions of present fact when we disagree about the real causes of teenage pregnancy rates in our big cities or the reasons for our lack of success on the tennis court. Questions of present fact focus controversy over what is factually true or false or probably true or false about our present world, and they encompass an interesting range of disputes, as the following examples illustrate:

> Can psychiatric evaluations determine whether an accused murderer was sane at the time of a slaying?
>
> Does frog urine cause warts?
>
> Does TV crime and violence contribute as a cause of juvenile delinquency?
>
> Is the Japanese government interested in promoting balanced trade with the United States?
>
> Does the televising of U.S. Senate deliberations have any effect on the Senate debate process?

The number of questions we could pose about present fact is perhaps limitless. Fortunately, however, most of us do not argue about everything, and we prefer to avoid the tiresome bores who do! But reasonable and sane people may disagree on a wide variety of questions concerning present fact, as our examples illustrate. We may decide, on the basis of the available evidence, that our planet is heading toward an overheated condition (the greenhouse effect), but we need to realize that our evidence yields only a level of probability for such factual judgments; factual questions of this sort cannot be answered with certainty.

Future Fact

The third type of factual question is concerned with predictions or arguments over what will happen in the future. Questions of this sort focus controversies over *what will be* true of future events, actions, persons, relationships, and so forth. If you think about it, many of the wagers people make are a form of argument about future events—such as which horse will come in first, whether our basketball team will make it to the playoffs, which baseball team will win the World Series, and so on.

On a personal level, all of us must make judgments about what will happen in the future. When we make decisions about whether we should change our college major, purchase a stereo, get married, vote for a particular candidate, or pursue a particular job, we are necessarily making judgments about what we think will happen as a result of our choices. Since we cannot know for sure what will happen, questions of future fact tend to account for a rather large share of the argumentation among family and friends, as well as in society in general. All of us must make judgments about what will happen. Consider the range of topics in the following examples of central questions of future fact:

> Will the large deficits in the budget of the federal government cause a resurgence of inflationary price increases?
>
> Will punitive tariffs against the goods of Japan force the Japanese to remove barriers to the sale of U.S. goods in Japan?
>
> Will employers avoid hiring Americans of Hispanic descent as a reaction to the federal penalties for hiring illegal aliens?
>
> Will the Broncos make it to the Super Bowl next year?
>
> Will the recision of the fairness doctrine by the Federal Communications Commission reduce the access of minority viewpoints to radio and television stations in the United States?
>
> Will U.S. colleges and universities experience a sharp increase in student enrollment within the next five years?

You may notice, once again, that people can have strong feelings about whether the *future facts* predicted in these questions are accepted or rejected, but the feelings are not, per se, an essential element of the questions. Just as we observed with questions of past and present fact, predictions are concerned with judgments on what is *true* or *false* about the real world. Their unique feature is that they focus on the future.

Questions of Value

There is a close relationship between questions of value and questions of fact. When we argue about the *value* of something, we are arguing about its worth, importance, or desirability. Notice, however, that in order to argue coherently over the worth of something, we must generally assume that the "thing" exists. Value disagreements, therefore, usually assume a factual foundation, or something which is thought to be factually real. I say "usually" because it is possible to argue about imaginary things. But the important value disputes in society are about things in the real world—whether past, present, or future.

In a sense, value questions contain questions of fact within them, but the focus of disagreement in a value question is not whether something is true; rather, the disagreement concerns whether a thing is good or bad. For example, if senators argue whether a proposed civil rights bill will be beneficial or harmful, their argument could include disagreement on two levels: (1) a question of future fact about what will happen if the civil rights bill is adopted and (2) a question of value on whether the alleged results will be harmful or beneficial.

The focus of disagreement in a value question usually is a critical *value term* that asserts a positive or negative response to the fact alleged or the thing evaluated. By "value term," I mean the words or phrases we use for expressing positive or negative reactions, feelings, responses, or attitudes toward objects, persons, ideas, events—in short, anything we can conceptualize or care about one way or another. Some of the value words commonly used to express such reactions include *good, bad, desirable, undesirable, great, lousy, beneficial, harmful, excellent, inferior,* and so on. Notice how such terms become the focus of the positive or negative evaluation in each of the following questions:

Is the media *unfair* in its treatment of Dan Quayle?

Are the efforts on some college campuses to curtail speech that is considered offensive to women or minorities an *undesirable restriction* on the rights of free speech?

Has the President done a *good* job (or *poor* job) in managing domestic policy?

I make no effort to list all of the value words or phrases because their potential number is limitless. But the examples here should help you to recognize other value terms that are used to express a positive or negative judgment. The key is that words and phrases become value terms when they move the focus of judgment in a question beyond what is true or false about the real world and into the realm of *how we feel* about what is true or false.

Many value terms, such as *unfair* or *beneficial,* have a pronounced emotive connotation, and this can be a useful quality to keep in mind as we gain experience in recognizing two different kinds of value questions. The first kind focuses on one subject and asks whether a positive or negative judgment is warranted. Many of our value disputes are of this sort, as the following questions illustrate:

Is the *Daily Tattler* a lousy (or excellent) newspaper?

Did the United States suffer a disastrous defeat in Viet Nam?

Do Affirmative Action programs foster unfair discrimination against white males?

In a second kind of value question, the dispute centers on a value comparison. In some cases, "things" are the focus of comparison, and the dispute is about which of them is better or worse. Is the new Plymouth van better than the Ford? Does State University offer a better program in communication studies than Private University? Are we worse off now than we were 10 years ago? Is American elementary and secondary education inferior to the education children receive in Japan?

In another kind of comparison question, the focus of the dispute is on competing values. For example: Will the benefits of oil exploration in wilderness areas of Alaska outweigh the costs to the environment? Is the public's right to know more important than the rights of the accused to a fair trial? Is a candid discussion of the issues more important than providing reporters with access to all meetings of public officials?

You should not feel discouraged if you find it difficult to distinguish fact and value questions. Distinguishing between fact and value is a troublesome business for many of us, partly because of a lack of experience and partly because value questions usually entail some factual assumptions. The key is to ask yourself if the question is concerned only with whether something is true or whether its principal focus is a judgment about the worth or importance of something.

Let's consider a question that contains both a factual and a value dimension to see if we can sort this out: Does the United States have a serious problem of functional illiteracy? The phrase "serious problem" is a value term. Why? Because things are judged to be a "serious problem" only in relation to our value standards for good and bad, desirable and undesirable. Even if we agree that functional illiteracy is undesirable (which would be a value agreement), at what point does the amount of it become a serious problem? Our criteria for setting a threshold for this will necessarily be based on our values. Not all cultures look at illiteracy in the same way. Notice, however, that the existence of illiteracy is a factual matter. Our question would be a factual question rather than a value question if its focus is on the amount of functional illiteracy or whether functional illiteracy is increasing or decreasing.

It becomes easier to see the difference between fact and value questions as you gain experience. One way to do this is to identify central questions whenever you read an editorial or engage in friendly arguments. Another useful activity is to phrase fact and value questions of your own.

Questions of Policy

Policy questions embody controversies over a proposed new course of action. On a personal level, we frequently deliberate policy questions with ourselves as we weigh the pros and cons of making a new purchase or electing to take a difficult course outside of our major. Similarly, the focus of most of the bills debated in the United States Congress, or any of the legislatures of the states, is a policy question. Such bills propose a new course of action, and the central question in dispute is whether legislative members should adopt a new law, program, policy, rule, or action. Consider the following examples of policy questions from some bills and resolutions that have been debated in Congress:

> Should the U.S. Congress increase taxes on all imported petroleum?
>
> Should the U.S. Congress impose criminal penalties on employers who hire illegal aliens?
>
> Should the federal government permit the states to increase the speed limit on rural stretches of interstate highway from 55 to 65 miles per hour?
>
> Should the Congress prohibit the use of federal funds for abortions?
>
> Should the Congress authorize the president to use military force to free Kuwait from the occupation by Iraq?

Because policy questions focus disputes over a proposed new action, most people find them easier to understand than disputes over questions of fact and value. Even little children seem to grasp the idea of pro and con argument about proposed actions, perhaps because they are required to justify their requests to stay up late and the like at an early age. Yet it is important to realize that policy controversies always involve subordinate disputes over questions of fact and value. We will explore this relationship in some depth in Chapter 3 when we examine the issues of policy questions. Here, it is important to realize that proposals for new actions are made because someone is dissatisfied with the present situation, and arguments about dissatisfactions are the focus of fact and value questions.

Members of Congress do not propose new laws merely for the recreational pleasures of debate. When a new law or program is proposed, it is because its advocates believe there is a significant motive for change: a serious problem, an unmet goal, an advantage, or some combination of these. Moreover, this principle applies in any arena where a proposed action is considered. For example, a physician would not propose surgery unless he or she believed there were a real need for it. But such a need could be argued. If a second physician argued that the alleged condition does not exist, the dispute would concern a question of fact. If the opposing physician agrees that there is a minor problem, but denies that it is harmful or harmful enough to justify change, then the dispute is a question of value.

Argument over a proposed new action or solution always entails the presence of some motive, but this is not to say that all of the advocates in favor of a proposed action will be concerned with the same motive. One member of Congress might favor a proposed 65 mph speed limit because he is personally irritated by the slower limit. Another member may believe it is a waste of her state's resources to try to enforce the 55 mph limit. And there could be still other motives for change. Nevertheless, there is considerable wisdom in the adage, "If it ain't broke, don't fix it." Policy questions become more difficult to analyze when the proposed new action is a solution in search of a problem.

Ways of Expressing Central Questions

Although central questions are generally perceived as a fair and clear way of expressing the nature of a disagreement, it is important to realize that the central point in a dispute can be phrased in various ways. In legislative bodies, members usually identify the policy questions of their debates by referring to a particular bill or resolution, or its number. In 1991, for example, the proposed civil rights bill was called H.R. 1. In our courts, attorneys may refer to the point in dispute as a complaint, if the case relates to civil law, or a charge if it is a criminal matter. When community or business organizations govern themselves with codes of parliamentary procedure, all of the topics for debate are presented as motions, and sometimes the motion may present a resolution.

Traditionally, argumentation textbooks have construed the topics of debate as propositions. The term *proposition* indicates that the pro side, which is called the affirmative, proposes something— either a judgment on a matter of fact or value, or a course of action—and the proposal therefore expresses the basis of the controversy. When propositions of fact, value, or policy are phrased for debate, they are usually framed as resolutions, as the following illustrate:

Resolved: That the United States should significantly reduce its military forces in bases outside the Western hemisphere.

Resolved: That the United States should support the creation of a Palestinian state.

Resolved: That activism in politics by religious groups harms the American political process.

Resolved: That the American judicial system has overemphasized the rights of the accused.

Principles for Phrasing Central Questions

Most of us have had the frustrating experience of discovering, after an hour or so of "friendly" argument, that our opponent is suddenly bewildered about our interpretation of the point in dispute. Of course, some opponents only pretend to have a different idea of the question in dispute because they realize they are losing the argument, and their bewilderment is a tactic to confuse the matter or to disengage without admitting defeat. There is also the genuine problem of differing interpretations, and this invariably stems from the failure to phrase the central question with precision.

We have now identified the three principal kinds of central questions that enable us to discern what kind of argument we are having with a friend or foe. The next step is to explicate the principles that help us to phrase the central questions clearly and fairly, so that both sides will agree that the question captures accurately what they disagree about. Five principles are helpful.

1. *The Crucial Yes and No.* Central questions should be phrased to elicit an answer of yes from advocates of change (from present policy or belief) and an answer of no from opponents of the change. It may be easy to initiate an argument by asking a question like: How do you feel about Donald Regan's insulting remarks about the intellectual capacity of American women in the arena of arms control? However, that sort of question does not focus the disagreement, if any, between opposing sides. A better version would be: Did Donald Regan reveal himself as a male chauvinist when he said that American women do not understand "throw weights" (of missiles) and "human rights issues"? The latter question poses a new value belief about Regan (President Reagan's White House Chief of Staff), and it requires a response of yes from advocates of the new belief and a response of no from opponents.

2. *Phrase in the Direction of Change.* Central questions should be phrased in the direction of change from present policy or belief. This principle stems from the need to clarify what the dispute is about, and it follows directly from the first principle—that is, the question needs to be phrased in the direction of change in order for the advo-

cates of a new policy or belief to respond yes. In addition, it is based on the natural sequence of events in the initiation of a conflict or controversy.

As long as everyone is satisfied with present policy or belief, there is no conflict. A conflict arises when there is a dissatisfaction of some sort—usually deriving from the perception that a problem needs attention—and when someone or some group proposes a change from present policy or belief. Notice that our criminal courts do not ask: Is Fred Fiend *innocent* of mayhem during fall registration? Rather, the courts consider the question: Is Fred Fiend *guilty* of mayhem during fall registration? The new belief—guilt—is advocated to replace the old or present belief of innocence. Similarly, it would likely confuse debate on policy questions to ask if the present system should be continued or retained. Policy questions come into being when someone proposes a new course of action. Supporters of present policy respond no to the question of whether a new policy should be adopted.

When questions of fact or value are argued within an institution, such as a court, there are rules of presumption and burden of proof (which will be discussed in Chapter 9) to indicate which belief is regarded as the established one and which is the proposed new belief. Outside of an institutional setting, the decision is more difficult; it may be up to either the participants or the audience.

3. *Clear Statement of the Nature of Change.* This simply means that everyone needs to know what new belief or policy is being proposed to replace the old. The nature of the proposed change is not clear when someone merely asks: Should the United States change its policy on troops in Europe? Change it in what direction? The change could be either to *decrease* the number of U.S. troops in western Europe or to *increase* U.S. troop strength. But there is another problem of clarity in this example. Even if we knew the direction of change proposed—say a decrease in the number of troops—we would still know very little about *what* is proposed. How much of a decrease? Opponents would surely care whether the proposed decrease were 10,000 troops rather than, say, 200,000. Does the proposed decrease in troops mean that the U.S. commitment to the defense of Europe has also declined? It may not be feasible to clarify all of the elements of a proposed change in the phrasing of a central question, but we cannot get into much trouble by trying to clarify as much as possible.

4. *Only One Central Idea.* Another principle that helps to achieve clarity in the phrasing of central questions is the principle of limiting a question to *one* central idea. This is a way to avoid the confusion that results when people try to argue about several matters at the

same time. Problems in society are often closely related to each other, at least in the minds of advocates, but the critical elements of similar kinds of problems may be quite different. One group of students discovered the consequences of ignoring this principle when they insisted on debating the question: Should the federal government ban all advertising of *alcohol* and *tobacco* products in the United States? Of course, it is true that alcohol and tobacco abuse are widely regarded as significant problems, and both problems have led to similar controversial proposals for bans on their advertising, but, as the students learned, the alleged problems of each product are quite different, and it was confusing to argue both in the same debate.

5. *The Rule of Fairness.* The words used in phrasing a central question should not, in themselves, favor one side or the other. On an analytical level, if a central question is phrased in a way that seems unfair to one side, then the question really does not fulfill its role of accurately indicating the nature of the disagreement. On a practical level, sponsors of public debates are often frustrated when one side or the other objects to the wording of the central question on the grounds that the wording favors the other side. The problem of slanted wording is aptly framed in the cliche question: When did you stop beating your spouse? When the central question is perceived as unfair, a public debate tends to generate more heat than light as advocates bicker about procedures rather than exploring the issues. Consider, for example, the following alternatives for a central policy question on a proposal to drill for oil in the arctic wilderness in Alaska.

> Should the federal government destroy our environment by allowing the greedy oil companies to drill for oil in the Alaskan arctic wilderness?

> Should the federal government permit oil exploration in the lands set aside for an arctic wilderness in Alaska?

Supporters of oil exploration would object, and with good cause, to the first version of the policy question. In contrast, the second version is phrased in terms that should, in themselves, be acceptable to both sides. A question meets the principle of fairness when both sides agree that the wording of the central question favors neither side, but nevertheless expresses what their disagreement is about.

The purpose of these five principles is to enable us to phrase the central question so that it is accurate, clear, and fair. These are important goals. If we are confused about the focus of a dispute, we will never make sense of its component issues, arguments, and evidence. The key to learning these principles is to apply them as you phrase central questions for the disputes or arguments you encounter.

Issues

After the central question in a dispute has been phrased accurately, the next major step in the process of analysis is to discover and identify the issues of the central question. The word *issue* is used in a variety of ways when people discuss conflict and controversy, and this variety of usage can cause confusion. In argumentation, *issue* has a technical meaning that is critical to the skills of analysis.[2]

> An issue is a vital, inherent question to which the advocates of change must say yes and the opponents of change may say no.

Relationship of Issues and Central Questions

As you examine the definition of *issue*, you may observe that we now have two kinds of questions in the anatomy of controversy: (1) central questions, which focus the dispute as a whole; and (2) issues, the subordinate questions in dispute. Issues are subordinate questions in the sense that they are the parts that, taken together, make up the whole of the central question. This whole-part relationship is illustrated in Figure 2.1.

Elements of Issues

Close examination of the technical definition reveals that an issue has five component elements. When all of the elements are understood, the task of discovering issues—which is essential in understanding a controversy—is considerably easier. The elements enable you to discover issues in a central question and to determine whether issues are correctly phrased.

Elements in the Issue Definition
1. An issue is a *question.*
2. The question is *inherent.*
3. The question is *vital.*
4. Advocates of change *must say yes* to the question.
5. Opponents of change *may say no* to the question.

FIGURE 2.1

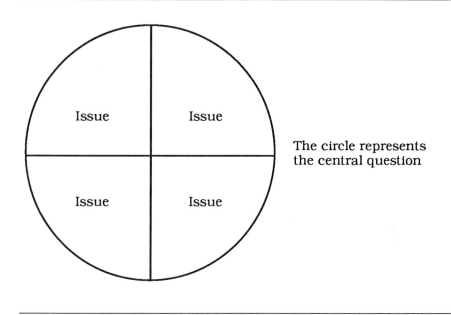

The circle represents the central question

1. *An Issue Is a Question.* The first defining element means that an issue must always be phrased as a question that will permit or require a response of yes or no. It would not be correct to phrase an issue as a declarative sentence or to refer to it as a point or argument or dispute. This means that you can apply a simple test to determine whether a purported issue is correctly phrased. Simply observe whether it is phrased as a question.

2. *The Question Is Inherent.* The term *inherent* means that issues are an intrinsic, inseparable part of a central question; they are derived from the meaning of the terms in the central question. By analogy, issues have the same relationship to central questions as the parts of a table have to the table itself. The parts are essential in order to have a table. Likewise, we would not have a dispute over a central question without its inherent issues. Issues inhere in a central question because they derive from the very meaning or definition of its critical terms.

An example may help to clarify this difficult idea. When a person is accused of murder in the first degree, the dispute yields a central question, which may be phrased as follows:

Did Jones commit first-degree murder in the killing of Smith?

To discover the issues, we must determine the meaning of the critical term *first degree murder*. Colorado criminal law stipulates three defining elements:

1. One person must have *killed* another.
2. The killing must have been *intended.*
3. The killing must have been *premeditated.*

Thus, to say that someone committed first-degree murder is to say that the three defining elements can be established in the actions of the defendant. In our example, these defining elements form the basis of three issues in the trial of Jones:

1. Did Jones kill Smith?
2. Did Jones intend the killing of Smith?
3. Was the killing of Smith premeditated by Jones?

Notice that the three questions are *inherent* because they derive from the very meaning of the critical term *first-degree murder,* and collectively they comprise what is meant by the central question.

3. *The Question Is Vital.* This element of the definition provides a basis for discerning which questions in a dispute may be issues. Some questions in a dispute may be trivial; some may be important but not vital. To label a question as *vital* in a controversy is to identify it as a critical and irreducible basis for decision in the dispute. By analogy, consider a simple object like a three-legged stool. Each of its legs is vital to its function because it could not stand if one of its legs were missing. Similarly, the charge of first degree murder would not stand if any one of the three issues were omitted. In our murder trial, one of the vital questions (issues) is: Did Jones kill Smith? If a jury decided that the answer to this question, or to any of the vital questions, is no, the change advocated—in this case the conviction of Jones—is defeated. The failure of one issue is thus similar to the failure of one leg of our three-legged stool; if one leg is lost, the stool will not stand up.

Other questions in the trial of Jones may be important but not vital. Some important questions could include: Did Jones have a motive to kill Smith? Did Jones threaten to kill Smith? Does Jones have a history of violent behavior? Although these questions are important, the decision to convict or acquit Jones does not really hang on the response to them. A jury could decide that the answer to all of these questions is no, and yet conclude that Jones is guilty of first-degree murder because the answers to all of the vital questions—the issues—are yes.

4. *Advocates of Change Must Say Yes to the Question.* The fourth element of the definition stipulates that the question must be

phrased so that the side that advocates a change in policy or belief is required to say yes. Notice, in the murder trial, that the advocate of change would be the prosecuting attorney and that the prosecution is required to say yes to all three of the issues in order to establish first-degree murder. A response of yes to only two of the three issues would fail to establish first-degree murder. Thus, advocates of change really have no choice in their response to the issues. In fact, one good way to determine whether an issue is correctly phrased is to ask whether the advocate of change would be required to say yes to the question in order to support the proposed change in policy or belief.

5. *Opponents of Change May Say No to the Question.* This final element specifies the relationship of advocates and opponents. The questions that frame the issues are the same for each side. It is the responses to the issues that determine the relationship of disagreement or agreement between the two sides. Use of the word *may* is intended to indicate that the two sides do not always disagree on all of the issues. Opponents of a change in policy or belief may sometimes agree with the advocates of change on one or more of the issues.

As we noted above, advocates of change *must* say yes to all of the issues, but opponents *choose* whether to say no to all of the issues or merely to one or more of the issues. In our murder trial, for example, the defense could possibly agree with the prosecution that Jones killed Smith, but disagree (respond no) on the issues concerning intent and premeditation. Of course, opponents must respond no to at least one issue or there would be no conflict—the matter would be resolved in favor of the advocates of change. And sometimes, that is precisely what happens. A defense attorney may advise her client, after examining all of the state's evidence, to plead guilty and pray for mercy. But when there is a dispute, it is the opponent of change who decides which issues will be contested and which will be admitted. Advocates of change must be prepared to support a response of yes to all of the issues.

Arguments, Premises, and Evidence

The third major step in the process of analysis is to find the arguments, premises, and evidence that are used by advocates and opponents to support their responses to the issues. As you may have noticed in the discussion so far, analysis depends on a clear perception of the complex parts of controversy. You cannot find issues unless you know what you are looking for in your search. Likewise, finding arguments, premises, and evidence is a frustrating task until you know how to recognize them in reading and in conversation.

Arguments

For more than 2,000 years, scholars in the fields of both rhetoric and logic (called *dialectic* by Aristotle) have shared an interest in the study of argument. It should not surprise anyone to learn that this mutual interest occasionally has produced conflict over disciplinary boundaries—that is, conflict over what part of the study of argument belongs preeminently or exclusively to each discipline. In some instances, such conflict over academic turf has been productive, but my perception is that the better logicians and rhetoricians borrow freely from any discipline that can enhance their understanding of argument and they do not worry much about overlap. Nevertheless, it may clarify the idea of persuasive argument to compare the general perspectives of rhetoric and logic.

The Concept of Argument in Logic

An argument, according to many logicians, consists of a *conclusion* (or claim) that is supported by *premises*. (Premise generally means the same thing as evidence, or the facts.) The discipline of logic, as we noted in Chapter 1, is generally concerned with the principles governing *correct relationships* between premises and conclusions. When the relationship between a conclusion and its supporting premises is correct, logicians say the argument is valid. When the relationship between premises and conclusion is incorrect, logicians judge the argument to be invalid.

A solid grasp of the principles of valid argument is essential for anyone who wants to master the rational elements of persuasive argument. The logician's way of analyzing argument is especially useful in helping to defend ourselves from the fallacious arguments of unethical persuaders. But the task of developing a faculty to discern all of the possible means of persuasion requires a perspective on argument that is, in some respects, more complex.

Perspectives of Rhetoric and Logic Compared

In rhetoric and argumentation, we can use the tests of validity provided by logic, but we are also interested in whether an argument will be perceived as sound and persuasive to a listener. It might be reasonable to say that logicians are interested in arguments that should persuade because they are valid—but it seems more accurate to say that logic, as a field of study, really has no direct interest or expertise in persuasion. Logic is not truly concerned with the persuasive power of arguments; its principles are solely concerned with the correctness or validity of an argument, whether or not it persuades anyone. Some arguments that are logically correct are unpersuasive. And some arguments that are invalid seem to persuade multitudes.

The goal of developing a faculty of discerning (or seeing) all of the available means of persuasion means that we are interested in the persuasive power of all arguments that persuade, even if they are invalid. Ethical persuaders, of course, do not use invalid arguments (at least, not purposely), and they will promote the use of valid argument by others. But it is nevertheless important to understand why invalid arguments are sometimes persuasive. In the real world, we can expect that we will need to recognize invalid arguments in order to defend ourselves from them.

The relationship of rhetoric and argument is clarified when we look at the components of the basic model of communication that we examined in Chapter 1: source, message, and receiver. Logicians are concerned solely with the properties of the message—and, even more precisely, with the relationships of terms and statements (words, premises, and conclusions) in the message. Rhetoric and argumentation also is concerned with the message, but our interest is not confined to its logical correctness; we are interested in what it is that makes a message persuasive, interesting, clear, appropriate, impressive, and sound to a particular audience.

Rhetoricians examine the nature of audiences (receivers) and share the interest of the psychologist in studying the reactions of audiences to persuasive messages. And finally, rhetoricians analyze the persuasive properties of speakers, or sources of messages, attempting to discover why some speakers seem always to be more persuasive than others, almost apart from the messages they present. Thus, the perspectives of logic are useful in rhetoric and argumentation but they are not sufficient for our purposes.

A Rhetorical Definition of Argument
In order to focus attention clearly on the persuasive dimensions of argument, while still paying proper attention to the logician's principles of correct reasoning, Karl Wallace suggested a rhetorical definition of *argument*. A rhetorical argument, according to Wallace, is *a claim that is supported by good reasons.*[3] As we examine the elements of Wallace's definition, it ought to become clear to you why this way of looking at an argument is superior in rhetoric and argumentation.

Claim is really just a synonym of *conclusion.* Each is a declarative sentence that asserts a judgment or policy position. This means that any of the central questions of fact, value, or policy may be converted to a claim simply by making them declarative sentences. For example, the value question—Do Affirmative Action programs foster unfair discrimination against white males?—may be converted to the claim: Affirmative Action programs foster unfair discrimination against white males. Likewise, any of the issues for policy, fact, or value questions may be converted to claims simply by converting them from questions to declarative sentences. The declarative sentence may be simple or complex, a generalization or a particular claim about a single case.

Components of Rhetorical Argument

A claim that is unsupported is merely an *assertion*, not an argument. A claim is an element of argument only when it is supported by good reasons—other statements offered by the speaker or writer to justify, explain, or support the claim. By itself, for example, the following claim is merely an assertion:

> The proposed use of toxic wastes for fuel in the cement plant is undesirable for the quality of life in our area.

The above statement is the claim of an argument when it is supported by reasons, such as (1) the use of such fuel will add tons of pollutants to the air, (2) our area already has a serious problem of air pollution, and (3) people are already scared stiff about environmental dangers caused by the cement plant.

Logically, any statement presented in support of a claim is a *reason*. In real-life persuasion, however, speakers support their claims in order to convince an audience. Just any old reason, therefore, will not do the job. Speakers need to support their claims with good reasons, as Karl Wallace suggests; that is, reasons that the target audience will consider "good." A good reason is therefore a supporting statement judged to be sound, convincing, adequate, and persuasive by the immediate audience to which it is presented.

Adapting Argument to an Audience

We need to stress the importance of the immediate audience as a way of highlighting one of the unique principles of our rhetorical perspective on argument: Supporting reasons considered sound or persuasive to one audience might, conceivably, be considered unsound and unpersuasive to a different audience. Thus, to an audience that believes air pollution is already a major threat to life on this planet, the statement that "the use of toxic wastes as fuel will put tons of pollutants into our air" would be considered a powerful reason for accepting the conclusion that "the proposed use of toxic wastes fuels is undesirable for the quality of life in our area."

A different audience, however, might not regard the potential air pollution as a major problem or might regard it as much less important than a possible loss of jobs if the cement plant is unable to expand. What makes a supporting reason a good reason, then, is partly a function of the correctness of its relationship to the claim (according to principles of logic). But it must also be considered sound, important, and persuasive to a particular audience. A reason is sound when it seems sensible, reliable, and based on the truth.

You may have noticed, in the toxic fuels example, that the good reasons presented could themselves be classified as claims. (Congratulate yourself if you noticed that!) What makes these statements "reasons" in our example is their *relationship of support* to the claim. The reasons could themselves be the claims of other arguments. Suppose, for example, that the audience is not inclined to accept the first reason, on pollution, merely on their faith in the veracity of the speaker. The speaker would then need to support the pollution statement, providing good reasons for the audience to believe that it is true. In our example, the good reasons probably would consist of factual and expert opinion evidence that has been gathered in a credible study.

At this point, you should have a reasonably clear idea of what is meant by the claim component of argument. We will now examine in greater detail the two primary sorts of material that comprise the components of good reasons: premises and evidence.

Premises

The term *premise*, in logic, usually means a statement of evidence. In rhetoric and argumentation, however, it is useful to distinguish between premises and evidence, even though these concepts are closely related. Here, the term *premise* will refer to those factual or evaluative beliefs that are widely shared in a community or audience to whom a persuasive argument is directed.

Factual Premises
When premises are factual, they comprise those beliefs we share about the nature of the real world as we (our friends, family, fellow students, community, etc.) experience it. Such beliefs may, of course, be incorrect. We know, for example, that the earth was not flat prior to the voyages of Columbus and other explorers of the fifteenth century. Nevertheless, the belief that the world was flat was widely shared in Europe during the fifteenth century, and the enemies of Columbus used this belief as a premise in support of their claims that his proposed voyage would end in disaster.

This sort of example makes it easy for us to feel smug about our superior twentieth-century knowledge, but such feelings are short-lived when we realize that much of our so-called knowledge has little certainty about it, and it may be as susceptible to change as the knowledge of the fifteenth century. The new theory of plate tectonics, for example, has supplanted much of the so-called knowledge in modern geology, and recent discoveries of the molecular structure of the genetic code have revolutionized the field of biology. Thus, to say that premises are factual beliefs does not necessarily mean that the beliefs are true—it is merely to say that premises of this sort are beliefs of a factual character and they are believed to be true by a particular group.

Persuaders are interested in the shared factual beliefs of their audiences because such beliefs can determine whether an audience accepts or rejects a persuader's arguments. What sorts of factual beliefs can make a difference? Suppose you were assigned the task of persuading the student body that they should favor an increase in student fees in order to provide additional funding for the athletic program. Although students might not be in favor of such a proposal initially, nevertheless, some of their beliefs about the facts of life concerning intercollegiate athletic programs could be used to support your point of persuasion. For example, if students believe that a successful athletic program increases "name recognition" of a school or that employers tend to be more inclined to recruit graduates from a school with a successful football program, such beliefs may be used as good reasons in support of argument claims that a modest fee increase is a good investment. On the other hand, some of the factual beliefs of the audience could work against your point of persuasion. Students may believe that past increases in fee support were not followed by any noticeable change in the records of the football or basketball teams or that the present coaching staff is incapable of doing any better, regardless of funding level. Such beliefs would clearly need to be refuted or shown to be inapplicable. The point is that you need to know what your audience believes to be factually true in order to present an effective argument for any point of persuasion.

One of the tricky things about the use of factual premises in persuasive argument is that frequently they are unstated or, more precisely, they often are unstated by the speaker. However, this does not mean such premises are really omitted from the discussion. The audience may be supplying the factual premises silently, to themselves, as the speaker is holding forth. Listeners are seldom passive. As a speaker is talking, the audience does not simply sit and absorb the message like some sort of recording device. Rather, listeners participate actively, adding their thoughts to those of the speaker, and sometimes the thoughts they add are silent refutation of arguments presented by a speaker with whom they disagree.

Shrewd persuaders know that listeners are wearied when the speaker plods along, telling listeners what they already know or believe to be true. So, the intelligent persuader allows the audience to "fill in the gaps," supplying some of the factual premises needed to make an argument complete. An advocate of increased expenditures for the U.S. military, for example, may not say explicitly that "weak nations get pushed around"—especially if that is already a strong, shared belief among the audience he or she is addressing. Such an audience probably would prefer to complete the speaker's argument by adding the unstated factual premise for themselves.

Value Premises

When premises are value beliefs, they consist of those widely shared standards of good and evil, fairness and unfairness, right and wrong, importance and unimportance—in short, all of those beliefs that form the basis of our positive or negative responses to any object, idea, event, and so on. Such shared beliefs in value standards, along with shared factual beliefs about the real world, actually define what we mean when we say that a group of people belong to a culture or that they are part of a community or family.

Curiously, while we find it difficult to perceive such shared beliefs in our own culture, they seem to leap out at us when we travel abroad or entertain foreign visitors here. One of the more interesting things I observed, in my experience as host of international debate teams at the university, was the genuine sense of shock experienced by American audiences as they listened to the arguments presented by the debaters from the former Soviet Union. The shock occurred when the audience suddenly understood the Soviets' *assumptions* about appropriate standards of good and evil in a civilized society. As an example, in one debate (before the perestroika reforms) the audience was shocked to realize that the Soviet team's argument on the merits of their system of government rested on the assumption that *any needs* of the state are more important than the merely personal freedoms or rights of the individual. Thus, if the state needs more workers in Siberia, it has an obvious and unassailable right to send workers to Siberia, regardless of the desires of the individuals. As they saw it, the state has the moral right to tell people where to live and what work they must perform, and they assume that all moral workers know that. Interestingly, the Soviets were seemingly unable to understand why Americans would object to such an exercise in "legitimate" power by the state.

The Soviets, of course, were not unique in believing that their values were superior to those of other nations and communities. The point here is that value beliefs are deep-seated facets of communities, families, and nations—and people tend to be unaware of them. Such value beliefs, which include our concepts of good and evil, right and wrong, tend to govern our response to any argument that urges a positive or negative evaluation of an event, person, idea—in short, anything that we can care about.

Perhaps the most important characteristic of fact and value premises is that they are beliefs—the common opinions of the group to whom the advocate presents his or her arguments. From the point of view of the audience, such fact or value premises do not require any support. The audience accepts them as true or appropriate before the speaker says anything, so the speaker does not need to present any evidence in support of these premises. The speaker simply uses fact and value premises as good reasons supplied by the audience in support of the speaker's claims.

Evidence

The literal meaning of the word *evidence* is that which makes another thing clear, plain, or easy to see.[4] Like a number of concepts in argumentation, "evidence" seems to have originated in the law courts of ancient Greece and Rome. Advocates for the prosecution and defense in the ancient courts were required to assemble and convey all of those items of support for their claims to a magistrate of the court—items including contracts, testimony, laws, oaths, witnesses, and any physical items such as swords or bloodstained clothing.

For our purposes, *evidence* may be defined as the factual foundation for the claims of the advocates. By "factual foundation," I mean all of the familiar kinds of factual materials we use to support the claims we make. Such factual materials include statistics, historical documents, examples, findings from studies, research reports, experimental results, survey reports, expert opinions, accounts of witnesses, and so on.

Classifications of factual materials can be useful as beginning students of argumentation initiate the process of research into a debate topic. When we understand that evidence consists of a variety of facts, such as statistics and examples, it can help us to understand what we are looking for. But any list of evidence types will probably be incomplete. As you gain more experience in finding and using evidence, it may be more productive to construe evidence as any kind of information that can provide a factual foundation for a claim.

The more interesting and fundamental question is not so much what constitutes evidence but whether the factual information presented as evidence is true, sound, reliable, sufficient, and persuasive. That is, what sort of evidence should be accepted or rejected? This question will be explored in Chapter 7.

Summary

1. Unless we are able to make sense of a controversy, we are especially vulnerable in arguments with others, and it will be difficult to develop a persuasive case in support of our own position. To make sense of a controversy is to understand what it is about and to grasp its major substantive parts.

2. Although we can have disagreements on any subject, the substance of a controversy can be analyzed in relation to four critical parts: (a) central questions, (b) issues, (c) pro and con arguments, and (d) premises and evidence.

3. When a controversy consists of a disagreement about something, it can be expressed as a central question of either fact, value, or policy. Factual questions express disputes in which the disagreement consists of opposing positions on what is actually real or true about some matter of either the past, present, or future. Value questions move beyond the level of what is true or false about the world; they focus disagreement on whether some thing or state of affairs is good or bad, important or unimportant. Policy questions focus disagreement on a proposed course of action. Whereas policy questions are usually easier to understand, their issues consist of fact and value questions.

4. A great deal of the bickering that sometimes accompanies our disputes is often caused by confusion over what the dispute is about. When the central question is poorly worded, frustration and charges of unfairness are virtually inevitable. Five principles for phrasing central questions help us to provide clarity and a sense of fairness in our disputes: (a) the crucial yes and no, (b) phrase in the direction of change, (c) clarity in the nature of change, (d) one central idea, and (e) the fairness principle.

5. Issues are the subordinate questions that constitute the critical components of central questions. To understand issues is to grasp the meaning of its technical definition: Issues are vital, inherent questions to which the advocates of change must say yes and the opponents may say no.

6. Persuasive arguments consist of good reasons in support of our claims. The reasons used should be considered "good" by the the audience as well as the advocate, and their relationship to the claim should be logically correct. Arguments are the critical components of proof that support a pro or con response to the issues.

7. Premises are the factual or value beliefs of the audience addressed by an advocate. Evidence is the factual foundation of supporting materials, consisting in examples, statistics, expert opinion, and the like.

We have now completed the initial discussion of the anatomy of controversy, and you should be able to identify the principal parts of any rational dispute. Your knowledge thus far equips you to make some sense of controversies that may have been confusing to you in the past, and your ability to recognize the critical elements in any rational controversy prepares you for the next stage—the methods for analyzing controversies.

Exercises

1. Consult one or more of the periodical indexes, such as the *Public Affairs Information Service* index, and find four topics that seem to be controversial. For each topic, phrase a central question of fact, value, and policy. Be sure your topics conform to the five principles for phrasing central questions.

2. Examine the editorials of your newspaper over a period of a week or so. Try to determine the persuasive claims of each editorial and then classify them as either fact, value, or policy. Assume that some readers would disagree with the claims in the editorials. As you examine the focus of disagreement, phrase the dispute as a central question.

3. Choose one of the editorials from the second exercise and identify the arguments that the writer presents in support of the persuasive claim.

4. Examine the central questions that follow and identify each as a question of either fact, value, or policy. Be prepared to support your identification in class discussion.
   a. Do recent Supreme Court decisions on civil rights indicate that the Court is less committed to the principle of affirmative action?
   b. Are American soldiers still being held as prisoners by the Vietnamese?
   c. Are American-made automobiles inferior to those made in Japan?
   d. Should the United States join with other nations in the Western Hemisphere to form a free trade zone?
   e. Should the federal government outlaw the possession and sale of "assault" weapons?
   f. Are the benefits of nuclear energy worth the risks?

g. Were the reports of American journalists, broadcast from inside Iraq, harmful to U.S. war aims?

5. Apply the principles for phrasing central questions and identify a flaw in each of the following:
   a. Should the United States continue its policy of guaranteeing the defense of Western Europe?
   b. Should Israel change its policy toward the Palestinians?

Endnotes

1. Other sources in argumentation and debate provide an alternative way of classifying the major kinds of disputes, and these alternatives can deepen your understanding of the nature of controversy. See, especially, Douglas Ehninger and Wayne Brockriede, *Decision by Debate* (New York: Harper & Row, 1978). Ehninger and Brockriede use both central questions and propositions in identifying disputes.
2. My definition of *issue* is a modest extension of the definition proposed by George Ziegelmueller and Charles Dause in their book, *Argumentation: Inquiry and Advocacy* (Englewod Cliffs, NJ: Prentice Hall, 1975). See also Ehninger and Brockriede, *Decision by Debate*.
3. For a more complete analysis of the concept of rhetorical argument, see Karl Wallace, "The Substance of Rhetoric: Good Reasons," *Quarterly Journal of Speech, 49* (1963): 239–249.
4. For an interesting discussion of the nature and functions of evidence, see Gerald Miller, "Evidence and Argument" in *Perspectives on Argumentation*, ed. Gerald Miller and Thomas Nilsen (Glenview, IL: Scott, Foresman, 1966).

3

Methods for Analyzing Controversies

Central Ideas in This Chapter

1. Discovering the issues, arguments, and evidence in a central question requires a method of analysis and in-depth research.
2. The stasis model provides a method for discovering issues in questions of fact and value.
   - Conjectural issues focus on the facts in dispute.
   - Definitional issues focus on the meaning of the facts.
   - Qualitative issues focus on mitigating circumstances.
   - Procedural issues focus on the rules for the conduct of a dispute over fact or value questions.
3. The stock issues model provides a method for discovering and phrasing the issues in questions of policy.
   - Motive issues focus on the rationale for any action.
   - Obstacle issues focus on the limitations of the present system.
   - Cure issues focus on the capacity of the proposed policy to satisfy the motive.
   - Cost issues focus on the advantages and disadvantages of the proposed action.
   - Comparison issues focus on the potential alternatives to the proposed action.
   - Procedural issues focus on the rules for the conduct of a dispute over policy questions.
4. Three kinds of issues emerge in the process of analysis: potential, contested, and admitted.
5. The stasis model provides a method for increasing depth of analysis for each of the issues in a policy question.

The goal of analysis is to discover the issues and to provide a kind of road map for the research process as you seek to discover the pro and con arguments, premises, and evidence used by the advocates in a particular controversy. To discover the issues, you need a combination of (1) in-depth research into the subject and (2) a method of analysis. Research without method generally results in disorganization and frustration—in much the same way that you might feel frustrated in trying to learn the layout of a strange city without a map. On the other side, use of analytical methods without research yields only a shallow understanding of a controversy—somewhat like trying to explore a city, such as London, by simply reading a map in your hotel room. You must walk about and get into the city!

The purpose of this chapter is to explore two analytical models for discovering and understanding the issues for central questions. The issues, in turn, clarify what we are looking for as we seek pro and con arguments and their supporting evidence.

Models for Discovering Issues

The earliest efforts to devise models for discovering the critical elements in disputes were made long ago, in the fifth and fourth centuries B.C. in Greece. As the ancient Greek rhetoricians studied the speeches of advocates in the courts and the legislative arena, they discovered that the central questions in dispute exhibited *persistent patterns* in the clash of persuasive arguments. Amidst the seeming chaos of particular facts in court cases or legislative debates, there was a surprising uniformity in the kinds of issues or vital questions that constituted the bases for decision.

Patterns of one sort seemed to emerge in the disputes of the law courts, where advocates argued matters of justice and injustice. Another sort of pattern was observed in the clash of arguments in the legislative bodies, where most of the argumentation concerned policy questions. In both settings, however, a rudimentary grasp of these uniformities, or patterns of issues, enabled the advocate to anticipate what would be important in future deliberations. Advocates in the deliberative assemblies and the courts could use these patterns to discover the potential arguments for each side, in advance of the debates, because they would know that the same kinds of issues would be important in future disputes of the same type.

Identification of the persistent patterns of issues and arguments enabled the early scholars in rhetoric and argument to develop two useful models for discovering issues. For questions of fact and value, the model is called the *stasis*. For policy questions, the model is called *stock issues*.

Stasis Model

The earliest efforts to develop an analytical system for fact and value questions seem to have been made by Corax and Tisias in the fifth century B.C. in the Greek city of Syracuse on Sicily. Aristotle added to these efforts in his *Rhetoric*, but the stasis model, as such, seems to have been perfected by Hermagorus of Temnos sometime in the second century B.C. In any event, the stasis model was a fully developed analytical tool by the first century B.C., during the time of Cicero, the greatest orator of the Roman world, and it has retained its essential form over the past 2,000 years with few changes.[1]

Like some of the other Greek words we have encountered, the term *stasis* has been adopted by the English language but its usage and meaning seem to be confined to medical and scientific fields. The ancient meaning of stasis is approximately translated as "a standing still"—a kind of dynamic pause that is created when opposing forces push against each other and neither is able to prevail, at least for the moment.

When this dynamic sense of standing still is applied to disputes over questions of fact and value, it refers to the kind of impasse that occurs when a charge is made ("You are guilty of assault") and a reply from the accused directly denies the charge ("I am not guilty of assault"). In a sense, the prosecution's charge sets up a kind of movement in the direction of a guilty verdict. If it is not resisted, there would be no dispute; the trial would be over. If it is resisted, the defendant's denial confronts the charge, producing a dynamic pause, or stasis.

Ancient Greek rhetoricians observed that when the accused offers a reason in support of his or her denial of the charge, the reason clarifies the nature of the stasis, or standing still, making it possible to discover the vital questions or issues.

Four Stasis Issues

We begin our discussion of this model by considering the kinds of issues we can anticipate in relation to four substantive categories of stases. As Cicero pointed out, the issues in criminal cases seem to fall consistently into four principal categories of questions.[2] These categories suggest the substance of the issues rather than the form of the questions. They alert us to what the questions will be about rather than how the questions will be phrased.

1. *Conjecture.* This issue is concerned with dispute over the alleged facts. If someone is charged with committing a crime, the conjectural issue would be concerned with: Did the event happen? Did it happen in the manner alleged? Who did it?
2. *Definition.* This issue is concerned with the meaning of the facts or the name that the facts should be called—for example, should a killing be defined as murder or self-defense?
3. *Quality.* This issue is concerned with the appropriate interpretation of the facts after they have been defined. Issues concerned with the quality of an act may ask if the act, though technically wrong, is justified or at least forgivable.
4. *Procedure.* This issue is concerned with the procedures followed in the conduct of an argument or dispute. The issue might be whether the charge has been properly drawn, whether the case is before the proper court, or whether the defendant's rights of due process have been violated.

Conjectural Issue

The first level of any criminal case derives from a charge that something (some action, event, factual matter, etc.) happened or is the case—giving rise to what the ancients called the *conjectural* stasis, an issue concerning the facts in dispute. In a famous case during the Roman republic, for example, Cicero defended Milo against the charge that Milo murdered Clodius. The conjectural stasis, or issue, was therefore concerned with the facts alleged, leading to the first vital question:

Did Milo kill Clodius?

Since Milo admitted killing Clodius, the conjectural issue was not contested. The two sides were in agreement on this issue.

Definitional Issue

If the critical facts are not contested—as in this case—the stasis analysis moves to a second level to determine whether the two sides agree or disagree over what the facts should be called. Killing is not always the same thing as murder. If one side says it was self-defense and the other side says murder, the dispute is focused on the definitional stasis. In this case, the definitional issue was:

Did Milo's killing of Clodius constitute a murder?

Cicero denied that the killing of Clodius was murder, claiming that Clodius laid in wait for Milo and attacked him. Prosecution and defense therefore argued for competing definitions of the same facts—one side claiming that the actions constituted murder and the other side claiming self-defense.

Ordinarily, we are tempted to think that criminal cases will be resolved when we have decided the conjectural and definitional issues, but life is more complex. The task of a law court is more than simply deciding matters of fact and definition; it is charged with determining justice and injustice in a case. If the court decides that a murder, or robbery, or an assault has been committed—based on its resolution of the conjectural and definitional issues—it may then be faced with another kind of issue, which the ancients called the stasis of *quality*.

Qualitative Issue

The central idea of the quality stasis is the notion that all of our rules and concepts have exceptions. Most of us have had the experience of arguing that some act we have committed is justified or at least not as bad as might normally be thought. We argue that something, some circumstance perhaps, makes our act an exception or provides an excuse. Thus, in ordinary circumstances, it is wrong to kill another person, and it is first-degree murder when the killing is premeditated and intended. But the condition of war seems to nullify the *first-degree murder* rule just presented. More generally, there may be exceptions to this or any other legal rule. A productive way to think about the stasis of quality is to ask: Are there unusual facts, competing values, or other criteria for judgment that might lead us to set aside ordinary standards for defining and interpreting the facts?

The stasis of quality is an explicit recognition that the real world frequently confounds the best efforts of human beings to define terms like first-degree murder with such precision and generality that the definitions will apply to all murders in a uniform and unambiguous manner, and for all time. Throughout the ages, courts have always had to decide cases in which they were forced to set aside their ordinary criteria for crimes such as murder, theft, fraud (in fact, criteria for any crime whatever) for what seemed to be unusual circumstances.

In criminal cases, the quality stasis could be initiated with the question: Was the action right or wrong? Or we might ask: Were there any extenuating or mitigating circumstances that might cause us to set aside our normal standards for defining or interpreting the facts? In Cicero's case, the qualitative issue was whether the killing of Clodius, even if it was technically a murder, should be excused because of Clodius's behavior. In other words, was the murder a good or a bad action, everything considered? Cicero argued that the killing of Clodius was a good act, even if the court decided it was a murder, because Clodius was a bad citizen who had plotted the overthrow of the Republic and had committed crimes against his fellow citizens.

Qualitative issues are not limited to ancient cases. What would courts do today with an admitted killer, Jones, who is 6 years of age? Even if there were no dispute over whether the facts of the killing met the ordinary definitional criteria for first-degree murder, children in the United States are not held to adult standards of criminal behavior. Alternatively, suppose that Jones is an adult who was certain in his own mind that killing Smith was the only way to prevent Smith from launching a nuclear missile at Russia. We must always recognize the potential for extenuating circumstances that could justify an action otherwise defined as wrong in our legal code.

In an effort to make sense of the complex idea of extenuating circumstances, Aristotle made the useful distinction between the written laws of a community and the unwritten universal law—or the idea that justice goes beyond the written code of any society. The concept of "equity," as Aristotle explained in his *Rhetoric*, makes up for the deficiencies in the written law:

> *Equity bids us be merciful to the weakness of human nature; to think less about the laws than about the man who framed them, and less about what he said than about what he meant; not to consider the actions of the accused so much as his intentions; nor this or that detail so much as the whole story; to ask not what a man is now but what he has always or usually been.*[3]

Procedural Issue

The stasis of procedure is concerned with arguments over the rules that govern the actions of all participants in a dispute. In ancient Greece, procedural issues could involve questions over whether the criminal charge against an accused was properly phrased, or whether the case was being tried before the proper court. Today, especially in the United States, procedural disputes seem to be even more important in criminal cases. Such disputes arise over whether the defendant was advised of his or her rights at the time of arrest (the Miranda rule), whether the accused was provided access to counsel before questioning, and so forth.

Strictly speaking, such disputes may not constitute vital questions that are inherent in the central question of whether the defendant committed the crime as charged. It may be more accurate to say that procedural questions are inherent in the court itself or its rules. But the resolution of procedural questions can determine the outcome of a trial. Moreover, in every arena, procedural disputes are potentially crucial in deciding a central question of fact or value, and we need to understand them if we are to make sense of the disputes around us.

Applying the Stasis Model

Students sometimes find it difficult to understand the stasis model at first, partly because it represents an unfamiliar way of thinking and also because it does not lend itself to easy formulas. You cannot learn the stasis model merely by memorizing the names of its categories. In order to develop proficiency with the stasis model, you must apply it to fact and value questions.

The stasis model suggests that we commence the analysis of any controversial question of fact or value by asking: What facts are either alleged or implied in the position of the pro side of the dispute? Does the con side deny these alleged facts? If so, the first issue is conjectural, focusing the dispute on the assertion and denial of the two sides in relation to the facts. Whether the two sides agree or disagree on the alleged facts, however, they may disagree over what the facts mean—leading to the definition issue or the meaning of the facts.

The Definitional Issue in an Ancient Case

One of the cases recounted by Suetonius, in the first century A.D., provides an interesting example of a dispute in which the two sides agreed on the facts but contested the definitional issue:

> Some young men from the city went to Ostia in the summer season, and arriving at the shore, found some fishermen drawing in their nets. They made a bargain to give a certain sum for the haul. The money was paid, and they waited for some time until the nets were drawn ashore. When they were at last drawn out, no fish were in them, but a closed basket of gold. Then the purchasers said the haul belonged to them, the fishermen said it was theirs.[4]

There was no dispute about the facts. Both sides agreed as to what was said and what happened. The dispute turns on the definitional issue. The fishermen, of course, would define *haul* as fish only, arguing that that was their intent in making the agreement. The young men countered that *haul* meant everything in the net.

As you reflect about the kinds of arguments you have had with family or fellow students, the stases of conjecture and definition, in particular, should help you to understand the positions of each side as well as what you might have argued if you had understood the stasis model. But the stasis model should also enable you to make sense of some public controversies in the news.

Applying Stasis to Contemporary Value Disputes

Consider the dispute over the value question: Is American elementary and secondary education inferior to that provided in Japan? The stasis of *conjecture* suggests that we look for the facts that people on the pro side point to when they compare education in the United States with Japan. Some of the alleged "facts" for the pro side include selected achievement test scores of Japanese and American school children at various age levels, the number of days spent in school each year, the percentages of school-age children who graduate from high school, and the like.

Although some of these alleged facts could be disputed, the controversy seems to be focused instead at the definitional level. The stasis of *definition* alerts us to ask what the critical terms in the value question mean. What are the appropriate standards or criteria for comparing educational systems among different cultures? What does it mean to say that one educational system is "inferior" to another? Does a difference in test scores, per se, constitute an adequate basis for a judgment of superiority or inferiority?

In addition, the stasis of *quality* should alert us to the potential for mitigating circumstances. Former Prime Minister of Japan, Yasuhiro Nakasone, created something of a storm of protest—though he apparently meant no insult—when he suggested that the relative educational successes of the Japanese could be understood as a predictable result of a highly homogeneous population, with very little immigration from the outside world, whereas the United States has an extraordinarily diverse population that would present educational challenges to any school system. Whether we agree with Nakasone or not, his point illuminates the qualitative issue. It suggests that unique features of either Japan or the United States might make it unfair or inappropriate to use ordinary test scores as the standard for comparing the education achievements of the two nations.

Using Stasis to Find Issues in Value Comparisons

The stasis model can also be used whenever the central question asks whether one thing is better or worse than another. Consider the rather banal situation of the salesperson who asserts that a Japanese-made car (Alpha) is better than an American-made car (Beta). The salesperson might commence her case by pointing to comparative "facts" for the two cars: (1) the Alpha gets 43 miles per gallon, whereas the Beta gets 35 miles per gallon; (2) the price of the Alpha is $1,000 less than the Beta; (3) the Alpha has been given a higher rating by an automobile club; and (4) for the past year's model, the Alpha had lower repair costs than the Beta.

At the *conjectural* level, any of these alleged facts could be contested. What is the evidence, for example, that the Alpha gets 43 mpg while the Beta gets 35 mpg? If the evidence comes from estimates of the Environmental Protection Agency, you might point out that such estimates have been widely criticized for their inaccuracy. Similarly, you might argue that the price difference is either misleading or untrue. Few buyers of American-made cars would be foolish enough to pay the list price, and data on purchase prices actually paid by consumers are notoriously unreliable. The third and fourth "facts" alleged could also be contested, but perhaps you get the idea of how the value claim that the Alpha is "better" than the Beta could be argued at the conjectural level, focusing on the factual claims from the pro side.

At the *definitional* level, we examine what the alleged facts mean. Even if the four factual claims regarding the Alpha and the Beta are true (or not contested), would the difference in gas mileage, price, and the like constitute sufficient reasons to judge the Alpha as "better"? At this level we begin to ask about the significance of the difference in gas mileage and the other alleged advantages of the Alpha. How much of a cost saving, for example, will the difference in 8 miles per gallon yield to the consumer? More importantly, perhaps, we may think about other criteria, or standards, that should be considered in judging which auto is "better." How about the ride, handling, dependability, and other performance items of each auto? What about the warranties? The point is that when we consider only the four alleged advantages of the Alpha, there is a tendency to assume that they reflect the only important bases for judging which auto is better.

The stasis of *quality* is perhaps a bit slippery here, but it suggests that we need to think about the relationship of this argument to its context. We should think about extenuating circumstances that might cause us to set aside our ordinary criteria for evaluating the merits of automobiles. Some would argue, for example, that we need to think about the trade imbalance between the United States and Japan, or the number of jobs exported to other nations when Americans buy foreign cars, or our own direct interest in a healthy U.S. economy.

In a somewhat different approach to the stasis of quality, some of the leaders of the U.S. auto industry have argued that a comparison of fuel efficiency and list price is unfair—that the industry has not emphasized fuel efficiency in its cars because the public has indicated, by its purchasing pattern, that gas mileage is not important. In addition, they argue that the Japanese have a price advantage because of unfair subsidies from the Japanese government.

As you gain experience with it, the stasis model should enable you to recognize the potential issues whenever anyone confronts you with a fact or value position (a central question of fact or value, in disguise). Moreover, as we shall point out later, the stasis model also provides powerful tools for deepening analysis of policy questions, to which we now turn.

Stock Issues Model

Stock issues are generalized forms of the vital questions that are inherent in any dispute over a policy question. While these generalized questions conform to all of the elements in our technical definition of *issue*, they are the generic models or archetypal forms for the issues in all policy questions. Like the stasis categories, the stock questions outline the vital substance of the actual issues in any dispute over a proposed course of action. In addition, stock issues suggest patterns or forms for phrasing the specific issues for any policy question, and they alert us to what will be important as we begin research.

If you surveyed some of the current textbooks in argumentation and debate, you would find that stock issues models are organized and phrased in several ways by various authors, suggesting that stock issues are more akin to an analytical concept than to any sort of precise mathematical formula. There is nothing harmful in this variety of models. The variety of "generic questions" merely indicates that analysis of policy questions is, like all arts, a matter of applying principles; it should not approached as if it were a set of recipes or the rote application of a formula.

As an analytical concept, stock issues will never be truly understood or mastered merely by memorizing a set of generic questions. Experience is the key. Initially, of course, you will need the experience of memorizing the stock issue questions, and you need to study the application of the stock issues that follows. But, to advance beyond mere memorizing, you need to move quickly to the second stage of experience, which involves applying the stock issues to a policy question of your own and evaluating the efforts of others as they use this model.

The stock issues model presented here has two components: (1) four *principal* stock issues and (2) two *subordinate* stock issues. We begin with an exploration of the four principal stock issues, so called because they outline the questions that are vital in any proposed new course of action. Next, we will examine two subordinate stock issues. They are subordinate because of their dependency on the way argument develops or on the rules for conducting a dispute. The subordinate stock issues seem to be less universal in their occurrence, especially when policy disputes are not contained in an institutionalized setting, like a legislative body. But it is useful to be aware of their existence.

The following version of the principal stock issues reflects the work of a number of argumentation theorists over the centuries, and it includes some modifications that I have found useful.[5] Study it carefully. Notice that there are alternative ways of phrasing the stock questions within the four categories. These variations in phrasing often help us to adapt the statement of issues to the needs or peculiarities of each policy question.

The Principal Stock Issues

Forms of the Questions

    Motive: Are the problems (or harms) of ＿＿＿＿＿＿＿＿
           significant enough to warrant action?
           Alternative: Are the unmet needs (goals, desires)
           of ＿＿＿＿＿＿＿＿＿ important enough to
           warrant action?

    Obstacle: Is the present policy (or system) of ＿＿＿＿＿＿＿＿
           incapable of solving the problem (or meeting the needs,
           desires, goals) of ＿＿＿＿＿＿＿?
           Alternative: is the present policy of ＿＿＿＿＿＿＿
           responsible for (or the cause of) the problem
           of ＿＿＿＿＿＿?

    Cure: Will the proposed new policy (course of
           action) of ＿＿＿＿＿＿＿＿ solve the problem
           of ＿＿＿＿＿＿?
           Alternative: Will the proposed policy
           significantly reduce the problem
           of ＿＿＿＿＿＿?

> *Alternative*: Will the proposed policy produce
> the advantage of _____?

> *Cost*: Will the benefits of solving the problem
> of _____ justify the costs of the proposed
> solution of _____?
> *Alternative*: Will the advantages of _____
> outweigh the disadvantages of the proposed
> change of _____?

Understanding the Logos of the Model

The first thing you need to understand about this or any other stock issues model is its assumption that the issues for *all* policy questions—regardless of their subject—always derive from the same set of persistent topics: motive, obstacle, cure, and cost. This means that there is an underlying logos of the model. The questions on the motive and the other stock issues are inherent in any policy question and they are vital in any decision to adopt or reject a proposed new action.

Motive Issue

To say that a new course of action should be adopted necessarily includes the idea that someone, at least, is dissatisfied with something at present. I refer to the potential range of dissatisfactions as the *motive* for change because this term includes all of the things that can move us to take action. Motive thus includes a problem or harm to be solved, a need or desire to be met, a goal or objective to be reached, or an advantage or benefit to be gained. At least one of these conceptions of motive is an inherent element in any decision to change from present policy, law, action, or whatever.

In a sense, this is simply a way of saying that a new course of action is a means to an end—and "end" is what we mean by "motive." But even if we think a new course of action is desirable in and of itself (i.e., the new action *is* the end) the idea of motive would still be important. Thus, for example, an action that we might consider an end in itself, such as the pleasure of a trip to Tahiti, is merely a kind of recasting of either the desire or goal dimension of *motive*.

The idea behind the motive issue is that we do not change our laws, policies, way of life, or whatever is being proposed unless there is either something unsatisfactory at present, like an unmet need, or some advantage to be gained that would be desirable to us. If there is no motive, there is no reason to consider any sort of change. So, the advocates of change must be able to say yes to the motive question; an answer of no, if judged to be correct, would defeat the proposed change.

Does this seem terribly abstract? Yes, of course! But we need only examine any of the relatively simple policy questions to clarify the idea here. Suppose Ralph is considering a central policy question for himself: Should I buy myself this new mountain bike? The stock issues model suggests that we cannot have a complete analysis of this proposed new action (purchase of the bike) unless we begin by considering the motive for doing anything at all.

The potential motive, in this case, would feature Ralph's present dissatisfactions that are relevant to the bicycle. What was it that led him to consider doing *anything?* Suppose, for this case, that Ralph's primary concern is his problem of transportation around campus. Accordingly, the motive issue would be: Are Ralph's transportation problems around campus significant enough to warrant action? Do you see why this question is vital? Even if Ralph is deliberating this question only with himself (meaning he is not asking his parents to buy the bike), the part of him that is advocating the new purchase would *have to* say yes to this motive question. If Ralph decided that his transportation problems are annoying but *not significant enough* to warrant action at the present time, then the potential new bike purchase is defeated.

Obstacle Issue

Even if it is clear that the motive question must be answered yes (Ralph's transportation problems are significant), the next vital question in any policy question is always the *obstacle* issue, in one or another of its guises. In this case, since Ralph already has an old bicycle, the obstacle question would be phrased: Is Ralph's present bicycle incapable of solving his transportation problems on campus? Notice, again, that the part of Ralph advocating the new bike *must* say yes to this question. If the old bike can handle his transportation problem, there is no need to make any change, including the purchase of a new bike.

Ordinarily, Ralph would not have said yes to the motive question unless there was some sort of problem connected to his present bicycle. However, it is possible to say yes to the motive and no to the obstacle. In part, this is because there are two closely related elements in the obstacle issue: (1) the inherent abilities or capabilities of the present system and (2) the causes of the problem. Suppose that Ralph's inability to get to classes or the library has been "caused" by two flat tires on his present bike. In this case, the causes of the transportation problems (which are serious) are not "inherent" because the present bicycle can solve the problems if its tires are repaired.

Of course, it may very well be that transportation is only part of the reason Ralph wanted the new bike; perhaps he also coveted its 18 speeds, its ultra-light frame, and its "campy" styling. But if these latter items are really an important part of Ralph's present dissatisfaction, they should be included in the analysis of his motive. In order to have a solid analysis of obstacle, we need to consider all facets of the motive.

Cure Issue

If Ralph decides that the old bike cannot solve his transportation problems, even with repairs, yet another vital question comes from the stock issue of *cure*: Will the proposed new bicycle solve Ralph's transportation problems on campus? Ordinarily, I suppose, we would not expect this question to be argued on a topic of this sort. We would think that only a nitwit would pick out a potential new bicycle, go through all of this analysis, and then discover that the bike would not solve his problem.

However, we should never assume that an issue will be uncontroversial or uncontested prior to our investigation. The cure issue is always a potentially vital question in any policy question—even in our simple bike proposal. People do, in fact, sometimes ignore whether the problems they have defined can be solved by their proposed solutions. Suppose Ralph goes to school in an area with icy roads or heavy snowfall throughout most of the school year. Ralph might find that his ability to get to classes has not been improved with the new bicycle—that he really needs an automobile or four-wheel drive vehicle to solve his transportation problems.

Cost Issue

The final stock issue, *cost*, is also a vital basis for decision, at least potentially, in any policy question that calls for a new course of action. The cost issue compares the value of the benefits we might get from solving our problem, plus any side benefits, to the cost (or disadvantages) of the new course of action. In our example, the primary cost element would be the purchase price of the new bicycle, but it is important to realize that the idea of cost includes any disadvantages of the proposed action. Likewise, benefits include any sort of advantage.

Although financial gain is certainly a kind of benefit, the primary advantages in our example have little to do with money. At least, it would be difficult to estimate the dollar value of solving Ralph's transportation problem, and even more difficult to place a dollar value on the aesthetic pleasure of owning and riding an 18-speed, ultra-light frame, "campy" marvel. Nevertheless, it is crucial to any rational analysis to ask: How much is all of this worth? More precisely, the cost issue for this topic would be: Will the benefits from solving Ralph's transportation problem (plus the aesthetic pleasures of ownership) justify the cost (or disadvantages) of the new bicycle?

Financial cost is the easiest to gauge at first. If the purchase price of the new bicycle is, say, $1,200, the cost issue asks whether it is worth that much to solve the transportation problem and to gain the pleasures of ownership. In effect, the cost issue suggests a kind of balance sheet, comparing benefits to costs, or advantages to disadvantages. It may be true, as the adage goes, that a cynic is a person who knows the price of everything and the value of nothing, but the price of a thing (including all disadvantages) needs to be related to its alleged value if we are to make wise policy decisions.

The idea of cost, as noted above, includes any disadvantage from the proposed new purchase. There is always an *opportunity* cost (i.e., if Ralph spends his money on the bicycle, he loses the opportunity to buy an automobile with it). In addition, there can be perverse disadvantages in riding a beautiful and expensive bicycle around campus. Ralph may be concerned that his new bike, unlike the old one, will be coveted by thieves and that he will worry about leaving it parked outside. Moreover, if it takes more time and trouble to lock it up, he may once again be late for class.

Simple policy questions, such as our bike example, are useful in several ways. First, these simple questions should help you to understand the logos, or the rationale, of the stock issues model, and why these four principal stock issues apply to all policy questions, regardless of subject matter or complexity. Second, this sort of example illustrates how the stock questions guide us in phrasing the specific issues for a particular policy question. Finally, I hope this example suggests how you can use the stock issues model in your personal decision making. You probably will not want to argue with yourself about every purchase you make (who would?), but it can be helpful to have a sense of all the potentially *vital* questions whenever you are making a major purchase or deciding anything of importance. As you become more adept at using it, the stock issues model also helps to expose weaknesses in the persuasive efforts of the unethical professional persuaders we discussed in Chapter 1.

Subordinate Stock Issues

The four principal stock issues apply to *all* policy questions, and they provide a more or less complete analytical tool for the initial investigation of most policy disputes. However, my studies of the legislative debate process in the U.S. House of Representatives have provided clear evidence of additional "persistent patterns" in the clash of arguments over policy questions, suggesting two additional stock issues. I call these additional stock issues subordinate because they seem to be dependent on the four principal stock issues.

Forms of the Questions

Comparison: Is the proposed change (or solution)

of _____ the best solution available for

the problem of _____?

Procedure: Have the advocates of change followed the appropriate

rules and procedures in advancing their persuasive

case for the proposed change of _____?

The subordinate stock issue of comparison clearly conforms to all of the defining elements of an issue; that is, it is a vital, inherent question to which advocates of change must say yes, and opponents of change may say no. But some might argue, as Greek and Roman rhetoricians argued centuries ago, that procedural questions are not inherent in a policy question; rather, they are inherent in the rules governing argumentation in the legislature. This is an important distinction, and it seems reasonable. But if the term *inherent* means an element is inseparable from the central question in dispute, my observations suggest that members of legislative bodies such as the U.S. Congress generally regard correct procedures as an inseparable part of decisions on policy questions. If members of Congress decide that the rules have been violated, that is enough to kill a proposed law or resolution. Let's examine how these issues would work in our bicycle case.

Comparison Issue

The comparison issue could easily surface if, say, a friend of Ralph's informs him that she knows of another bicycle on sale that has all of the features that are most important to him, and it is being offered at half the price of the bicycle he has been deliberating about. Accordingly, the comparison issue might be phrased: Is the proposed new mountain bike the best bicycle available in relation to Ralph's transportation needs and financial resources? Even if Ralph has decided that the answers to the issues of motive, obstacle, cure, and cost are yes, a response of no on the comparison issue would be sufficient to cancel the purchase of the bike.

Procedural Issue

The final stock issue is perhaps a bit more difficult in relation to our bicycle example, but it could emerge if Ralph were having a serious dispute over what we call *rules of fairness* or *correct dealing* between merchant and customer. What sort of dispute? Suppose there is only one shop in town that carries the proposed mountain bike that has elicited a judgment of yes on all of the other five issues. Ordinarily, we would expect that Ralph would purchase the bike at this point. But what if Ralph decides that the merchant is being manipulative or unethical in his methods of persuading college students or that he has an insulting and arrogant attitude? This decision, by itself, might be enough to cancel Ralph's proposed purchase.

Procedural issues seem to be most important when argumentation takes place within a rule-governed institution, such as Congress. At least, that is where they seem to be most important in the outcome of a policy debate. In the U.S. House of Representatives, procedural issues seem to surface with every bill that is debated, and members frequently begin their speeches with arguments on whether the sponsors of a bill have followed House rules, including the appropriate deference to committee jurisdiction, unwritten standards of decorum, and a host of other procedural items.

A bill can be defeated if its sponsors are found to be in violation of House rules of parliamentary procedure. Conversely, although it seems bizarre, some members of Congress apparently decide to vote for a bill merely on the grounds that it has followed all the correct or appropriate channels and has received the blessings of particular committees. One congressman told me of an incident in which a member of his own party was threatening to block an important bill granting "wild and scenic" status to a river in the West. He later relented and even voted for the bill when he was informed that the "appropriate committee" had spent about 1,000 hours on the bill— which was merely to say the bill had been considered according to standard House procedures!

Three Categories of Issues: Potential, Contested, and Admitted

As we noted in the discussion of the concept of issue (in Chapter 2), it is not necessary for all of the issues to be argued. You may recall that the advocates of change must respond yes to all of the issues, but opponents have a choice either to say no or to agree with the pro side. Because of the choice available to the opponents of change, issues can be grouped in three categories: potential, contested, and admitted.

For a policy question, all six of the principal and subordinate issues are potential until the opponents of change decide to contest them. The term *potential* refers to all of the vital questions that may be argued by the pro and con sides in a dispute. The term *contested* refers to those issues on which the two sides disagree and there is a clash of arguments. If the two sides agree on a vital question, it is an *admitted* issue.

Using the Stock Issues

In using the stock issues, it is helpful to think of analysis and research as interrelated processes. Both are essential for two major tasks: (1) phrasing the specific issues for a policy question and (2) finding the important arguments and evidence for each issue. Research and stock issues illuminate each other.

The example in Figure 3.1 provides an extended illustration of how the stock issues are used to perform each task. Study this example and use it as a model.

The example does not attempt to provide a complete analysis of its policy question (it omits the comparison and procedure issues), but it should clarify how the stock issues help us to phrase the particular issues for the proposal to resume use of DDT. Notice that a specific issue is phrased for each of the stock issues of motive, obstacle, cure, and cost, and the analysis proceeds by providing a preliminary sampling of pro and con arguments in relation to each issue. Notice as well that the arguments for each side consist of a claim and supporting evidence.

The model analysis in Figure 3.1 is not intended to provide a complete development of all of the argument claims or supporting evidence in relation to any of the four issues. Typically, advocates for each side have a fairly large number of arguments in their arsenal that they could present in relation to each issue. Your goal in analyzing your own policy question is to discover all of the arguments and supporting evidence rather that just a specimen or two for each issue, as I have illustrated in Figure 3.1. The sample brief in Chapter 8 illustrates the kind of complete analysis you should assemble for your topic. However, the model shown in Figure 3.1 should help you to see the relationship of pro and con arguments and evidence in relation to each issue.

By following the stock issues model, you should be able to phrase the *specific issues* for your policy question. These specific issues, in turn, will help to focus your research efforts; it will become easier to find the pro and con arguments and evidence because you will know what you are looking for.

FIGURE 3.1   *Model Analysis: Stock Issues*

Policy Question: Should the use of DDT be resumed to control insect damage to farm crops?

Motive: Is there a significant problem of insect damage to agricultural crops in the United States?

Pro Change

Claim: We are incurring serious damage to grain crops due to insects.

> *Evidence*: USDA study, "In 1984, U.S. farmers lost $95 million in insect damage to corn and wheat."

> *Evidence*: Agricultural Prof. Jane Doe says, "Damage to grain crops of all types exceeds the range of tolerance for a country like the United States."

Against Change

Claim: Insect damage is not a serious problem.

> *Evidence*: Agricultural economist Prof. John Doe says, "The loss attributed to insects is exaggerated—a true estimate is about $5 million."

> *Evidence*: The Earth Club reports that "damage to grain crops is well within the limits of tolerance projected by the United Nations."

Obstacle: Are present methods of controlling insects incapable of holding damage to crops within acceptable levels?

Pro Change

Claim: Many insects are developing immunities to the insecticides used.

> *Evidence*: (should be here)

Claim: Organic farming appears to be an economic impossibility.

> *Evidence*: (should be here)

Claim: Insect sterilization attempts have limited application.

> *Evidence*: (should be here)

Against Change

Claim: Development of immunities does not occur with correct use.

> *Evidence*: (should be here)

Claim: Large-scale programs of organic farming may yet prove successful.

> *Evidence*: (should be here)

Claim: Programs of insect sterilization show promising signs.

> *Evidence*: (should be here)

Continued

FIGURE 3.1   *Continued*

Cure: Will resuming the use of DDT provide a remedy to the alleged insect damage?

Pro Change

Claim: DDT is effective against the entire range of insect pests.

    Evidence: (should be here)

Against Change

Claim: Many varieties of insects have built up an immunity to DDT due to its indiscriminate and uncontrolled use in the past.

    Evidence: (should be here)

Cost: Will the benefits of increased control over insect damage justify the costs of using DDT again?

Pro Change

Claim: Proper use of DDT would increase crop yields by $150 million per year.

    Evidence: (should be here)

Claim: We now know enough about DDT that proper use would not result in any significant harm to the environment or other life forms.

    Evidence: (should be here)

Against Change

Claim: We cannot expect any significant increase in crop yield due to the use of DDT.

    Evidence: (should be here)

Claim: There is no "proper" use of DDT that would avoid extensive killing of birds, fish, and other animals—including people.

    Evidence: (should be here)

Actually, phrasing issues and conducting research is a reciprocal process. The issues guide research, and the discovery of specific arguments and evidence used by pro and con advocates helps to refine the statement of the specific issues so they reflect more precisely the vital questions for decision. The motive issue in the sample analysis on DDT (Figure 3.1), for example, identifies "insect damage to *crops*" as the alleged problem in dispute. However, if you examine the specific arguments and evidence presented by pro and con for that issue, you may notice that both sides focus their arguments on *grain crops* rather than *crops* in general. Thus, the pro and con arguments discovered in the research process indicate that the motive issue should be restated: Is there a significant problem of insect damage to agricultural *grain crops* in the United States?

As you sort out arguments and evidence in relation to the four stock issues, you may discover that one or both sides fail to back up some of their claims with evidence, that some of the evidence cited is flimsy, or that the evidence really does not support the claim for which it is used. Also, you may begin to see some new arguments that could be used to make a stronger case for one side or the other, but which the active participants in the dispute do not seem to be using. Or you may notice weaknesses in the reasoning of one or both sides that do not seem to be apparent to the active participants. If any of these things occur for you, it is cause for self-congratulations rather than worry. It means that you are gaining insights, along with your experience, in the use of the analytical methods. In fact, you are learning what Aristotle defined as the art of rhetoric: the faculty (power, ability) of discerning in any case the available means of persuasion.

The Relationship of Stock Issues and Stasis Models

The stock issues model is a useful tool but, like all tools that are properly understood, it has a limited application. The stock issues model applies only to the analysis of policy questions. It does not help us to discover the issues in questions of fact or value, and the effort to make it work will result in confusion. Avoid the syndrome of the young boy who has just learned how to use a hammer—and then seems to find that everything needs a pounding. Many students are similarly inclined to apply the stock issues model to *all* disputes, perhaps out of a similar kind of exuberance.

On the other hand, analysis of fact and value questions, using the stasis model, can be a productive way of deepening analysis of the issues in policy questions. The stasis model can be used to deepen your analysis of any of the principal or subordinate issues in questions of policy. All of the issues for policy questions may be analyzed independently as questions of fact or value.

Consider the motive issue phrased for the sample analysis on the DDT topic in Figure 3.1:

> *Motive*: Is there a significant problem of insect damage to agricultural crops in the United States?

If you think of this question as a central question rather than as an issue, you should see at once that it is a question of value. As such, the stases of conjecture, definition, and quality can be applied to deepen our understanding of potential pro and con arguments.

At the *conjectural* level, what are the alleged facts concerning insect damage? What sorts of agricultural crops are being damaged? By what kinds of insects? How is insect damage measured or distinguished from damage caused by a virus or fungus?

At the *definitional* level, the most important question is what constitutes a "significant problem" of insect damage? What is the threshold beyond which we move from an ordinary, tolerable problem of insect damage to a "significant" problem? What are the criteria for determining significance? To whom is it harmful, for example?

Surely, in a century of consistent overproduction by U.S. farmers, it would seem difficult to argue that consumers have been harmed by losses to insects. Similarly, to the extent that large agricultural surpluses cause a decline in the prices farmers receive for wheat, corn, and so on, it would seem difficult to establish that the losses in grain crops, at any rate, constitute a problem for farmers in general.

The stasis of *quality* also suggests some intriguing questions about the motive issue. The idea here is to ask about the sorts of circumstances that might lead us to set aside our ordinary criteria for judgment on losses of agricultural crops. Even if we assume that the losses of agricultural crops to insect damage are substantial, and certainly harmful in some respects, the question here might be whether such losses could be viewed merely as a price we are willing to pay for an approach to agriculture that is more in tune with natural processes, and that is striving for lesser reliance on chemical poisons in providing what we need. This, at least, seems to be the sort of argument advanced by champions of organic farming as well as by a sizeable group of biologists concerned about the unknown long-term effects of the tons of insecticides routinely used by farmers year after year. To such organic farmers and biologists, a $95 million loss in corn and wheat might even be considered a small price to pay for a ban on DDT.

You may have noticed that my application of the stases categories to the motive issue is slanted somewhat toward the con side of this dispute—and you would be correct. But no matter; it is simply easier to work one side at a time. We could apply the stases from the pro side with equal ease, and it would be useful for you to do that. Or you might try to use the stases of conjecture, definition, and quality on the obstacle, cure, or cost issues. Your ability to see argument possibilities and to make sense of controversies increases as you gain experience with each of the analytical methods.

Summary

1. Mastery of the methods for analyzing controversies does not result merely from memorizing models or key elements. Like all of the arts of rhetoric, analysis is learned through an effective blending of theory, practice, and criticism.

2. In this chapter, we have discussed the stock issues model, the stasis model, and applications of these tools to discover the issues in questions of fact, value, and policy.

3. The stasis model is based on the idea that the issues of fact and value questions will be found in four categories: the conjectural, the definitional, the qualitative, and the procedural.

4. The stock issues model applies only to policy questions, and it provides the generalized questions that can be adapted to any policy dispute to frame the issues. There are four principal stock issues: the motive, the obstacle, the cure, and the cost. In addition, there are two subordinate stock issues: the comparison and the procedural.

5. There are three kinds of issues: potential, contested, and admitted.

6. The stock issues model applies only to policy questions. The stasis model applies to questions of fact and value. However, because the issue of policy questions are themselves fact or value questions, the stasis model can be used to deepen the analysis of policy disputes.

There is, to be sure, a body of new information here, and some time is required to master it at the level necessary to apply it effectively in analyzing disputes. Most students find that it is helpful to think of the concepts and methods in this chapter as conceptual *tools*, analogous to the tools of an automobile mechanic. The analogy is apt at least to this extent: We would be worried about trusting our auto to a mechanic who did not know at least the names and the uses of each tool of the trade—and we would certainly prefer a mechanic who had actually used the tools prior to the repair job on our car.

Likewise, a student who does not know at least the names and uses of the conceptual tools discussed here is simply lost in attempting to analyze a policy question. However, real excellence is achieved only when the tools are used a number of times. Experience is the key to understanding analysis. You need to apply the methods and concepts we have discussed in this chapter to controversies of the real world.

Exercises

1. Apply the stasis categories to the following case and phrase the issues of conjecture and definition.

Near the end of a term in a statistics class, a student named Sam was charged with bribery. His professor told police that late one afternoon, when he returned from class, he found an envelop under his office door containing $500 in cash and a note, signed by "Sam," requesting a passing grade in the class.

2. Use the stock issues model as your guide, and phrase the four principal issues for two policy questions. It would be useful to select questions that are suitable for debate in class.

3. Select the motive issue from one of the policy questions you analyzed for the exercise above. How would the stasis categories of conjecture, definition, and quality enable you to deepen your analysis or focus your research? Compare your results with those of other students.

4. Apply our definition of issue, and the stock issues model, to identify which of the following are correctly phrased issues for the policy question: Should the university increase tuition by $100 per year to pay for improvements in the library?
    a. Is the present level of tuition more than many students can afford?
    b. Why should students have to pay for the library?
    c. Are the problems of student complaints about tuition significant enough to warrant action?
    d. Would an additional $100 per year from each student provide the needed improvements in the library?
    e. The benefeits of a fine library would justify the costs.

5. Find an editorial in your local paper that either supports or opposes a proposed new course of action. Identify the major arguments in the editorial and classify them according to the stock issues. Are any of the four principal stock issues ignored by the writer? If so, do you think the writer's silence on a particular issue indicates that it is an admitted issue?

Endnotes

1. The work of three scholars has been especially helpful for our understanding of the ancient stasis system as well as the beginning of a stock issues model: Otto Dieter, "Stasis," *Speech Monographs, 17* (1950): 345–369; Lee Hultzen, "Status in Deliberative Analysis," in *The Rhetorical Idiom,* ed. Donald Bryant (Ithaca, NY: Cornell University Press, 1958); and Raymond Nadeau, "Some Aristotelian and Stoic Influences on the Theory of *Stases,*" *Speech Monographs, 26* (1959): 248–254.

2. Cicero, *De Inventione. De Optimo Genere Oratorum. Topica*, trans. H. M. Hubbell (Cambridge, MA: Loeb Classical Library, Harvard University Press, 1960).
3. Aristotle, "Rhetoric," in *Aristotle: Rhetoric and Poetics*, trans. W. Rhys Roberts (New York: Modern Library, Random House, 1954).
4. Cited in D. L. Clark, *Rhetoric in Greco-Roman Education* (New York: Columbia University Press, 1957), pp. 239–240.
5. The stock issues model presented here builds on the work of George Ziegelmueller and Charles Dause, *Argumentation: Inquiry and Advocacy* (Englewood Cliffs, NJ: Prentice Hall, 1975).

4

The Research Process

Central Ideas in This Chapter

1. The goals of research are to understand a controversy, discover the pro and con arguments, and find the evidence.
2. Issues guide research for arguments and evidence.
3. Six key elements in the background of a controversy help to deepen research of the issues and to understand the dispute.
4. Identification of key words in a central question focus the initial search for sources.
5. Effective use of reference sources is essential for building a bibliography.
6. Efficient reading enables the investigator to find evidence and arguments quickly.
7. Four guidelines help the investigator to record evidence in an ethical and efficient manner.

In Chapter 2, we observed that analysis without research yields only a superficial understanding of a central question in dispute. Without a command of the evidence that provides the factual foundation for pro and con arguments, the claims of an advocate are mere assertions. Without real knowledge of the topic, the advocate can only mislead an audience. Therefore, research is the ethical and rational foundation for persuasive argumentation. But what is research and what are its goals?

In rhetoric and argumentation, research is a process of investigation that seeks to achieve three goals: (1) to understand the background of a controversy, (2) to discover the pro and con arguments for each issue, and (3) to find the evidence that provides the factual foundation for arguments. Of course, these goals are not entirely separable. It would be rather difficult to search for evidence unless we had some idea of the major pro and con argument claims. Likewise, as we deepen our understanding of the background of a controversy, we gain a better sense of what factual materials are important.

Many students find that the most troublesome part of the research process is how to begin it. In some cases, getting started seems daunting because students have not developed skills in using a library. Doing research is both inefficient and frustrating for anyone who has not learned to use their own campus library. If you are merely unsure of your expertise, this is a good place to begin learning to research. Reference librarians at many colleges provide tours and instructional materials that explain how to use such vital tools as the reference sections, government documents, microfilm, interlibrary loan, and the use of computers for search and retrieval of materials.

Efficiency in research is not, however, merely a matter of knowing how to find books and journals. To search efficiently for anything, we need to have a clear idea of what we are looking for, we need to understand some of the major tools available for locating high-quality materials on the topic, and we need to understand how to gather and record the fruits of the investigation. Thus, our purpose in this chapter is to understand the major steps in developing and implementing a research plan. Specifically, we will examine (1) what we are looking for, (2) how to find it, and (3) how to record the products of research.

The Focus of Research

Fortunately, the foundations for determining what we are looking for have been discussed in a general way in the preceding chapters.

Determining the focus of research, then, can commence with what we already know—the issues in a central question.

Issues Focus Research

Issues provide a kind of map for the research process, suggesting the kinds of factual materials that are important. In Chapter 2, we examined the major substantive elements in central questions: issues, arguments, premises, and evidence. And in Chapter 3, we explored methods of analysis and the logos of the different kinds of issues. On a general level, the stock issues and stasis categories point to the kinds of arguments and evidence that would be useful to advocates on either side of a central question. This means that you do not need to be engaged in the inefficiency of miscellaneous reading. Before you begin to read anything, you will already have a fairly good idea of what you are looking for—namely, the major argument claims used by the pro and con sides to back up their yes and no responses to each issue, and the specific evidence and premises used to support their argument claims.

A clear statement of each issue, even in a preliminary form, enables us to generate a series of more specific questions to focus our search. Consider how this works with a motive issue that asks: Are the problems of unemployment significant enough to warrant action? This issue can immediately suggest a number of questions that are answered only by investigation. At the general level, we ask: What sorts of arguments and evidence will support the pro side's response of yes to this question? What kinds of factual materials are available for describing the size of present levels of unemployment? How is unemployment measured? Is there any evidence to show that the problem is growing? Who is effected by the problem? How are they harmed? Are there any generally accepted standards for determining when the size of a problem is really serious?

Such questions will inevitably be rather general in the early stages of research. As you learn more about the topic in dispute, you will be able to refine your research questions. For example, by finding answers to the preliminary questions about unemployment, we will learn that there is a distinction between long-term and short-term joblessness, based on the number of weeks that a person has been out of work. The harms of long-term unemployment are much more serious, but there are fewer people involved. So we may want to ask: How many people are among the long-term group? What sorts of harms do they suffer? What happens to their families and their communities? What is the relationship between long-term unemployment and such problems as crime, family instability, and drug use?

Notice that so far we have looked at the motive issue primarily from the pro side perspective. But we will not stop there. Arguments and evidence on the pro side actually provide a very specific research agenda for the con side. How does the con side respond to these arguments and evidence? Are there any flaws in the factual materials (especially statistics and studies) that describe unemployment? Is it true that long-term unemployment always results in the alleged harms? Are there any problems in the criteria for long-term and short-term unemployment? In the chapters that follow, we will examine methods for testing arguments and evidence, and these will suggest a variety of specific research questions that are especially useful for the con side.

Key Elements in the Context of a Controversy

Although issues help us to recognize evidence and argument claims, there is a more direct way to develop an understanding of a dispute. To understand a dispute is to know its history, why the central question is controversial now, and who is involved. More specifically, there are six key elements that need to be investigated:

1. Definitions of critical or ambiguous terms
2. Immediate causes of the controversy
3. Participants in the controversy
4. Present policy or belief—its nature and history
5. Proposed policy or belief—its nature and history
6. Common ground between participants in the controversy

Definition of Terms

An essential early focus for research is the identification and definition of critical or ambiguous words or terms. How many times have you been involved in an argument, only to discover after an hour or so that your opponent does not share your understanding of one or more of the critical words or terms in the dispute? We feel frustrated when we are misunderstood and we feel even more frustrated when the misunderstanding results in an unnecessary or unproductive argument.

Failure to define terms is not the only cause of misunderstanding, of course, but it is often a major cause. Consider the potential for confusion in the ongoing national debate over the quality of education in the United States. Will everyone mean the same thing when they use terms such as *incompetent teaching, functional illiteracy,* and *basics* (as in "back to the basics")? What do people have in mind when they propose to "abolish tenure"? Do they mean that teachers would be stripped of all job security so they could be fired at the whim of an administrator? Can anyone imagine that the sort of talented and intelligent young people we need to attract into teaching could be attracted if all job security were eliminated?

A fuzzy grasp of core words and terms in a dispute produces muddled discussion and frustration. Thus, whenever you engage in argument on any level, it is always worthwhile to ask: What do the words or terms in the central question mean? And, as an argument progresses, it can be enlightening, and even strategically potent, to ask yourself or your opponent what is meant by the words and terms used in the argument claims. In many cases, the superior analysis of a dispute over fact, value, or policy will be based directly on definitions that establish criteria or standards. Clear definition of key terms in a dispute is therefore a crucial goal of research.

Immediate Causes

This element reminds us that disputes are, in a sense, provoked by events in the world. To understand the immediate causes of a controversy is to identify the events that seem to be the catalysts for making people aware of a significant danger, problem, or potential benefit.

Recall, from earlier discussions of central questions, that legislators ordinarily do not propose new laws unless someone thinks there is a problem that requires a solution. Frequently, such proposals occur when the public's attention has been focused or refocused on a problem by some dramatic event. For example, when the Iraqis invaded Kuwait in 1990 and the United States was moving toward war in the Persian Gulf, many people began to reexamine our dependency on imported oil, and the seemingly forgotten question of a national energy policy resurfaced on the national agenda. In addition, questions of fact were argued about the "real" causes of Iraq's invasion and the reasons for U.S. determination to get Iraq out of Kuwait. Questions of value were argued about whether it was worth the risks of war and the loss of American lives in order to restore an undemocratic government in Kuwait.

Attention to the immediate causes of a controversy especially helps to deepen investigation of the motive issue of a policy question. Dramatic events seem to provide a focus for the dissatisfactions that lead to a call for change, and they remind us of previous debates. For example, when John Hinckley, Jr. attempted to assassinate President Reagan, the problem of violence with handguns was once again brought to the attention of the U.S. public, and numerous proposals to curb deaths and injuries from handguns were presented in the U.S. Congress shortly thereafter.

For controversies over questions of fact or value, immediate causes can provide crucial context for the conjectural and definitional issues. Shocking events, for example, such as the videotaped beating of Rodney King by Los Angeles police in 1991, can come to dominate national arguments over the extent and severity of police brutality. Such events become potent symbols. They seem to point to the kinds of factual evidence that will be important on the conjectural level and deepen our understanding of the definitional and qualitative issues.

Immediate causes can be a powerful aid in focusing research. Whenever there is a dispute over a question of fact or value, we should ask: Why is this question being argued now? What made people feel concerned about contradictory views on what is true or important? In disputes over policy questions, we should ask: What has happened to make people think we need a new course of action, policy, or solution?

Participants in the Controversy

When a question of fact or value is argued, it is necessarily argued by someone or some group. Likewise, a proposed new course of action is proposed by someone. The participants in a controversy therefore include all of the pro and con advocates. Participants also include the people who provide information or expert opinion cited as evidence by one side or the other. Identification of the persons or groups can be vital to understanding both the nature of a proposed change as well as the arguments in support of it. On the con side, recall that it is the opponents of change who determine which issues are to be contested.

The question you need to ask as you begin your research is: Who are the advocates and opponents of change in this controversy? Later, as your investigation deepens, you need to know the identity of the major sources of evidence for both sides—that is, who found out the facts used by advocates to support their arguments and who are the so-called experts providing testimony for each side?

Nature and History of Present Belief or Policy

Before you can expect to argue effectively either that a new policy or belief is needed or that a present policy or belief should be kept, you must have a clear grasp of the nature of present policy or belief. You cannot expect to mount an effective attack on present beliefs or policy unless you know what they are. An experienced insurance salesperson, for example, knows that his or her pitch that a client needs additional coverage must be based on the argument that the client's present insurance is inadequate. Frequently, mastery of this element of background research is the major difference in the preparation of the successful and the unsuccessful advocate.

When disputes over questions of fact and value take place within an institution, such as our courts, there are often rules that guide us in identifying the present beliefs. In a scientific discipline, the relevant present belief may be an established theory or accepted description. If the dispute is over a question of policy, we need to discover both the elements of present policy and its history. That is, how did present policy evolve to its present form? What were the reasons the present policy was adopted? This sort of background deepens analysis of the obstacle issue and it is essential for both the pro and the con sides of the dispute.

Nature and History of Proposed Belief or Policy

Knowledge of the proposed belief or policy is also essential to advocates on both sides of a central question. How can one argue that a proposed policy either will or will not solve a problem unless the advocate knows what is being proposed? Advocates on both sides need a detailed understanding of how a new policy or program is to be administered as well as a grasp of the principles of the policy.

A group of students in a recent class debated the question: Should the United States adopt the policy of comparable worth? The question neatly focused an important, timely topic, but the pro side (also called the *affirmative*) was embarrassed in the first debate as the audience witnessed their inability to answer questions about how so-called male and female jobs would be evaluated and what would be done to resolve major inconsistencies in the worth of these jobs that seemed inevitable as they were evaluated by different people.

The effective advocate must know how a new proposal will be implemented and administered as well as what the new proposal entails. If a new policy requires enforcement, such as a proposed revocation of the driver's license for any high school dropout, then both sides must know the details of how such a law would be enforced. And finally, as with present beliefs and policies, we need to understand the history of a proposed policy or belief. Has the fact or value position been advocated in the past? Has the policy been proposed in the past? If a proposed change was rejected at some previous time, why was it rejected? If it was adopted in the past, what were its effects and why was it abandoned? On fact or value disputes, questions of this sort generally deepen analysis of definitional or qualitative issues. In policy disputes, such questions deepen our understanding of the cure and cost issues.

Common Ground

When the opposing sides agree on any of the issues, arguments, facts, or values in a dispute, their agreements are called *common ground*. Contrary to the general view, pro and con advocates often agree on one or more of the issues. For example, both sides of the long-term policy debate on mandatory airbags for automobiles have generally agreed on the motive issue that there is a significant problem in the number of deaths and injuries caused by head-on collisions on our highways. But even when pro and con disagree on all of the issues, they may nevertheless agree on many of the facts and values related to the policy dispute.

Consider, for example, the dispute over the comparable worth proposal. Both sides appear to agree that the average earnings of women are substantially less than the earnings of men. Further, they seem to agree that low income for women who are heads of their households results in a serious problem of poverty for the women as well as their children. Understanding the potential for such agreement on some of the facts and values in a controversy helps us to avoid the shallow bickering of the immature and the pig-headed and it also helps us to deepen our understanding of the issues.

How to Find Research Materials

After you have outlined what you need to investigate—the strategy of your research focus—the next step is to locate the best resource materials available on your topic. The problem of research usually is not a matter of finding enough sources. Even the more modest university library either contains or provides access to large numbers of books, articles, government documents, and other sources of information on almost any question of fact, value, or policy. The beginning researcher can easily feel overwhelmed by the sheer quantity of sources. The primary need is to devise a plan for finding high-quality sources of pro and con arguments and evidence and to avoid wasting time with aimless browsing.

In addition to quality, resource materials should also provide a reasonably balanced view of both sides of a dispute. A major goal of research on a controversy is to find all of the major argument claims and their supporting evidence for both sides on each issue, or at least to come as close to that ideal as possible. Even though we may not plan to argue on both sides of a central question, we need to know what arguments and evidence are available to our opponents. Professional advocates, such as courtroom attorneys, always want to know what the arsenals of their opponents contain.

Initially a research strategy should consist of a working bibliography and a preliminary statement of the issues. The issues, as we have noted, help us to recognize what we are looking for. A working bibliography of sources enables us to plan our research, concentrating effort on the sources that appear to be most productive for each of the issues. But how do we begin?

Identification of Key Terms

One of the most important things to understand about all college and university libraries is that they are designed to enable patrons to find resources through the use of two principal search strategies: author's name and topic. For example, card catalogs are usually organized into separate files for authors and subjects. A topical or subject strategy usually is best suited to the early stages of the research process on a central question. You can make the library work for you if you begin your research by listing the key words and terms (the topics) in your central question and its issues. To some extent, you can also generate topics by anticipating pro and con argument claims as well as concepts that are important to arguments from each side.

The better the quality of key words, the more efficient your search is likely to be; therefore, do not hesitate to seek help in identifying key words. Reference librarians are an excellent source of help. They are often expert in isolating search patterns, and they are usually happy to assist students who approach them with the proper respect, especially when students have invested reasonable effort and thought into their research task. Another valuable resource in finding good key words is experts in the general subject area of the debate topic. In addition to faculty experts, do not overlook experts in the professions that are related to your topic. For example, local attorneys can provide valuable assistance on any debate topic that concerns legal issues. And finally, do not overlook bibliographic aids in the library. An especially useful source of key words is *The Library of Congress Subject Heading List.* It provides subject matter headings as well as synonyms that are used in various indexes.

You do not need to wait until you develop a complete set of topics in order to begin your bibliographic search. In fact, many bibliographic sources suggest alternative key words under most subject headings, so the development of key words and the bibliographic search can be simultaneous once you get started. In addition, when you work with quality books and articles, the authors will often suggest additional sources of information in their notes and bibliographies.

Bibliographic Sources

The following list of bibliographic sources contains some of the more useful aids for research into important public controversies. It is not intended to be a complete listing, but it should provide most of what you need. When you have exhausted this list, it is time to seek the aid of a reference librarian.

1. *Card Catalog.* The card catalog of a library provides a listing of the books and journals it contains. As noted earlier, card files are organized by subject and by author. One of the best places to begin your research is in the portion of the index that lists sources by subject matter. Index cards frequently indicate whether a particular source includes a bibliography. If a book is recent, its bibliography can be a valuable resource of quality materials on your topic. Within the past decade, many college libraries have incorporated their card catalogs into computer databases, permitting a faster search of library holdings on the subject. Some libraries also use databases that access holdings of other libraries in their region.

2. *Public Affairs Information Service (PAIS).* The PAIS is one of the most useful indexes for research into important public controversies. This index is a publication of the New York Public Library, and it is designed to provide bibliographic resources on contemporary topics for debate. It lists books, some government documents, and articles in journals and periodicals. The PAIS is incorporated in some databases used by college libraries.

3. *Readers' Guide to Periodical Literature.* This is a useful index for the more popular magazines and a few of the better-known journals. Because the articles referenced are intended to appeal to a wide audience, they tend to be short and rather general. Although the *Readers' Guide* does not include academic journals, its wide listing of articles in news magazines, in particular, can provide useful summaries of information that is recent and easily understood.

4. *Infotrak Database.* Many college libraries have installed computer databases such as Infotrak, and many of these are available to students without charge. Infotrak is a useful example of this resource. It provides a large number of sources of the same general type as *Readers' Guide* and it is easy to use. I will not attempt to list all the kinds of databases here. Consult your reference librarian to find out what is available in your library.

5. *The New York Times Index.* This is an index to all of the articles carried in one of the most comprehensive U.S. newspapers. Most

libraries carry all back issues of the *New York Times* on microfilm. Many libraries carry other newspaper indexes, such as the *Official Washington Post Index* and the *National Newspaper Index*.

6. *CIS Index.* Compiled by the Congressional Information Service, this index is probably the most useful source for locating hearings conducted by congressional committees. Because congressional committees conduct hearings on seemingly every policy question debated nationally, the *CIS Index* is an excellent resource for most controversial subjects. It is published monthly and it includes abstracts of all congressional publications with the exception of the *Congressional Record*.

7. *Monthly Catalog of U.S. Government Publications.* This index lists publications issued by agencies of the U.S. government, including reports and studies on topics that span virtually the entire range of public policy questions. It includes indexes for subject, author, title, and series/report number.

8. *Index to U.S. Government Periodicals.* This resource provides a quarterly index to articles in 170 government periodicals that span most of the topics for public debate.

9. *Social Sciences Index.* This index references periodicals in the fields of anthropology, economics, law and criminology, psychology, medical science, politics, and sociology.

10. *Humanities Index.* This index includes a wide range of journals in such fields as literature, philosophy, music, and the arts.

In addition to the general indexes, there are specialized subject indexes in virtually every area of knowledge or argument. Some of the more important indexes in particular are listed here, but there are many others. If you find that your topic is not covered in any depth by the references included here, you should consult the *Bibliography Index* and your reference librarian.

11. *Education Index.* This bibliography provides a valuable index to books and journals concerned with the general subject of education.

12. *Business Periodicals Index.* This resource provides a subject index for articles published in English language periodicals.

13. *Index to Legal Periodicals.* This is a standard index for law review journals and legal periodicals published in the United States,

Canada, United Kingdom, Ireland, Australia, and New Zealand. Articles are listed by subject and by author. It is a valuable resource for investigating any controversy that has a legal dimension.

14. *Index Medicus.* This index provides a helpful subject index for articles on medical topics.

Special Resources for Background Material

So far, our search for resources has been focused on the problem of building a bibliography of books and articles on the topic in dispute. But another early task in research is to get "grounded" in the topic with material that provides a good overview of the pro and con arguments. There are two very useful sources for disputes on policy questions. The *Congressional Digest* is a commercial monthly publication that features controversies in Congress and the major pro and con arguments on a wide range of public disputes. *Congressional Quarterly Weekly Report,* also a commercial publication, contains a summary of the activities in Congress each week, highlights of major legislation, and discussions of the relations between Congress and the executive and judicial branches of government.

Reading and Recording Research Material

When you have a working bibliography assembled, the next decision is where to begin your reading! Early reading on the topic should be more concerned with understanding the controversy than with gathering argument claims and evidence. However, the most efficient approach to research will depend somewhat on the complexity of the topic as well as your background and abilities as a researcher. As you gain experience in the process of research, you will become more efficient in all of the tasks. Initially, however, it is helpful to think about an approach to working through your bibliography. What should you read first?

Efficient Reading

If you do not know much about your topic, it may be wise to begin with a relatively short article that attempts to provide an objective presentation of the major pro and con arguments, such as the *Congressional Digest.* News magazines such as *Newsweek, U.S. News and World Report, Time,* and others of this sort can be helpful in providing an overall perspective on the central question in dispute. One or two general articles may help you to recognize argument claims and evidence in the more in-depth sources.

It may not be literally true that reading one article in the popular news weeklies is like reading all such articles, but their value drops off quickly after one or two, and you need to get into materials of greater depth and quality. Government documents may seem intimidating, but they are often among the more efficient resources to investigate. Congressional committee hearings, for example, often feature testimony from the most interesting and knowledgeable experts—on both sides of a question. Moreover, the testimony is often preceded by a short position paper full of information and arguments, which is comparable in length to some magazine articles. Once you have an overview of the topic, the issues and the questions you have developed in relation to each of them can guide the order in which you investigate materials in your bibliography.

Recording Evidence

The most efficient approach to collecting the argument claims and evidence is by recording as you go. Whether you are reading in the library or elsewhere, you will want to avoid wasting your time in rewriting evidence and background material. Most libraries provide ample access to photocopy machines, and these can save a great deal of time. But lengthy articles can be unwieldy in debate, and a single article may contain a number of distinct arguments and pieces of factual evidence. To put this material into a more convenient form, many students find it is efficient to record evidence and argument claims on standard 4 x 6 index cards. Whatever system you use, it is very important to safeguard the integrity of evidence. The following guidelines help to ensure efficiency as well as integrity in the recording of evidence.

1. Evidence should be quoted accurately. In most circumstances, the requirement for accuracy means quotations will be verbatim. But the most important thing is to be faithful to the context and the author's meaning. When evidence must be edited or paraphrased, an ethical advocate will be careful that the changes do not distort its original meaning. In such cases, it is wise to have a copy of the original material.

2. It is very important to know the source for each piece of evidence. If you record your evidence on 4 x 6 cards, you should include complete documentation on each card. This may seem terribly redundant, but as you gather quantities of evidence, you will need to organize it according to issues and arguments rather than by source. Unless the crucial source information is recorded on each card, there is considerable risk that you will lose track of evidence sources.

Proper documentation means that the top of each card should record (1) the name of the author or person quoted; (2) the qualifications of the person on the subject; (3) the title of the article, journal, book, or document (in proper bibliographic form); (4) the date of the publication; and (5) the page(s) from which the evidence is quoted. Figure 4.1 is an example of an evidence card.

3. Ideally, each piece of evidence will concern one idea. In part, this guideline is concerned with the practical problem of sorting evidence when it wanders from subject to subject. If the evidence is recorded on cards, you will want to file each under an appropriate subject heading, and this is an easier task when the evidence is concerned with one idea. But the single idea principle is also important when we use evidence in support of an argument claim. When expert testimony addresses several ideas at once, it is likely to confuse rather than persuade an audience.

Actually, the expert probably does not discuss several ideas at the same time. Usually, the problem of multiple ideas in a quotation reflects the beginner's failure to distinguish and to separate an author's argument claims and factual evidence.

4. In general, the length of quoted material should be related to its intended use. If a quotation is too long, you will not be able to use it in a debate. Audiences are often impatient with the reading of lengthy quotations or lists of statistics. At the same time, however, some materials need to be recorded in full in order to prevent loss of critical detail. Charts and tables, for example, can be ruined if shortened, and you may be unable to shorten some arguments or evidence without distorting it. In these situations, it is usually best to photocopy the material.

The sample evidence card in Figure 4.1 illustrates all of these rules, and it includes a heading that describes the content/importance of the evidence quoted. Notice, as well, that the evidence is recorded with a typewriter, facilitating its easy use. Typewritten evidence is usually easier to read than handwritten materials.

Summary

1. Research on a central question in dispute is a process of investigation that seeks three goals: (a) to understand the controversy, (b) to discover the pro and con arguments for each issue, and (c) to find the evidence for each argument.

FIGURE 4.1 *Sample Evidence Card*

>   Family background most important to educational suc-
> cess
>
>   Interview with Dr. James S. Coleman, professor of
> social relations at Johns Hopkins University, Director of
> U.S. Office of Education study, "Equality of Education Op-
> portunity," <u>Saturday Review</u>, 27 May 1982, p. 59.
>
>   "All factors considered, the most important variable—
> in or out of school—in a child's performance remains his
> family's educational background. The second most impor-
> tant factor is the educational background, the social
> class background, of the families of the children in
> school. These two elements are much more important than
> any physical attributes of the school."

2. Efficiency in research requires an investigator to know what he or she is looking for, how to find it, and how to record it for its intended uses.

3. The focus of research, or knowing what we are looking for, is guided initially by the issues an investigator has phrased for the central question. Issues enable us to identify the pro and con arguments and evidence. In addition, six key elements in the context of a controversy enable the investigator to deepen research of each issue and to gain an understanding of the controversy. The six key elements include (a) definition of terms, (b) immediate causes, (c) participants in the dispute, (d) present belief or policy, (e) proposed belief or policy, and (f) common ground.

4. Finding research materials requires, first, the identification of key terms or words to guide investigation of bibliographic sources. Second, the investigator builds a bibliography of quality sources by using such reference sources as the card catalog, *PAIS, Readers' Guide to Periodical Literature, CIS Index,* the *New York Times Index, Social Sciences Index,* and the *Humanities Index.*

5. Efficient reading may require you to begin with overview materials if the topic is not well understood. However, it is not efficient to read only short, generalized articles. Use the issues and key elements to identify high-quality sources, and read with a purpose.

6. Four guidelines help the investigator to record evidence in an ethical and efficient manner: (a) quote accurately, (b) record sources systematically, (c) focus on single ideas, and (d) strive for brevity.

Exercises

1. As a class project, arrange for a tour of the campus library and examine at least six of the reference resources discussed in this chapter. Ask the reference librarian about the availability of databases and on-line computer searches.

2. Select one or more central questions of fact, value, or policy for class debates, and phrase the issues. As a class project, generate key words for the central question and issues that could be used to find research resources in the *PAIS*, the *Readers' Guide to Periodical Literature*, and the *CIS Index*.

3. Submit a working bibliography of 20 sources for a central question of fact, value, or policy. Include at least two entries for each of the following categories: books, newspaper articles, newsmagazine articles, government documents, and journals or professional periodicals (such as a law review).

4. Following the four guidelines for recording evidence, submit 10 pieces of evidence that are recorded on 4 x 6 cards.

5

Rhetorical Argument: The Logic of Good Reasons

Central Ideas in This Chapter

1. Rhetorical argument consists of good reasons in support of a claim.
   - An argument claim expresses an advocate's conclusion or belief.
   - Good reasons consist of persuasive support for a claim.
2. Three general tests of argument examine the truth, relevance, and sufficiency of the reasons.
3. Inductive reasoning is based on probability.
   - Evidence is always incomplete.
   - Inductive reasoning moves from known to unknown.
   - Two common patterns are particulars to generals and particulars to particulars.
   - Induction is based on the assumption of uniformity.
   - There are four useful concepts of probability: classical, frequency, degrees of confirmation, and degrees of belief.
4. Deductive reasoning provides complete support for claims.
   - Conclusions are contained in their premises.
   - Conclusions follow necessarily.
   - Validity means the form of the argument is correct. Validity and truth are not the same.
   - One kind of deduction is the syllogism.
   - The enthymeme is a rhetorical syllogism.
   - Acceptance is a crucial standard for major premises.

Continued

5. Toulmin's critique points to deficiencies in traditional induction and deduction.
  ■ The Toulmin model provides a functional analysis of the six elements in argument.
  ■ Toulmin's "field" standards clarify argument evaluation.

Unless we are in some way incapacitated, all of us engage in reasoning and argumentation. Even little children in our society are called on to justify their opinions, requests, and actions. From about the time children acquire language, parents expect them to provide supporting reasons for such ordinary requests as permission to stay up after the normal bedtime. And when a child violates a rule of the home or the school, a parent or teacher may demand an explanation or justification ("Why did you do that?"). The child, in turn, is expected to justify his or her behavior with a kind of argument, providing reasons that are likely to pass muster with the parent or teacher. As children mature, we think their ability to reason and to argue, providing reasons to justify either their behavior or their claims, should also improve.

If even small children are required to support their claims, it seems only fair to expect adult college students to be quite proficient in justifying their beliefs and actions. To be considered an educated person in Western societies is to be able to support claims effectively and to respond to the arguments of others—sometimes agreeing, sometimes opposing. The adequacy of our education will be assessed according to the quality of our responses as we decide whether the arguments of others are sound or unsound, trustworthy or misleading.

Unfortunately, despite these general expectations, many adult college students are unable to reason or argue very well, mainly because our schools provide very little systematic instruction in argumentation, and few people are naturally good at it. So, like most people, there probably have been times when you felt overwhelmed or manipulated by the persuasive arguments of others, even when you knew, deep down, that their arguments were flawed. Unless we learn to apply principles in evaluating argument, our ignorance condemns us to proceed randomly, relying on intuitive powers that seem to abandon us at important moments.

What sorts of principles enable us to determine whether arguments are sound or unsound, reliable or deficient? What is it that we need to learn? This chapter will examine principles of rhetorical argument in relation to two major questions:

1. What is the *nature* of rhetorical argument? How should it be defined? What are its elements?
2. How does the *structure*, or *form* of rhetorical argument provide insights into its strengths and weaknesses?

The Nature of Rhetorical Argument

What is a rhetorical argument? In Chapter 2, *argument* was defined as "good reasons in support of a claim."[1] Perhaps the most important feature of this definition is its emphasis on the persuasive functions of argument. Not only is persuasion the central focus of rhetoric but also, as Perelman put it, "every argumentation is addressed to an audience . . . which the speaker seeks to persuade."[2] Perelman did not mean to ignore the occasional playfulness or recreational functions of argument transactions. Rather, his point was that whenever we attempt to use argument to prove our point, or support our position, or justify our conclusion, we are necessarily trying to persuade someone that our claim or position or conclusion is true, correct, or well-founded, and thus worthy of our listener's acceptance. Neither philosophers, nor advertisers, politicians, attorneys, scientists, or even lovers want to find or use arguments that are unpersuasive to the person or group they are addressing.

Does this central focus on persuasion mean that we are not concerned with unethical argument or that we would wish to persuade by any means? Not at all. Nothing about this approach diminishes our disapproval of fallacious argument or unethical tactics of persuasion. But much of our concern would vanish if fallacies and unethical methods were not persuasive to people, and the focus on persuasion may enable us to learn why untrustworthy arguments sometimes have the power to influence people. However, while part of our goal is to learn self-defense against flawed arguments, good critical tools should also enable us to recognize sound arguments that are worthy of our acceptance.

Since all serious uses of argumentation are intended to be persuasive, as Perelman noted, the term *rhetorical argument* is perhaps redundant. If so, it is a harmless redundancy. We can easily afford a little redundancy if addition of the term *rhetorical* helps us to maintain the persuasive focus of our analysis. So let us return to our opening question: What is a rhetorical argument? To answer this question, let us turn to our definition and commence our response with an examination of its parts: An *argument* is "good reasons in support of a claim."

This definition, proposed by Karl Wallace, can help us to perceive and understand the form as well as the materials of argument, and it provides a useful way of thinking about audience standards for argument evaluation. You may recall that we explored the elements of Wallace's definition, in a preliminary way, in Chapter 2. Here, we will examine it in a bit more depth, incorporating material from earlier chapters. We begin by looking at the two major components of argument that are included in the definition: (1) the claim and (2) good reasons.

The Claim

The term *claim* refers to any statement of a conclusion, position, or belief an advocate is trying to establish or justify to another person or group. Initially, the only difficulty most people have with this element of argument is that we use a variety of words to introduce or identify our claims.

Consider the range of terms used in introducing the following argument claims. A child "insists" that she should be permitted to stay overnight at her friend's house. A foreign policy expert "contends" that it was a mistake for President Bush to threaten Saddam Hussein with ground forces instead of a preemptive air attack in order to force Iraq out of Kuwait. An official from NASA "maintains" that the space agency has not become incompetent, despite the embarrassments of leaky space shuttles, a major flaw in the Hubble space telescope, and difficulties in maintaining control over the spacecraft *Magellan* in its mission to map the planet Venus. An expert meteorologist "argues" that average global temperatures are increasing faster than at any time in the past 10,000 years, when the last Ice Age ended. A legislator "proposes" that 16- to 18-year-olds should not be allowed to drive automobiles unless they are making satisfactory progress toward high school graduation.

Claims Should Be Stated in
Complete Sentences

These illustrations should help you to recognize that argument claims usually follow whenever someone is insisting, contending, maintaining, arguing, or proposing. Such terms should not be confused with the claims themselves, however. Notice in the preceding examples that each claim is a complete sentence; it is a statement that presents someone's belief, position, conclusion, or judgment. A mere phrase or single term may be sufficient for a quick reference to a claim, providing it with a kind of label, but a belief, opinion, judgment, or conclusion cannot be fully expressed with anything less than a complete sentence. Moreover, reliance on the use of single terms as shorthand labels for claims should be avoided; it is a major source of confusion about arguments.

The Subject Matter of Claims Is Unlimited

Since human beliefs span the entire range of matters that our species can conceptualize or care about, people make claims about any and all aspects of reality as they perceive it or would like it to be. When an advocate is advancing a claim, he or she is urging another person or group to accept a judgment that something is true or false, good or bad, justified or unjustified, wise or foolish, expedient or inexpedient. The range of subject matter in our illustrative claims is intended to show that argument claims can be made about anything; the topics of argument are unlimited.

Good Reasons

The term *good reasons*, the second element in Wallace's definition of rhetorical argument, is almost instantly intelligible to any normal person in Western culture because it coincides with our ordinary ways of thinking and talking about supporting or justifying our claims. Whenever our claims are doubted, or even likely to be questioned by our listener, we understand the need to back them up, to support them, and to provide good reasons that will show they are worthy of belief.

Suppose you are concerned about the health of your friend, who seems to be neglecting the need for adequate exercise, and so you say to him:

> **Claim**: "You are really out of shape, Joe."

"Why do you think that?" Joe replies. Notice that Joe's question will be understood by any normal person as a request for you to provide support or justification—that is, good reasons why Joe should accept your claim. Therefore, you would probably respond, without even thinking that you were engaged in any sort of complex argument process, with what you take to be two good reasons in support of your claim:

> "Because, Joe, (1) you are out of breath after climbing only one or two flights of stairs, and (2) when a person your age has difficulty with a couple flights of stairs, it is a sure indication of poor physical conditioning."

Good Reasons versus Ordinary Reasons

At first, *good reasons* may seem to be a rather redundant term, and someone might ask: What is the difference between a *reason* and a *good reason*? If we were interested only in the "correctness" of the relationship between a claim and its support, the more neutral term *reason* would be satisfactory. Logicians, in fact, typically use the even more neutral term *premise* for those statements that support argument conclusions. But arguments, from our rhetorical perspective, are always intended to be persuasive. Just any old reason or premise suggests a casual attitude, or even disregard, toward the audience we want to persuade, even if the premise or reason is correctly related to the claim according to standards of logic. An advocate seeks to support his or her claims with reasons that the immediate audience is likely to regard as "good." Such good reasons should, of course, be relevant, true, and sufficient in order to meet the requirements of logic. But good reasons must also meet rhetorical requirements: They must be perceived by the listener or reader as important, interesting, and convincing. If the immediate audience finds the reasons to be unimportant, boring, or unconvincing, the argument will fail to meet its persuasive goal, even if the reasons are correctly related to the conclusion according to standards of logic.

Do All Claims Require Support?

Is it absolutely essential to provide good reasons in support of all your claims? The short answer is yes, with qualifications. If a claim is in any way doubted by the audience, the support of good reasons is essential. In Chapter 2, we noted that an unsupported claim is merely an assertion, not an argument. "Merely an assertion" is generally meant to be a criticism. It means that the point of an unsupported claim is in dispute or is doubted, and any attempt to presume its truth will be resisted or even regarded as an unfair or unethical move. For example, a defense attorney may criticize a prosecutor's case for "merely asserting" a point that is disputed by the defense—namely, that the defendant had a motive for murdering the deceased victim. In sum, then, a fair statement of our rule is that any claim that is controversial or doubted by the listener will require support.

However, we do not object to all assertions or require that all claims be supported. In some cases, we are simply indifferent to a claim. In other cases, we do not object to an unsupported claim because we agree with it, and we see the advocate's assertion as merely a sensible effort to articulate what we already believe or know to be true, or wise, or correct about the world. In fact, when we agree with an assertion, we may be surprised that someone else thinks that it needs support.

All of this means that it is the audience that determines whether a claim needs to be supported, at least from a persuasive standpoint. Our listeners are never merely passive creatures, absorbing our words like some mechanical recording device. Rather, they participate actively as we speak, accepting claims without support when they agree with them, and rejecting other claims, even when they are supported with evidence that the advocate considers to be sufficient. To be persuasive, the audience must consider the reasons "good," or at least good enough.

Problems with Audience Evaluation of Good Reasons

From our discussion thus far, it may have occurred to you that there is a problem in centering the evaluation of rhetorical argument on the audience. The problem stems from two central facts that are in conflict:

1. From a persuasive standpoint, the audience determines whether an argument is sound or unsound, trustworthy or flawed.
2. Some audiences are less competent than others and may be unable to make wise judgments about arguments.

Whether we like it or not, these statements simply express the reality of the persuasive situation: The immediate audience judges for itself whether arguments are acceptable or trustworthy, and the audience may or may not be competent in its judgments. However, no self-respecting rhetorician would say that an argument is satisfactory merely because an ignorant audience says it is. Rather, the rhetorician would argue that this is the very reason why people need to be as competent as possible in understanding argument. Everyone should receive education in argument evaluation.

Education on the general standards of evaluation will not provide a complete solution by itself, of course. Sound evaluation of some arguments will always require expertise in their subject matter, and none of us can have expertise in everything. But that does not make us helpless. We can make use of experts whenever an argument exceeds our own evaluative capacities. If the best standards for evaluating legal arguments are provided by the field of law, and the field of economics provides the best standards for economic argument, and the same is true whenever the subject matter of an argument can be referred to the experts in a particular field, then we need not be limited to our own intellectual resources. If an education does not provide any of us with all of the knowledge or answers that we need, it should at least provide us with the ability to find answers and to use the expertise of others.

The Structure of Rhetorical Argument

An argument has structure in more or less the same sense that we think of a house as having structure or form. What sorts of structure? And what does an understanding of structure help us to see? Just as the blueprints of a house help us to see how its parts are related, providing a model that reveals its potential flaws, analysis of argument structure helps us to see potential problems in the relationships between good reasons and claims.

General Tests of Argument

What kinds of problems or flaws can make a difference? Just as a house can be unsound if it is constructed of inferior materials, or the builders are incompetent in putting it together, or there is insufficient material to build a completed house, an argument can be defective if it fails to measure up to any one of three general tests:

1. Are the good reasons true or acceptable?
2. Are the good reasons properly related to the claim? Are they relevant?
3. Are the good reasons sufficient to establish the claim?

An interesting feature of these tests is that they have both a logical and a rhetorical dimension; they are a way of getting at the reasons why an argument is unpersuasive as well as why it is flawed according to principles of logic. We shall commence our discussion of structure by examining some of the logical and rhetorical implications of our general tests, and then we shall see how they illuminate the more useful modes of argument structure: induction, deduction, and the Toulmin model.

Truth or Acceptance of the Good Reasons

Initially, this is the simplest test. Even little children understand that their claims will be rejected quickly if they are supported with reasons that are untrue. But is it always easy to determine whether a supporting reason, or item of evidence, is true? Well, we find it easy to assess the truth of some reasons, and not so easy in the case of others. Suppose Abner's physician presents him with this sort of argument:

> "Abner, you need to cut down on your coffee consumption. You are drinking eight cups a day, and that much coffee can cause heart disease."

Notice that Abner's physician provides two good reasons in support of his claim: (1) Abner drinks eight cups of coffee a day and (2) that much coffee can cause heart disease. Abner can easily determine the truth of the first reason, of course—he either drinks that much coffee or he doesn't. But what of the second reason? Is it really true that eight cups of coffee a day can cause heart disease?

Here, the truth is not so easily determined. Research on the relationship between coffee consumption and heart disease seems to offer inconsistent findings. One massive study, published in 1990, found essentially no relationship between coffee consumption and heart disease, apparently contradicting the findings of previous studies. But the findings of future studies may or may not agree. Moreover, even if Abner is aware of these coffee/heart studies, he must also weigh the credibility of his physician who may know something about Abner's condition that would make caffeine consumption more hazardous in his case.

From a purely logical standpoint, a supporting reason is either true or false, and a false reason cannot provide support for a claim. But logic itself does not determine the truth of argument premises or reasons. As logician Wesley Salmon put it, "Logic deals with the relation between premises and conclusion, not with the truth of the premises."[3]

If logic does not determine the truth of "good reasons," then, we might ask, where is it done? Who is responsible? From a persuasive standpoint, it is the audience of listeners and readers who decide the truth or acceptability of the good reasons, and their judgments seem to be made on at least three bases: (1) people can rely on their own assessment of factual evidence, (2) they can consult the experts or authorities of whatever field seems to have jurisdiction over the subject of the argument, or (3) they can look to the prevailing views of their community, engaging in what Willard calls a "social comparison process" of argumentation.[4] Logicians focus their attention purely on whether a premise is true or false and they tend to ignore the audience that judges the premise. Persuasively, however, what is crucial is whether the audience accepts the reasons as true. If Abner rejects the truth of his physician's statement that eight cups of coffee increases risk of heart disease, the argument is unlikely to be persuasive.

Relevance of the Good Reasons

Whether the reasons offered in support of a claim are properly related to the claim is a major concern of logic. In fact, as Wesley Salmon put it, "The logical correctness or incorrectness of an argument depends solely upon the relation between premises and conclusion."[5] From this standpoint, statements either support a claim or they do not. Not just any statement can be a reason in support of a claim. Even if a statement is true, or accepted as true, it may not be relevant to the statement in a claim.

We will explore some of the logical standards of relevancy when we discuss inductive and deductive reasoning. Here, however, we should observe that relevance is not a matter that can be left entirely to logic. Relevance is also something that we judge by our experience. When we consider the persuasive potential of argument, relevance is very much a rhetorical as well as a logical matter. That is, from a purely persuasive standpoint, members of the audience decide whether an advocate's good reasons really do provide support for the claim.

Sufficiency of the Good Reasons

The test of sufficiency asks whether the good reasons offered by an advocate provide enough support for us to accept a claim. Has the claim been supported, justified, or established to a level that meets our standards for its acceptance? Here again, this test has a rhetorical as well as a logical dimension. From a rhetorical perspective, we might ask: Sufficient for whom? Persuasively, an advocate's good reasons may be sufficient for some members of an audience and inadequate for others. In our criminal courts, for example, some members of a jury may find the good reasons (evidence, explanations, reasoning) of a prosecutor to be more than enough to find the defendant guilty. But other members of the same jury may find the prosecution's case to be insufficient to meet the standard of "beyond reasonable doubt" for a guilty verdict. Persuasively, the test of sufficiency is applied by members of an audience, and their judgments may or may not agree.

Unlike the persuasive standards of sufficiency, logical standards are concerned solely with the relationship between premises and a conclusion. When the relationship between premises and a conclusion is logically correct, there remains the question of the degree to which the premises support the conclusion. The degree of support for argument claims is analyzed in relation to two kinds of reasoning: deductive and inductive.

Traditional logic distinguishes between *deductive* arguments, which provide complete support for their claims, and *inductive* arguments, which can provide only incomplete support for conclusions or claims. As we examine each of these forms of reasoning, we shall be especially concerned with the ideas of sufficiency and relevancy.

Inductive Reasoning

The key idea of induction is *probability*. The claim of an inductive argument is supported by evidence that establishes a certain level of probability for it, but the evidence for inductive claims is always *incomplete*, or unable to establish the truth of a claim to a level of complete certainty. To put it another way, the claim of an inductive argument always goes beyond the evidence in support of it.

Incompleteness of Evidence

To clarify this idea of incompleteness, consider the case of a scientist who wants to determine the boiling point of a watery-appearing liquid she has found. Sensibly enough, our scientist heats the liquid until it boils and then takes its temperature. But is one trial enough? Clearly, if she concludes that whatever boiling temperature she obtained in her first trial is *the* boiling temperature (from now on) for the liquid, her conclusion or claim would go considerably beyond the evidence in support of it.

Thus we might suggest that the scientist perform additional trials. But how many trials? Even if she was very careful and heated the liquid for 100 trials, finding that it boiled at, say, 115 degrees centigrade each time, the conclusion that the boiling temperature of the liquid is 115 degrees would go beyond the evidence in support of it. To be sure, 100 trials would provide excellent evidence for the conclusion; however, we can never be certain that the liquid would boil at the same temperature for the next 100 trials. Indeed, since there is a potentially infinite number of times this sort of liquid could be boiled, any number of trial cases would be less than the infinite universe of possible cases. Therefore, our inductive evidence can never be complete.

The idea of incompleteness is well understood in society, and we incorporate it into our criteria for deciding claims about matters of fact in a wide range of situations. For example, juries are not expected to say that it is a "certainty" the defendant is guilty. Rather, juries use the standard of "beyond reasonable doubt" (which is a very high level of probability). Likewise, a scientist may be considered justified in concluding, on the basis of all the available evidence, that there is no life on the other planets in our solar system. Yet, to call the conclusion "justified" does not preclude the possibility that evidence of life could be discovered at a later time.

The idea of incompleteness helps us to understand that the arguments of experts are not necessarily flawed or defective merely because other experts disagree. It is possible to have good inductive arguments on both sides of an issue. This may be especially clear when the claims are predictive. Prior to the war with Iraq, for example, military experts who were interviewed on national news networks made a rather large number of contradictory predictions about such matters as how long a war might take and the numbers of U.S. casualties. Although many of these predictions turned out to be incorrect, the inductive arguments in support of them, at the time, may nevertheless have conformed to the best available standards. Predictions are always based on evidence that is incomplete.

Notice that in each of these cases the most we can expect is that the evidence will provide strong support for the respective claims, making it highly probable that the claims are true. In each case, if we looked closely, we could see that, despite its evidence, which may be true and reliable, it would always be possible for the claim of an inductive argument to be false, and more than possible when two people support contradictory claims. If the claims are contradictory, at least one of them must be false, even though the inductive arguments in support of them conform to the best available standards. Inductive arguments may provide strong support for their claims but they cannot guarantee their truth absolutely.

Reasoning from Known to Unknown

Even little children reason inductively from the known to the unknown. Perhaps you have seen a mother try to feed her child a new spinach-squash vegetable. She spoons some of the greenish-colored mush into her child's mouth, which the child promptly spits out. The mother tries in vain to coax her child to accept another bite, but her most skillful presentations of the mush are unable to penetrate the child's tightly closed lips, and the mother finally admits defeat. Without any formal instruction, the infant has engaged in a fairly sophisticated inductive inference—reasoning from the known to the unknown. On the basis of a rather small sample of spinach-squash—the "known," which was despised—the child has concluded that *all* spinach-squash in the universe—the "unknown"—will also be unfit for human consumption.

Making inferences from a known sample to an unknown—the more general universe from which the sample has been drawn—is a mainstay for human beings; it is a crucial method for learning about the world around us. We use it whenever we sip a bit of wine (the known) to decide whether the rest of the bottle (the unknown) will be to our liking. We use it in deciding whether we like a particular activity, such as tennis, by giving it a try. We may conclude that we like it or that we are good at it on the basis of one trial. And students decide, on the basis of their first day or two in a class, whether they will find the course difficult or easy, interesting or boring.

Patterns of Inductive Argument

Particulars to Generals. You may have noticed that, in many of the examples of induction we have surveyed so far, the conclusion is a generalization that is based on particulars. This pattern is typical of a large number of inductive arguments, and it is useful to understand. We use this pattern whenever we argue or claim that something is true in general because it is true in the particular cases we have examined. Thus, John argues that he can do well in mathematics (generalization) because he has performed well in three math classes (particulars). Mary supports the generalization that students have a very low participation in voting by pointing to low student-voting levels in the past three elections.

Particular to Particular. Some people have suggested, incorrectly, that particulars to generals is the only pattern of induction. But inductive arguments can also have a pattern of particular to particular, which is the pattern used when we reason by analogy that what is true of case one is also true of case two. Thus, Harry says to his friend, Mike, "I know that you can pass this class in calculus, Mike, because I passed it, and your ability in math is at least equal to mine." On a slightly more complex level, we can see this same pattern in the argument of some environmentalists that the auto industry can improve gasoline mileage and reduce auto pollution in the 1990s (particular) because it was able to do this during the decade of the 1970s (particular).

You should notice, at this point, that both patterns of argument are used in everyday reasoning and they are a mainstay for any persuader who needs to support generalizations or to make predictions. It should also be clear to you that, in each pattern, the evidence is incomplete; the claim goes beyond the evidence in support of it.

Assumption of Uniformity

What is it that permits the conclusions of inductive arguments to go beyond their evidence and to say something new? The infant in our earlier example concluded that *all* spinach-squash is inedible (a generalization) on the basis of a very limited sample—one spoonful. How does a child know that all of the spinach-squash in the universe will taste like the sample? How does a student know that an entire course will be easy or difficult on the basis of the first day or two? How does a physician know that a patient's cholesterol level is high on the basis of the cholesterol level found in a small sample? The short answer is that we do not *know* for sure. In all of these cases, we must *assume* that what is true of our sample will be true in general. This assumption is known as the *assumption of uniformity.*

What is this pervasive assumption and where does it come from? Assumption of uniformity is a shorthand way of saying that we must assume that reality as we know it, all of the universe, has a rather high degree of order, regularity, consistency, and dependability. We cannot actually prove that the universe has this uniformity, as the philosopher David Hume demonstrated in the eighteenth century, but we find that we must accept this assumption because without it we could not make much sense of the world in which we live. We must accept that there are such things as physical laws that cause water to boil at 212 degrees Fahrenheit, and these laws will continue day after day, year after year. In truth, if there were no uniformity in nature, science and superstition would be in the same boat; knowledge would be impossible. At the same time, however, reliance on the uniformity assumption is a major reason why the claims of inductive reasoning can never be more than probable.

Probability Concepts in Induction

What does it mean to say that the conclusions of inductive arguments are probable? We considered some of the elements of probability when we looked at the reasons why the conclusions of inductive arguments always go beyond the evidence in support of them, and that the support for inductive claims is always incomplete. These elements have led some philosophers, such as Rudolph Carnap, to construe induction as the "logic of probability."[6] But what does *probability* mean, other than the idea of incompleteness in the support for a claim? In its technical usages, the term *probability* has four more or less distinct meanings, all of which can increase our understanding of rhetorical argumentation as well as inductive reasoning: (1) classical probability, (2) frequency probability, (3) degrees of confirmation, and (4) degrees of belief.

Classical probability is most easily understood in relation to simple objects such as coins, dice, or cards. All of these objects are capable of producing a known number of events that seem to be equally possible. An unbiased coin, for example, is capable of producing two events—either heads or tails—and both seem to be equally possible or likely. Therefore, according to the classical concept, the probability of heads turning up is determined by dividing the number of times that heads can happen in a single flip (once) by the number of possible results (two). Thus, the probability of heads is 1/2, or 50 percent.

In similar fashion, we can determine the probability of a particular number turning up with the roll of a set of dice or with a single die. One die is a six-sided cube with the numbers 1 through 6 on its sides. Since each side of the die seems to have an equal chance of turning up, the probability of any particular number turning up is 1/6. If we roll a set of dice, the probability of any particular number will be based, first, on the number of possible combinations, which is 36 (6 x 6). Then we will need to know how many times a particular number can occur out of the 36 combinations. Thus, suppose we want to know the probability of rolling a 7 with our dice. As the illustration below shows, 6 of the 36 combinations produce the number 7.

Possible Combinations of the Dice to Produce a 7

Die #1		Die #2		
1	+	6	=	7
2		5		
3		4		
4		3		
5		2		
6		1		

Thus, the probability of a number 7 turning up with a roll of the two dice is 6/36, or 1/6. The number 12, however, can be produced with only 1 of the 36 combinations, when the number 6 turns up with both dice. So, the probability of a 12 is 1/36. Thus, the number 7 is six times more likely to turn up than the number 12.

The classical concept of probability is useful but it is rather limited to the sorts of things, like coins, that seem to have a number of equally likely possibilities, and few things in the world are so uniform. In addition, the assumption that heads and tails are equally likely when a coin is flipped is also troublesome. There is the old story of a student who used a coin each evening to decide whether he should study. If the coin came down heads, he went to see his girlfriend; if it came down tails, he went out with the guys; if it stood on its edge, he studied! This student's decision method is not likely to overcome the rather well-founded general belief that coins do not land on their edges, but perhaps it helps us to see the problematic assumption of the classical probability concept: namely, the assumption that we can tell by looking whether events like heads and tails are equally likely. How do we know that the coins or dice are not biased?

Frequency probability theorists, such as Hans Reichenbach, argue that probability always has a statistical meaning, and that the frequency idea solves the weakness of the classical concept.[7] According to the frequency concept, the only way to know the probability of heads is to flip the coin a sample of flips. If we flip the coin 100 times, and heads turns up 70 times, the frequency notion says the probability of heads is 70 percent, not 50 percent as the classical concept indicated. Likewise, the probability of a 7 turning up for a set of dice can be determined only by rolling the dice and counting the number of times a 7 turns up in a particular series. If we roll the dice 100 times, and the number 7 turns up 10 times, then the probability of a 7 with those dice is 10/100, or 1/10, not 1/6.

The frequency concept of probability seems to dominate in statistical or mathematical applications, but it applies only to a series of events—it really does not apply to single events. For example, when insurance companies need to determine rates for male drivers between the ages of 16 and 20, the frequency concept provides an exact idea of the probability for accidents in this age group. The number of 16- to 20-year-old males who are driving is known, and the insurance companies also know how many accidents these drivers have. So, the probability for accidents in this age group is exactly equal to the percentage of accidents the group is now having. Insurance rates can then be set at a level that prevents the companies from losing money when they insure these young drivers. However, the frequency concept does not tell an insurance company anything about the probability that a particular driver in this group will have an accident; it only informs them about the group.

Degrees of confirmation probability, as proposed by Rudolph Carnap, permits us to make sense of the probability concept with unique events as well as events in a series. Carnap maintained that probability refers to the logical relationship between a claim and the evidence in support of it. A particular body of evidence can be said to confirm a claim, or to support it, or to substantiate it to a certain degree, and that degree of support is its probability. The more evidence we have for a claim, the greater is the degree to which the claim is confirmed. To see how this might work, consider three arguments in support of the same claim.

1. *Claim*: Maude killed her husband, Abner.

    Evidence: 1. Maude had a motive (to get Abner's insurance).

Our evidence for argument #1 certainly supports the claim that Maude killed Abner, though probably not enough by itself for a jury to convict Maude. As Carnap might put it, evidence of a motive confirms the claim to the degree of plausibility, perhaps, but juries want more than mere plausibility to convict.

2. *Claim*: Maude killed her husband, Abner.

    Evidence: 1. Maude had a motive (insurance).
    2. Maude told her friend she intended to kill Abner.
    3. Maude's fingerprints are on the knife that killed Abner.

Notice how the additional evidence in argument #2 increases the probability, or the degree to which the claim is confirmed. Some juries might convict when the evidence is at this level.

3. *Claim:* Maude killed her husband, Abner.

   Evidence: 1. Maude had a motive (insurance).
   2. Maude told her friend she intended to kill Abner.
   3. Maude's fingerprints are on the knife that killed Abner.
   4. Ada Mae says she saw Maude do it.
   5. Maude has confessed that she killed Abner.

The two additional items of evidence surely yield a higher level of probability for argument #3, even though we might find it difficult to say exactly how much higher. Carnap's degree of confirmation does not have the apparent precision of the frequency concept because it does not consist merely of numbers. And it would undoubtedly sound perverse for the prosecution even to attempt a quantitative probability estimate, suggesting that the evidence established, say, a 95 percent probability of guilt. However, it might seem reasonable to say that argument #3 could establish guilt "beyond reasonable doubt," which is a very high degree of probability.

Although both the classical and frequency concepts of probability are illuminating, Carnap's degrees of confirmation provides the most useful way of thinking about logical probability in persuasive argumentation. Unlike the other concepts, it allows us to assess probability with any kind of evidence and it provides a basis for decision with unique events. In our example on Maude, degree of confirmation permits a logical comparison between two opposing claims: Claim #1 is that Maude killed Abner. Claim #2 is that she did not kill Abner. We can decide which claim is more probable by comparing the degree to which each is confirmed by its supporting evidence.

Degree of belief is a mental, or psychological, concept of probability that is concerned with the extent to which an audience or an individual believes a claim is true. Notice that our first three concepts are logical, based solely on the relationship of evidence and claim, apparently independent of what anyone might think of it. In contrast, the degree of belief concept is psychological; it construes probability as the degree to which an audience believes or feels that a claim is true or false. A person's degree of belief in a statement can therefore range anywhere from absolute disbelief through various levels of uncertainty, to general confidence that a statement is true, and finally to a feeling or belief that it is certainly true.

In the case of crazy people, or perhaps any of us at certain times, the degree to which one feels that something is true might have nothing whatsoever to do with any evidence. Witness those people who buy lottery tickets and then report that they feel absolutely certain that they will win! Clearly, such feelings can have little to do with evidence. Yet, there is nothing about the degree of belief concept that makes it incompatible with the other concepts. In fact, it can help us to make sense of the probability concept in persuasion.

Probability judgments of an audience are unlikely to be antiseptically distinct from their feelings and attitudes about the subject of an argument. Thus, although the degree of belief concept of probability is generally shunned by logicians, it is an important concept for rhetoricians. We need to realize that the probability of a persuasive claim will be assessed by an audience (and there are probably few logicians in a jury box).

Deductive Reasoning

A useful way of understanding deduction is to examine how it differs from induction. Recall our initial distinction on the completeness of support. Inductive conclusions can be established only to a level of probability because their support is always incomplete. In contrast, deductive arguments support their claims completely. Partial support is not an option. If a deductive conclusion is established at all by its supporting reasons, it is established completely.

To a certain extent, the abstractness of deductive argument for beginning students is unavoidable. But we can reduce the level of abstraction in the concept of completeness by comparing examples of deductive and inductive arguments that have the same conclusion. Examine the following arguments closely, noting similarities and differences.

Deductive:	All humans are mortal.	(premise)
	Agnes is human.	(premise)
	So, Agnes is mortal.	(conclusion)
Inductive:	According to our records, every human from the past has been mortal.	(premise)
	Agnes is human.	(premise)
	So, Agnes is mortal.	(conclusion)

Although the conclusions of our illustrative arguments on Agnes are identical, the nature of the support provided by their premises (or good reasons) is quite different. This difference reflects two basic distinctions between induction and deduction:

Deduction	Induction
1. The conclusion is, in a sense, contained in the premises.	The conclusion goes beyond the premises or evidence in support of it.
2. If the premises are true or accepted and the argument has correct form, the conclusion necessarily follows.	If the premises are true or accepted and have a correct relationship to the conclusion, the conclusion is supported to some degree of probability.

The Containment Principle

The principle of containment means that whatever is said in the conclusion of a deductive argument must, in reality, be *in* its premises or supporting reasons; the conclusion cannot truly say anything new or go beyond what is already in the premises. Thus, in the preceding example, the conclusion that "Agnes is mortal" is *contained* in the premises in the sense that it is an implicit part of their meaning. It would be impossible to know that our first premise, "All humans are mortal," is true unless we also know that Agnes is mortal, providing that she is human. Another way to see this containment is to convert our premises to a simple model (see Figure 5.1).

Notice that the first premise locates humans within the category of all things that are mortal. The second premise places Agnes *within* the category of humans, all of which have the property of mortality. Thus, our conclusion is contained in the premises, according to our models of the statements. Essentially, the idea of containment has to do with the meaning of argument premises. A deductive conclusion is contained in its premises because the meaning or ideas they express include the idea expressed in the conclusion. In a sense, the conclusions of deductive arguments merely make explicit what is expressed implicitly in the premises.

In contrast, though the claim of our inductive argument is identical to our deductive claim, it is not contained in its supporting premises; it goes beyond them to say something new. Neither the statement "Every human from the past has been mortal" nor the statement "Agnes is human" contains the idea that "Agnes is mortal." The evidence in our premises is very strong but the meaning of our inductive claim is not implicit in its evidence. It goes beyond the evidence.

FIGURE 5.1 *Syllogism Model*

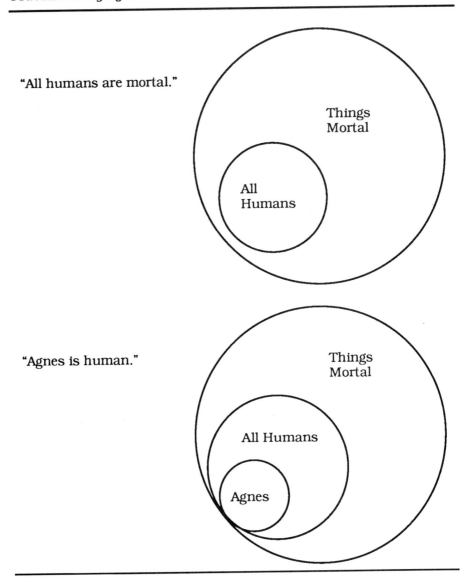

"All humans are mortal."

Things Mortal

All Humans

"Agnes is human."

Things Mortal

All Humans

Agnes

The Necessity of Deductive Conclusions

Whereas probability is the central concept of induction, the key idea of deduction is necessity. The idea of *necessity* means that it is logically impossible for the conclusion of our deductive argument to be false if its premises are true or accepted. Why impossible? Logical impossibility means that we would be contradicting ourselves if we accepted the premises of our correct deductive argument about Agnes and then denied its conclusion. If we agree that all humans are mortal and we also agree that Agnes is a human, we would contradict ourselves if we deny that she is mortal.

Validity Means Correct Form

To say that a deductive argument is valid is to say that its form is *correct*. More precisely, validity means that the premises and conclusion of the argument are correctly related. Whereas real arguments must have content as well as form, the concept of validity is concerned only with the formal relationships between premises and conclusions, and these relationships are, in a sense, separable from what an argument is about. Thus, we can extract the formal elements of our Agnes example and we can reduce the argument to symbols representing its components.

Complete Argument	*Formal Elements*
All humans are mortal.	All *A*s are *B*.
Agnes is a human.	*C* is an *A*.
So, Agnes is mortal.	So, *C* is a *B*.

Validity and Truth

Our Agnes argument is valid because its underlying formal relationships are correct. Moreover, any argument with the same relationships among its formal elements will also be valid. But the concept of validity does not tell us whether the premises of an argument are *true* or whether they will be accepted. Because validity is concerned only with the formal relationships in deduction, an argument can be valid even though its premises are false, as the following argument illustrates:

All reptiles are dictators.
Saddam Hussein is a reptile.

Therefore, Saddam Hussein is a dictator.

You should see that this argument is valid because it has the same formal relationships as our Agnes example. Moreover, its conclusion is true (as a matter of fact and definition) even though its premises are false. Correct relationships between premises and conclusions are essential for a valid or trustworthy deductive argument but they are not enough by themselves. The premises must also be true or accepted as such by the audience.

Deduction and the Syllogism

A *syllogism* is a deductive argument composed of two premises and a conclusion. One form of syllogism, called the *categorical syllogism*, is used by virtually everyone. In fact, the categorical syllogism is illustrated in our argument on Agnes and her mortality. We use this pattern whenever we apply definitions, rules, precepts, theories, or other kinds of generalizations to particular cases.

Such applications do not require an exotic setting, such as a court of law. In fact, some of the more interesting examples of categorical syllogisms can be encountered in our applications of rules and definitions in the arguments of ordinary conversation. Suppose, for example, that Boris and Oscar are discussing some of the events at a recent college football game.

> "Those students at the south end of the stadium are real jerks!" Boris stated.
>
> "Why do you say that?" Oscar asked.
>
> "Well," said Boris, "you saw them throw snowballs at those kids in the high school marching band. Any college student who does that is a jerk."

Boris, of course, is applying a social rule that comes from what we might call the penumbra of our shared social concept of "jerkness." His application of this rule yields a formal syllogism that can be presented as follows:

> *Major Premise*: Any college student who throws snowballs at kids in a high school band is a jerk.
> *Minor Premise*: Those students at the south end of the stadium threw snowballs at the kids in the high school band.
> _____
> *Conclusion*:   Those students are jerks.

Enthymeme: The Rhetorical Syllogism

An *enthymeme* is a syllogism that has been adapted to the needs of persuasive argument.[8] Like all syllogisms, it consists of two premises and a conclusion, but persuasive advocates seldom present all of these components explicitly. As Aristotle pointed out, if one of the premises in an argument is based on familiar facts or notions possessed by everyone, "there is no need to mention it; the hearer adds it himself."[9] Thus, to support the claim that Ann is a very fine student, it would be enough to state that she has been awarded an academic scholarship to one of the academically elite universities in the United States. There would be no need to add that such an award is given only to very fine students, a fact that most listeners would know.

Aristotle thought that such audience participation was an essential feature of the enthymeme. Active listeners and readers generally add their own beliefs to an advocate's persuasive argument, filling in what may appear to be gaps or omissions of premises. Thus, our syllogism from Boris is an enthymeme if its major premise is unstated:

> "Those students at the south end of the stadium are real jerks!" Boris stated.
>
> "Why do you say that?" Oscar asked.
>
> "Well," said Boris, "you saw them throw snowballs at those kids in the high school marching band."

Notice that this version of the argument invites Oscar to complete it by adding the unstated major premise—that "any college student who throws snowballs at kids in a high school band is a jerk." If Oscar agrees with the major premise, he becomes a participant in the argument, contributing one of his beliefs as a good reason in support of the claim by Boris.

Such audience-supplied good reasons help us to understand how authoritative testimony works. Even when a claim is controversial, we may require no other support than the knowledge that it was presented by a person whose authority or expertise we respect. In effect, the ethos (or credibility) of the source of a claim can serve the function of good reasons, and sometimes provides the primary support for the claim.

Suppose that one of the claims (considered earlier in this chapter) about the mistake of using ground forces rather than relying on air power in a war with Iraq has been made by Henry Kissinger, who served as Secretary of State during the presidencies of Richard Nixon and Gerald Ford. The claim may be accepted if listeners believe that Kissinger made this statement and if the listeners regard Kissinger as an expert in international conflict. In effect, the claim would appear to be an unsupported assertion only when it is examined out of its context—namely, the particular audience to which it is addressed. If the audience respects Kissinger's expertise, his claim would be supported in their minds by two implicit (unstated) good reasons: (1) Henry Kissinger said this is true and (2) Henry Kissinger is an expert whom we believe to know the truth (or to have trustworthy views) about conflict in the international arena.

Truth versus Acceptance
of Deductive Premises

Usually, the terms *true* and *false* are reserved for those statements that purport to be in accord with fact or with objective reality. Social rules, however, go beyond fact; their purpose is to guide behavior and to provide grounds for expressing approval or disapproval. Moreover, if we try to construe social rules as true or false statements, what shall we do about the fact that different communities and cultures have rules that conflict and sometimes contradict each other? It makes far more sense to say that social rules can be accepted or rejected by a particular community or by the person with whom we are talking.

The distinction between truth and acceptance is quite abstract, of course, so it will be useful to look again at our simple argument from Boris. This argument helps us to see that it is sometimes more pertinent to ask whether the audience accepts the premises than to ask whether they are true. Of course, there is no difficulty in asking whether it is true that the students threw the snowballs, because that is a purely factual matter. But to ask whether the rule about "jerkness" is true tends to produce confusion over the meaning of the term *truth*.

In this case, Oscar can either accept or reject the social rule articulated by Boris. If he rejects it, or deems it inappropriate in the circumstances, Boris's argument will have no persuasive force despite its valid form. However, if Oscar accepts the rule, and also agrees that the students threw the snowballs, he must accept the conclusion that the students are jerks or he will be contradicting himself.

Audience acceptance or rejection also seems to be the relevant standard when one premise of an argument is a definition. At least it seems more intelligible to say that definitions can be accepted or rejected by audiences than to say that they are true or false—and especially when a conflict between communities or groups seems to center on a dispute over definition. Pro-life groups, for example, define abortion as the murder of unborn babies. Pro-choice groups, however, dismiss such definitions as emotional and simplistic, and see abortion as the private right of a woman to choose whether or not to permit her pregnancy to continue. We will not make much sense of arguments from these groups by asking whether these definitions are true or false—but we can learn something about persuasion with argument if we examine whether an audience accepts or rejects a particular definition, and their reasons for accepting or rejecting.

Whenever a definition becomes a crucial premise in an argument that people care about, it makes more sense to ask whether it is accepted or appropriate in the circumstances than to ask whether it is true. Consider, for example, how the definition of plagiarism functions in the following argument:

"I know it makes you feel bad, Carl, but the historian, Clayborne Carson, reported that the doctoral dissertation of Martin Luther King, Jr., contains lengthy passages copied from the writings of other people, and these sources were not credited or cited," said David. "So, he was clearly guilty of plagiarism."

"You may be right," said Carl, "but we don't want to be too harsh in our judgment of the great civil rights leader."

"This has nothing to do with being harsh or lenient, and I don't think it has anything to do with Martin Luther King's great achievements in civil rights," said David. "It has to do with plagiarism. By definition, plagiarism is taking another person's writings and passing them off as one's own, and King did that."

You should be able to see that this argument has a valid form, which means its conclusion that Martin Luther King, Jr.,"was clearly guilty of plagiarism" follows necessarily from these two premises:

1. Anyone who takes another person's writings, passing them off as his or her own, is guilty of plagiarism.
2. King took another person's writings and passed them off as his own.

Therefore, King is guilty of plagiarism.

However, even though the form of this argument is valid, it can be considered sound or trustworthy only if its premises are either true or accepted. But which standard—truth or acceptability—is most intelligible here? It would, of course, make sense to ask whether the second premise is true. As it happens, the truth of this premise seems to be generally accepted. It is based on the testimony of a highly credible source—Stanford University history professor, Clayborne Carson, who was appointed by Coretta Scott King to edit the papers of her slain husband. Moreover, King's dissertation can be inspected by anyone who doubts Professor Carson.

The first premise, however, is another matter. It generally makes little sense to question the truth of a definition. Definitions can be useful or not and they can be accepted or rejected within a community, but it makes little sense to ask if they are true. In this case, the definition of plagiarism presented in the argument is a rather standard, generally accepted definition within the academic community. But most definitions are open to exceptions or arguments about their application to particular facts. One could ask, for example, did King intend to pass off another person's work as his own? Was it merely an oversight or sloppiness that led to his failure to cite sources or was it deliberate? Would another term, such as *bad judgment*, be more appropriate for the facts of this case?

Toulmin's Critique of Induction and Deduction

Some of our questions about the definition of plagiarism point to a more general problem in the traditional classification of all arguments into the categories of induction and deduction. A number of argumentation theorists, including Toulmin, Perelman, Gottlieb, and Willard, have identified a variety of problems in traditional logic, and each has argued for an approach to the analysis of argument that is more in line with the way people actually justify their own claims and criticize those of others.[10] Beginners in argumentation do not need to be overwhelmed with all of the complexities in this ongoing ferment in argumentation theory, but two of the contributions of Toulmin, in particular, can extend our understanding of argument: (1) the Toulmin model of argument and (2) the concept of an argument field.

The Toulmin Model of Argument

Toulmin argued that the traditional structures for deductive and inductive arguments fail to illuminate some of the important functions in the real argumentation of persuasive advocates. He maintained, first, that it is confusing to use the single name *premise* for the different kinds of supporting reasons in argument. The term *premise* tends to blind us to the varied functions that supporting reasons serve. Second, Toulmin argued that the traditional model of deductive argument, with only two premises and a claim, has fewer parts than the elements we can easily see in the arguments of real advocates. Toulmin therefore proposed an argument model with six elements, all of which serve distinctive functions.

Grounds, Warrant, and Claim. The first three elements of Toulmin's model are grounds, warrant, and claim. Although these core elements initially look very much like the minor premise, major premise, and conclusion of the traditional syllogism, there are some important differences in the ideas of grounds and warrant.

The term *grounds* refers to the factual basis of support in the argument. It answers the question, What do you have to go on?

Toulmin's idea is that arguments must be grounded in something that is real—namely, the facts that serve as the foundation of any inference. Thus, if I claim that tomorrow is going to be a beautiful day, you could reasonably ask me why I think so, and your question would prompt me to respond with my grounds: the factual information that I heard in a weather forecast. The term *grounds* has an advantage over *minor premise* because it indicates more clearly the function of this element in an argument. Whenever one makes a claim, it is reasonable for the listener or reader to ask what the facts are that support it or that led the advocate to make the claim.

The term *warrant* is also an effort to get at function in a clearer way than the term *major premise*. Toulmin says that a warrant functions to answer the basic question, How do you get from the grounds to your claim? Warrants justify inferences and provide the basis for going from grounds to claim. Warrants seem to function as rules or principles that guide our inferences, decisions, or actions. When warrants are very strong, they may take the form of rule statements, which looks like these:

If *A* is present, we can be sure that *B* is also.

When the grounds *A* are in evidence, we can conclude that *B* is the case.

The concept of warrant is, of course, rather abstract at this point, but we are now in a position to see what an argument would look like according to the Toulmin model, using just our three basic elements of grounds, warrant, and claim. Suppose that a defense attorney argues that her client could not possibly be guilty of murder because he was in San Francisco at the very time that the victim was killed in Detroit. As is often the case with real argument, we find that this argument presents only two explicit elements—grounds and claim—which we can present as follows:

Grounds ———————————— *Claim*

My client was in San   My client could not be
Francisco at the time the   guilty of murdering
victim died.   the victim in Detroit.

The warrant here is unstated, but it is the clearly understood general rule that "a person cannot kill someone in Detroit if he is in San Francisco." Thus, when we insert the warrant into the model, the argument looks like this:

Grounds ————————————————— *Claim*

My client was in San Francisco at the time the victim died.	My client could not be guilty of murdering the victim in Detroit.

Warrant

A person in San Francisco
cannot kill someone in Detroit.

Backing, Rebuttal, Qualifier. The other three elements in Toulmin's model are not reflected in traditional deductive argument structure. *Backing* provides support for the warrant, or reasons why the rule in the warrant is true or in force as an operating rule. In our argument example, backing for the warrant is the fact that "a person cannot be in two different places at the same time." Although it is unlikely that our attorney would ever need to state explicitly either the warrant or its backing for our illustrative argument, backing can be a crucial function in some inferences.

The concept of *rebuttal* is unique. The idea is that the general rules in warrants may not always hold good in every situation; there may be exceptions that would invalidate the warrant's justification of the inference from grounds to claim, causing us to set aside a rule that would generally hold good. Thus, in our illustrative argument, although the rule statement in our warrant that "a person in San Francisco cannot kill someone in Detroit" would generally hold good, we can think of exceptions, and these exceptions would comprise the rebuttal element of the argument. Suppose, for example, that the victim was killed by an explosive device that could be detonated electronically, even over very large distances. There may be many other possible exceptions to our warrant rule.

The term *qualifier* is also unique. Toulmin argues that claims vary considerably in their strength, and we therefore need to qualify, or express, the extent to which our argument claim is confirmed by its support. If the claim is confirmed completely, we can use the qualifier *necessarily* in relation to it. Thus, our defense attorney might say that it is "necessarily true that my client could not have killed the victim." But in the case of claims that are not so certain, we might need to select qualifiers such as *possibly, probably, most likely*, and so on.

Toulmin suggests that the rules implicit in most argument warrants generally hold good, but not always. For example, we may generally accept the social rule that "anyone who tells your secrets, after promising not to do so, is not your friend." But when such a rule appears as the warrant of an argument, we would surely disagree with any suggestion that there are no exceptions to it. Under the rebuttal, we might note that other priorities of friendship, such as saving a friend's life or protecting a friend from great harm can surely constitute exceptions to an otherwise acceptable rule.

Now that the six elements in Toulmin's model have been examined in brief, note how all of them would look with our original example.

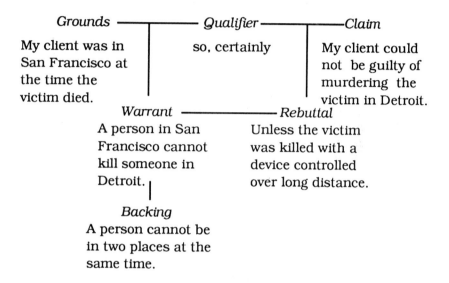

Grounds ———————— *Qualifier* ———————— *Claim*

My client was in San Francisco at the time the victim died.

so, certainly

My client could not be guilty of murdering the victim in Detroit.

Warrant ———————— *Rebuttal*

A person in San Francisco cannot kill someone in Detroit.

Unless the victim was killed with a device controlled over long distance.

Backing

A person cannot be in two places at the same time.

Among its many virtues, the Toulmin model helps us to understand how rules that are usually true or acceptable, but not always, are used in arguments. As Gottlieb has noted, reasoning with such rules does not seem to fit either the traditional inductive or deductive forms we have examined, and yet this sort of reasoning is characteristic of much of the argumentation in law courts as well as the political arena.

Aristotle observed that, the materials of argument, which Toulmin calls grounds, warrant, and backing, are largely comprised of propositions (or reasons) that are "only usually true." Aristotle called the materials of persuasive argument *probabilities* and *signs*. A probability, he wrote, "is a thing that usually happens," which is reasonably close to our notion of a rule that is generally true.[11] For example, our culture may generally agree on what normal people do under particular circumstances, and these agreements comprise what we think of as human nature. But we would likely be shocked if anyone thought that such shared ideas about human nature would hold for all people, in any situation.

Likewise, we seem to prize maxims, or those gems of cultural wisdom that advise us generally, "If it ain't broke, don't fix it" and "Never wrestle with a skunk." But we well understand that there are many exceptions to these general guidelines. However, as soon as we include the idea of exceptions to these potential premises or reasons, there are difficulties in using traditional logic. Unless we construe such materials in all-or-nothing premises, they seem not to measure up to the strictures of formal deductive logic. And if we make them fit the requirements of deduction, they seem to be untrue, or at least exaggerated.

Unlike many of the critics of traditional logic, however, I think it is unwise simply to discard the disciplines of induction and deduction merely because they cannot include every kind of argument. There are many arguments that are clearly inductive or deductive, and the concepts and rules of these two forms of reasoning are valuable in helping us to see what it is that makes such arguments sound and trustworthy. While Toulmin and other argumentation theorists have framed many of their contributions as an attack on the older standards of logic, I think it is more productive to view their work as additions rather than replacements for traditional logic. Both explanations of argument structure have value for anyone who wants to understand how argument works.

Field Standards for Argument

It is helpful to think of argument in relation to specific subject fields such as law, physics, sports, medicine, and so on. For example, the standards for evaluating arguments in tennis can be very different from the standards we would use in the field of law or atmospheric science. The idea of field includes more than just the subject area of an argument, however, Field can refer as well to the logical type of an argument in the sense that predictive arguments about future events are of a different type than arguments about the present or the past.

In addition, the concept of field ultimately extends to audiences. Throughout our analysis of argument in this chapter, we have found that, persuasively, it is the audience that decides whether an argument measures up to the appropriate standards—that is, whether the reasons presented by an advocate are true or acceptable, relevant to the claim, and sufficient. Thus, in a very real sense, argument standards may vary from one audience to another. This is not an entirely appalling prospect, however. Consider how such concepts as the assumption of uniformity, which we considered earlier, might be applied in relation to the field concept.

Here is the problem: In one case, we may concede that it is perfectly reasonable for a physician to assume that the level of cholesterol in a patient's blood is identical to the level found in a sample of blood taken from the patient. In this case, it seems reasonable to assume that the patient's blood is uniform. But suppose a small child concludes that (all) dogs are friendly, gentle creatures that do not bite. This conclusion is based on the child's sample— namely, all of the dogs the child has been around so far. The inductive process of reasoning from particulars (the sample of either blood or dogs) to the respective generalizations appears to be the same. Both cases rely on the assumption of uniformity. However, the first appears to be sound; the second, as the child will discover, is quite unsound. So how do we know when it is reasonable to rely on the assumption of uniformity?

From the standpoint of traditional logic, it is difficult to articulate general rules that provide satisfactory distinctions between our two cases, let alone all of the cases of inductive argument. However, Toulmin's field concept makes it clear that we do not need to rely on general rules that apply to every kind of inductive argument. Subject matter experts in the field of medicine, for example, should be far more adept in judging an inductive argument about cholesterol than any ordinary patient. Likewise, experts in the fields of law, physics, ethics, sports, chess—or any subject field—will have developed standards for evaluating arguments that come within their subject and that are based on the collective wisdom and experience of the best thinkers in their subject area. Thus, whenever we can determine the relevant field of an argument, we can consult its experts for the best standards for judging the trustworthiness of any inductive reasoning that falls within its jurisdiction.

On a less exulted level, all of us apply the standard of our experience to differentiate sound from unsound arguments. Thus, a child may be excused for inferring that all dogs are gentle beasts that never bite, but if an adult makes a similar inference, we are inclined to conclude that he or she is naive or mentally weak. In a sense, our experience, including all facets of our education, allows us to develop critical standards for induction for a range of fields, as Toulmin might say, that increase our ability to distinguish sound from unsound inductive argument.

Summary

1. In our society, an educated person should be able to support claims with effective arguments and to evaluate the arguments of others.

2. The major principles of rhetorical argument divide into two categories: the nature of argument, and its form.

3. The nature of rhetorical argument is focused effectively by Wallace's definition: good reasons in support of a claim.

  a. Claims are complete sentence statements of any conclusion, position, or belief of an advocate.
  b. The subject matter of claims is unlimited.
  c. To be persuasive, the reasons must be considered "good" by their intended audience.
  d. Good reasons should be provided for any claim that is likely to be doubted by the audience.
  e. Audience evaluation of argument can be inadequate if the audience lacks knowledge of the subject or the nature of argument.

4. Traditional logic provides three kinds of general tests for argument: (a) truth of the reasons, (b) relevance of the reasons, and (c) sufficiency of the reasons. All of these tests also have a rhetorical dimension.

5. The standards of induction provide a way of understanding arguments in which the evidence for a claim is necessarily incomplete.

  a. Evidence is always incomplete in inductions.
  b. Inductive reasoning moves from known to unknown.
  c. There are two common patterns of induction: particulars to generals and particulars to particulars.
  d. Induction assumes that the universe is uniform, at least to some extent. Without this assumption, science and superstition would be in the same boat.
  e. There are four useful concepts of probability: (1) the classical concept, (2) the frequency concept, (3) degrees of confirmation, and (4) degrees of belief. Of these, degrees of confirmation is the most useful for assessing the probability of a claim in relation to its evidence, but the persuasive dimensions of probability also rely on degrees of belief.

6. The standards of deduction help us to understand arguments in which the premises provide complete support for the claim.

  a. The conclusions of deductive arguments are contained in the meaning of their premises.

b. The conclusion of a correct deductive argument follows necessarily from its premises. It would be contradictory to accept its premises and deny its conclusion.

c. The standard of validity refers to the form of an argument. An argument is valid if the relationship between its premises and its conclusion is correct.

d. Because validity refers to the form of an argument, it would be possible for the premises of a valid argument to be untrue.

e. Syllogisms are one kind of deductive reasoning. Syllogisms consist of two premises and a conclusion.

f. The enthymeme is a rhetorical syllogism. Enthymemes have the syllogistic form but they draw their premises from the notions possessed by everyone. Thus, enthymemes can seem to be incomplete syllogisms unless we understand that the audience contributes the unstated elements.

g. When we apply rules, definitions, social values, or principles deductively, the standard of acceptance of the premises often makes more sense than the truth standard.

7. Toulmin's critique of induction and deduction provides insights into the elements of argument and an alternative way of thinking about standards for evaluating our reasoning.

a. The Toulmin model consists of six functional elements. Grounds, warrant, and claim resemble the traditional deductive elements of premises and conclusions, but they help us to understand the various functions of supporting reasons in argument. Backing, rebuttal, and qualifier isolate elements that have no clear counterpart in traditional logic.

b. Toulmin's concept of argument fields provides a useful way of understanding how standards for evaluating argument are developed by the communities of experts in various subjects, as well as how audiences utilize their own sense of experience for evaluating arguments.

The principles and concepts in this chapter are among the more difficult ones for beginners in the study of argument, so you should not feel discouraged if the ideas here seem abstract at first. And yet, how disappointing it should be for anyone to graduate from a university and find himself or herself unable to make sense of reasoning forms that even children use. The core ideas of rhetorical argument are intended to help you understand argument that is designed to persuade others. As you gain experience in examining arguments and in composing your own, you should find that the ideas here become less remote.

It will help you if you study this and the next chapter together, even though they cover quite a lot of ground. Analysis of the specific forms of argument and the tests that advocates have developed for them over the centuries are the topics for Chapter 6. These forms of argument provide a direct way to gain experience with Toulmin's concept of field. More importantly, these concrete, everyday forms of argument will deepen your understanding of argument as good reasons in support of a claim. The major points developed in this chapter about inductive and deductive reasoning, the concepts of probability, and the Toulmin model can all be examined in relation to the argument forms that everyone uses.

Exercises

1. Letters to the editor in local newspapers typically address one point or support one central claim. Examine the editorial page of your local paper and pick out two or three of the more interesting letters. Identify in each of these the claim and the "good reasons" in support of the claim.

2. Classify the arguments you found in the exercise above as either inductive or deductive. If you have classified them as inductive, which of the four concepts of probability would be most useful for explaining the degree of support the evidence provides for the claim? If your arguments are deductive, has the writer stated both premises explicitly or is there an unstated premise that the reader is expected to supply?

3. As a class project, apply Toulmin's model to the arguments you or your classmates found in letters to the editor. Can you identify Toulmin's elements of grounds, warrant, and claim? Ordinarily, we will not find Toulmin's elements of backing or rebuttal explicitly stated in arguments, but we can determine what they might be. Can you find either backing or rebuttal in your arguments?

4. As a class discussion exercise, consider the following argument and decide whether it is deductive or inductive. You should be prepared to support your answer in relation to the characteristics of induction and deduction.

"Well," said Harry, "I think it is clear that big awards by juries in malpractice cases against obstetricians cause these physicians to give up the practice of obstetrics."
"Why do you believe that?" asked Bill.

"For one thing," Harry continued, "a study by the American Medical Association shows that the number of physicians practicing obstetrics has declined as jury awards have increased in malpractice cases concerning obstetrics. For another, my old friend, Doctor Joe, said he just couldn't afford to deliver babies anymore, what with all these high jury awards."

Endnotes

1. Karl Wallace, "The Substance of Rhetoric: Good Reasons," *Quarterly Journal of Speech, 49* (1963): 239—249.
2. Chaim Perelman, *The Realm of Rhetoric* (Notre Dame: University of Notre Dame Press, 1982), p. 101.
3. Wesley Salmon, *Logic* (Englewood Cliffs, NJ: Prentice-Hall, 1963), p. 4.
4. Charles Willard, *Argumentation and the Social Grounds of Knowledge* (University: University of Alabama Press, 1983).
5. Salmon, *Logic,* p. 4.
6. Rudolph Carnap, *Logical Foundations of Probability* (Chicago: University of Chicago Press, 1962).
7. Hans Reichenbach, *The Theory of Probability* (Berkeley: University of California Press, 1949).
8. Lloyd Bitzer, "Aristotle's Enthymeme Revisited," *Quarterly Journal of Speech, 45* (1959): 399–408.
9. Aristotle, "Rhetoric," in *Aristotle: Rhetoric and Poetics*, trans. W. Rhys Roberts (New York: Modern Library, Random House, 1954), p. 28
10. Stephen Toulmin, *The Uses of Argument* (Cambridge: University Press, 1964); Gidon Gottlieb, *The Logic of Choice* (New York: Macmillan, 1968). See also Perelman, *Realm of Rhetoric*, and Willard, *Argumentation.*
11. Aristotle, "Rhetoric," p. 28.

6

Analysis of Forms of Argument

Central Ideas in This Chapter

1. Analysis of argument forms requires three kinds of abilities.
   - It recognizes the common persuasive argument forms.
   - It sees clearly the pattern of reasoning in each form.
   - It masters the tests that enable us to see possible weaknesses and to refute arguments of each form.

2. Six forms of argument, and their respective tests, are analyzed in this chapter.
   - The argument by example has three tests: number test, representativeness test, and contradiction test.
   - The argument by analogy has two tests: comparison test and description test.
   - The argument by causal correlation has four tests: consistency test, strength test, time test, and coherence test.
   - The argument by sign has three tests: necessity test, number test, and contradiction test.
   - The argument by causal application has three tests: truth test, sufficiency test, and intervention test.
   - The argument by applied generalization has two tests: acceptance test and exceptions test.

The ability to invent arguments and to respond to the arguments of others, either by nodding in approval or by pointing to flaws, is perhaps as universal as the ability to use language—and both seem to be acquired without great effort, at least initially. Most children learn their own language, including its basic grammar, by about the age of 3 years. We know that 3-year-olds have learned basic grammar because otherwise they would be unable to use the language as they do—that is, to understand and to produce novel utterances. They say things they have never said before and they understand sentences they have never heard before. Yet, we would be surprised if anyone should think that 3-year-old children ought to be able to explain any of the rules of the language they use, let alone its complete grammar. Children evidently acquire their language merely by communicating with others.

Apparently, we learn to make persuasive arguments in more or less the same way that we learn other uses of language—namely, in the give and take of communicating with others. Children seem to acquire the ability to make arguments and to evaluate the arguments of others merely by participating in a family or group in which people are expected to justify their actions and assertions. As John Locke maintained, none of us learns to argue, initially, through the formal study of argument rules and structure; our ability to reason does not come from books in logic, such as Aristotle's works in syllogistic logic:

> *If syllogisms must be taken for the only proper instrument of reason . . . it will follow that, before Aristotle, there was not one man that did or could know anything by reason; and that, since the invention of syllogisms, there is not one in ten thousand that doth.*
>
> *But God has not been so sparing to men to make them barely two-legged creatures, and left it to Aristotle to make them rational.*[1]

The fact that we learn to argue without formal instruction in rhetoric or logic, just as we learn language prior to any formal instruction in grammar, should in no way diminish the value of these studies. It seems to be a universal in all of the human arts that practice precedes theory. The art of rhetoric began with the realization that some speakers were consistently persuasive, while others were not, and it gradually became apparent that success and failure could be explained in relation to principles of rhetoric. Furthermore, our natural abilities to speak and to argue persuasively can be developed and improved through systematic study of the principles of rhetoric and argumentation. Thus, the goal of this chapter is not to teach you to argue. You could hardly be an adult college student and be unable to make arguments or respond to the arguments of others. Rather, our goal is to develop your ability to use argument, to discern the persuasive possibilities among the more important forms of reasoning and argument, and to see the persuasive options for testing, criticizing, and refuting the arguments of others.

More specifically, this chapter will explore the six forms of argument that are frequently used and abused in many arenas of persuasion:

Argument by example
Argument by analogy
Argument by causal correlation
Argument by sign
Argument by causal application
Argument by applied generalization

Many more than six forms of argument have been identified by rhetoricians and logicians, of course. Aristotle, for example, described 28 valid "lines of argument" (many of which are argument forms) in his *Rhetoric*, and there is no reason to suppose that Aristotle thought his list was exhaustive. However, there is no need to attempt a complete survey of argument forms here. As you gain experience in recognizing and using the more common patterns of argument, you will develop the facility for recognizing other patterns and extending your arsenal.

The ability to recognize argument forms is an essential first step for argument evaluation, and it requires a good grasp of our analysis of the nature of argument from Chapter 5. You will have mastered this step when you can readily identify the arguments you read or hear, and explain your identification in relation to the essential features of each argument form.

The second step in argument evaluation is to master the tools for testing each form. As we describe each form of argument, we will examine the tests that have been found useful in determining whether these arguments are sound, reliable, sufficient, or otherwise up to the best standards available. All of the tests of specific argument forms are based on our discussion of the nature and form of rhetorical argument in Chapter 5.

Argument by Example

One of the most common ways to establish a generalization is to cite examples in support of it. Thus, if Bill Moyers claims that the term *student athlete* is an oxymoron in intercollegiate athletics, we would expect him to support his claim by pointing to representative examples of athletes whose college experiences are contrary to the very idea of being a student. Argument by example operates on the assumption that what is true of representative examples, or typical cases, is true in general. Pay special attention to this assumption as we examine the form of this argument.

The Form of Argument by Example

Argument by example has one of the archetypal forms of the inductive process of reasoning we explored in Chapter 5. It is what people have in mind when they say that inductive reasoning moves from particulars to generals. Whenever we support generalizations by citing particular cases, the argument form always has a kind of whole-part relationship between the claim and its support. Notice in each of the following arguments that the claim is a generalization—especially in relation to the good reasons in support of it. The claim says that something is true in general, whereas the examples provided as support show that the claim is true or probably true in particular cases.

1. ***Claim:*** Air pollution is a serious problem in U.S. cities.

     Good Reasons: 1. Air pollution is serious in Denver.
                       2. Air pollution is serious in Los Angeles.
                       3. Air pollution is serious in Detroit.

2. ***Claim***: The failure of nations to stand up to aggression only encourages an aggressor.

     Good Reason: 1. When England and France failed to stand up to aggression from Germany, it merely encouraged Hitler to attack them.

3. ***Claim:*** Negative political ads are a major feature of modern presidential campaigns.

     Good Reasons: 1. Negative advertising, such as the Willy Horton ad, was a major feature of the Bush-Dukakis campaign of 1988.
                      2. Negative ads were a major feature of the Nixon-Humphrey campaign of 1968.
                      3. Negative ads were a major feature of the Johnson-Goldwater campaign of 1964.

As you examine these arguments, consider how they manifest all of the characteristics of induction we discussed in Chapter 5. First, in each case the examples provide incomplete evidence for the generalization they support. It would always be possible for each of the generalizations in the conclusions to be false even though the examples that support them are true. Second, this means that the examples can establish only a level of probability for each claim. If the examples are true, they confirm each claim to a certain degree. Third, the reasoning for each argument moves from the known to the unknown, or at least the truth of the examples is better known than the generalization they support. And finally, each of the arguments relies on the uniformity of nature principle.

It may occur to you that there is a very close similarity between our argument by example and the kind of reasoning involved in public opinion polling—and you would be quite right. The pattern or form of reasoning is identical. Public polls never ask everyone in the population what they think about an issue. Rather, they ask a sample of the population (which is a kind of example) what they think and then infer that the opinions found in their sample are the opinions of the general population.

The A. C. Neilsen ratings for television programs provide an interesting example of public polling. How does Neilsen determine what television programs are being viewed in U.S. households? It would be terribly expensive, even if it were possible, to ask everyone in the nation what programs they view each evening. Hence, Neilsen monitors the viewing preferences of approximately 1,200 households nationwide and infers that the viewing preferences of this sample accurately reflect the viewing preferences of all households. The 1,200 homes are, in a sense, examples (presented in a rather compact way) that are used to support generalizations about what people in millions of homes are viewing.

Notice the similarity between Neilsen's reasoning and each of our illustrative arguments. All of them share the same whole-part relationship between their claims and their supporting examples and they all assume that what is true of the examples is true in general. Thus, our first illustrative argument assumes that the examples cited of pollution in Denver, Los Angeles, and Detroit are representative of big cities everywhere in the United States.

You may have noticed that the number of examples presented varies from one argument to another. In persuasive argument, there is no general rule on a minimum or maximum for the number of examples required to support a claim. In some cases, there may be few examples available to an advocate. In others, it may be a matter of how much time is available or how likely the audience is to accept a particular generalization as true. One example can be persuasive if it rings true to the audience; many examples can seem weak if the audience is hostile to the generalization or doubts its truth.

Argument by example is persuasively powerful because it reflects an inductive pattern of reasoning that everyone uses. We really cannot avoid it. As we observed in Chapter 5, reasoning from particulars to generals is one of the major ways we come to know what the world is like. Children use it when they try okra or squash one or two times and then conclude (a generalization) that such foods taste awful, or okay, or great. In a similar way, all of us make general conclusions about the world around us on the basis of examples. As you begin to realize how many ways we rely on this form of reasoning, you should become more effective in distinguishing it from other argument forms.

In order to recognize argument by example, or any of the other forms of argument, the trick is to begin by locating the claim, or conclusion, and then determine what support is offered as reasons why the claim should be accepted. See if you can isolate the claim and the support for the following argument.

> Pete was trying to persuade Mike to vote in the presidential primary election. "Don't you realize," said Pete, "that every vote can be crucial?" "What makes you think so?" said Mike. "Well, just look at all the elections where the outcome turned on just a few individual votes," said Pete. "In 1960, John Kennedy won the presidential election by getting less than 1 vote per election precinct more than Nixon. In 1968, Nixon beat Humphrey by only seven-tenths of a percent of the popular vote. And right here in our own county, several elections have been decided with the victor getting fewer than 10 votes more than his opponent, out of more than 60,000 votes cast. If one of those candidates you call 'bozos' winds up winning the nomination by just a few votes, you're going to feel awful!"

Can you distinguish the claim of Pete's argument from his supporting examples? The claim is the generalization: "Every vote can be crucial [to the outcome of an election]." Once the claim is identified, most people have no trouble in locating the examples presented in support of it. But it is also important to realize that not everything presented in connection with this argument is relevant. The last sentence, on possible consequences of not voting, is irrelevant to the generalization.

Tests for Argument by Example

Each of the tests for argument by example serves as a critical tool or probe. Such tools enable us to probe the use of examples as persuasive support for a claim and to see clearly the possible defects in arguments of this sort. The tests are framed as questions because they are intended to provoke inquiry along lines that advocates have found to be useful. The questions are helpful in debate because they provide us with the means of exposing defective reasoning in opposing arguments. But their value is not limited to debates or refutation. These tests also help us to ensure that our own arguments are sound and worthy of belief. The three general tests for argument by example are number, representativeness, and contradiction.

1. *Number.* Is the number of examples sufficient to support the generalization in the claim?
2. *Representativeness.* Are the examples typical?
3. *Contradiction.* Are there any negative instances?

1. *Number.* Is the number of examples sufficient to support the generalization in the claim? This test is based directly on the general test of sufficiency for any evidence-claim relationship, which we explored in Chapter 5. However, to ask How many examples are required to support this claim? is a rhetorical as well as a logical question. Enough for whom?

The number of examples needed will vary in relation to the subject of the claim, the situation, and the audience. The nature of the audience can be crucial. An opposed or critical audience, for instance, can be expected to require more supporting examples than a favorable audience. Thus, if an audience is opposed to a speaker's point of persuasion and thinks we already spend too much on the military, one example (such as the case of Hitler's aggression after the appeasement efforts of Britain and France) would probably be regarded as inadequate to establish the generalized claim that "the failure of nations to stand up to aggression only encourages an aggressor." But a favorable audience that already believes we must remain militarily strong in order to keep our freedom would probably be more than satisfied with one example of that sort.

Adequacy in the number of examples provided is very much like the problem of sample size for a public opinion poll. Just as we would not expect Neilsen to sample all U.S. homes in order to find out what people are watching on television, we would not want a speaker to cite all of the cities in supporting the claim that "air pollution is a serious problem in U.S. cities." But whether three examples (Denver, Los Angeles, Detroit) are sufficient will probably depend on the application of the generalized claim.

2. *Representativeness.* Are the examples typical? This test is also concerned with the sufficiency of support provided by the examples, but its focus is just a bit different. Even a rather large number of

examples can be unsatisfactory if they are atypical. Witness the advertised claim that "*anyone* can earn $50,000 per year selling our product." Initially, it may seem impressive to us if this claim is supported with the examples of, say, 10 people who have earned that much while selling the product. But is this the typical experience? Are these folks really representative of all the people who have worked on the sales force? What if a large number of people—say 10,000—have tried to sell the product? In that case, 10 examples of success would then seem less impressive—especially if it is difficult to discover the earnings of the other 9,990.

3. *Contradiction.* Are there any negative instances? Since the claim of an argument by example is a generalization, it usually purports to be true in all cases. Thus, one negative instance is sufficient to refute it, or at least to require that it be modified. Instead of "(all) military weakness invites aggression," perhaps it is reasonable to say that this is true of only "some" military weakness. And if there are enough negative cases, they may nullify any sort of generalization or even support a contrary generalization.

Argument by Analogy

As a kind of inductive reasoning, analogy is based on our capacities to compare things, to see resemblances and similarities, and to expect consistency and uniformity in the world. Even little children expect similar things, like two different flavors of ice cream, to have similar properties. This expectation is one of the foundations of argument by analogy. An argument is an analogy whenever its reasoning is based on a comparison, and the support for its claim depends on the essential similarities between two things.

The Form of Argument by Analogy

Argument by analogy has the second archetypal form of inductive reasoning we examined in Chapter 5: It reasons from particular to particular. The claim of an analogy is particular, at least insofar as the cases compared are particular. Thus, we argue in an analogy that if two cases resemble each other in essential points, whatever is true of case one will be true of case two. Likewise, we argue that if something is fair, or good, or appropriate in one situation, it must be fair, or good, or appropriate for another situation that is comparable to it. Consider these examples of argument by analogy that reveal its diverse uses.

1. One common use of analogies is to support a claim that a present law or policy is doomed to failure by comparing it to another law or policy that is generally viewed as a failure:

> "Failure of the policy of prohibition (of alcohol) in the United States shows that similar policies, such as the laws against marijuana, cocaine, and other drugs, are doomed to failure."

Claim: The laws against marijuana, cocaine, and other drugs are doomed to failure.

> *Good Reasons*: 1. These laws are essentially the same as former laws prohibiting alcohol.
> 2. Prohibition laws were a failure.

2. Another common usage of analogy is to support the claim that a proposed law will work by comparing it to a similar law already on the books that is working effectively:

> "Mandatory seat-belt laws are working in other countries which are much like us, such as Australia, so a seat-belt law will work in the United States."

Claim: A mandatory seat-belt law will work in the United States.

> *Good Reasons*: 1. The seat-belt laws of other countries, such as Australia, are working effectively.
> 2. The seat-belt laws of Australia and other nations are essentially like the law proposed for the United States.

3. To support a claim that a foreign policy is likely to result in disaster, an advocate might compare it to a policy widely thought to have been a disaster:

> "U.S. policy in Central America has all of the earmarks of the policies that led us into the disastrous war in Viet Nam. If we continue in our present policy, we will be drawn into another disastrous war."

Claim: If we continue our present policy in Central America, we will be drawn into another disastrous war.

> *Good Reasons*: 1. U.S. policy in Central America is essentially like the policy that led the United States into war in Viet Nam.
> 2. The Viet Nam War was a disaster for the United States.

4. To support the claim that a proposed method for evaluating different colleges is purely arbitrary and lacks good sense, it may be compared to another evaluative system that appears foolish:

> "The proposal reminds me of the way some people weigh hogs in Texas. They put a hog on one side of a balance scale and then pile rocks on the other side, until the scale is in balance. Then they guess the weight of the rocks!"

> ***Claim***: This proposed evaluation system is foolish.

> ***Good Reasons***: 1. The proposal is essentially like the method some people use to weigh hogs in Texas.
> 2. The method of weighing hogs is foolish.

You may have noticed that our hogs analogy is somewhat unlike the first three arguments. When we are comparing two laws, or any two things that are really in the same class, the argument is called a *literal* analogy. When the two things compared come from different classes, the argument is called a *figurative* analogy. Thus, it is figurative to compare a proposal for evaluating colleges to a method for weighing hogs because the speaker does not mean that the two things are really the same. Rather, a figurative analogy suggests that two things from different classes share an essential feature—in this case, foolishness in achieving their objectives. Figurative analogies are often regarded as merely a kind of stylistic device, like metaphor, and therefore deficient as logical argument. (It is a metaphor to call a fighting man a tiger, for instance.) However, figurative analogies, unlike metaphors, provide support for an argument claim, and the support is sometimes powerful.

Argument by analogy, like argument by example, is persuasively powerful because all of us rely on the comparison process of reasoning as we try to sort out the world around us. Even small children quickly learn that analogy is a powerful way to argue about what is fair or unfair, just or unjust—especially if they have brothers or sisters. Parents can expect to be confronted with an impressive array of analogies as little Suzy uses comparisons to support her claims that she should be allowed to stay up late, see a particular film, or have a particular toy because her sister, or brother, or a child down the street has the particular freedom or toy.

The operating concept of such analogies is that the children are essentially the same and should therefore receive similar rights or freedoms if justice is to prevail. Moreover, children are in good company here. Our courts rely on precedent (or similar) cases in order to determine how a present case should be handled. The idea of a precedent is that similar cases should be resolved in more or less the same way.

Tests for Argument by Analogy

There are two tests for argument by analogy: comparison and description. Like other tests of argument forms, these tests are sometimes used alone and sometimes in combination. Both provide useful tools for spotting flaws that can render an analogy unsound, whether it is our own or our opponent's.

1. *Comparison.* Are the compared cases really alike in their essential features?
2. *Description.* Are the two cases accurately described?

1. *Comparison.* Are the compared cases really alike in their essential features? What is an essential feature? There would be no need for an analogy if two cases were identical in every respect, and probably most analogies compare two cases that have many real differences. The question is not whether there are differences between two cases but whether the differences are important in relation to the claim. Little Suzy certainly is not identical to little Mary. Even if Mary were Suzy's identical twin sister, they could have important differences in relation to a particular claim. If the claim concerns whose turn it is to help with the dirty dishes, an essential difference between the girls could be the fact that Mary helped with the dishes yesterday and so today it is Suzy's turn.

Suppose two states are compared to support the claim that a law that works in Michigan will work in Colorado. Proponents argue that raising the drinking age in Michigan from 18 to 21 resulted in a decrease in drunken driving, so Colorado lawmakers could get the same result by raising the drinking age to 21. Obviously, the two states have many rather striking differences as well as similarities. The comparison test asks: Are these two states similar in their essential features in relation to the claim? To answer this, we need to ask: What are the essential features of the two states for this argument? Are the mountains of Colorado or the great lakes of Michigan relevant here? Probably not, but the fact that Colorado permitted 18- to 20-year-olds to purchase a low-alcohol beer for many years could be an important difference.

What if the two states are West Virginia and California? Suppose a group of California legislators argue that a proposed law to deny a driver's license to any 16- to 18-year-old who drops out of school will reduce the number of high school dropouts in California. As support for their claim, they point to West Virginia's success in reducing dropouts with a similar law. Once again, we could identify many differences as well as similarities between these two states. The key for the comparison test is whether the two states are essentially the same in relation to teenager response to the proposed law.

Pointing to essential differences can be a powerful method of refuting an analogy—especially when the differences can be focused in relation to the original cases. Steven Cahn used this method effectively in supporting his claim that the teaching effectiveness of university professors should be evaluated by their peers rather than by students.

> Students, by definition, do not know the subject matter they are study- ing, and so they are in a poor position to judge whether it is being well taught or whether the instructor's presentation is shallow, inaccurate, incomplete, or biased. Students know if teachers are likeable, not if they are knowledgeable.
>
> Proponents of student ratings claim that students are the best eval- uators . . . , drawing an analogy to the restaurant patron who is a better judge of the food than the chef. While we would all agree that those who eat food know how it tastes, whether it is nourishing or not is most reli- ably judged by a nutritionist, just as educational value is best judged by an educator.[2]

Notice how Cahn begins by pointing to important differences between students and faculty in the first part of his argument. The second part of his refutation confronts a figurative analogy on its own terms to refute the claim that students are the best evaluators.

2. *Description.* This test poses two kinds of questions that are closely related. The first question asks: Are the two cases accurately described? Alternatively, are the facts alleged of each case true? The second question asks: Is the description of the two cases complete? Have any of the important (or essential) features of either case been left out? Notice that all of these questions are concerned with the descriptions of two cases. The focus of this test is whether the description is really truthful.

Earlier, we cited the analogy used by opponents of the former U.S. policy in Central America—namely, a comparison between Viet Nam and Nicaragua. Those who disagreed with this analogy used the description test, arguing that neither of the two cases were being described accurately. In relation to Viet Nam, they disagreed on what it was that led to the disasters experienced by the United States, and they also disagreed on the nature of the disaster. Opponents argued that the causes of U.S. failures in Viet Nam were wrongly attributed to the policy to prevent a communist takeover. Instead, they argued, the disasters of Viet Nam were the result of ambivalence and vacillation in the way the war was conducted. On the other side, they also disagreed with the way Nicaragua was described.

Wise parents also use this test, questioning the accuracy of alleged facts in the cases cited by their children. Do 5-year-old Johnny's parents really let him stay up to midnight anytime he wants to do it? If so, are they sane? Do all of the other teenagers at high school really get sports cars for their sixteenth birthdays? Whenever compared cases seem just a bit too good to be true, it may be that they are. Check the facts alleged.

Argument by Causal Correlation

The search for cause-effect relationships is, in some respects, as universal in our daily lives as it is in science. In medicine, we search for the causes of disease and attempt to correlate them with their effects. In economics, we examine such phenomena as inflation, unemployment, and economic growth and try to find their causes. In daily life, we search for causes as we try to understand how things work and what actions are likely to accomplish the goals we seek. Whenever we try to predict what will happen in the future, or explain what is happening or has happened, we are tied to causal reasoning.

The Form of Argument
by Causal Correlation

Argument by causal correlation is an inductive form of argument that shares the archetypal pattern of particulars to generals, but its particulars are more complex than argument by example. How do we distinguish causal correlation from example?

As noted earlier, whenever we need to identify the form of an argument, we should always begin by locating its claim—and then we should seek out the reasons or evidence in support of it. This procedure is especially important here. The claim of a causal correlation argument is always a generalization of the form that *A causes B*. This is the easy part. Whenever you find an argument in which the claim states that one thing causes another, you will know that it is a causal correlation argument. The nature of the support, however, is much more complex. People use a wide variety of evidence, such as statistics, examples, authoritative testimony, and studies— to mention only the more common types—in support of *A causes B* claims. To see how this works, let's look at some examples of cause-effect claims.

1. ***Claim:*** Smoking causes lung cancer.

   Good Reasons: 1. Statistical comparisons show that the number of lung cancer cases is far greater among smokers than among non-smokers.
   2. Mice exposed to the components of tobacco smoke in laboratory studies contracted cancer at a rate significantly higher than mice who were not exposed.
   3. National studies of smokers show that as the amount of smoking increases, the amount of cancer increases.

2. ***Claim:*** Chlorofluorocarbons destroy (cause destruction of) the protective ozone layer in the atmosphere.

   Good Reasons: 1. Studies of the "hole" in the ozone layer in Antarctica show a decline in atmospheric ozone as the amount of chlorofluorocarbons (CFCs) in the atmosphere has increased.
   2. Expert chemists testify that CFCs react chemically with the oxygen in ozone to form other compounds.

3. ***Claim:*** Negative political campaigning increases (causes) media attention on the candidates.

   Good Reasons: 1. Campaign professionals in Texas offer specific examples of candidates who were ignored by the media until they began to use negative campaign tactics.
   2. Two candidates in Virginia report that media coverage of their campaign increased dramatically as they and their opponents increased the usage of negative campaign tactics.

4. ***Claim:*** Large tuition increases result in (cause) a drop in non-resident enrollments.

   Good Reasons: 1. Public University reports a decline in non-resident enrollment after tuition was increased by 20 percent.
   2. State University reports a decline in non-resident enrollment after they increased tuition by 10 percent.

  3. Western Public University did not increase tuition and reports no decline in nonresident enrollment.

5. ***Claim***: An increase in seat-belt usage results in (causes) a drop in automobile injuries and fatalities.

  Good Reasons: 1. A study in New York shows that injuries and fatalities declined as seat-belt usage increased.
  2. A study of automobile accidents in Ohio shows a much higher rate of injuries and deaths among drivers and passengers who were not wearing seat belts.

6. ***Claim***: Any significant threat to the supply of a petroleum produces (causes) an increase in its price.

  Good Reasons: 1. The price of petroleum more than doubled when the Iraqi invasion of Kuwait in August 1990 threatened the supply of oil.
  2. As the threat to the supply of oil diminished, the price of oil declined to below the preinvasion level.
  3. Various experts testify that the futures market, which sets the price of oil, responds dramatically to news of any significant threat to supply.

As you study these illustrations of argument by causal correlation, pay special attention to the two elements of argument: the claim and the good reasons that support it. The claim in each causal correlation argument is a generalization that some *A* causes some *B*. Second, examine the variety in the good reasons, or the kinds of particular evidence, used as support in these arguments. Some of the evidence, such as the studies and laboratory experiments, has a pronounced scientific quality about it. But studies and experiments are not always available for causal claims.

The claim in the last argument, on the price of oil, is supported by the specific example of what happened in connection with the 1990–91 crisis in the Persian Gulf, plus the testimony of experts. Similarly, support for the claim that "negative political campaigning increases media attention on the candidates" consists of reported examples of campaigns from two states in which media attention increased as the candidates began to hurl mud or point out the flaws of their opponents.

Despite the variety in the evidence, all of it tends to reflect John Stuart Mill's three methods for discovering causation:[3]

1. The method of concomitant variation
2. The method of agreement
3. The method of difference

Let's see how these methods clarify how the evidence in our illustrative arguments works.

The *method of concomitant variation* means that we have direct evidence (often statistical) that *A* and *B* vary together. If *A* stands for smoking cigarettes and *B* stands for cancer, a concomitant variation means that as smoking increases, cancer also increases. Another sort of concomitant variation occurs when there is an inverse relationship between *A* and *B*: We have an inverse relationship if *A* goes up as *B* goes down, or if *A* goes down as *B* goes up. Seat-belt usage and highway deaths provide one example of inverse relationships between a claimed cause and effect. As seat-belt usage goes up, highway deaths go down. Similarly, we see an inverse relationship when a decrease in the supply of oil results in an increase in prices.

The following summary may help you keep in mind the ways a possible cause (*A*) and its alleged effect (*B*) might vary together:

Direct Relationships

A goes up, *B* goes up   (smoking and lung cancer)
A goes down, *B* goes down   (study time and grades)

Inverse Relationships

A goes up, *B* goes down   (exercise and heart disease)
A goes down, *B* goes up   (seat-belt use and injuries)

The mere presence of a concomitant variation between *A* and *B* does not, by itself, prove a causal relation. A concomitant variation could simply mean that *A* and *B* are both responding to (or caused by) some *C*. For example, there is a well-established statistical correlation between ice cream consumption and burglaries: As ice cream consumption goes up, burglaries also go up. Yet, common sense seems enough to tell us that ice cream does not *cause* crime!

The *method of agreement* means that we try to find the cause by looking for a common element or circumstance in cases where an effect occurs. This is a difficult idea for most people, so let's look at a reasonably clear example. One afternoon, an elementary school had to send about half of the children home after they began to experience severe stomach cramps, vomiting, and high temperatures. What caused this? Mill's method of agreement directs us to ask:

What did all of the sick children have in common that day? As the investigation proceeded, it became clear that all of the sick children had selected the burrito special at the school cafeteria that day.

The *method of difference* is frequently used in conjunction with the method of agreement. When two groups are quite similar, except that one group becomes ill and the other one does not, the method of difference directs us to ask: In what ways are the two groups different? In our school case, recall the information that half of the children became ill. This tells us that the other half of the students remained healthy. More specifically, the method of difference suggests that we ask: What was different in the experience of the sick and the normal children? The answer in this case was that none of the healthy children had eaten the burrito special that day.

Mill's three methods for discovering causation provide a powerful way of discerning the common thread in the variety of evidence used for causal correlation arguments. It will help you to gain experience with these methods if you try to classify the good reasons for each of our illustrative arguments in relation to them. In addition, it is important to see how they are related to the tests for arguments that support causal claims.

Tests for Argument by Causal Correlation

There are four tests for causal correlation arguments: consistency, strength, time, and coherence. All of them can help us to probe the weaknesses of our own reasoning as well as to find the flaws in the arguments of our opponents.

1. *Consistency.* Is the relationship between the alleged cause and effect consistent?
2. *Strength.* Does the alleged cause have the power to produce the alleged effect?
3. *Time.* Does the alleged cause always occur before the alleged effect?
4. *Coherence.* Does the alleged cause-effect relationship make any sense?

1. *Consistency.* Is the relationship between the alleged cause and effect consistent? If the world were a completely tidy place, this would mean that *A* should produce *B* in *every* instance if *A* is the cause of *B*. However, the world is not so tidy, and the consistency test does not mean that a cause must produce an effect every time. Some people manage to smoke cigarettes their entire lives without contracting lung cancer, and seat belts do not always prevent fatal injury.

The consistency test simply means that cause and effect are related in a stable and perhaps predictable way. For example, the findings of one study (by Alan Rozanski and colleagues) indicate that "public speaking . . . can be as potent as hard exercise in disrupting the heart's blood supply when people have underlying heart disease."[4] Rozanski found that "asking people to give a five-minute talk in front of two observers about their personal faults and habits" produced harmful mental stress, called *ischemia*. If public speaking does cause this sort of mental stress, with potential for heart damage, we should expect that a similar study would produce similar results. If other studies find no such effects, it would weaken the causal claims from Rozanski's study.

2. *Strength*. Does the alleged cause have the power to produce the alleged effect? This test is especially important where there are multiple causes involved. Many of our social problems, especially, seem to be the result of several causes. Does television crime and violence produce juvenile delinquency? Many of the studies that have examined this question indicate a fairly complex range of factors involved in juvenile delinquency, including stability of the home, family income level, neighborhood environment, mental stability of the youth, and so on. Apparently, few researchers think television crime and violence, by itself, is sufficient to cause delinquency. But many (such as Alfred Bandura) argue that television program content is a strong causative factor for the relatively large numbers of youth who suffer from unstable homes, poverty, and poor environments.

3. *Time*. Does the alleged cause always occur before the alleged effect? This is a relatively simple test, although it sometimes appears that cause and effect happen at virtually the same time. Obviously, if *A* is supposed to cause *B*, then *A* must occur first. For example, if a consumer claims that the mouse he found in his can of beer made him nauseous, it would be rather embarrassing to learn that he was nauseous before he opened the beer.

On the other hand, it would be a mistake to assume that whenever one thing consistently follows another, the first *must* be the cause of the second. Such assumptions can lead to a fallacy of reasoning called the *post hoc* fallacy. (The complete name is *post hoc ergo propter hoc*, which means "after this, therefore because of this.") For example, just because many heroin addicts used marijuana before turning to heroin, some people have concluded that marijuana use leads to (causes) heroin use. Although there may be some truth to this argument (the evidence is not yet clear), do you see why it could be fallacious? Many heroin addicts also drank milk before turning to heroin. Would it make sense to say that milk use leads to heroin use? Heroin addicts used many things before turning to heroin.

4. *Coherence.* Does the alleged cause-effect relationship make any sense? This is what we might call the commonsense test, and it is always worthwhile to probe causal correlations with it. Especially when a statistical relationship is the basis for a causal claim (that *A* causes *B*), we should ask ourselves if it makes sense in relation to our own experience.

Earlier, we noted that ice cream consumption is positively correlated with burglaries, so that burglaries increase in an almost direct proportion to the increase in ice cream consumption. But our common sense should tell us that it would be rather silly to conclude that ice cream causes burglaries. Rather, we should look to another factor that might account for (or cause) both effects. In this case, the factor is warm weather. As summer temperatures increase, it is easier for burglars to get into homes because people tend to leave windows open and doors unlocked. And when do we consume the largest quantities of ice cream?

Argument by Sign

Sign reasoning is pervasive in every facet of our lives. When we see dark clouds gathering into a thunderhead, we infer that it will rain. Hunters look for droppings or tracks as reliable signs that a particular animal has been in the area. Economists looks to the leading indicators (signs) in predicting future behavior of the economy. Physicians gather symptoms (signs) of a patient in order to diagnose illness. And all us tend to think we can determine (or conclude) how people around us feel by looking to their more or less reliable signs: facial expressions, tone of voice, posture, or body language. Notice, in each case, that the presence of recognizable signs allows the hunter, physician, or any of us to infer the presence of whatever is associated with the signs.

The Form of Argument by Sign

Arguments from sign are based on our understanding of the way things are associated or related to each other in the world around us. When we reason from signs to the thing associated with them, we conclude that the thing is present if its signs are present. The claim of a sign argument is invariably a statement that something is or is not the case. Thus, a psychiatrist uses signs (or symptoms) such as indifference, withdrawal, hallucinations, and delusions of persecution and omnipotence as support for a claim that Harry suffers from schizophrenia. In this case, the thing is schizophrenia, and it is inferred from its signs. But such sign reasoning could also take the reverse path—reasoning that the presence of the thing allows us to conclude that its particular signs are present, or have been present, or will be present. So our psychiatrist might argue that if Harry suffers from schizophrenia, then he will manifest its signs.

Consider the two paths of sign reasoning in the following outline of our arguments about Harry's schizophrenia:

> ***Claim***: Harry suffers from schizophrenia.
> > ***Good Reasons***: 1. Harry has symptoms of indifference, withdrawal, hallucinations, and so on.
> > 2. These are the recognized symptoms of schizophrenia.
>
> ***Claim***: Harry will manifest symptoms of indifference, withdrawal, hallucinations, and so on.
> > ***Good Reasons***: 1. Harry suffers from schizophrenia.
> > 2. Schizophrenics will manifest a recognized set of symptoms.

No doubt this seems to be a fairly complex and abstract form of reasoning so far. However, it is one of the more universal forms of reasoning and argument, and we use it many times each day. If it seems unfamiliar, it is only because we take sign reasoning for granted so much that we hardly recognize it as a reasoning form. It will be helpful to you to try to become aware of your own sign reasoning here. Think of all the conclusions based on signs that we make about the emotional state of our friends or even strangers. When we infer that another person is bored, happy, angry, curious, sad, tired, depressed, in love, or envious, we base our inferences on their facial expressions, manner of communicating, body posture, tone of voice, and many other signs, perhaps without even realizing consciously that we have gathered and read such signs. Consider this argument:

> "You don't want to ask your mother for that favor right now," said Dad. "She's in a bad mood."
> "Why do you say that?" asked Marty.
> "Well, she snapped at me when I asked what was for dinner, and she even hollered at the dog when he scratched at the door to go out."

This example shows us the rather typical way that sign arguments come up in ordinary conversation. In arguments of this sort, if you can identify the claim, it is rather easy to see the signs used as good reasons in support.

> **Claim**: Your mother is in a bad mood.
>
> **Good Reasons**: 1. She snapped at me when I asked what was for dinner.
> 2. She hollered at the dog.
> 3. (unstated) She only behaves like that when she is in a bad mood.

In addition to the feelings of another person, how would you or your friends support the claim that someone is bluffing? Intelligent? Stupid? On drugs? What kinds of signs would support the claim that someone is flirting with you? How do you decide that you are doing well in a course other than by "signs of doing well"? Do you begin to see how pervasive our use of this form of reasoning is? It will probably be helpful for you to try to list some of your other ordinary uses of sign reasoning, but for now let's complete our analysis of its form.

One of the complexities of sign argument is that its form is sometimes inductive and sometimes deductive. To see this, it is essential to recall the key distinction between inductive and deductive arguments:

> Inductive arguments provide *incomplete* support for their claims, and the claims can be established only to a degree of probability.
>
> Deductive arguments provide *complete* support for their claims; if the good reasons are true or accepted, the claim follows necessarily.

If a farmer claims that it will rain on the basis of black clouds and a certain smell of rain in the air, his argument is inductive. The signs provide support for his claim but the support is incomplete; the claim has only a degree of probability. However, in other sign arguments, the presence of the signs may provide complete proof, yielding a deductive argument. As Aristotle noted centuries ago, some signs are infallible, or invariable, meaning they are always associated with a particular thing. "The fact that she is giving milk," says Aristotle, "is a sign that she has lately borne a child."[5] Another apparently invariable sign relation is the color of litmus paper after it is exposed to a liquid: If the paper turns red, the liquid is acid; if it turns blue, the liquid is a base.

When sign arguments are deductive, the reasoning process seems to rest on an unstated generalization that a set of signs *A* invariably indicates some *B*. Thus, red litmus paper is thought to be an invariable sign of acid, and it is accepted as a complete proof. When arguments are inductive, there is also an unstated generalization, but it says that the signs *usually* enable us to infer the thing with which they are associated. Could we conclude from a red sky this evening (the sign) that we will have fair weather tomorrow (the claim) if we did not believe in the generalization that red skies are fairly reliable signs of fair days? Likewise, a physician could hardly infer anything about Mary's physical health unless her symptoms (signs) were consistently associated with a particular disease, or at least with illness. But neither our weather forecast nor the physician's diagnosis follows necessarily from the signs.

There seem to be few of the infallible or invariable signs in the arguments we encounter. More often, signs are usually reliable, but not always. Thus, we would normally think that smiling and maintaining eye contact are signs of friendliness, but we know that these signs are not always reliable. Not only are such signs subject to manipulation by unscrupulous people feigning friendship but they also are rather peculiar to Western society. In other cultures, a smile may signify grief, and eye contact can indicate disrespect. It is primarily these fallible or variable signs that direct us to the major tests of sign argument.

Tests for Argument by Sign

The three tests for sign argument are necessity, number, and contradiction. They focus primarily on the underlying variable or fallible generalization between the sign and the thing signified.

1. *Necessity.* Is the sign invariable or infallible?
2. *Number.* Is there a sufficient number of signs?
3. *Contradiction.* Are there negative or contradictory signs?

1. *Necessity.* Is the sign invariable or infallible? This test confronts the underlying generalization directly. Thus, in Aristotle's example of an infallible sign, modern physicians might clear their throats and gently suggest that they are aware of cases, admittedly rare, of women and even young girls who gave milk without having borne a child. So it can be rather surprising to us when we see or hear someone present a claim from a sign argument in a strident way when it is based on a weak sign relationship. For example, what is invariably signified by tears when a candidate withdraws from office? In the following letter, the author evidently believes that tears

infallibly signify weakness, instability, lack of ability to lead, and lack of poise—to mention only the most salient.

> *Editor: The tearful, disgraceful announcement by Rep. Pat Schroeder not to run for the Democratic nomination for president was the most devastating blow to equal women's rights in my memory.*
>
> *Many people, both male and female, have vigorously fought for years to elevate women to a status equal to men in business and political life.*
>
> *For several terms in office, we have seen Schroeder's smiling countenance on TV and in personal appearances, giving us the illusion of a stable, upwardly mobile individual. Now on national television we see this maudlin, pathetic performance showing her total lack of poise and stability.*
>
> *Thank God she didn't elect to run or be elected, as this class of female lends credibility to some people's image of women as suitable only to make grocery lists and brew coffee in the morning.*
>
> *I request here to Pat Schroeder, please don't ever run for higher office, because of your aberrant conduct. I also suggest you resign your current elected position for the same reason.*[6]

2. *Number.* Is there a sufficient number of signs? Especially in cases where one sign, by itself—such as Congresswoman Schroeder's tears—could be misleading, the prudent advocate attempts to gather as many signs as possible that point in the same direction. A police detective, for example, would probably say that a sign such as a motive to kill the victim is good evidence that a particular suspect is guilty, but generally insufficient if it is the only sign of guilt. However, the sign evidence of motive is strengthened when it is combined with other *circumstantial* evidence (another term for signs) such as fingerprints on the murder weapon, footprints in the area where the victim was killed, and lack of an alibi.

In some cases, when the number of signs is small, advocates try to make up for this deficiency by using the method of logical division, arguing that the signs can be interpreted in only so many ways—*A, B,* or *C*—and that the truth must be one of these. The following editorial presents an example of this sort of argument, as its author interprets the actions (signs) of administrators in the Department of Housing and Urban Development.

> *Although they evicted the squatters who occupied a HUD-owned house in Northeast Denver, HUD officials essentially surrendered to the group's demand that scores of units be released for long-term housing for the homeless. Fifty-five vacant HUD homes will be rented for $1 a year to organizations that provide shelter to the poor.*

This episode reveals HUD bureaucrats as weak or previously derelict in their duty, or both. *They already were leasing a handful of homes to groups serving the homeless. If 55 additional homes are appropriate for that use, why weren't they opened before now? Why did it take civil disobedience to prod HUD to expedite its program?*

On the other hand, if HUD had good reason for moving slowly in leasing additional houses, the present speedup is management by panic.[7] *(emphasis added)*

3. *Contradiction.* Are there negative or contradictory signs? All of us have experienced the sense of confusion that comes from mixed signals, when some signs point in one direction but other signs point in an opposite direction. What should Fred conclude when Doris says she cares only for him (a positive sign) and then goes out with Doug, his chief rival (a most negative sign)? Fred may not be prepared to abandon his conclusion that Doris cares for him, but the negative sign diminishes his confidence in its truth. Similarly, when the so-called leading indicators point in opposite directions, economists become less confident in making predictions about future behavior of the economy. Negative signs weaken the claim of a sign argument in more or less the same way that a negative example weakens the generalization of an argument by example.

Argument by Causal Application

This is another of those forms of reasoning that seem baffling initially, but you can master it if you see clearly how all of us use it in our everyday lives. Many of our actions are undertaken because of our beliefs in cause and effect. We push a button on our alarm clock in the morning (cause) in order to produce the desired effect—silence. We select a particular cereal for breakfast (cause) since we have found it tasty and nutritious (effect) in the past. In fact, as you think about it, just about everything you do in order to produce a particular result is based on your beliefs/knowledge about causality. When we apply our knowledge of cause and effect to particular cases, we are using argument by causal application.

The Form of Argument by Causal Application

It is easy to confuse causal application with the argument by causal correlation, which we discussed earlier. So it is very important to be clear about their similarities as well as their differences. They are similar because both are concerned with cause and effect statements. How are they different? Recall that the purpose of *causal cor-*

relation argument is to *establish claims* that are *generalizations* that *A* causes *B*. They reason from a body of evidence (as support, or good reasons), and the evidence reflects one or more of Mill's canons of causation. But the most unmistakable feature of a causal correlation argument is its claim. If the claim is a generalization that *A* causes *B*, you have a causal correlation argument.

The purpose of *causal application* arguments is to *apply generalizations* that *A* causes *B* to a *particular case*. The claim always concerns a particular case. The generalization that *A* causes *B* always appears as a premise, or part of the support for the claim. Let's examine two of the principal patterns of this form in the categorical syllogisms that follow. The first pattern reasons from cause to effect.

A causes *B*.
A is present.
_____

Therefore, *B* is present or will occur.

The second pattern reasons from effect to cause.

A is the only cause of *B*.
B is present.
_____

Therefore, *A* is present.

The first pattern of causal application argument is especially common in the sciences. For example, a weather scientist might argue that because chlorofluorocarbons (CFCs) destroy ozone, and large quantities of CFCs have been released into the atmosphere, we will therefore find destruction of the ozone in the atmosphere. The pattern of this argument becomes clear when we outline its elements.

Claim: We will find destruction of the ozone in the atmosphere.

Good Reasons: 1. Chlorofluorocarbons destroy ozone. (*A* causes *B*)
2. Large quantities of chlorofluorocarbons have been released in the atmosphere.

Notice especially the location of the causal generalization (CFCs destroy ozone). This argument is causal application because the cause-effect generalization appears as one of the reasons in support of the claim.

Cause-effect generalizations are applied extensively when people make predictions. Knowledge of cause-effect relationships enable us to predict that if a cause is present, its effect will occur. Thus, many people worry that lower-income students will be excluded from our universities if tuition and other costs continue to escalate. What is the cause-effect generalization here? If we outline the implied argument, it becomes:

> **Claim**: Lower-income students will be excluded from our universities.
>
> > **Good Reasons**:1. Escalating tuition and other cost increases can exclude lower-income students from our universities. (causal generalization)
> > 2. Tuition and other costs are continuing to escalate.

Or consider the argument presented to Smokestack Sally by her sister, that if she doesn't quit smoking, she will get lung cancer. What is the unstated cause-effect generalization?

Perhaps the only tricky thing about spotting causal reasoning is that people do not always use the word *cause* when they present one or the other pattern of causal application arguments. Learn to spot the alternatives we use for the term *cause*, such as *lead to, result in, produce, bring about, effect, make, induce, produce,* and *secure.*

The following arguments illustrate how cause-effect generalizations function as major premises, or good reasons, in arguments by causal application.

1. **Claim**: Large numbers of people in central African nations will contract AIDS.

   > **Good Reasons**: 1. Unprotected sexual contact with carriers causes the spread of AIDS. (causal generalization)
   > 2. Large numbers of people in central African nations have unprotected sexual contact with carriers of AIDS.

2. **Claim**: Teens in our inner cities will continue to have a high incidence of venereal disease.

   > **Good Reasons**:1. Ignorance about sex leads to venereal disease. (causal generalization)
   > 2. Teens in our inner cities continue to be ignorant about sex.

3. ***Claim***: Harry is increasing his risk of heart disease.

    Good Reasons: 1. High-cholesterol diets increase the risk of heart disease. (causal generalization)
           2. Harry has a high-cholesterol diet.

4. ***Claim***: Texas will gain better instruction in its classrooms.

    Good Reasons: 1. Minimum competency testing for teachers produces better classroom instruction. (causal generalization)
           2. Texas has instituted minimum competency testing for teachers.

Tests for Argument by Causal Application

There are three tests that help us to determine the soundness of argument by causal application: truth, sufficiency, and intervention.

1. *Truth.* Is the cause-effect generalization true, or established, or generally accepted as true?
2. *Sufficiency.* Is the cause sufficient to produce the effect?
3. *Intervention.* Will intervening factors prevent the cause from operating?

1. *Truth.* Is the cause-effect generalization true, or established, or generally accepted as true? In some respects, this can be the most powerful way to attack a causal application argument. When someone argues that we should institute a program of minimum competency testing for all teachers as a way of improving the quality of instruction in our classrooms, frequently the cause-effect generalization—that minimum competency testing for all teachers will produce improved classroom instruction—is unstated. To ask whether this causal generalization is true or established is to allow us to examine the causal correlation argument that must have been used to establish it, and we can then examine the evidence.

2. *Sufficiency.* Is the cause sufficient to produce the effect? In complex matters, there are often multiple causes at work, and sometimes they work in opposite directions. Thus, although it may be generally true, according to economists, that the reduction in the price of a product leads to increased consumption, such a decline in price may not be sufficient to increase consumption in a particular case. Most of us use gasoline in our automobiles, for example, and we may use more gasoline if its price drops. But an increase in our consumption may depend on other causal factors as well, such as

whether we have an automobile or whether we have time to do any more driving.

3. *Intervention.* Will intervening factors prevent the cause from operating in this case? Ordinarily it may be true that you will get burned if you put your hand in a fire, but not if you wear protective gloves. In almost every field, we must qualify any cause-effect generalization, and the qualification usually reflects the possibility that intervening factors can prevent the cause from producing its effect. Thus, we worry about escalating costs of higher education preventing students from attending college—but there are a variety of factors that could intervene, trumping the cost factor. Loans, scholarships, and work study are some of the more obvious intervening factors. We also know that a student's desire for an education, and parents' determination to find a way can often overcome the apparent barriers of high cost.

Argument by Applied Generalization

In one sense, this category merely covers all of those generalizations that are not included in our causal application argument form. However, there is nothing "mere" about the range of arguments involved. Whenever we apply a general standard, or criterion, or definition, or concept, or rule to a particular case, we are using applied generalization.

The Form of Argument by Applied Generalization

Since we have already explored the idea of applying generalizations to particular cases, let's begin by examining some specimens of this argument form.

1. "Well," said the President, "you know that fella is a brave man. He risked his own life by jumping into the freezing Potomac to save drowning passengers from the airplane crash, and only a brave person would do that."

Claim: That fella is a brave man.

> *Good Reasons*: 1. He risked his own life by jumping into the freezing Potomac to save drowning passengers from the airplane crash.
> 2. Only a brave person would do that. (generalization that is applied)

2. "That Harry is such a nitwit!" Mabel said to her friend Zoe. "Do you know what he tried to do?" "What now?" asked Zoe. "He tried to claim his pet snake as a dependent on his income tax. I told him, too. I said, 'Harry, only a nitwit would try a stunt like that.'"

   Claim: Harry is a nitwit.

   > ***Good Reasons***: 1. He tried to claim his pet snake as a dependent on his income tax.
   > 2. Only a nitwit would try a stunt like that. (generalization)

3. Jesse Jackson said Wednesday that George Bush is not "morally fit" to be president: "Mr. Bush opposed the Civil Rights Restoration Act. Anyone who opposed the Civil Rights Restoration Act is not morally fit to lead this nation."

   Claim: George Bush is not "morally fit" to be president.

   > ***Good Reasons***: 1. Mr. Bush opposed the Civil Rights Restoration Act.
   > 2. Anyone who opposed the Civil Rights Restoration Act is not morally fit to lead this nation (i.e., to be president). (generalization)

You should notice in the above examples that each claim is based on two supporting elements: (1) the alleged actions of an individual and (2) a generalization that functions as an operating standard, criterion, or rule that governs the alleged actions. All of our moral rules and values operate this way, allowing us to make judgments about particular cases, situations, or individuals. Some of our value rules are general, covering a wide range of situations; others are quite specific. For example:

4. Any college student who would tear articles out of magazines in the library is an immature jerk.

If we accept this value rule, and we know of a college student who has torn an article from a library magazine, we would conclude that the student is an immature jerk.

Our examples so far have been concerned with judgments about people, but our value systems typically cover just about any situation or object. In fact, we usually have evaluative rules to cover the entire range of our experience, including our vicarious experience from reading, listening, or viewing the experiences of others.

In addition to generalized value rules, we also use a wide range of definitional and regulative rules in argument by applied generalization. Consider, for example, the exclusionary rule of evidence established by the Supreme Court in *Mapp* v. *Ohio*. According to the rule, state and federal courts must exclude from consideration any evidence that has been illegally obtained. Thus framed, the exclusionary rule is a generalization that can be used in specific arguments, as follows:

5. "Your honor," said the defense attorney, "I request that the court rule that this confession is inadmissible. My client's alleged confession was obtained by the police before they read him his rights, which is illegal. Since illegally obtained evidence is inadmissible, this confession must be thrown out."

   Claim: The confession is inadmissible as evidence.
   > *Good Reasons*: 1. Illegally obtained confessions are inadmissible as evidence. (general rule)
   > 2. The confession was obtained illegally.

We also apply generalizations that are distilled from our collective experience, providing us with rules for avoiding trouble or making mistakes. For example, during congressional hearings over the so-called Iran-Contra scandal (during the Reagan administration), a number of speakers condemned the trading of weapons for hostages as a clear violation of the generally accepted rule against negotiating with terrorists. Such rules are thought to embody the wisdom of our collective experience and to have been validated by painful lessons— so that everybody knows they are not to be violated. Ironically, former President Reagan himself had repeatedly affirmed the rule against dealing with terrorists.

Tests for Argument by Applied Generalization

Apart from the various rules concerning the formal relationships between the premises of an applied generalization and the conclusion they support, we previously explored two tests that are helpful in deciding whether an argument of this sort is sound or unsound: acceptance and exceptions.

1. *Acceptance.* Is the generalization true, or accepted as true, or appropriate?
2. *Exceptions.* Are there any exceptions to the rule in the generalization?

1. *Acceptance.* Is the generalization true, or accepted as true, or appropriate in this sort of case? If we are concerned with a rule of evidence, the question is whether the court hearing the case has adopted the rule. I was surprised to discover, during my observations of criminal proceedings at the Old Bailey in London, that Her Majesty's Courts had only recently adopted a version of the exclusionary rule of evidence we discussed earlier—but with apparently much greater discretionary power for judges to determine whether police actions were a violation of the spirit rather than merely the letter of the rule. The important point here is that a rule must be accepted as such in order to have any value in argument. This is especially true of the generalized rules derived from the values of our audience, but it is also true of other generalizations when they are applied to particular cases.

2. *Exceptions.* Are there any exceptions to the rule in the generalization? Are there any circumstances in which we would be inclined to say that a generalization, normally accepted, does not apply in this case? Perhaps the most extreme of our foreign policy experts would say that there are no exceptions to the rule that we can never negotiate with terrorists, but I suspect that most would agree that unusual circumstances could cause us to set an otherwise sound rule aside. Suppose the terrorists were in a position to explode nuclear weapons, destroying the cities and inhabitants of New York and Washington, DC? Even the most widely accepted rules can admit of exceptions. Whenever they are applied to particular cases, it is useful to see if there might be exceptional circumstances or facts that would lead us to set the rule aside.

The best way to understand the tests of applied generalization is to use them. Examine the preceding examples. Can you think of any audiences that might reject one or more of the generalizations listed? Certainly, we could expect that many Republicans might reject the value generalization that Jesse Jackson used to support his claim that George Bush is morally unfit for the presidency. You ought to be able to find some potential exceptions to the other generalized rules used in the illustrative arguments.

Summary

1. All of us use a variety of argument forms. You could hardly be an adult college student if you were unable to make arguments or respond to the arguments of others. But our abilities to use argument effectively, to defend ourselves, and to see persuasive possibilities can be enhanced by learning to analyze the more important, yet common, forms of argument.

2. Effective analysis of argument forms requires three kinds of abilities:

    a. The ability to recognize the form of an argument when we hear it or read it

    b. The ability to see clearly the pattern of reasoning involved in each form

    c. The ability to apply the tests that enable us to see weaknesses or flaws in each argument form

3. This chapter analyzes six of the more common forms of argument that are widely used as people support their own claims or refute those of others. The six forms are example, analogy, causal correlation, sign, causal application, and applied generalization (see Figure 6.1).

FIGURE 6.1 *Summary Analysis of Argument Forms*

Argument Form	Reasoning Pattern	Nature of Claim
Example	Particular to general: What is true of the particular examples is true generally.	Claim is a generalization
Analogy	Particular to particular: What is true of case one is true of case two.	Claim is particular
Causal Correlation	Particular to general: Evidence of cause and effect in one of Mill's canons supports a general cause-effect claim.	Claim is a generalization that A causes B
Sign	Particular signs to the thing signified: If the signs are present, the thing is present.	Claim is either that the thing or the signs are present
Causal Application	Causal generalization to particular case: If the cause is present, the effect is present.	Claim is particular
Applied Generalization	General to particular: Any rule, definition, or general principle is applied to a particular case.	Claim is particular

4. The first step in analysis is to see clearly the pattern of reasoning in each form. The second step is to master the tests that enable us to evaluate each form of argument (see Figure 6.2).

5. Argument by example relies on a pattern of reasoning that infers that what is true in particular cases or examples is true generally. There are three useful tests for this form:

    a. *Number.* Is the number of examples sufficient to support the generalization in the claim?
    b. *Representativeness.* Are the examples typical?
    c. *Contradiction.* Are there any negative instances?

FIGURE 6.2 *Argument Forms and Their Tests*

Argument Form	Argument Test
Example	1. *Number.* Is the number of examples sufficient to support the generalization in the claim? 2. *Representativeness.* Are the examples typical? 3. *Contradiction.* Are there any negative instances?
Analogy	1. *Comparison.* Are the compared cases really alike in their essential features? 2. *Description.* Is the description of the two cases accurate and complete?
Causal Correlation	1. *Consistency.* Is the relationship between the alleged cause and effect consistent? 2. *Strength.* Does the alleged cause have the power to produce the effect? 3. *Time.* Does the alleged cause always occur before the alleged effect? 4. *Coherence.* Does the alleged cause-effect relationship make any sense?
Sign	1. *Necessity.* Is the sign invariable or infallible? 2. *Number.* Is there a sufficient number of signs? 3. *Contradiction.* Are there negative or contradictory signs?
Causal Application	1. *Truth.* Is the cause-effect generalization true, or established, or generally accepted as true? 2. *Sufficiency.* Is the cause sufficient to produce the effect? 3. *Intervention.* Will intervening factors prevent the cause from operating?
Applied Generalization	1. *Acceptance.* Is the generalization true, or accepted as true, or appropriate? 2. *Exceptions.* Are there any exceptions to the rule in the generalization?

6. In an argument by analogy, an advocate maintains that what is true or correct in case one is true or correct in case two, which is similar. Analogies may be either literal or figurative. For either, there are two useful tests:

   a. *Comparison.* Are the compared cases really alike in their essential features?
   b. *Description.* Is the description of the two cases accurate and complete?

7. Argument by causal correlation seeks to establish a generalization that *A* causes *B* on the basis of particular evidence that reflects one or more of Mill's canons: concomitant variation, agreement, and difference. There are four useful tests for this form of argument:

   a. *Consistency.* Is the relationship between the alleged cause and effect consistent?
   b. *Strength.* Does the alleged cause have the power to produce the effect?
   c. *Time.* Does the alleged cause always occur before the alleged effect?
   d. *Coherence.* Does the alleged cause-effect relationship make any sense?

8. Argument by sign is based on our associations between particular signs and the thing they signify. Typically, we claim that the thing is present if its signs are present or that the signs will be present if the thing is present. There are three important tests:

   a. *Necessity.* Is the sign invariable or infallible?
   b. *Number.* Is there a sufficient number of signs?
   c. *Contradiction.* Are there negative or contradictory signs?

9. Argument by causal application always has a generalization that *A* causes *B* as its major premise. The claim of this argument is always particular. There are three useful tests for this form:

   a. *Truth.* Is the cause-effect generalization true, or established, or generally accepted as true?
   b. *Sufficiency.* Is the cause sufficient to produce the effect?
   c. *Intervention.* Will intervening factors prevent the cause from operating?

10. Argument by applied generalization includes all of those claims that rely on the application of a general standard, rule, definition, or value to a particular case. Its claim is always particular. There are two useful tests for this form:

a. *Acceptance*. Is the generalization true, or accepted as true, or appropriate?

b. *Exceptions*. Are there any exceptions to the rule in the generalization?

Gaining the ability to recognize argument forms and to detect potential flaws is perhaps as difficult to acquire as it is valuable. Analysis of the forms enables us to become more sensitive to our persuasive choices. The tests empower us to anticipate objections to our arguments and they provide an arsenal of probes for detecting weaknesses in arguments of our opponents. Few people find it easy to acquire these tools, however.

Experience is the key. If you are persistent in looking for these forms in the persuasive discourse of editorials, in sales pitches, and in arguments from friends, you will soon discover that you are beginning to recognize them. Recognition of an argument form is the first step. Then, it is just a matter of gaining experience with the next step—applying the tests we have discussed to determine whether the argument is sound or unsound, worthy of belief, or fatally flawed. Persevere! It is worth it.

Exercises

1. Identify the form of argument for each of the following passages. Be sure to start by locating the claim of the argument. Next, examine the nature of the support and its relationship to the claim. Answers may be found immediately following the chapter endnotes.

   a. "Lands sakes," Aunt Martha exclaimed, "anyone can tell that poor child is starving. Look at the way he's chewing on his suspenders. He is only 2 years old, and his mother said he hasn't had anything to eat since breakfast—more than eight hours ago."

   b. "I don't know about you," Mort said to Homer, "but I think newspaper stories on spouse killings just lead to more spouse killings. Why, the first of the year a man killed his wife. The newspaper ran the story on page one for several days, and the first thing you know another man kills his wife. Then a wife shoots her husband. No telling who's going to get shot next."

   c. "You just can't predict the weather in New England," George said to Bob, as Herb was trying desperately to keep from falling off his bar stool. "What?" Herb asked. "It just can't be done with any accuracy," George continued. "Our local weatherperson has predicted snow 20 times this spring, and it snowed only one day he predicted. The other 3 times we got snow, he had predicted clear skies."

d. "Mary has a crush on the tennis pro," Hazel whispered to her friend Mildred. "No, it can't be," Mildred replied. "Oh, yes," said Hazel, "didn't you notice the way she looked at him last night? And look at how she's smiling at him now, for heaven's sake. She doesn't even realize he's telling her she's hopeless in tennis—and probably everything else!"

e. "I don't understand why you would oppose the idea of distributing free condoms to high school students," said Bert. "Because," said Dr. Noble, "passing out condoms to teenagers is like issuing them squirt guns for a four-alarm blaze. Condoms just don't hack it. We should stop kidding ourselves."[8]

f. "According to recent studies," said Larry, "mild consumption of beer and wine produces about as much cholesterol-inhibiting chemicals in the body as jogging does." "Really?" asked Tim. "How did they determine that?" "Well," said Larry, "the studies measured the presence of HDL (inhibits cholesterol) in the blood of three groups: joggers, mild chuggers, and a boring control group. The joggers and chuggers (mild beer and wine consumers) had approximately equal levels of HDL in their blood, and both groups had significantly higher levels of HDL than the control group."

g. "How in the world did that jury decide that the defendant was insane?" asked Mary. "Well," said Susan, "I was there, and it seemed very clear. The judge told the jury that the rule was that people who are unable to appreciate or understand the wrongfulness of their actions are insane. Every one of the expert psychologists and psychiatrists testified that the defendant really wasn't capable of appreciating or understanding that his actions were wrong."

h. "So how do you know that the price of petroleum will go down after this war is over?" Albert asked. "Nothing mysterious about it," said Robert. "When the demand for a product is steady, an increase in supply causes a decrease in price. As soon as this war is over, there will be a big increase in the supply of petroleum."

2. As we observed in Chapter 5, people often leave out one of the premises in their arguments, especially when it is something that the audience knows and can fill in for themselves. Examine the following argument by applied generalization. What is the unstated premise, or unspoken rule, that is assumed in Sue's argument?

Once again, you may find the answer following the chapter endnotes.

"You are a dirty rat," Sue said to Rita.

"Why?" Rita asked. "What did I do?"

"You promised me you wouldn't tell anyone about my drinking the other night, and then you told my mother about it."

Endnotes

1. John Locke, *An Essay Concerning Human Understanding* (vol. 2), ed. Alexander Fraser (New York: Dover Publications, 1959), pp. 390–391.
2. Steven Cahn, "Faculty Members Should Be Judged by Their Peers, Not by Their Students," *Chronicle of Higher Education*, 14 October 1987, p. B3. Reprinted with permission of Steven M. Cahn.
3. John Stuart Mill, *A System of Logic* (London: Longmans, Green and Co., 1895).
4. Alan Rozanski, quoted in "Stress Can Hurt Bad Heart, Study Shows," *Rocky Mountain News*, 21 April 1988, p. 38. Reprinted with permission of the *Rocky Mountain News*.
5. Aristotle, "Rhetoric," in *Aristotle: Rhetoric and Poetics*, trans. W. Rhys Roberts (New York: Modern Library, Random House, 1954), p. 29.
6. Byron E. Hall, *Coloradoan*, 4 October 1987, p. B5. Reprinted from the Fort Collins *Coloradoan*.
7. Editorial, *Rocky Mountain News*, 18 August 1988, p. 56. Reprinted with permissionof the *Rocky Mountain News*.
8. Adapted from Robert C. Noble, "There Is No Safe Sex," *Newsweek*, 1 April 1991, p. 8.

Answers for Exercises

1. Argument identifications: (a) sign, (b) causal correlation, (c) example, (d) sign, (e) analogy, (f) causal correlation, (g) applied generalization, (h) causal application.

2. The unstated premise is: Anyone who promises not to tell, and then tells a person's mother, is a dirty rat.

7

Testing Evidence and Premises

Central Ideas in This Chapter

1. Value premises are essential support for any argument that claims that something is good or bad, important or unimportant.

2. We can test value premises with three kinds of questions:
   - The so what? test
   - The value comparison test
   - The value application or interpretation test

3. The factual support for argument claims consists of two sources:
   - Factual premises
   - Evidence

4. There are four tests for the evidence-claim relationship:
   - The test of assertion
   - The test of relevance
   - The test of recency
   - The test of sufficiency

5. There are three tests of the evidence source:
   - The test of source identification
   - The test of source expertise
   - The test of source bias

6. There are four tests of the evidence substance:
   - The test of integrity
   - The test of context
   - The test of consistency
   - The tests of statistics

When people ask what is most essential among the concepts and skills of argumentation, occasionally there is a temptation to engage in reductionist slogans or metaphors. But if such questions are properly focused, they can sometimes help us to synthesize our study or clarify its objectives. Thus, for this chapter, we might ask: What does an educated person really need to know about testing evidence and premises? What is essential? The response I find most insightful was offered by Ernest Hemingway some years ago. When Hemingway was pressed by an interviewer to name one essential ingredient for becoming a great writer, he replied, "In order to become a great writer a person must have a built-in, shockproof crap detector."

On a general level, Hemingway's response identifies a major goal for all of the concepts and methods of argumentation. But it provides an especially useful way of understanding what is essential in studying the principal tests for evidence and premises. Advocates offer a wide assortment of support for their argument claims. Some of it is solid, relevant, and trustworthy. In other cases, listeners and readers are taken in by supporting evidence that is inaccurate, outdated, false, irrelevant, misleading, biased, or flawed in some other way. Therefore, if someone asks what an educated person really needs to know, the essential ingredient is to become skillful in separating sound support from its counterfeits.

Developing expertise in detecting flawed support for argument requires mastery of two categories of testing tools. First we will examine the three major tests of value premises, and then we will explore the major tests for evidence and factual premises.

Tests of Value Premises

You may recall from Chapter 2 that the term *value premise* refers to the beliefs that are widely shared in a community, and especially those beliefs that function as standards or criteria to determine whether something is good or bad, fair or unfair, important or unimportant. Such premises are a critical element in any argument in which the claim asserts that something is good or bad or that one thing is better or worse than another. Value premises are crucial in any dispute over a central question of value or policy. Indeed, it is virtually impossible to make much sense of the definitional and qualitative issues in a value question or the motive and cost issues in a policy question without confronting value premises.

However, most people seem to be troubled by the idea of arguing about values, let alone analyzing them. When it becomes clear that the decision in a dispute turns on a choice among values, there seems to be a general tendency in our society to shrug and simply give up on the idea of a rational process of conflict management and resolution. It is as if there were a widespread notion in our culture that we cannot reason about values, or even make sense in talking about them. People seem to think that if there is a value disagreement, one side or the other must surrender, or both sides must simply resign themselves to having different opinions. This attitude impoverishes our analysis, and it is essentially misguided.

One purpose of this discussion, then, is to help you see other options. As you become familiar with the tests of value premises, you should begin to see how to analyze your own values as well as to scrutinize premises in arguments. We will explore three tests for value premises:

1. The so what? test
2. The value comparison test
3. The value application or interpretation test

The So What? Test

The so what? test of value premises asks: Is there really anything bad or harmful in the situation described? Or, alternatively, is the alleged benefit really "good"? This test applies to any argument in which the claim states that something is good or bad, important or unimportant, desirable or undesirable, and so forth.

The phrase *so what?* is a kind of linguistic probe that is widely used in our culture as a challenge to value claims. Little children seem to master the so what? test shortly after they learn to talk, and to use it as an all-purpose way of confounding the reasoning of parents—especially the sort of reasoning in which parents try to discourage or encourage behavior by pointing to harmful or beneficial consequences of the behavior.

> "Brush your teeth," the mother says, "or they will turn black and fall out."
> "So what?" says the child. "I don't want my teeth."

> "Don't be mean to your little sister," says the father, "or you'll make her cry."

"So what?" says the child. "I don't care if she cries. In fact, I like her to cry!"

So What? Test Reveals Underlying Values

The *so what?* phrase demands additional support for a value claim that is implicit but unstated in an argument or assertion. In our examples above, the mother and father will discover that almost any response to a so what? challenge, including a response of punishment for the child, reveals the parent's underlying value premise. And when the underlying value premise is exposed, it becomes possible to assess whether it is warranted—that is, whether it ought to be accepted in the argument and whether it needs qualification.

Exposure of a value premise is akin to a process of exploratory surgery in the sense that the purpose of both is to reveal potential problems. The surgeon uses exploratory surgery to discover whether the patient has, say, a malignant tumor that does not show up on other nonintrusive tests. Advocates use the so what? test to determine whether an argument has a hidden defect in an assumed value premise that is unwarranted. Let's look at an example of how the so what? test might work.

When former President Reagan argued that a failure to provide military aid to the freedom fighters (also known as Contras) would mean there would be no chance to overthrow the marxist Sandinista regime, he was relying on an unstated value premise—namely, that overthrowing the Sandinista regime in Nicaragua was desirable. The so what? challenge alerts us to such unstated value premises and leads us to consider in an explicit way whether we subscribe to them.

Accept the Description, Deny the Harm

Notice that the so what? test seems to agree, at least provisionally, that the factual elements described or pointed to in the argument are true. Its focus instead is on the assumed goodness or badness of the factual elements. Thus, in our example from President Reagan, the so what? challenge does not deny his contention that "there would be no chance to overthrow the Sandinista regime." Rather, the challenge focuses on the *assumed evil* of Reagan's prediction, and it says, in effect: If you wish to be successful in this argument, you must support your underlying value premise that the overthrow of the Sandinistas is desirable. This is not to say that Reagan was either unwilling or unable to support his value premise. But as he offered support, he simultaneously opened up his reasoning to his opponents, providing an opportunity for the general public as well as his opponents to see any weaknesses in his argument.

The so what? probe of value premises can provide a powerful method for uncovering persuasive counterarguments, called *refutation*, for both the pro and the con sides in any dispute. For example, in a debate over a question of policy, the so what? probe is especially valuable in analyzing potential methods of refutation for the motive and the cost issues because these issues are always heavily dependent on value premises. The motive issue, as we know, is concerned with pro and con arguments over whether an alleged problem is significant enough to warrant action, and our concepts of terms such as *problem, significance*, or *importance* are inextricably connected to our values. Put another way, a phenomenon like drug use is a problem because it violates one or more of our values. Similarly, the ideas of cost and benefit are also based on our values of what is good or bad, desirable or undesirable.

Since the so what? test provides a way to uncover assumed values of good and bad, the con side always has a direct way of probing potential weak points in any argument the pro side might use to establish a significant problem. How does this work? Let's say the pro side wants to show there is a significant problem in the trade imbalance between the United States and Japan. Typically, an advocate for the pro side would support the claim that the trade imbalance is a significant problem by describing its size and pointing to its growth. Notice that both forms of support are purely factual and descriptive and neither really gets at why this state of affairs is evil or harmful. It is usually easier to describe factual matters than it is to prove harm, which involves values. So when an advocate for the con side responds to the description of the trade imbalance, not by challenging the description but by using some version of the so what? challenge, our con speaker forces the pro side to get beyond mere statistics, and to discuss underlying values.

Do not be dismayed if the so what? test seems initially rather abstract. The idea is really not far removed from the methods you probably have used since you were a child to confound the arguments and pronouncements of your parents, and maybe brothers or sisters as well. A good first step in using this test is to keep in mind its core notion: The idea is to accept a description of some state of affairs (e.g., "I agree that if the United States refused to escort Kuwaiti oil tankers, Kuwait would probably turn to Russia for this assistance"), but deny that there is anything bad (or good) about the affairs described ("but there is nothing harmful about letting the Russians escort Kuwaiti oil tankers, if they are foolish enough to do so!").

Variations of the So What? Test

The phrase *so what?* can sometimes seem offensive to other people, and there may be better choices for the way we actually want to phrase it in a dispute. If an argument seems to assume that the situation described is harmful, we can ask:

- Is there anything really harmful about the situation de-scribed?
- Who or what is really hurt?
- Is there actually an evil in this state of affairs?

Alternatively, if we are urged to agree to a belief or an action because of some implied benefit, we can ask:

- Is there really anything beneficial that results from this belief or action?
- Is the alleged benefit really "good"?

The Value Comparison Test

The value comparison test asks: Is there a more important value in this situation? This test reminds us that in the real world things are seldom so simple that only one value is important in an argument. Our more difficult disputes and decisions usually are troublesome because there is more than one value and we must choose between them.

We value our families and wish to spend time with them, but we also value our work and wish to be successful. Students value recreation and dating but also value the necessity of study for learning and achieving good grades. When these values conflict, we understand that we must choose between them. The nature of this choice can be framed as a general question: Which is the more important value? Thus, when a student is faced with a choice of going out with a special person for dinner and dancing or going to the library to study for a final examination, the basis for the decision should be: Which is the more important or valuable use of the time? Such decisions may be difficult to make, but at least we understand what is involved.

Comparison Questions Reveal Other Values

The tricky thing about the value comparison test in argument is that advocates frequently are either unaware of other important values or they do not think to apply them because an individual argument seems to have a single value focus. Newspaper editors, for example, are inclined to argue vigorously for the "public's right to know" whenever they are denied information or access to any meeting in which public business is being conducted. However, they seldom mention the fact that there are other values involved in a decision to open meetings to the press or to provide the press with particular information for publication.

The comparison test suggests that we probe such arguments with the question: Is there a more important value? We do not need to argue that the public has no "right to know" or that this right is unimportant (as the so what? test might suggest). Rather, the comparison test might prompt us to ask, in the case of information sought from the Department of State, for example, if the value of national security in this case is more important than the public's right to know? Suppose the information is about current arms control proposals, including secret information about monitoring equipment our government has recently developed as well as proposals the U.S. government has made to the Russians. This example is admittedly hypothetical, but perhaps it shows why there is seldom merely one value—such as the public's right to know—in a policy dispute. In our example, we need to consider as well the value of national security, and perhaps whether an arms control agreement is more important than instant access to information by the press.

Accept the Value, Challenge Its Priority

The value comparison test provides another useful approach to the analysis of arguments in relation to the motive and cost issues. On the motive issue, the pro side typically chooses to discuss only the problem that is the focus of the central policy question. In some cases, it may not be reasonable to respond with a so what? kind of challenge to the problem presented by the affirmative.

For example, from 1985 until their release in 1991, even the most callous among us would not have said "So what?" to the problem of U.S. hostages who were being held in Lebanon. However, the plight of the hostages was not the only value to consider. When members of Congress discovered that operatives in the Reagan administration had traded weapons to Iran in exchange for the freedom of some of the hostages, their criticism was based on the idea that there were other, more important values. Surely, they argued, it was important to ask if the value against trading arms with the sponsors of terrorism, or the value against doing anything to make terrorism a successful strategy, thereby endangering other citizens, is more important than even our concerns for the hostages.

The value comparison test, like the so what? test, is an abstract, difficult idea only if we think about it as something exotic and new. Most people have used one or more versions of the value comparison test for a good part of their lives without being aware that they were doing so. Adding this method of probing values in argument to your arsenal is therefore best accomplished by thinking of the ways you have used it already in social arguments with family and friends.

The Value Application or Interpretation Test

The value application or interpretation test asks: Is the value being correctly applied in this case or is the interpretation of the value reasonable in this case? People in any particular culture generally agree on a wide range of values, and this agreement means that they will tend to see the same sorts of things as good or evil. However, many of the values used to decide what is good or bad, desirable or undesirable, are high-order abstractions, and it is not always so clear whether a value has been applied correctly or appropriately in a particular case.

Interpretation Is Based on Value Criteria

Murder is an evil according to the values of most societies, but there is substantially less agreement about the kinds of killings that should be interpreted as murder. In our own society, some groups interpret any abortion, performed for any reason, as murder. Others are not inclined to go so far, and therefore apply the value against murder only to those abortions that are a form of delayed birth control. Still others do not interpret any abortion as murder unless the fetus is capable of independent life outside the womb. For each group, the definition of *murder* is important, of course, but we will not make much sense of their disagreement on abortion unless we discover their standards for this value. This seems to be a case where people choose a definition that is compatible with their interpretation of abortion rather than the other way around.

Accept the Value, Deny Its Application

Whenever a more general value is used in argument to support a positive or negative response to any kind of thing, we can test the argument by asking the question: Is the value being correctly applied in this case? Suppose you are confronted with the charge that you violated the trust of your spouse (or significant other) because you told a rotten lie. Most of us would agree that telling a rotten lie would constitute a violation of trust among close friends or lovers. But you might argue that this shared value that condemns rotten lies is irrelevant in this case.

By applying the interpretation or application test, you maintain that the standards for rotten lies do not apply to your statements or actions. Suppose your "fib" (it is not significant enough to qualify as a "lie," you argue) was a response to a query from your spouse who asked, "How do you like my new hairdo?" You might argue that fibs such as your response should not be interpreted as "rotten lies"; really, they should be seen as the survival strategies of a thoughtful but judicious mate!

Like the other tests of value premises, the interpretation or application test is most useful in analyzing pro and con arguments in relation to the definitional and qualitative issues of central questions of value, and the motive and cost issues of policy questions. Consider the Congressional debate in 1991 over the use of U.S. military force to push the Iraqis out of Kuwait. Some of the supporters argued that it was crucial to preserve the right of the Kuwaiti people to self-determination; Opponents did not deny the value of self-determination; rather, they argued that restoring Kuwait to its monarch, the Emir, who had suspended the parliament and constitution of Kuwait in 1986, was hardly a case of providing self-determination for the Kuwaiti people.

The key to learning the three tests of value premises is to apply them. You will not have learned them at all if you simply memorize their names. Look for the supporting reasons in the arguments of newspaper editorials, and listen for the arguments of friends that claim that something is good or bad. All of these arguments rely on values, and frequently their premises are unstated. The tests of value premises are especially potent when you can use them in conjunction with the tests of evidence, our second set of detection tools.

Testing Evidence and Factual Premises

The factual foundations for an argument come from two major sources: factual premises and evidence. Factual premises derive from a community's beliefs about what is true or false in the real world. They include what we call the *common knowledge* of a community, and they tend to change over time as our general consensus on what is true or false about the world changes. *Evidence*, as we observed in Chapter 2, refers to the materials advocates present in support of their claims, and such materials are generally organized into two major categories: factual and opinion. *Factual evidence* includes examples, statistics, descriptions (of events, objects, and persons), studies, historical documents, survey reports, experimental results, and the reports of witnesses.

Opinion evidence usually means expert opinion. Experts interpret the facts or draw inferences from the facts, providing a dimension of support unavailable from any other kind of evidence. Many of us, for instance, may be familiar with some of the facts that have been published on the terrifying disease of AIDS (Acquired Immune Deficiency Syndrome), but we find ourselves in the frustrating position of not understanding the information at our disposal and unable to make sense of deliberations over proposals to safeguard the public from exposure to the AIDS virus. In complex matters of this sort, the opinions of experts become a major source of support for the pro and con claims presented by advocates.

Our grouping of factual premises and evidence here does not mean they are the same thing. Premises, as we have said, come from the community or audience judging an argument. In contrast, evidence typically comes from sources that are independent of either audience or advocate. Trustworthy evidence, at least, ought to be independently verifiable. However, although these differences are important, factual premises and evidence are functionally identical when they serve as good reasons in support of an argument claim. Both provide support for argument claims by purporting to indicate what is factually true or false about the real world.

The functional identity between premises and evidence is not merely convenient; it means that we can analyze both in relation to the three general tests of argument discussed in Chapter 5: (1) truth, (2) relevance, and (3) sufficiency. When these general tests are applied to our rhetorical definition of argument (good reasons in support of a claim), they suggest a more specific threefold evaluation of factual support: The test of truth is applied by examining the reliability of the source of good reasons (evidence or premises) as well as the substance of the evidence itself. The tests of relevance and sufficiency are applied by examining the relationship between evidence and claim. Accordingly, we will explore three categories of evidence tests: (1) the evidence-claim relationship, (2) the evidence source, and (3) the evidence substance.

Tests of the Evidence-Claim Relationship

The tests of the evidence-claim relationship are all concerned with whether, or how well, a piece of evidence supports the claim in an argument. There are four important tests of the evidence-claim relationship:

1. The test of assertion
2. The test of relevance
3. The test of recency
4. The test of sufficiency

Your goal, as you follow the discussion here, should be to learn the names and meaning of each test, thinking of each as a valuable tool that provides you with a powerful means of self-defense and a way of ensuring that your own evidence is of the highest quality.

Test of Assertion

The test of assertion asks: Is the claim supported by *any* evidence? Professional persuaders can be marvelously creative in their efforts to invent tactics that cause listeners to accept assertions as if they have been supported, when in truth no evidence has been presented. One such tactic is the attempt to confuse the listener about who is responsible for providing the evidence when a claim is doubted. This tactic is sometimes combined with an assumed air of authority in which an assertion is presented as its own support. Perhaps you will recognize this tactic in the case of the egotistical lawyer, cited in an early argumentation text:

> A man who offers his own statement as sufficient evidence may have something in common with a certain lawyer. When asked, "Who is the most eminent lawyer in this city?" he replied, "I am."
> "But where is your proof?" rejoined the other.
> "I don't require proof," said the lawyer; "I admit it."[1]

Another common, though less interesting, tactic of assertion is the effort to bully listeners into submission. Parents occasionally resort to this tactic, especially when wearied of argument with a contentious teenager, by offering the pseudoevidence of self-authority: "Because *I said so*, that's why!" Parents and teens sometimes attempt to strengthen assertions by shouting them, as if vehemence is a workable substitute for evidence. People who do this seem to expect that their assertions will be regarded as complete proof if they are forcefully expressed.

A subtle variation of the bullying tactic is the attempt to silence opposition by making it costly for a listener or an opponent to challenge the bully's assertion. You may recognize some of your opponents in the following:

> *Washington Irving says, in the* Salmagundi Papers, *that Straddle "became at once a man of taste, for he put his malediction on everything; and his arguments were conclusive, for he supported every assertion with a bet." Straddle's method was not original, and it is not obsolete. On the contrary, it is the main reliance of people who are unable to prove their contentions with evidence.*[2]

In the social arguments we have with family and friends, assertions usually are about some question of fact: Who won the Super Bowl in 1975? When did the United States adopt the income tax? And the assertion of a claim may be accompanied by phrases such as "I read somewhere" (who can remember the exact place?), "All of the experts say . . . ," or "*They* have discovered. . . ." These phrases are intended to give the impression that the assertion is backed "somewhere" by authorities whose expert credentials are unassailable, and who agree with the present advocate. But you do not need to be fooled by such pseudosupport as the "they say. . ." tactic. Instead, such phrases can function as red flags, providing you with an easy way to recognize a mere assertion.

The key to the assertion test is to ask: Is there *any* evidence in support of the claim presented? Note that you do not want to become tiresome by challenging all of the assertions of your friends. Some assertions are reasonable and may very well be based on evidence that is merely assumed to be common knowledge (our factual premises). Moreover, people do not usually present evidence for claims that they perceive to be uncontroversial. However, when there is controversy about a claim, it is reasonable to ask for the evidence in support of it. Like all tests of evidence, it is important to know when to use the test of assertion.

Test of Relevance

The test of relevance asks: Does the evidence actually support the argument claim for which it is offered? Sometimes, material presented as evidence is, in itself, reliable, sound, and true, but these virtues do not necessarily mean that the material supports the claim in question. The test of relevance, by its nature, cannot be absolute, but its application can indicate flaws in the evidence-claim relationship that are not revealed by any other test. One of the useful ways to apply this test is to ask: Does the evidence really provide a good reason why the claim is true or should be accepted? Put another way: Would you run any risk of contradicting yourself if you accepted the statement of the evidence as true, but denied the claim? Suppose you are confronted with an argument that runs as follows:

> **Claim**: No one in the United States suffers from hunger or malnutrition.
>
> **Evidence**: Professor Fatbelly, an expert on food and eating, states that "every county in the United States is set up to provide food stamps to the needy."

Although the evidence (quotation) from this "expert" concerns the general topic of hunger, the statement does not provide support for the claim. Fatbelly's statement that "every county in the United States is set up to provide food stamps to the needy" could be true, but it does not support the factual claim that "no one in the United States suffers from hunger."

Ideally, the test of relevance would be strictly a logical matter; that is, logically, evidence either supports a claim or it does not. The reality of argument, however, is not quite so simple. Cultures and social institutions have a great deal to do with the way we decide whether factual material is or is not relevant to an argument claim. Some examples may clarify this distinction. If the defendant in a burglary case has previously been arrested or convicted of burglary, is such information relevant to the present charge? Many people seem to think it is. Yet, although there are some exceptions, U.S. courts generally apply the rule that such information is irrelevant and prejudicial and therefore may not be presented to a jury.

Is the prior sexual activity of a victim relevant to a claim that she or he was or was not sexually assaulted? In the past, the sex life of a victim was considered relevant in a sexual assault case, and especially when a defendant admitted to having sex with an alleged victim but argued that there was consent. Because of this standard of relevance, women and men could be asked all sorts of embarrassing questions about their sex lives by defense attorneys. The effect was to make it "open season" on the victim, as one attorney put it, and many victims declined to press charges against their attackers because they did not want to face questions about their past in open court. As a result, many states have revised their statutes, and the prior sexual behavior of a victim is ruled irrelevant in assessing whether she or he was sexually assaulted.

Criminal cases seem to provoke numerous challenges on the relevancy of evidence, but the test of relevance is not confined to the legal arena. Consider the application of the relevancy test in the following:

The objections now being voiced to the proposal to assign disruptive students to a single school facility have focused on the issue of race. That is unfortunate, because it obscures the real point, which is whether or not particular students will be allowed, through disruptive behavior, to deprive other students of their opportunity to get as good an education as possible. . . . It doesn't matter if they are black, Hispanic or Anglo—they have no right to make it difficult or impossible for others to learn.[3]

Test of Recency

The test of recency asks: Is the time referent of the evidence consistent with the time referent of the claim? Alternatively, is the evidence recent enough to support the claim? When an argument claim maintains that something is true at the present time, the evidence cited in support of the claim should also be current or as current as possible. Suppose the claim is that women earn approximately 59 cents for every dollar men earn. How recent should the evidence be for this sort of claim? Certainly, the older the evidence, the less it can be regarded as reliable support for a claim about what is true right now. Suppose further that the evidence consists of data on male and female income gathered in the 1970 census. We should say that these statistics provide powerful support for a claim about disparities in income in 1970, but they are almost irrelevant as support for a claim about the relationship of present earnings of men and women.

Evidence for a current disparity in income between men and women should be as recent as possible. But how recent is recent? If the claim concerns a topic such as the present levels of inflation or unemployment, the evidence should consist of the most current measurement that is regarded as reliable. The Department of Labor provides monthly statistics on the numbers of unemployed in the labor force, but these monthly statistics, though most recent, are not thought to be reliable, or not as reliable as statistics released for each quarter (three-month period). Thus, in the case of unemployment, the most recent reliable measurement would be the most recent quarterly statistics.

When the evidence consists of an expert opinion, it should be the most recent opinion the particular expert has published. Experts, like the rest of us, change their minds or perhaps refine their opinions as events unfold. The future is inherently uncertain, and any expert predictions about the future will necessarily be based on assumptions about weather patterns, how people will behave, and other highly changeable matters. Who could have predicted with any certainty the so-called glut of oil on the international market in 1985–87, with the resultant decrease in gasoline prices? Certainly, such a prediction was beyond the powers of major investors in the stock market! If expert opinion is to be used fairly and effectively, the opinion quoted should be the most recent in relation to the claim that is being made.

The concern for a consistent time relationship between evidence and claim should make it apparent why it is so important to provide the date for all evidence. However, the date of publication frequently is not the same as the date of origin for the evidence. Statistics from the 1950s, for example, do not become recent merely by virtue of being published this year in a book or article. Likewise, experts are sometimes chagrined to discover a previous, discarded opinion quoted in contemporary works, as if they had just made the statement.

Although the test of recency generally seems to make it essential for all of our sources to be current, even ancient sources can pass the recency test if the claim supported is concerned with a timeless principle. Consider my quotations of Aristotle and other ancient sources in this book. It is the time referent of the claim that determines how recent the evidence needs to be. If the claim concerns principles of argumentation or virtue, for instance, the age of the evidence may be unimportant. In fact, older sources are sometimes more highly regarded.

Test of Sufficiency

The test of sufficiency asks: Is there enough evidence? Does the evidence provide enough support for you to decide that the claim has been justified, established, or supported to a level that is sufficient to accept it as true? In some respects, this is the most interesting and difficult of the four tests of the evidence-claim relationship. How much evidence is enough? Enough for whom?

Surely we would not expect a defense attorney, for example, to agree that the prosecution has presented enough evidence on any of the contested issues. But the prosecution does not need to worry about what the defense attorney thinks. In most criminal cases, a jury decides whether the evidence is sufficient to warrant a guilty verdict, and their standard of sufficiency is applied as they ask themselves whether the evidence proves guilt "beyond a reasonable doubt." The evidence would be insufficient to establish a guilty verdict if, instead of "beyond reasonable doubt," the jury decided that the evidence made the criminal charge merely possible or plausible.

Suppose our favorite defendant, Jones, is accused of attempting to bribe a professor to give him a passing grade in statistics (based on an actual case). The test of relevancy, discussed earlier, would help us to decide the kinds of evidence that could support the claim—but how much evidence would be required? If you were a member of a jury hearing this case, how much and what kind of evidence would be required to constitute sufficient proof of the bribery charge? Would a written proposal from Jones be required, or would an oral request (based on testimony of the professor) be sufficient?

Clearly, the nature of the request would be important. There is a big difference between a request for compassion, for example, and an attempted bribe. If Jones couched his request in rather vague terms, the request per se might not be sufficient to support the claim of attempted bribery. Likewise, there could be a problem of ambiguity with any money offered. In this case, the professor claimed he found an envelope with $500 in new $50 bills that had been slipped under his door. The envelope also contained a note, signed by Jones, requesting a passing grade. What if the note had not been included? Would the money, by itself, have been sufficient evidence of attempted bribery? What if the note simply suggested the money was a gift from this student or an expression of appreciation?

Although this example is admittedly a fairly special application of the sufficiency test, it illustrates the way the test would be applied to almost any claim. In a policy question, for instance, how much evidence is required to establish a significant problem of drug abuse? What about illegal immigration, unemployment, poverty, or any other problem? The test of sufficiency applies to the evidence-claim relationship in any argument on any subject.

Tests of the Evidence Source

Just as the value of testimony in a court of law is no better than the witness who provides it, the value of any kind of factual or expert opinion evidence can be no better than its source. Thus, we need some methods to test, systematically, the credibility of the source of any sort of evidence or factual premise, just as an attorney needs to have standard methods for examining the credibility or trustworthiness of a witness. Three tests of the evidence source are especially useful:

1. The test of identification
2. The test of expertise
3. The test of bias

Test of Identification

The test of source identification asks two different but related questions about the credibility of evidence: (1) Who is the author/source of the evidence (whether factual or opinion)? and (2) Where is the evidence published? Both of these are important tests of source identification, and many people seem to confuse one with the other.

Identifying the Author

The first concern we have with source identification is: Who said it or reported it? Because factual evidence consists of a statement by someone that something is so, its credibility depends on its author—the person who found out the facts and then communicated them to others. Source identification becomes a bit complex when the person who communicates the factual statement is not the same as the person who found or observed the facts, and this complexity has led to strict rules in our criminal courts limiting the use of what is called *hearsay* evidence (one person attempting to testify about what another person supposedly observed or heard). But even without such complexity, we need to be aware of the difference between an original observation—say, my observation of a burglar breaking into my neighbor's house—and the factual statements I might make in communicating my observation.

Clearly, there are potential problems in both the observation and the reporting of factual matters. Not all observers are equally competent. Professional police are trained to be precise in their observations and, not surprisingly, when police testify as eyewitnesses of criminal events they are generally regarded as more reliable than the average person. Reporters also vary widely in their ability to communicate factual observations. Thus, in order to assess the reliability of any factual evidence, the very least we must know is the identity of the observer and the reporter.

Consider the problem of source identification with factual material such as statistics. How can we determine the reliability of statistics on problems such as student poverty unless we know something of the person or group that investigated the problem and made the measurements? In addition to the potential for incompetent measurement or reporting, unscrupulous advocates have been known to invent statistics to suit their purposes. Suppose you read in a newspaper article that U.S.-funded Contras in Nicaragua violated the human rights of several thousand civilians in 1984, committing 2,973 murders and over 3,500 rapes. You should immediately ask: Who found that out? Who reported those figures? Whenever you see statistics used in support of a claim, if the source of the statistics is not identified, you should remember Disraeli's advice: "There are three kinds of lies—lies, damned lies, and statistics!"

If the evidence is expert opinion, someone who claims expertise must have expressed the opinion. Expert testimony is an important form of evidence in a wide range of disputes. Congressional committees, for example, typically invite experts to testify on such matters as the causes of the tragic explosion of the spaceship *Challenger* in January 1986. Similarly, experts frequently are invited to express their opinions in courtrooms on such matters as the sanity of a defendant, the cause of death of a victim, fingerprint identification, and the like.

Opinion evidence is generally factual in the sense that the experts make statements about what they believe to be true of people or events of the real world, but their statements frequently go beyond the merely observable facts. Expert opinion usually consists of factual statements that are inferences from the observable facts, and sometimes these inferences include the expert's interpretive powers and intuitive judgment. A coroner, for instance, may present factual statements concerning the cause of death in a murder trial, testifying that the victim died from only 1 of 27 stab wounds—that 26 of the wounds were merely superficial whereas the fatal wound punctured an artery. A layperson could observe and report that the victim suffered 27 stab wounds, but the factual statement about the cause of death is an inference from an expert. The value of such an inference clearly depends on the credibility of the expert, and we cannot assess this credibility unless the identity of the alleged expert is known.

Identifying the Primary Source

The discussion thus far has concentrated on the more obvious, commonsense applications of the source identification test. Less obvious, but frequently important, is the problem of secondary sources who seem to pose as the primary source of evidence. A *primary source* is the person or group that originally observed or reported a particular fact. A *secondary source* is the person or group that repeats a factual statement, and may or may not cite the primary source.

News magazines are typical examples of secondary sources. The articles they publish generally are written by journalists, and the articles contain quantities of facts and opinions on virtually every topic of interest to the public. Although such articles may be informative and well written, their authors generally are not experts on the topics and they are seldom the primary source of the factual material presented.

We do not want to say that secondary sources are unreliable in general, but whenever a message is restated there is always potential for distortion, and important information may be omitted. Thus, insofar as it is possible, it is desirable to determine the primary sources of evidence. At the very least, we need to be aware of the potential for distortion in secondary sources. As a rule of thumb, we should prefer to use primary sources of evidence if they are available.

Identifying the Place of Publication

In addition to the problem of identifying the author/source, the second test of source identification asks: Where was the evidence published or presented? In general, evidence used in debates should come from published sources. The principle is that the evidence should be available to any of the parties involved in a debate and it should be open to their inspection. Emphasis on the place of publication helps to ensure the integrity of the debate process, and it also provides us with a way to protect ourselves against unethical persuaders who are willing to invent any kind of "evidence" in order to deceive us.

We need to train ourselves to be alert to speakers and writers who cite statistics or any other evidence without, at the same time, indicating where such material is published. Some speakers and writers, of course, may simply neglect to inform us of the place of publication, or may omit such information because they want to save time or avoid tiring the audience. We must be cautious about challenging anyone's honesty, but we have the right to expect that any persuader will be able and willing to provide publication information when it is requested—and it is always a good idea to request it. The place of publication encompasses (1) the name of the author; (2) the title of the article, journal, book, or document where the evidence is published; (3) the date of the publication; and (4) the page number where the evidence may be found.

Test of Expertise

The test of expertise asks: Is the source an expert in relation to his or her statement of fact or opinion? When evidence is factual, we need to know whether the source had the ability to get at the facts and to report them accurately. More generally, was the source in a position to be able to discover and report what is true or most probable? With opinion evidence, we want to know whether the source knows what he or she is talking about. Does the source have special qualities of expertise that provide an ability to explain the facts and to make inferences from them?

What sorts of special qualities are thought to indicate expertise? In general, the qualities or signs of expertise are the same as the elements of "good sense" in Aristotle's concept of ethos: intelligence, knowledge, experience, education, official or professional position, and manifest wisdom. Moreover, as we noted in our discussion of ethos in Chapter 1, the test of expertise is concerned with both the real and the apparent qualities of expertise. When expert testimony is used to support an argument claim, the purpose is to persuade someone (the audience) to accept the claim. This means that expertise is a quality that is perceived and judged by an audience. Readers or listeners decide whether the source of an opinion or factual statement is knowledgeable or competent.

Some audiences, of course, have greater ability to assess expertise than others. Usually, the more educated or knowledgeable the audience is about the expert's subject, the more competent is the evaluation of expertise. However, debate processes provide a crucial remedy for the less knowledgeable audience. Competent advocates in a debate are eager to challenge the expertise of sources cited by their opponents, and the clash of their mutual efforts can provide listeners with a critical basis for evaluating source qualification.

In some arguments, the test of expertise is applied to the credentials or qualifications of only one source, and the initial question is whether the source measures up to the minimum standards or "threshold" for expertise. In an interesting murder case, I saw a defense attorney demolish the credibility of a coroner who was testifying about the cause of death of the murder victim. The attorney acknowledged that the witness had been elected to the office of county coroner, but argued that he was lacking in the most rudimentary credentials for his post—he was not a licensed physician and he did not have a medical degree. Minimum standards of education and licensing can provide a convenient and easily understood basis for questioning the qualification of an alleged expert.

Comparative Expertise

Although the fate of an argument sometimes depends on the expert qualifications of just one source, frequently we need to compare the relative expertise or competence of two or more experts in order to decide which of two competing claims is more solidly supported. In virtually any arena of dispute, so-called experts can be marshalled for at least two sides—generally to the dismay of lay listeners and readers.

Was John Hinckley, Jr. legally insane at the time that he attempted the assassination of former President Reagan? Some expert psychiatrists testified that he was—some said that he was not. Hinckley's jury no doubt felt frustrated by the disagreement of the experts, but it is important to realize that such disagreement is not unusual. It is typical of almost all disputes on important questions. Can the United States trust the various Russian states to abide by the provisions of a treaty on nuclear arms limitations? Some experts say that we can—some say that we cannot. The listener or juror, as the case may be, must decide which expert is more credible.

The Problem of Corporate Expertise

The concept of expertise is most intelligible when it is applied to individuals, but we must also be ready to assess the expertise of groups, institutions, and publications. Increasingly, it seems, important news articles, studies, and reports are published under a corporate group name or are unsigned by the author. If expertise is a quality that we normally associate with a person—the author/source of a statement of fact or opinion—how do we assess expertise when we do not know the identity of the author?

When statements of fact or opinion come from an unsigned article in a news magazine, for example, we can usually assume that the reason the author's name was not provided is that the author has no expertise in the subject, and the credibility of material from this article should be reduced accordingly. But how much shall it be reduced? Any evidence is probably better than none, but if there is a clash between two pieces of evidence, we should prefer evidence from a known author whose credentials can be determined.

Someone might object that the publications themselves stand behind the accuracy of their articles, and this objection sounds reasonable at first. Undoubtedly, magazines such as *Time* are firmly committed to factual accuracy in their articles, and their editors do their best to ensure such accuracy in articles submitted for publication. But notice how this complicates the matter of primary and secondary sources. If it is an editorial board that vouches for the accuracy of facts reported in articles, such a board must do so either from firsthand knowledge of the facts (which probably never happens) or on the basis of trust in the statements of their reporter.

Do you see how this puts us in the hearsay evidence quandary? To complicate matters, if the reporter is not a primary source of facts quoted (he or she is relying on another source that may or may not be primary), the editorial board is at least at a third level removed from any direct observation. Even though reputable news magazines and newspapers try to protect the credibility of the process by requiring "independent verification" of facts reported, errors in such a system are inevitable.

If factual statements are at least suspect in unsigned articles, what of the opinions? In some respects, we are simply unable to escape reliance on corporate entities because they may be the only known author identification of important evidence such as studies and reports. This sort of reliance clearly is not ideal. But we can discriminate somewhat among corporate sources, attempting to discern the more and the less credible. For example, the credibility of corporate authorship seems to be quite strong in relation to agencies of the federal government, such as publications of the Departments of Defense, Labor, and Health and Human Services. Federal agencies publish numerous reports and studies without identifying authors by name, and such reports and studies tend to be highly regarded. Perhaps the best approach is always to seek out the best evidence. If everything else is equal, an article with the author identified is better than an article unsigned, and a source whose qualifications are known is better than a source we can identify only by name.

Test of Bias

The test of source bias asks: Does the source of evidence have a conflict of interest? Does this person or group have any sort of stake in the outcome of a dispute that might cause you to doubt the objectivity of their statements of fact or opinion?

At its most basic level, the test of bias is concerned with honesty. Unethical persuaders, as we have noted, do not hesitate to distort evidence whenever it is in their interest to do so. We have only to consider the stereotype of the used-car dealer who is incapable of even a blush as he baldly lies to his customer. But the problem of bias is a potential problem for any human source, even the most honest. Any of us may have our perception of facts or the meaning of facts distorted by our preconceived notions of what is true or important, and we should be careful in equating prejudice with dishonesty.

Should anyone be surprised that ethical attorneys oppose proposals that might limit their income or freedoms, or that physicians generally see themselves as innocent victims of high rates for malpractice insurance? People tend to see the world in a way that is compatible with their vital interests. Virtually all U.S. industry groups that have suffered losses of market share to vigorous competitors from Japan tend to see themselves as victims of unfair competition, and it is quite understandable that so many of them call for protective legislation in the form of tariffs and quotas. Thus, while self-interest should not be equated with dishonesty, the potential for bias in any source of information should alert us to a corresponding potential for distortion in the statements of the source.

Probably most of us are instinctively wary of statements that are obviously self-serving—such as a statement from an executive officer of an automobile company that its manufacturing department has not had sufficient time to comply with federal gas mileage requirements in its current models. A more difficult problem occurs when the bias of a source is not so apparent. Consider the problem of bias in the following report by Anne Roark:

> *Six of the 15 members of a National Academy of Sciences panel that recently urged healthy Americans to stop worrying about fat and cholesterol in their diets have acknowledged that they have financial ties to the food industry.*
>
> *Partly because of those connections, critics have charged that the board's 20-page report on food and nutrition is inaccurate and misleading and represents a serious conflict of interest between science and industry. . . .*
>
> *The man who wrote the final report of the nutrition study—Robert E. Olson, a biochemist from Saint Louis University School of Medicine—earns approximately 10 percent of his income as a consultant for the American Egg Board. . . . Two [other] members are food industry executives. . . .*[4]

The shock in this report is not that people who have financial ties with the egg industry would have a conflict of interest, but rather that the conflict was disguised behind the prestigious National Academy of Sciences—a private organization chartered by Congress to provide scientific advice to lawmakers and the public, and therefore thought to be an objective, independent source of scientific information.

Bias is a potential problem with any source of evidence, but the nature of the bias can differ markedly. Certainly, not all bias is caused by financial interests. Friendship, pet ideas, prior public statements, experiences, and many other factors can distort judgment or even perception. Most of us, for example, are inclined to overlook personal flaws in the people we love, to the extent that we do not even notice such flaws—no matter how obvious they may be to others. Thus, as we apply the bias test to evidence, the question we need to ask is: Is there anything about the source that might distort judgment or perception in relation to this subject?

Tests of the Evidence Substance

Tests of the substance of evidence are concerned with probes for examining directly the trustworthiness of objects, or statements of fact or opinion offered as evidence. There are four such tests we shall discuss here:

1. The test of integrity
2. The test of context
3. The test of consistency
4. The tests of statistics

Test of Integrity

The test of the integrity or honesty of evidence necessarily has a broad sweep. If the evidence is a physical object of some kind—say, a driver's license—this test would ask: Has the object been altered in a way that would distort its true meaning? Probably every college student, past and present, could provide examples of friends or acquaintances who used altered or fake identifications in their quests for cultural enrichment. But the test of integrity is not limited merely to faked documents.

Whenever evidence consists of an object, the test of integrity asks if the object is authentic: Is it truly what it is purported to be? *Objects*, of course, may have an almost infinite variety. The Black Skull unearthed in remote Kenya in 1985, which was said to constitute direct refutation for many current theories on the origin of the human species, could hardly be more different as an object than a driver's license. Yet, critics will ask essentially the same sorts of questions about its authenticity as might be asked about an indentification card that indicates an age of 21 for a high school senior.

In a more general way, we are concerned with integrity if there is any question about whether the evidence is fake. Unscrupulous persuaders are sometimes quite willing to fabricate statistics or examples to support their claims, and we need to be alert to such dishonesty. If the facts or expert opinions seem to be too powerful to be true, it may be that they are.

Application of the test of integrity is not limited to evidence. It is also a useful tool for examining any factual premises that support the claim of an argument. As we noted earlier, communities share large numbers of beliefs about what is true or false about the world, and such beliefs can provide powerful support for an argument. At the same time, such beliefs can also be quite wrong. Thus, we apply the test of integrity to factual premises when we confront them directly, asking if they are really true.

Test of Context

The test of context asks: Is the quotation of factual material or opinion consistent with its original meaning? In many respects, this test is a subspecies of the test of integrity. When evidence consists of quoted statements of fact or opinion, the test of integrity is concerned with authenticity of the statements quoted. Initially, we need to ask: Did the source really make this statement? Or, alternatively, is the quotation accurate? But accuracy is not just a matter of repeating verbatim what was said by a person; it is also a matter of context.

The term *context* refers to all of the parts of a sentence, paragraph, or discourse that occur before and after a quotation, and that determine its exact meaning. Thus, when public officials complain that they have been quoted "out of context," they mean that a quotation may, perhaps, accurately report some of what they said, but it distorts their meaning—either by leaving out portions of what they said or by omitting significant events or statements by others that clarify the meaning of the quotation.

The reputed experience of an Anglican Bishop from London illustrates the problem of context. As the story goes, on the Bishop's first trip to the United States, he was met by a bevy of newspaper reporters at the airport. One of the reporters asked, in a rather disrespectful tone, "Bishop, do you plan to visit any nightclubs in New York?" Attempting a sarcastic reply, the Bishop retorted: "*Are* there any nightclubs in New York?" The next morning the Bishop was horrified to read the headline of the reporter's account: British Bishop's First Question upon Arrival: "Are There Any Nightclubs in New York?"

Test of Consistency

The test of consistency has two variations. The first, called the test of *internal consistency*, asks: Is this particular piece of evidence or its source inconsistent with itself or in any way self-contradictory? The second variation, called the test of *external consistency*, asks: Is this evidence or source inconsistent with other evidence or sources on this matter?

Although the tests of consistency may not seem familiar initially, they are probably used by all of us whenever we engage in disputes. Even small children realize that consistency is considered a virtue, and they become very upset when parents allow a brother or sister to get away with behavior for which they have received punishment. Children also understand that inconsistency in stories about what happened ("Who broke the window?") is a surefire test used by parents to spot fibs. When the inconsistency is solely in the tale of one child, it would be called an *internal* inconsistency. But if one child says the window was broken by the cat, and a second child says a burglar did it, the inconsistency would be called *external*.

The uses of consistency tests by parents are elementary, of course, but they provide valuable insights into the way these tests help us to discern the truth in any particular subject. Truth is by its very nature complex and difficult to discover. Falsehood, however, is sometimes easier to discern because of its particular tell-tale signs, such as inconsistency and contradiction. Whenever two statements are directly contradictory or inconsistent, at least one of them must be false. This means we can sometimes discover what is true by a process of elimination—eliminating, one by one, alternatives that are false. Parents do this as they reject a child's story on the grounds that it is inconsistent or self-contradictory. (This works until the little devils learn to invent consistent lies!) Likewise, police detectives use the test of external consistency when they question suspects separately and then compare the stories.

In the arena of public policy, the tests of internal and external consistency become important as we assess whether a proposed course of action, such as mandating seat-belt usage by all auto passengers, will in fact result in reduced injuries and deaths. Over a number of years, studies on seatbelt usage seemed to provide consistent findings: Wearing seat belts reduces injuries and saves lives. However, in August 1986, the National Transportation Safety Board (NTSB) caused shockwaves with the announcement that their study found that lap belts for rear-seat passengers "induced severe to fatal injuries that probably would not have occurred if the lap belts had not been worn."[5] The NTSB finding was immediately disputed by other groups—providing an example of external inconsistency:

> The NTSB findings were immediately disputed by the National High-way Traffic Safety Administration, which issues auto safety regulations. The agency called the study "a specific search for cases in which belts failed" and not statistically valid.
>
> The highway safety agency added, "In numerous studies involving thousands of cases, lap belts have been found to reduce the risk of death or serious injury" and should continue to be worn.[6]

Whenever such prestigious sources of evidence come to opposite conclusions, the inconsistency ought to suggest that the topic warrants further study—that we do not yet know the truth about the capabilities of lap belts in preventing injuries and deaths for rear-seat passengers. It should also prompt the researcher to go beyond the conclusions of the conflicting sources and to examine the reasons or facts in support of the conclusions.

Another dimension of the newspaper account of the lap-belt controversy provides an interesting example of internal inconsistency. Although the NTSB study indicates that lap belts may do more harm than good, Patricia Goldman, the NTSB's vice chairman, acknowledged that "we don't know whether it is best for rear-seat passengers to ride with only a lap belt or without one."[7] Such an admission suggests at least a lack of confidence in the NTSB findings, and it reveals a problem of internal inconsistency within the agency.

Tests of Statistical Evidence

The final test of evidence substance is, in reality, a group of tests for statistical evidence. Few types of evidence seem to be more confounding to students, and few are so critical in modern controversy. We shall begin with a brief description of two major types of statistics, and then we will discuss some of the more important tests for statistical evidence.

Descriptive and Inferential Statistics

When statistics are used as evidence, they are almost invariably based on one of two major types: (1) statistics drawn from a complete numerical count or (2) statistics based on an inference or a projection from a sample. The first type is called *descriptive* because it is based on a complete numerical count of all items in a particular class or population. Descriptive statistics tend to be the most reliable, mainly because they are less complex in derivation. For instance, the U.S. Census, conducted every 10 years, attempts to provide a complete count of all citizens and resident aliens in the United States, and it provides a wealth of data on the size of each age group, location of the population, number and location of the unemployed, income levels, occupations, and so on. Similarly, universities generate complete counts, providing data on the numbers of ethnic group members, men and women, on- and off-campus residents, majors in each college and department, and many other items.

Data from the census, and similar sources, are seldom troublesome in themselves so long as there is confidence in the counting process. But problems in counting are not unknown. The accuracy of the 1990 census, for example, has been challenged by a number of cities and by various ethnic groups who have charged that the Census report understated their populations. Likewise, universities occasionally have internal disputes over the numbers of students in each major. However, the more typical problem with the complete count type of statistics concerns the inferences or conclusions that are drawn from them. For example, at what point does a decrease or an increase in student enrollments constitute a trend? How much of an increase is a significant increase? We will return to these questions as we discuss statistical tests.

The second type of statistics is called *inferential* because it is based on an inference or projection from a sample to the entire population. Public opinion polls, for example, are almost always based on samples. When the polls reported in March 1991 that 90 percent of the voters were satisfied with the way President Bush handled his job, we can be very sure that the polls were not based on a complete survey of all U.S. voters. Complete counts are generally avoided because they are expensive in time and money and they are often impossible. So the Gallup poll, for example, usually selects a sample of the population—approximately 1,500 respondents for national opinion polls—and then infers that the opinions reflected in the sample are representative of the more than 248 million Americans in our population. Such inferences are often troublesome, and they are the chief concern of our first major test of statistics.

Representativeness of the Sample

The first test for any statistics that are inferred or in any way based on a sample is the question: Is the sample representative of the population? The question seems straightforward enough, but pay special attention to the term *representative*. To say that a sample is representative is to say that what is true of the sample is also true of the entire population from which the sample is drawn. In our Gallup example, this means that if the 1,500 in the sample are truly representative, then the opinions or preferences of the people in the sample will be the same as the opinions of the entire population. Thus, if 20 percent of the prospective voters in the sample say they prefer candidate X for president, then we infer that 20 percent of all prospective voters in the United States also prefer candidate X.

The concept of representativeness seems simple enough, but how do we know whether a sample is representative? This question is not so simple. The short answer is that we do not know. No matter how carefully a sample is selected, it is always possible for the sample not to be representative. However, there are some principles that guide the process of sampling, and these principles can help us to spot problems in sampling—that is, samples that are unlikely to be representative.

The first principle is concerned with the *size* of the sample: The smaller the sample, the more concerned we are about its representativeness. We would probably doubt the representativeness of an opinion poll purporting to reflect the views of the student body on a campus of, say, 20,000 students if only 20 students were interviewed. Our doubt derives in part from our knowledge of the diversity of opinion among students, and we would question whether 20 students could represent that diversity. Yet, a sample of 20 students is proportionately much larger than the 1,500 prospective voters in the Gallup sample, or the 1,200 homes in the Nielsen survey, and both the Nielsen and the Gallup polls are considered adequate in size. However, neither Nielsen nor Gallup samples are defended solely on the basis of their size, which leads us to the second principle.

The second principle is concerned with the *critical characteristics* of the sample: A small sample can be representative if its critical characteristics match the characteristics of the population. The Nielsen sample is defended largely on the basis that the U.S. Census provides a broad base of information about the critical characteristics of homes with televisions for the entire population. The Nielsen sample is said to have, in microcosm, proportionately the same characteristics. Perhaps. But someone could reasonably ask how can we be certain that the U.S. Census identifies all of the critical characteristics important to viewing habits? This sort of misgiving leads us to the third principle.

The third principle is concerned with the *method of sample selection*. A sample is more likely to be representative if the method for its selection tends to ensure proper distribution. One such method is called *random selection*, which is a strategy of using chance to ensure that all members of a population have a more or less equal chance to be in the sample or out of the sample. Thus, in our example of the 20-student opinion sample, the 20 students are more likely to be representative of the student body if they are selected in a purely random way than if they are all members of the same fraternity.

A special case of difficulty in sample selection involves what is called the *self-selecting* sample—individuals who have an unusual interest in the subject and who volunteer themselves. For example, some television news programs conduct occasional polls of their viewers by asking people to call one of two or three telephone numbers (depending on the topic) as a means of registering their opinions. ABC-TV's "Nightline" host, Ted Koppel, used this method in 1980 as a way to get an immediate response from viewers on who they thought had "won" the presidential debate between Ronald Reagan and Jimmy Carter. The poll was a dramatic success, but many worried, and with good reason, about the possible impact of an admittedly invalid polling method on the presidential election. The polling method was invalid because the people who call in are those who are most intensely involved in an election, and there is no way to determine whether their views are in any way representative of all viewers or all voters.

Appropriateness of the Statistical Unit

The second major test of statistical evidence is important for either descriptive or inferential statistics. This test concerns what is called the *statistical unit*, and it asks a basic question of any statistical measurement or comparison: Is the statistical unit appropriate?

One of the more common misuses of statistics involves deceptive use of averages. The term *average* is concerned with central tendencies and with what is deemed normal or usual. Thus, we speak of average age, income, exam scores, height, weight, prices, intelligence, and so on. But the term *average* has three different meanings: It can refer to the *mean* average, or the *median*, or the *mode*.

To be clear about these different meanings, suppose we were interested in determining the average income for a hypothetical baseball team. The mean average income could be obtained by adding up all of the salaries paid to players, and then dividing that by the number of players. The median would be the middle salary: Half the players earn more than the median and half earn less. The mode is the most frequently occurring salary. Thus, if there are 25 players on the team, each of the averages would work out as follows:

Players at Salary	Salary	
1	$900,000	
1	300,000	
2	200,000	
1	114,000	Mean Average
3	100,000	
4	74,000	
1	60,000	Median Average
12	40,000	Mode Average
Total 25	$2,850,000	

It should be apparent from our example that it would be misleading to say that the "average" salary for a player on this team is $114,000. Even though that is an accurate figure for the mean average, only one player earns that salary. Likewise, only one player earns the median salary of $60,000. But the essential point is the potential for distortion when we are unclear what is meant by the term *average*.

Another common misuse of statistical units involves what I call *percentage increase and decrease games*. When the deceptive persuader wants to show that a problem is increasing or decreasing, one favorite device is the use of percentages with a hidden or faulty base. Some years ago, for instance, an athletic director supported his claim that he was making great progress in equalizing the funding between female and male sports by citing a 50 percent increase for the female programs over the previous year. The faculty senate was impressed—initially. Then some members began to wonder: What did the 50 percent really represent? As it turned out, in the previous year, women's athletic programs had received 5 percent of the budget, and that had increased in the current year to 7 1/2 percent. The reported increase of 50 percent, while technically true, clearly distorted the reality of funding for the women's sports by concealing the base for the percentage comparison.

Distortion in the Basis of Comparison

Manipulation of statistical units is a favorite tactic of the deceptive, and it is probably one of the things Disraeli had in mind when he said there are "lies, damned lies, and statistics!" Do we want to show that voter participation is increasing or decreasing in our country? It may surprise you that it is possible to do both—depending on the unit selected as the basis for comparison. A newspaper article published just after the 1984 presidential election, for example, reported that the percentage turnout of the *voting age population* increased from 52.6 percent in 1980 to 53 percent in 1984. Although not impressive, an increase is at least an increase—right? Well, the same article noted a decline in percentage turnout of *registered voters* in the same two elections, from 75.2 percent in 1980 to 72.4 percent in 1984. Which is the most appropriate basis of measurement?

It is important to realize that statistics can be misleading even though they are numerically accurate. A study released by the Justice Department in 1985 provides an interesting example of how accurate statistics may suggest a misleading view of reality. The study reported statistics that seem to show that whites have a greater risk of receiving the death penalty than blacks:

> *The department's Bureau of Justice Statistics found that for every 1000 whites arrested for murder . . . almost 16 went to prison under sentence of death from 1980 through 1984. Fewer than 12 blacks arrested for the [same crime] were sent to death row in the same period.[8]*

Notice that the statistics are based on those "arrested for murder." Yet, to be "arrested for murder" is not at all the same as to be "guilty of murder" or "convicted of murder." The Justice Department's figures could be interpreted to mean that relatively more blacks than whites who are arrested for murder are found not guilty by the courts. What sort of statistical picture develops if the basis of comparison is the relative number of whites and blacks in the U.S. population? In the 1980 census, blacks comprised 11.7 percent of the U.S. population. Yet, according to the Justice department study, blacks accounted for 41 percent of death sentences.

Appropriateness of Time Period

The question of whether the statistics cover an appropriate time period is also important for descriptive and inferential statistics, and it is closely related to the matter of statistical unit. If we want to know whether voter turnout in national elections is increasing or decreasing, what is an appropriate time period for making a comparison? In the previous example, the writer compared the turnout in 1980 to 1984. Such a comparison is reasonable in itself, but a four-year period and two elections may not tell us much about about whether the trend in voter interest in elections is really changing one way or another. But how large does the time span need to be? In one sense, as the time span increases, we become more confident in the observed trends. At the same time, we need to be aware of potential difficulties in what is selected as the base year, or first election. The election of 1960, for example, had a record turnout of 62.8 percent. If that is the base year, later elections would suffer by comparison. Moreover, the voting age was changed from 21 to 18 years in 1969, which means a comparison between 1960 and 1984 would be based on different voting populations.

Our discussion of methods for testing statistical evidence is not intended to be exhaustive. Rather, the idea is to introduce some of the more common problems and to provide a perspective on the nature of statistical evidence for a beginning level. At the same time, you should also see that the tests of the evidence-claim relationship and the source apply to statistics. The test of recency, for example, is frequently of major concern with statistics, and it is always important to know source identification—the person or group responsible for the statistical information. The tests for evidence and premises are separable, but all of them work together to help us become expert in detecting counterfeit claims.

The tests of evidence and value premises, like most of the concepts we have discussed so far, must be applied to arguments in order to be learned. You have not learned them at all if you simply memorize their names. All principles of rhetoric and argumentation are learned as you gain experience in their use. The key is to apply these tests as you read research materials for class debates and to deepen your understanding of value premises as you participate in the ordinary activities of campus life. Practice is key to understanding.

Summary

1. Expertise in detecting flaws in value premises requires mastery of three test questions: (1) the so what? test, (2) the value comparison test, and (3) the value application or interpretation test (see Figure 7.1).

  a. The *so what? test* is a kind of linguistic probe that unmasks the arguments that have an assumed value that makes something described either good or bad, important or unimportant.

  b. The *value comparison test* alerts us that there are usually conflicting values as we examine any alleged problem or benefit. This asks: Is there a more important value?

  c. The *value application or interpretation test* suggests that we can accept a value, but deny that it applies in this case. This test examines the criteria for a value and asks: Is the value correctly applied or interpreted in this argument?

FIGURE 7.1 *Tests of Value Premises*

Test Name	Test Questions
So What?	1. Is there really anything bad or harmful in the situation described? or
	2. Is the alleged benefit really "good"?
Value Comparison	1. Is there a more important value in this situation? or
	2. Is value X more important than value Y?
Value Application	1. Is the value being correctly applied in this case? or
	2. Do the standards for the value fit this situation?

2. Expertise in detecting the flaws of factual support covers both factual premises and evidence. Although factual premises derive from audience beliefs, and evidence is usually external to advocate and audience, they are both subject to three general categories of tests: (1) tests of the evidence-claim relationship, (2) tests of the evidence source, and (3) tests of the evidence substance (see Figure 7.2).

3. There are four useful tests of the evidence-claim relationship:

    a. The test of *assertion* asks: Is there any evidence in support of the claim?

    b. The test of *relevance* asks: Does the evidence (or factual premise) really support the claim?

    c. The test of *recency* asks: Is the evidence recent enough in relation to the claim it supports?

    d. The test of *sufficiency* asks: Is there enough evidence in support of the claim?

FIGURE 7.2   *Tests of Evidence Summary*

Tests of Evidence-Claim Relationship

---

1. Assertion	- Is the claim supported by any evidence?
2. Relevance	- Does the evidence actually support the claim?
3. Recency	- Is the evidence recent enough to support the claim?
4. Sufficiency	- Is there enough evidence?

Tests of the Evidence Source

---

1. Identification	- Who is the author/source? Where was this published?
2. Expertise	- Is the source an expert on this subject?
3. Bias	- Does the source have a conflict of interest?

Tests of the Evidence Substance

---

1. Integrity	- Is the evidence authentic or true?
2. Context	- Is the quotation true to its original meaning?
3. Consistency	- Is the evidence consistent with itself and other sources?
4. Statistics	- There are several test questions:
	a. Are the statistics descriptive or inferential?
	b. Is the sample representative of its population?
	c. Is the statistical unit appropriate?
	d. Is the basis of comparison distorted?
	e. Do the statistics cover an appropriate time period?

---

4. Three tests help us to detect potential flaws in the source of evidence:

   a. The test of *source identification* asks two questions: (1) Who is the author/source? and (2) Where is the evidence published?

   b. The test of *source expertise* asks: Does the author/source know what he or she is talking about?

   c. The test of *source bias* asks: Does the source have any conflict of interest that would interfere with perceiving or reporting the truth?

5. There are four useful tests for the substance of evidence:

   a. The test of *integrity* asks: Is the evidence (or factual premise) really true?

   b. The test of *context* asks: Are the facts or opinion presented in a way that is consistent with their original meaning?

   c. The test of *consistency* asks: Is the evidence consistent with itself (internal) and is it consistent with other evidence or sources (external)?

   d. *Statistical* tests ask: (1) Are the statistics descriptive or inferential? (2) Is the sample representative? (3) Is the statistical unit appropriate? (4) Is the basis of comparison distorted? and (5) Are the time periods appropriate?

Exercises

   1. Suppose you found the following arguments on the editorial page of your local newspaper. How could you apply each of the three tests of value premises to expose possible weaknesses? (See answers following the chapter endnotes.)

   a. "The university should not install condom dispensers in the dormitories. If they do that, it will put the university in the position of condoning illicit sexual activities among students."

   b. "There are lots of reasons that I'm opposed to the sort of national health care program proposed by Senator Kennedy—but the most important is that it is just one more step down the road to socialized medicine."

   2. How would you apply tests of the evidence source to the following evidence concerning the "winner" of the first Kennedy-Nixon debate? (See answer following the chapter endnotes.)

> *As far as the television audience was concerned, Claude Robinson and the other pollsters recorded a clear edge for Kennedy. . . . Radio reaction was just the opposite from that on television. All the polls gave me a clear advantage. (Richard Nixon, Six Crises [Garden City, NY: Doubleday, 1962], pp. 341–342.)*

3. Select two editorials or letters to the editor from the editorial page of your local newspaper. Alternatively, locate an argumentative piece in the *New Republic* (generally liberal) and the *National Review* (generally conservative). Identify the supporting material for the argument claims presented and apply the tests of evidence-claim relationship, evidence source, and the evidence substance to each. What flaws or potential defects do you find?

4. As a class project, try to identify the major kinds of value and factual premises that function as assumptions for important arguments in your class debate topics. If your topic is a value question, what are the underlying value premises for arguments on the definitional or qualitative issues? If you are debating a policy question, what are the value premises for arguments on the motive and cost issues?

Endnotes

1. William T. Foster, *Argumentation and Debating* (Boston: Houghton Mifflin, 1917), p. 95.
2. Ibid, p. 92.
3. Randall Perkins, "Race Irrelevant," *Rocky Mountain News*, 14 December 1983, p. 56. Reprinted with permission of the *Rocky Mountain News*.
4. Anne Roark, "Report on Nutrition Fuels Conflict-of-Interest Debate," *The Chronicle of Higher Education*, p. 8. Copyright 1986, *The Chronicle of Higher Education*. Reprinted with permission.
5. Associated Press, *Rocky Mountain News*, 12 August 1986, p. 2. Reprinted with permission of the *Rocky Mountain News*.
6. Ibid.
7. Ibid.
8. Robert Engleman, "Execution More Likely for Whites, Study Says," *Rocky Mountain News*, 26 August 1985, p. 30. Reprinted with permission of the *Rocky Mountain News*.

Answers for Exercises

1. Apply tests of value premises
   a. Argument on condom dispensers in the dorms:

(1) *So what? test.* This asks whether there is really anything harmful if the university is put in the position of "condoning illicit sexual activities among students." Is that really a problem for the institution? If so, how exactly is it hurt?

(2) *Value comparison test.* This asks whether there is another more important value. In this case, we need to get at the unstated value (goal) of putting the condom dispensers in the dorms—namely, to prevent unwanted pregnancies and venereal diseases. So, the value comparison test becomes: Is the value of preventing unwanted pregnancies and venereal diseases among students more important than any harm from the university being put in a position of "condoning"?

(3) *Value application test.* This asks whether the placement of condom dispensers in the dorms really does put the university in the position of condoning anything.

b. Argument on socialized medicine and health care:

(1) *So what? test.* This asks whether there is necessarily anything harmful about socialized medicine. The assertion that socialized medicine would result from the health insurance program implies that this would be harmful. The test asks for explicit harm.

(2) *Value comparison test.* This asks whether the value of providing health care to people is more important than the implied harm of socialized medicine.

(3) *Value application test.* This asks whether a national health care program really is a step down the road toward socialized medicine.

2. Apply tests of source

(1) *Source identification.* The author and place of publication are provided, but notice the reference to "all the polls." What polls? The only poll Mr. Nixon cited was a weak survey by Ralph McGill who said that he asked "a number of persons" to listen to the debate. A phrase like "all the polls" indicates potential problems of primary source identification.

(2) *Source expertise.* We should not be picky about Mr. Nixon's expertise, but we cannot assess expertise in "all the polls" since they are not identified. Ralph McGill may or may not have had expertise, but the polling of an unknown "number of persons" does not suggest the approach of an expert.

(3) *Source bias*. It should not surprise anyone that Mr. Nixon would have a conflict of interest in accounting for his evident loss of the debate as well as the election. His claim that the radio audience thought he won is clearly self-serving. (See David Vancil and Sue Pendell, "The Myth of Viewer-Listener Disagreement in the First Kennedy-Nixon Debate," *Central States Speech Journal* 38 [Spring 1987]: 16–27.

8

Organizing the Analysis: The Brief

Central Ideas in This Chapter

1. Briefs are a useful tool for synthesizing research, providing a storehouse of argument resources, and anticipating opposing argument.

2. Six rules help us to construct a quality brief:
   - Use issues to structure the brief.
   - Use complete sentences.
   - Use consistent symbol systems and format.
   - Place items of comparable importance on the same level.
   - Follow the principle of logical subordination.
   - Include only the evidence that provides distinctive support.

3. An illustrative brief can serve as a model and help us to see the relationships of issues, arguments, and evidence.

Analysis is the process of breaking down a controversy into its simpler components—the issues, the pro and con arguments, and the premises and evidence. A clear grasp of larger components—the central question and the issues—provides guidance in the research process in much the same way that good map helps us to get about in a new city. And if the process of research and analysis is done well, you will soon possess a substantial amount of evidence and a large number of arguments for each side. Knowing how to use the materials discovered is another matter, however. It is rather like the problem a child faces in trying to make sense of a new puzzle. The pieces of the puzzle are individually interesting perhaps, and certainly provide plentiful material for the construction of "something," but unless the child has a means to discern the pattern for the completed puzzle, the plentiful pieces are a box of confusion and not much fun at all. Likewise, the student of argumentation needs to discern a pattern for the quantity of arguments and evidence gathered in the research process. The idea is to organize the material into a cohesive framework; the pattern needed for this task is called the *brief.*

The task of constructing a brief often inspires an almost unique form of anxiety for the beginner, principally because a finished brief seems to be a complex document and the result of considerable labor. *The brief is a complete outline of all the issues, arguments, and evidence for both pro and con sides on a central question.* But a brief only seems complex to a person who is unfamiliar with the process of analysis discussed in previous chapters. Most students find that the labor is uncommonly rewarding—most immediately in preparing them for the class debates, and later when students realize they have learned important skills of organization that can be used for any kind of composition.

Developing the Brief

The final brief is organized as a logical outline. In the early stages of its development, however, it is helpful to have a visual model for keeping track of what you are discovering and seeing where research is weak as well as strong. This visual model is comparable to the model presented in Chapter 3 (Figure 3.1), which displays the arguments and evidence for each issue on the DDT policy question. One simple method is to write each issue at the top of a separate piece of paper that has been divided into two columns: one column for the pro side (affirmative) and one for the con side (negative). The issues guide the search for argument claims and evidence because they indicate what the affirmative must prove and what the negative may choose to refute.

As you find argument claims that seem to support a response of yes or no to each of the four issues, record them in the pro or con column for the appropriate issue. If you are using quality research materials, you will soon see a pattern emerging in the pro and con arguments, with evident clash between pro and con on some points. You will also notice a lack of clash on other arguments, suggesting areas where your research is incomplete or where an argument from one side is apparently unanswered by the other side. You may also think of some potential arguments for pro and con yourself— arguments that you have not found in your research thus far but that seem to be relevant to one of the issues. Usually, of course, such arguments will be found as you deepen your research, but the ability to anticipate pro and con arguments is a sign that you are developing analytical skills. And students occasionally discover new arguments that have not been used or invented by participants in a controversy.

As you record pro and con argument claims for each issue, you will also want to keep track of factual or opinion evidence that supports the claims. However, in the early stages of research and analysis, it can be tiresome and of little value to write all of the evidence under each claim. A more useful technique, illustrated in Figure 8.1, is to number evidence cards and record the numbers under the statements of argument claims the evidence seems to support. When your research is complete and you are ready to compose the finished brief and type it as a logical outline, the evidence can then be incorporated under each claim.

Although the brief is a logical outline of all the important components of a controversy, its format and structure can vary considerably according to its purpose. Attorneys, for example, use briefs for at least two purposes: to prepare themselves for trial and to appeal decisions to a higher court. In preparing themselves for trial, attorneys use the brief to organize their arguments and evidence for effective oral presentation of the case. Thus, the best format for this purpose is virtually whatever method of logical outlining is most effective for the individual attorney. But legal briefs are also used as a means of persuasion. When the decision of a lower court is appealed to a higher court, the brief is intended to persuade the judges. Such briefs are more formal, and the arguments and evidence are presented in a more complete, paragraph form.

There is no one, correct way to assemble all argument briefs. However, for the beginning or the advanced student of argumentation, the brief is a practical instrument that should meet three kinds of objectives: (1) it should synthesize research on the topic, (2) it

FIGURE 8.1   *Visual Model for Early Stage of Brief*

Policy Question: Should the federal government ban all advertising for alcoholic beverages on radio and television?

   Motive Issue: Is there a significant problem of alcohol abuse in the United States?

Affirmative	Negative

1. Alcohol is a very harmful substance
   a. evid. #1—the body
   b. evid. #3—brain damage
   c. evid. #4—liver
   d. evid. #5—other
	1. Alcohol does not cause harm when used in moderation.
	   a. evid. #2—moderate use

2. Alcohol causes deaths.
   a. evid. #6—overdose
   b. evid. #8—highway
   c. evid. #9—drownings
   d. evid. #10—killings
	2. Alcohol has health benefits.
	   a. evid. #7—heart disease

3. Alcohol causes economic harm.
   a. evid. #11—total economy
   b. evid. #12—work time
   c. evid. #13—welfare costs
   d. evid. #14—property damage
	3. ???

4. Alcohol causes social harm.
   a. evid. #15—family trauma
   b. evid. #17—skid row
	4. Alcohol has social benefits.
	   a. evid. #16—breaking ice

5. Alcohol is addictive for some.
   a. evid. #18—studies
   b. evid. #19—examples
	5. ???

Notice that the affirmative side has considerably more evidence. This is not uncommon in the early stages of analysis, but it also probably reflects the truth about this issue. The affirmative is frequently in a stronger position on the motive issue. One of the values of the model is that it reveals gaps for one side or the other, and these may prompt additional inquiry. On this topic, much seems to depend on the idea of moderation in consumption of alcohol.

should serve as a storehouse of resources for developing an affirmative or negative case, and (3) it should help a debater anticipate the major arguments and evidence of the opposing side. The illustrative brief presented later in this chapter shows one way of meeting these objectives. By incorporating the major lines of argument and evidence for pro and con under each issue, this sort of brief virtually assures that students will anticipate arguments from their opponents in a debate and thus have time to think about the best answers or means of refuting them.

Rules for Constructing a Brief

The formats for briefs can vary, but the principles of logical outlining are universal. Moreover, the traditional rules for constructing briefs help to provide a clear and useful synthesis of research and analysis.

1. *The Brief Should Be Organized by Issues.* The parts of a brief should correspond to the number of issues. When the central question is one of policy, the brief will have at least four parts corresponding to the motive, obstacle, cure, and cost issues. In some cases, the brief may require the addition of the comparison or procedural issues. When the central question is either fact or value, the number of issues can vary. A first-degree murder case, for example, typically has three issues, but a burglary case may have four or five.

2. *Use Complete Sentences.* Argument claims and issues should always be stated in single, complete sentences. Because single-word topics or short phrases are useful for naming our arguments, students are sometimes tempted to use them instead of sentences as a kind of shortcut in the brief. This is a bad idea, however. First, anything less than a complete sentence does not actually express an argument claim, so a mere phrase or label can mislead us and produce fuzzy thinking. If you have difficulty in expressing a claim as a complete sentence, it means that you really have not crystallized the thought; you are uncertain about the claim of the argument. Second, complete sentences are essential in order to see the logical relationships among arguments and the issues. Phrases or one-word topics do not enable us to see how one thing supports another.

The complete sentence rule applies to issues and claims, but it may or may not be useful in relation to supporting evidence. Evidence should be expressed in complete sentences wherever possible, but statistics may require a different format, and expert opinion often cannot be limited to one sentence. We need to include enough of a quoted opinion to make it clear how it supports the claim and to avoid the problem of quoting out of context.

3. *Symbol Systems and Format Should Be Consistent.* The relationship of all components in the brief should be indicated by the consistent use of symbols and indentation. When a brief is typed as a logical outline, we need to use symbols to indicate the relationships between issues, argument claims, and evidence. When the symbols are used consistently, it is easy to see the relative importance of argument claims and evidence, and the relationships of support. Inconsistent use of symbols can produce a visual mess. There are a

variety of symbol systems, but you should use one that provides a standard, generally understood method for assigning a symbol to components at each level of the outline, commencing with the issues.

Issues should be identified with roman numerals that are placed at the left margin of the page. When the brief format includes both pro and con arguments, such as our illustrative brief later in this chapter, the major responses of the pro and con sides to each issue should be identified by the capital letters *A* and *B*, and these should be indented five spaces in relation to the roman numerals. The claims that constitute the reasons in support of the pro and con responses to the issues should be identified by the arabic numerals 1, 2, 3, and so on, and these should be indented five spaces in relation to the capital letters *A* and *B*.

Usually, the next level in the brief will be the evidence, but sometimes, in the case of a complex argument, there may be subordinate argument claims for the reasons identified with arabic numerals. In either case, items for the next level in the brief should be identified with lower case letters *a, b,* and so on, and these should be indented five spaces in relation to the arabic numerals. The result of this pattern will appear follows:

    I. (the motive issue)
        A. (pro side response to the motive issue)
            1. (first reason why pro response is true)
                a. (evidence why reason is true)
                b. (evidence why reason is true)
            2. (second reason why pro response is true)
                a. (evidence)
                b. (evidence)
            3. etc.
        B. (con side response to the motive issue)
            1. (first reason why con response is true)
                a. (evidence)
                b. (evidence)
            2. etc.

    II. (the obstacle issue)
        A. etc.
            1. etc.
        B. etc.

This pattern should continue with roman numerals III and IV for the cure and cost issues, and the numerals V and VI if there are comparison and procedural issues. This pattern provides sufficient flexibility for most briefs, but if an additional level is needed, it should be identified with the symbols *(1)*, *(2)*, and so on, and these items should be indented an additional five spaces in relation to the lower-case letters. The idea is that the relationships among items should be clear to anyone who looks at the brief.

4. *Items of Comparable Importance Should Be on the Same Level.* Statements at any given level of the brief should be comparable in importance or scope. This rule is followed easily by simply attending to the identification provided above for each level of the brief. All of the issues are comparable in importance, for example, so they all are identified by roman numerals and none is indented. Likewise, it would be confusing to place evidence at the same level as argument claims within the same portion of the brief.

5. *Follow the Rule of Logical Subordination.* Any statement in the brief should support, justify, or explain the statement to which it is subordinate. This means that a statement identified as *1* that is indented and placed under a statement at point *A* should be a *reason why* statement *A* is true or should be accepted. Thus, for example, we should not find arguments and evidence that belong to the obstacle issue placed under the motive. Suppose that the central question asks whether the United States should adopt a national competency test for high school teachers. If the pro side is arguing that there is a significant problem of poor educational achievement among high school students in the United States, all of the arguments and evidence placed under that claim should provide reasons why that it is true. The principle of logical subordination would be violated if we found arguments concerning the *causes* of poor achievement placed under the motive issue. Causes of the problem belong to the obstacle issue.

For some, this is a difficult principle to follow. To test your brief for logical subordination, you may find it helpful to ask whether each statement in the brief is *a reason for* (or a response to) the statement it is placed under.

6. *Follow the Rule of Efficiency.* Include all of the evidence that is separate and distinct for each argument claim. Students frequently find that they have some redundancy in their evidence, so that they have the same facts reported in evidence from several sources. Such redundancy is almost inevitable, and even desirable since it is hard to know in the early stages of research which sources will be the best. But there is no value in repeating the same facts in your brief. At the same time, you should include all evidence that contributes distinctive support to an argument claim.

Illustrative Brief

The brief that follows is intended to illustrate the structure, format, and relative depth of analysis needed for an excellent brief that is reasonably complete. Since the purpose of this illustration is to help you to see the relationships between issues, arguments, and evidence, the material has been compressed a bit for clarity and documentation has been omitted. A complete illustrative brief, in final form with its bibliography, is included in Appendix E. As you examine this illustration, notice especially how the negative side for each issue tries to provide a response to affirmative arguments. Notice as well the variety in the kinds of harms under motive, and the various kinds of costs or disadvantages under the cost issue.

Argument and Evidence Brief

Policy Question: Should the possession and use of all alcoholic beverages be banned on the campus?

I. Is there a significant problem of alcohol abuse on campus?
    A. Advocates of a ban on alcohol argue that alcohol abuse is a serious problem on campus.
        1. The student body consumes enormous amounts of alcohol.
           a. The Walker study found that 88.7 percent of the student body consumes alcohol.
           b. The Walker study also found that 54.2 percent of students on campus drink from 1 to 3 times a week.
           c. The Hill and Bugen study found that men were twice as likely to drink 4 to 5 drinks at each episode than were women.
        2. The heavy drinking syndrome seems to be self-perpetuating among students.
           a. A study by Doyle surveyed freshmen and found that 88 percent drink alcohol.
           b. Many students in the Doyle study reported that it was difficult to abstain at the university because all of the other students seem to drink.
        3. Increasing numbers of students on campus are becoming alcoholics.
           a. Campus officials at the student health center report that the number of students with problems of alcoholism has been increasing over the past five years.
           b. Student Assistants from the dorms report more alcoholics this year than last.

4. Alcohol use is a major factor in auto accidents involving university students.
   a. Statistics from the university police and the city police show that alcohol was a factor in 70 percent of the accidents involving students last year.
   b. Local insurance agencies report that alcohol is almost always involved in the more serious accidents involving university student drivers.
5. Alcohol use is a major source of the problems students experience with roommates and other students in the dorms.
   a. The Walker study reported that students' fights with roommates involved alcohol in the majority of cases.
   b. The Student Assistants Association reports that alcohol is almost always a factor in the more serious interpersonal problems in the dorms.
6. Alcohol abuse is a major factor in academic problems of students.
   a. A study of party noise reported that many students said that they could not study in their dorms on weekends due to parties involving the drinking of alcohol.
   b. A survey of students on academic probation revealed that alcohol abuse is a major cause of academic difficulty for some of the students.
7. Alcohol abuse has been one of the major problems associated with the Spring Fest.
   a. The campus police chief said that every instance of property damage and excessive noise complaints involved excessive drinking.
   b. A report of the Faculty Council Committee on Student Life identified the problem of alcohol abuse as part of its rationale for abolishing the Spring Fest.
B. Opponents argue that the problems of alcohol abuse on campus have been exaggerated.
   1. The extent of alcohol consumption at the university is about the same as at other universities of comparable size and atmosphere.
      a. A study at the University of Maryland reported that 87 percent of the students drink alcohol.
      b. A survey at Iowa found that 92 percent of the students consume alcohol.
   2. Student drinking habits seem to be relatively stable over time.

    a. Studies of student drinking in the 1960s showed essentially the same levels of beer consumption per student as we see now.

    b. The former head of the student center says, if anything, students nowadays seem to be less wild in their drinking of alcohol.

3. Although alcoholism is a serious problem, it does not seem to be related to the level of drinking at this university.

    a. The number of alcoholics per thousand college students is approximately the same as for noncollege people of the same age.

    b. An expert on the disease of alcoholism says that there is no clear evidence that partying at the university causes students to become alcoholics.

4. The relationship between alcohol and auto accidents is the same for all young people.

    a. Statistics on the incidence of alcohol-related accidents among 18- to 20-year-olds in the United States are essentially the same as those for university students.

    b. A local insurance executive says he finds no difference between university students and other young people in the number of alcohol-related accidents.

5. The relationship between alcohol and interpersonal problems among dorm residents is not clear.

    a. Some Student Assistants say that roommate fights occur with or without alcohol. Boyfriend and girlfriend visitations are often the cause of roommate fights.

    b. A social worker says the problem is irresponsible drinking rather than drinking per se.

6. The relationship between alcohol consumption and academic problems is not clear.

    a. One psychologist in the Counseling Center says that moderate drinking may help to relieve the stress of academic pressure and test anxiety.

    b. A local fraternity president says that alcohol does not cause poor grades; rather, poor grades cause drinking.

7. The problems of alcohol abuse associated with the Spring Fest are unclear in recent years.

      a. Data on the arrests for the last five Spring Fest weekends indicate that many of those arrested were not university students.

      b. The former director of the student center says that steady progress has been made in curbing alcohol abuse during the Fest.

II. Are the present policies governing alcohol consumption on the campus responsible for the problems of alcohol abuse?

    A. Advocates of a ban argue that present policies either encourage alcohol abuse or do nothing to prevent it.

      1. The absence of a formal drinking policy results in an atmosphere that supports excessive drinking.

        a. Dorm policy on hard liquor is essentially "out-of-sight, out-of-mind."

          (1) Students under the age of 21 conceal and consume hard liquor in their rooms.

          (2) Student Assistants make no effort to stop underage drinking unless they see it.

        b. Students are allowed to have beer in the dorms, the student center, and on the campus grounds during Spring Fest.

      2. A number of university-sanctioned activities actually promote alcohol consumption.

        a. Dorm parties provide free beer, and many students are inclined to take advantage of anything that is free in order to get their "share."

        b. Beer is sold to students in the student center, which operates under the authority of the governing board.

        c. Beer companies are allowed to promote their beverages in a variety of programs on campus.

      3. University officials have opposed raising the state drinking age to 21.

    B. Opponents of the ban argue that alcohol abuse on campus is caused by many other factors unrelated to university policy.

      1. The atmosphere that supports drinking pervades the entire society; it is not the result of lax rules at the university.

        a. The Assistant Residence Hall Director said he found that a dry campus has about the same problems of alcohol abuse as this university.

        b. A sociologist says that heavy use of alcohol is the cultural norm.

2. University policy places the responsibility for drinking where it belongs—with the individual.
    a. The Assistant Residence Hall Director said that students need to learn that they are responsible for their use of alcohol.
    b. Resident hall parties provide a choice to students by making alternative beverages available; students are not forced to drink beer.
3. The problem of alcohol abuse is caused by many other factors.
    a. (evidence—quotation from alcohol abuse expert who states that alcoholism is a disease, and that some people become alcoholics with their first drink.)
    b. (evidence—quotation from sociologist who states that use of alcohol is caused by peer pressure.)
    c. (evidence—quotation from psychologist who states that the glorification of alcohol use in the film and television media contributes to alcohol abuse among youth.)

III. Will a ban on the possession and use of all alcohol beverages solve the problems of alcohol abuse at the university?
   A. Advocates of a ban argue that it would help to reduce many of the problems of alcohol abuse.
      1. Some students think it would provide a better climate for the pursuit of educational goals.
          a. One female dorm resident said, "If we could get rid of those Friday and Saturday night partyers, we'd all get a lot more study time in."
          b. (evidence—quotation from a Student Assistant on his experiences in a nondrinking dorm floor.)
      2. Some university officials believe it would reduce auto accidents and other student problems with the law.
          a. A police sergeant says, "After 8 1/2 years on the department, I've seen a lot of kids who wouldn't have gotten in trouble if they hadn't been drinking."
          b. (evidence—quotation from staff member of the residence halls that students who do not drink have fewer auto accidents.)
      3. A ban would reduce the amount of alcohol consumed on campus.
          a. Currently, beer sales on campus amount to almost $200,000 per year, and this would be ended.
          b. The elimination of beer for dorm parties would reduce beer consumption.

         c. A ban on possession would significantly reduce consumption.

    4. Even if alcoholism were not reduced, it would at least not be abetted by university policy.

  B. Opponents of the ban argue that it would not solve any of the significant problems.

    1. There is no clear evidence that the quantities of alcohol consumed would be decreased.

        a. The number of bars and liquor outlets in the vicinity of campus would not be reduced, and they would reap a bonanza of increased sales.

        b. (evidence—statistics on beer consumption for "dry" campuses in comparison to "wet.")

    2. A ban on possession and use is almost impossible to enforce without the use of unthinkable "police-state" methods.

        a. Dorm rooms would have to be searched on a regular basis to stop concealment and consumption of liquor.

        b. Informers would have to be employed.

    3. There would be no net reduction in auto accidents.

        a. (evidence)

        b. (evidence)

    4. There is no evidence that alcoholism among students at the university would be reduced.

    5. There is no evidence that alcohol-related academic problems would be reduced.

    6. Past experience with Spring Fest indicates that problems of alcohol abuse are worse when beer is not available on campus.

        a. The former director of the student center said, "At the last Spring Fest without beer, we pretty much lost control. Hundreds of drunk students packed downtown bars, and the weekend was near riot-level in the city. No one in their right mind wants to encourage this."

        b. (evidence—quotation from a city police that Spring Fest drinking is easier to control on campus.)

IV. Will the benefits of reducing alcohol abuse justify the costs of a ban on possession and use of alcohol at the university?

  A. Advocates of the ban say the benefits of reduced use and availability of alcohol would outweigh any costs of a ban.

    1. Although it might take some time, eventually the consumption of alcohol by students would be reduced significantly.

      a. New freshmen would not be entering an "alcohol-approving" environment.

      b. The dorms, at least, would not be the site of drunken parties.

  2. The university would not be in the position of abetting alcohol abuse among students.

  3. Any loss of revenue from beer sales is insignificant in comparison to the well-being of the students.

  4. The enforcement of a ban need not result in any significant violations of the civil rights of students.

      a. (evidence—quotation from a student leader from a campus with an alcohol ban, stating that most students simply follow the rules.)

      b. (evidence—quotation from a university president citing the lack of any student complaints about the alcohol ban.)

  5. The rights of some students, whose religious convictions make beer consumption a sin, would be enhanced, whereas the rights of other students would not be significantly reduced.

B. Opponents argue that the disadvantages from a ban on alcohol far outweigh any alleged benefits.

  1. The ban is subject to an enforcement dilemma.

      a. Serious enforcement of the ban would result in a "police-state" environment.

      b. Lax enforcement would simply encourage students to break the rules, and this could lead to problems in compliance with other university rules.

  2. The university does not now "abet" problems of alcohol abuse, any more than the laws of the state "abet" alcohol abuse.

      a. University policies place responsibility on the individual, in the same way that society places responsibility on the individual.

      b. The principle that the university abets any undesirable behavior unless it expressly prohibits it is absurd.

  3. The university would suffer financial loss.

  4. The ban could result in more alcohol-related accidents.

      a. Inability to get a beer on campus would inevitably drive some students to bars off campus.

      b. An increase in the number of students driving to and from bars probably would increase the number of alcohol-related accidents.

    5. A ban on alcohol would diminish the joy of college life.
      a. One of the joys of college life is the sense of being treated as an adult.
      b. Some may not understand it, but having a beer in the congenial atmosphere of college is one of the adult joys that students prize.
    6. It is a basic injustice to punish the many for the sins of the few.
      a. Most students are responsible drinkers.
      b. The ban punishes everyone, not just the irresponsible.

Summary

1. The brief is a complete logical outline of all the issues, arguments, and evidence for a central question of fact, value, or policy. Since briefs serve different purposes, their formats can vary, but there are three general objectives for beginning students: (1) to synthesize research, (2) to serve as a storehouse of resources for case development, and (3) to anticipate opposing arguments and evidence in preparing for a debate.

2. Six rules for constructing briefs help us to develop a clear logical outline of arguments and evidence:

    a. The parts of a brief should correspond to the number of issues in the central question in dispute.
    b. Use of complete sentences clarifies claims and supporting reasons, and enables us to determine logical relationships in the brief.
    c. Symbol systems and format for the brief should be consistent so that it is easy to find issues, arguments, and evidence. Issues, for example, are always identified by roman numerals.
    d. Items of comparable importance should be placed on the same level in the brief. Thus, major reasons in support of the pro side's response to an issue should appear on the same level and should not be mixed with supporting evidence.
    e. The rule of logical subordination says that anything that is placed under another item in the brief should either explain it or provide a reason why it is true or should be accepted.
    f. The rule of efficiency suggests that we avoid redundancy and include only the evidence that provides distinctive support for each argument claim.

Exercises

1. As a class project, select one of the following central questions and outline the issues and major lines of argument that might be available to each side:

   a. Should the university increase its requirement in English composition?

   b. Should the university require all students to enroll in a course in human diversity?

   c. Did the U.S. government betray the Kurds in their fight to overthrow the government of Saddam Hussein in Iraq?

   d. Does the decline in SAT and ACT scores since the 1960s reveal a decline in the level of education among college-bound high school students?

2. Prepare a brief on a central question selected for class debates. It may help you to look to the brief in Appendix E for a model.

3. Outline the arguments and evidence in an article in an opinion magazine. Magazines such as the *New Republic* or the *National Review* are especially useful, but you may also find interesting articles for this purpose in science or sports magazines.

9

Procedural Rules in Advocacy

Central Ideas in This Chapter

1. Understanding the process of advocacy requires a grasp of three kinds of rules:
   - Constitutive and regulative
   - Presumption and burden of proof
   - Debate rules
2. Constitutive rules define concepts, moves, and behaviors in rhetoric and argumentation.
3. Regulative rules govern behavior, indicating what is prohibited, required, or permitted.
4. Presumption is an automatic decision rule that tells us what to consider correct in the case of a tie in the argument.
5. Burden of proof tells the advocates what must be proven and who must do it.
6. A case is prima facie when it initially meets the burden of proof.
7. Existing beliefs or policies usually have the advantage of presumption, but social institutions govern the rules of presumption and burden of proof.
8. The general rules of debate enable us to focus on the purposes of advocacy and adjust specific rules so that debates are useful, fair, and illuminating.

Making sense of persuasion in conflict requires a clear grasp of both *structure* and *process*. In Chapter 2, we analyzed the structure of conflict by breaking it down into its component parts and examining their relationships to each other. According to this view, the substance of a conflict has a kind of whole-part structure: A central question represents a dispute as a whole, and its parts consist of issues, arguments, and evidence, respectively. However, when we shift our focus from the *substance* (what a dispute is about) to the *process* of argumentation and persuasion in conflicts, we need another way of making sense of conflict.

Process is concerned with the actions and moves of the persuaders in a dispute. Thus, to make sense of the process of argumentation is to grasp the rules that govern the actions of advocates in disputes, enabling them to understand their moves and counter-moves in more or less the same way that the rules of a game clarify the behavior of its players.

One of the more productive analytical perspectives in contemporary social psychiatry is the notion that human communication, like game activities, is *rule governed*. This is not to suggest that communication is a frivolous process or that the term *game* implies only an entertainment activity—though there certainly are some kinds of communication that are entertaining and frivolous. Rather, as Eric Berne put it in his provocative book, *Games People Play*, "Significant social intercourse most commonly takes the form of games."[1] For Berne and his colleagues in psychiatry, analysis of communication games and their rules provides a powerful means of understanding transactions among people (which is one way of thinking about persuasion). The game perspective suggests that persuasive argument is a rule-governed activity, and if we want to make sense of argument tactics and strategy, we must learn the rules of various argument "games."

The purpose of this chapter is to survey three important categories of rules that illuminate the process of argumentation and enable us to begin thinking strategically about how advocates attempt to persuade others by means of argument:

1. Constitutive and regulative rules
2. The rules of presumption and burden of proof
3. The general rules for debate

Constitutive and Regulative Rules

Rules perform two major functions in any sort of game: (1) they *constitute*, or define, the important elements of a game and (2) they *regulate*, or govern, the behavior of the participants. Let's begin by looking at these two functions of rules in games that all of us know reasonably well, and then we will look at them in relation to the process of persuasive argumentation in conflict.

Constitutive Rules Define Elements

By defining all of the important elements in a game, constitutive rules essentially tell us what game we are playing. In the game of football, for example, constitutive rules define such things as a *touchdown*, *field goal*, *offsides*, *roughing the kicker*, and all of the other elements that would differentiate this game from, say, soccer, basketball, or other ball games. Constitutive rules are not limited to games played with a ball, however.

All games seem to require rules that define their elements. Consider the constitutive rules we need to understand in order to play any of a number of board games. In chess, constitutive rules define *check*, *checkmate*, the kinds of chess pieces and their powers of movement, features of the chessboard, and all of the elements of chess that make it different from other board games, such as checkers. If you think about it, any kind of game we can imagine will need constitutive rules to define its concepts, moves, methods of scoring, termination points, and so forth. When we say we understand or know how to play a certain game, we mean at the very least that we understand the constitutive rules that define its elements.

Definitions May Seem to Be Arbitrary
Particular constitutive rules are, of course, arbitrary in a sense. In U.S. interscholastic and professional football, for example, a constitutive rule decrees that the proper length of the playing field is 100 yards. Why 100 yards? Why not 200? Our Canadian neighbors have adopted a constitutive rule that decrees a field of 110 yards for their professional football games. Moreover, when enthusiasts in our country play touch football in a backyard or at a park, the length of the playing field usually is decided by the adoption of a constitutive rule on the spot—and the rule typically will define a playing field of substantially less than 100 yards.

Definitions and Good Reasons
The constitutive rules that define elements of chess and other games can vary at least as widely as our example of the rule for a football field. However, to say that constitutive rules are, in one sense, arbitrary is not to say that they lack a rational foundation. Constitutive rules are arbitrary only in the sense that they are not fixed by natural laws of the universe; they can be framed in alternative ways. But there are usually good reasons for framing a constitutive rule in one

way rather than another. The good reasons for the length of our touch football field, for example, may include such rational factors as natural barriers (trees and rocks), available space, and the age of the players.

Constitutive Rules in Rhetoric
and Argumentation

Constitutive rules are abundant in rhetoric and argumentation, and we have examined a number of them in preceding chapters. In Chapters 1 and 2 in particular, I presented constitutive rules in defining terms such as *rhetoric, central question, issue, argument,* and *evidence.* And in the case of *rhetoric* and *argument,* I surveyed some of the alternative definitions or constitutive rules for these terms, along with the consequences of the alternatives. Like the various constitutive rules for the length of football fields, the definitions adopted for the core concepts of rhetoric and argumentation tell us, in effect, what game of persuasion we are playing.

To extend our game analogy, alternative definitions of rhetoric yield different conceptions of an art of persuasive discourse just as variations in the constitutive rules for football yield different games of football. We have already noted the enormous difference between the "games" of rhetoric as defined by contemporary U.S. politicians and the rhetoric defined by Aristotle. Are the differences in the definitions arbitrary? Well, yes, in the sense that certainly it is possible to define rhetoric in various ways, and we can decide to adopt one definition or the other. But there is also a rational foundation—a set of good reasons—for adopting one definition rather than another.

Aristotle's definition of *rhetoric* delineates an art that is essential for any citizen of a democratic society. A faculty of discerning the available means of persuasion enables citizens to distinguish good arguments from bad and to recognize unethical persuasion. Thus, if we did not have the term *rhetoric* for Aristotle's conception, we would need to find another term to represent it. In contrast, the definition of *rhetoric* that is implied when politicians and journalists use it to refer to unethical persuasion seems confused: It mistakes unethical uses of persuasive principles for the knowledge of the principles, which is tantamount to confusing torture, an evil use of medical knowledge, with the art of medicine.

As you deepen your understanding of the constitutive rules for rhetoric and argumentation, you should attempt to get beyond merely the definitions that are offered in this or any other textbook and to understand the reasons for preferring one conception of a constitutive rule to another.

Regulative Rules Govern Behavior

Regulative rules are intended to govern the behavior of participants in a game. Although they are closely connected to the constitutive rules that define elements, concepts, and behaviors in a game, regulative rules govern or guide the behavior of participants by indicating (1) what is *required*, (2) what is *prohibited*, and (3) what is *permitted* in a game.

Recall in our example of football that constitutive rules define such actions as *roughing the kicker*. That is, the rule would tell us what constitutes roughing as opposed to, say, insulting the kicker. A regulative rule, in turn, would indicate whether the defined behavior of roughing is required, permitted, or prohibited. At present, regulative rules in football stipulate that roughing the kicker is *prohibited*, but for much of this century, roughing the kicker was permitted.

A great deal of violence is *permitted* in U.S. football if it occurs after the ball is put in play and before an official signals the end of a play by blowing a whistle. Regulative rules also permit a wide range of strategies, substitutions, and plays. For example, teams are not required to pass the ball nor to run with it—and they frequently will elect to do neither if they hold a commanding lead in the waning seconds of a game. However, some behaviors are *required*. Thus, in order to initiate a play, the ball must be snapped by a center to a player in the backfield, usually the quarterback.

Regulative rules, like constitutive, are universal in all games and are essential in order to understand how a game is played. Have you ever observed young children attempt to play a game like chess? Usually they have some notion of the rules of play, having watched adults staring intently at a chessboard, but their ideas about what sorts of behaviors are permitted, required, and prohibited are seldom consistent with standard chess rules. The result can be entertaining. If the children are old enough to grasp the idea of regulative rules, they may invent a set that permits them a shared sense of an interesting game that they call *chess*, even though they are the only players in the world who know its unique rules.

Regulative Rules and Good Reasons

There is an arbitrary quality to regulative rules, which is reminiscent of the sense of alternative choice we found with constitutive rules. That is, if we have a rule concerning some sort of defined behavior, we have a choice as to whether our rule will prohibit, require, or permit the behavior—and the choice is discretionary, based on the preferences of the parties involved. Once again, this is not to say the choice is without a rational foundation of good reasons, however. The decision to prohibit roughing the kicker in U.S. football seems to be based on the sound reasons that too many kickers were getting injured, and injuries per se are considered an undesirable feature of the game.

Argumentation Rules in Institutional Context

The number of regulative rules in persuasive processes, as well as their relative importance, seems to depend on the context within which the persuasion takes place and the power of a rule-enforcing agency. When persuasive argument is presented in an institutionalized setting, such as a courtroom, there tend to be large numbers of formal regulative rules governing the behavior of participants, and the enforcer of the rules is principally a judge. Attorneys, witnesses, the defendant, and any observers are subject to rules that permit, require, or prohibit a wide range of behaviors. For example, attorneys are *required* to follow rules of courtroom decorum, rules for the introduction of evidence, and rules for the questioning of witnesses. At the same time, regulative rules of the judicial system *prohibit* particular behaviors and practices, even though they might be persuasive to a jury. Thus, the rules may prohibit the introduction of certain forms of evidence that could be persuasive to a jury: Examples include illegally obtained evidence, prior sexual behavior of an alleged victim of sexual assault, and prior arrest record of a defendant.

In general, the regulative rules that require or prohibit behavior are more readily apparent than the rules that permit behavior. In most institutionalized circumstances, such as courts and legislative bodies, advocates are permitted to do or not do whatever is neither prohibited nor required in the rules. A defense attorney has a choice, for example, as to whether the defendant should testify in his or her own behalf, and each side is permitted an enormous range of choice in the selection of arguments used to persuade a jury.

Institutionalized settings for persuasive argument, such as courtrooms, give heavy weight to regulative rules, so much so that judges are often reluctant to allow defendants to plead their own cases without the professional assistance of attorneys. However, we should not make the mistake of thinking that regulative rules are important only in courts; they operate in all persuasive situations.

Rules in Informal Context

Consider the importance of rules of decorum in persuasive arguments with your parents. Most parents are willing to participate in persuasive argument with their children, and some parents are fairly flexible in their willingness to tolerate heated argument. But few parents are willing to tolerate a lack of respect from their children. What constitutes lack of respect may be defined in somewhat different ways, but its regulative rule is generally that it is prohibited. In almost any situation we can imagine where persuasive argument is used, there are rules of decorum that govern the way we present arguments, as well as what kinds of arguments are permitted or prohibited.

Variations in parental style lead to an extraordinary range of methods for communicating to children that they have crossed a threshold, violating family standards of "appropriate" argumentation. Some mothers use the guilt method effectively; others are better with threats or angry expressions, such as, "You can't talk to *me* that way, you little devil!" Parents and other family members generally have ways of indicating when a family rule governing behavior in argumentation has been violated. And there is almost always at least an implied sanction: Unless the violation of the rule is repaired in some way, perhaps with an apology, no persuasion is possible.

Regulative rules governing the process of persuasive argument with family, friends, coworkers, and even employers usually are informal, meaning they are not formally written down anywhere, or voted on, or even directly enacted. In some cases, parents may formally articulate rules for appropriate argumentation to their children, such as, "I don't care how angry you are, you can't use that tone of voice with me." And most of us, at some time, have had friends object to our manner of arguing, or even a particular kind of argument, by stating a rule of fairness, such as, "It isn't fair to reject all of my authoritative evidence as simply 'opinion' and then insist that your authorities must be accepted." But the more typical situation is that the rules for arguing with parents and friends are unstated; they are simply understood by all of the members of a family or among a group of friends.

Regulative rules governing persuasive argument can vary widely from one context to another. There is an enormous difference between the rules for persuasive argument in a formal debate before an audience and the sort of informal debate we enjoy with our friends. And the rules for formal debate also vary from one setting or institution to another. For example, the rules governing debate in the U.S. House of Representatives are somewhat different from the rules of debate for the U.S. Senate. We shall explore some of these differences in our discussion of the rules governing debate format and decorum, but here we shall begin with two of the more universal formal rules: the rules of presumption and burden of proof.

Presumption and Burden of Proof

One of the troublesome features of argumentation in the process of social conflict is that argument exchanges are frequently *inconclu-*

sive. That is, an impasse results when neither side of a dispute provides a set of persuasive arguments sufficiently strong enough to settle the matter. In our arguments with family or friends, settling the matter usually means that one side or the other voluntarily agrees that his or her argument is in error or that the good reasons of the opponent must prevail because of their superior strength, soundness, or wisdom. (The agreement must be voluntary if we are talking about a *persuasive* process.) But what do we do when the good reasons from both sides are thought to lack such strength, soundness, or wisdom? What happens if neither side is willing to concede? How do we decide or even terminate a dispute if there is a tie in the arguments and evidence from each side?

Lewis Coser suggests that the natural tendency of social conflict is to continue and even to escalate.[2] We need not look very far to see evidence for Coser's position. Whenever we have a disagreement with a friend or a family member, our egos quickly become involved and it is hard to admit that we are in error or that the other person is more correct than we are. So, in many cases, we either continue the argument or we elect to terminate the dispute by some form of avoidance: One or both simply stop talking about the matter or cease contact with the other person. But what if the dispute must be settled with a decision, one way or another? In some situations we are simply unable to avoid a disagreement; a decision must be made.

If we want to terminate a dispute on rational grounds, we must have rules that tell us how to do this, and the rules must be understood by advocates for each side. Such rules would inform the advocates what is required of them in the way of arguments and evidence and would spell out what will be decided if there is a tie—or when neither side manages to present a superior persuasive case. There are a number of rules that perform these functions, but we will commence here with two of the most important: the rules of presumption and burden of proof.

Presumption

Like most rules, the rule of presumption has both a constitutive and a regulative dimension. What is a rule of presumption? This question directs us to the constitutive dimension, and we define the rule as follows:

> *Presumption:* An automatic decision rule that governs which beliefs or policies will be considered correct unless rejected by positive action

This definition is necessarily broad because it is intended to cover all of the presumption rules in various institutions, such as courts and legislatures, as well as informal settings, like our arguments with friends. However, we can clarify the definition by examining its three component parts.

1. *Presumption Is an Automatic Decision Rule.* This element of the definition suggests that the purpose of any rule of presumption is to provide an automatic decision whenever there is an impasse (or a tie) in the arguments from the advocates. In some situations, a decision must be rendered. Criminal courts, for example, must at some point say either guilty or not guilty. They cannot avoid decision forever the way some married couples seem to do. Thus, a rule of presumption ensures that a decision will be reached when arguments and evidence are inconclusive.

2. *Presumption Governs Which Beliefs or Policies Will Be Considered Correct.* Whenever there is a dispute over a central question of fact, value, or policy, a rule of presumption tells us to automatically accept one side or the other in the case of an impasse or a tie. In other words, if a dispute concerns a question of fact (for example: Did Smith kill Jones?), a rule of presumption would specify, in the absence of convincing proof, which of two possible beliefs or judgments will be considered as correct (Smith killed Jones or Smith did not kill Jones).

The word *considered* is important here. It means that we will behave in all practical ways as though the belief selected by our presumption is really correct, but not because we know it is true. To *consider* a belief correct means that we accept it because *we do not know* it is false, and we think it is better to err in one direction rather than the other.

In our criminal courts, we have adopted a particular regulative rule of presumption that dictates that a defendant will be presumed innocent until proven guilty. This means that of the two possible beliefs about Smith—that he killed and that he did not kill—the latter belief will be considered correct unless and until the prosecution proves Smith is guilty. Our system of justice is based on the idea that if evidence is inconclusive, it is better to err by allowing a guilty person to go free than to convict an innocent person.

3. *Unless Rejected by Positive Action.* This phrase means that a belief or a policy is to be presumed or considered correct only so long as we do not make a decision to reject it. Thus, the presumption of innocence for our hapless defendant, Smith, would continue only up to the point that a court *decides* that he is guilty. A verdict

from a court is what we mean by a positive action. Once a guilty verdict has been rendered, there would be a new presumption —namely, that Smith did kill Jones.

Our analysis of presumption has been focused thus far on its operation in institutions like courts of law, but the same elements can be seen in its function in a legislative body. In a policy dispute, a rule of presumption indicates whether the existing policy or the proposed policy will be considered correct. You may notice that our definition does not require a presumption in favor of present policy— it stipulates only that we must consider either the present or the proposed policy as correct. However, a presumption in favor of proposed policies certainly would confuse debate in a legislative body, not to mention the confusion it would create in the meaning of votes on proposals. In legislative bodies, as a practical matter, existing laws continue in effect until they are changed, and a new policy does not go into effect until it is enacted by a positive vote. This means that if no action is taken, either because the legislature postpones decision or merely fails to bring a matter to a vote, existing laws or policies will continue in effect. So, in debates over questions of policy, present policy usually is presumed correct until it is rejected by a positive action—namely, a vote.

One of the useful ways of thinking about regulative rules of presumption in society is that they usually favor the *status quo*, a Latin term that means the existing state of affairs, or whatever belief or policy was thought to be correct before the outset of a dispute.

Burden of Proof

The rule concept of burden of proof, like the rule of presumption, has both a constitutive and a regulative dimension. What is burden of proof? This question calls for a constitutive rule that defines this concept:

> *Burden of Proof*: A rule that stipulates and assigns requirements for overturning the presumption on a belief or policy

Notice that the definition for the burden of proof concept initially includes the idea of presumption. This means that it will be intelligible only if we begin with a solid grasp of presumption. But we can clarify the definition by examining its two principal components.

1. *Burden of Proof Is a Rule That Stipulates Requirements for Overturning the Presumption.* An advocate who has the task of trying to overturn a belief or policy presumed to be correct needs to know

what must be done or proved in order to do that. If a defendant is presumed innocent until proven guilty, then a prosecutor needs to know what is meant by proof of guilt in relation to a particular charge.

In general, burden of proof is stipulated by a *statement of the issues*. If a dispute is about a criminal charge, the burden of proof is precisely delineated by the issues or the vital questions that are inherent in the charge against the defendant. Thus, in our example of the charge of first-degree murder against the defendant Smith, the three defining elements of first-degree murder yield three issues that indicate precisely what must be proved:

a. Did Smith kill Jones?
b. Was the killing intended?
c. Was the killing premeditated?

Notice, however, that although the issues indicate *what* must be proved, they do not tell us *who* must do it. Must the prosecution prove an answer of yes, or must the defense prove an answer of no.

2. *Burden of Proof Rules Assign the Requirements for Overturning the Presumption.* Assigning the task of proving to one side or the other is the second vital element in a burden of proof rule. In other words, the rule tells us who has the burden, which is indicated by the issues. Usually, the advocates of change in belief or policy are assigned the burden of proving that the new belief or policy is warranted. In our criminal courts, the advocate of change is the prosecution. So, in our murder case, the prosecution must respond yes to all of the issues and must provide sufficient argument and evidence to support each response of yes. Similarly, if the charge were, say, vehicular assault, the issues would derive from the elements that constitute the definition of vehicular assault, and the prosecution would be required to establish a yes response to each of the issues.

In disputes over policy questions, burden of proof is stipulated (or made specific) by the categories of the stock issues, and advocates of change are required to support a response of yes to the specific issues derived from the stock issue categories. If some of the issues are not contested by the opponents of change, either because they agree with the pro side or because they regard a particular issue as unimportant or uncontroversial, the burden of proof for the advocates of the new policy is accordingly narrowed to whatever issues are contested.

Issues clarify the burden of advocates by stipulating what must be established, but they fall short in one important respect: The issues do not tell us *how much* argument or evidence will be required from a prosecutor in order to prove or establish the yes response for each issue. This is a thorny problem. We say the prosecution must support a response of yes to each issue, but it is up to the jury to decide whether the support provided is adequate. In effect, each juror must be persuaded that the evidence is adequate, and any method we use to specify a level of proof required from the prosecution must necessarily be applied by a jury. However, we do provide juries with standards for determining whether the evidence and argumentation is sufficient or insufficient in relation to the issues.

The Prima Facie Case Standard of Proof

In our courts, we try to objectify the level of support required in relation to the issues by saying that the advocates of change (the prosecution in criminal matters) must provide a prima facie case. The term *prima facie* means a case that, "on the face of it" or "at first look," would be considered sufficient to meet the burden of proof by any reasonable person, at least until it is refuted by opponents of change. Thus, if Harry Thug is on trial for burglary, the prosecution must respond yes to two issues:

1. Did Mr. Thug break into building X?
2. Did Mr. Thug enter the building to commit a theft or other felony?

A prima facie case supports an answer of yes to each issue with argument and evidence at a level that would be accepted by a reasonable person unless or until the arguments and evidence are refuted. Failure to support any of the issues would mean that the prosecution has failed to meet its burden of proof or, to put it in the more formal way, the prosecution has failed to present a prima facie case.

Other Burden of Proof Standards

In our criminal courts, we do not say that the prosecution must support a yes response to each issue to a level of *certainty*. Rather, we say the prosecution must support its yes response to each issue to a level of *beyond reasonable doubt*. Of course, such a standard must be applied by each juror. But we assume a kind of broad cultural agreement on what *beyond reasonable doubt* means and we also assume that a jury of 12 will develop a consensus on its meaning that is fair. Moreover, the consensus of one jury is thought to approximate what another such jury would develop in relation to the same case.

The standard for *beyond reasonable doubt* is less than *certainty*, but a somewhat higher level than the standard used for trials in our civil courts, which is called the standard of a *preponderance of evidence*. If it were possible to present these standards in numerical terms, we could approximate their difference by saying that *beyond reasonable doubt* means that the evidence makes us, say, 95 percent sure that a defendant is guilty. Preponderance of evidence would mean that evidence from the plaintiff is judged to be stronger than evidence from the defense—by a margin of, say, 55 to 45 percent. In reality, however, each juror must decide what *beyond reasonable doubt* and *preponderance of evidence* means in relation to each case.

Applying Rules of Presumption and Burden of Proof

Now that we have sketched general definitions for *presumption* and *burden of proof*, we are in a position to examine how these rules operate to govern behavior in disputes.

Regulation of Speaking Order

One practical consequence of presumption and burden of proof is that their assignment dictates format whenever argumentation occurs in a rule-governed setting. Since a defendant is presumed to be innocent until proven guilty, the prosecution must open a trial and must provide an adequate case in relation to the issues before the defense needs to say anything. Likewise, in policy debates, the burden of proof is on the side that advocates a change from the present policy or system. This means that advocates of change should speak first, at least outlining their arguments and evidence in relation to the issues before the con side replies. If the pro side is unable to provide argument and evidence to support a response of yes to any of the issues, the rule of presumption would award the issue to the con side, and the loss of any one issue, as we have seen, is sufficient to defeat a proposed change.

Rules of Presumption Are Fixed by Social Institutions

It should be apparent to you that it can be a major advantage for an advocate to have presumption on his or her side in a dispute, but does the advocate ever have anything to say about what will be presumed correct, or is this always dictated by the situation? In general, presumption and burden of proof are more likely to be fixed and beyond the control of advocates whenever disputes are managed and resolved in a social institution like a court or a legislative body. Institutions are required in order to determine and enforce rules of any sort. Thus, in the less formal or rule-governed disputes we have as we argue with family and friends, it becomes less clear what has presumption, if anything, and who must bear a burden of proof.

In an argument with your parents over a policy question, such as whether they should purchase a new sports car for you, their presumption might be that your old car (the present system) is adequate to your needs until proven otherwise. You would probably expect to have the burden of proof on all four of the issues of motive, obstacle, cure, and cost—and the comparison issue could surface if your parents suggested a used car in place of the new model you have in mind. This sort of policy dispute makes the application of presumption and burden of proof reasonably clear. But what if the policy dispute is over what college you should attend or what your major should be? If you are in college and have declared a major, we would expect that presumption would consider these as correct choices until proven otherwise. But what if you are not yet in college or have not yet declared a major? When there does not seem to be a present belief or policy or when it is not clear what present policy is, presumption and burden of proof rules may not be available.

Most rules of presumption are framed in favor of existing beliefs or policies, probably because it is simply more sensible to consider our present beliefs and policies (actions, etc.) as correct than to be always in a posture of questioning everything. And it would be downright dangerous to presume that any proposed change or new action is correct until proven otherwise. But one of the tricky elements in applying these rules is in recognizing the difference between a proposed new belief or policy and an established belief or policy. However, if we realize that presumption and burden of proof rules are almost always important in our informal arguments, we are in a better position to gain the advantages of presumption and to prevent others from unfairly placing the burden of proof on us.

Unfair Attempts to Shift Burden of Proof

Have you ever had the experience of being wrongly accused of cheating, or stealing, or lying? It is a disconcerting experience. We know that in our courts an accused is presumed innocent until proven guilty, but does this rule of presumption also operate in our families, our schools, or our workplaces? Suppose you were accused of cheating on an examination. Would the accuser need to prove you cheated or would you need to prove you did not cheat? It makes a great deal of difference, and universities seem to vary in their assignment of presumption and burden of proof in such cases. If the rules permit it, you would be well advised to point out that you should be presumed innocent until proven guilty.

It is also important to recognize that your opponents in arguments will sometimes attempt to usurp presumption and shift the burden of proof to you. Suppose you are in an argument with the local leader of a group advocating that marijuana be legalized, and she presents this sort of statement:

> The fact that marijuana is harmless is well known. If you want to argue that marijuana is harmful, you're going to have to prove it.

You should recognize that this is a classic attempt to claim presumption for a proposed new belief. Some people believe marijuana is harmless, but the official position of society is that it is harmful, and the official position (or majority position) normally has the presumption. You should inform your opponent that she has the burden of proof for her assertions and that she cannot shift the burden to you, the defender of established beliefs.

A tricky element in arguing with parents and other loved ones is that they can be offended by what they perceive to be arbitrary decisions concerning presumption and burden of proof on your part. You might be tempted to say something like, "Since I have always had a messy room, that is the present system, and therefore you have the burden of proof if you are advocating that I clean my room, because that's a change in policy." You could say this, but it would not be wise. In all of our less formal arguments, we need to understand that formal rules, like presumption, must be used in a way that is perceived to be fair by our argument opponents.

The Social Basis of Presumption and Burden of Proof

All rules of presumption provide an automatic decision in case of an impasse in the argumentation, but particular rules of presumption can vary widely as to *what* belief or policy will be considered as correct. In U.S. courts, the rule directs us to presume innocence until guilt is established; however, if we wished, we could have a rule of presumption that directed our courts to presume guilt until proven innocent. In fact, the courts of some totalitarian governments do utilize a presumption of guilt—in their practice if not in their formal rules. When the Shah of Iran was overthrown by the followers of the Ayatollah Khomeini, for example, thousands of members of the Shah's government, and many other Iranians, were brought to trial under a rule in which they were presumed guilty until they could prove their innocence to the satisfaction of the court!

Regulative rules, such as presumption, are framed according to the objectives of their framers. If we choose to presume innocence in our courts, it is not because this makes trials easy or cheap but because this sort of presumption fosters our ideas of criminal justice. Totalitarian regimes, however, tend to be less interested in justice than in power, and more interested in a court process that is cheap and efficient in disposing of their potential enemies than in fostering a just society. However, it is important to realize that rules of presumption are not entirely uniform in our own society—and in some situations there is a conflict of rules.

One of the more dramatic examples of a conflict among rules of presumption and burden of proof came in the trial of John Hinckley, Jr., who was charged with several counts of attempted murder, including the attempted assassination of former President Reagan. Hinckley's defense, based on a plea of insanity, raised a perplexing question: Should Hinckley be presumed sane or insane?

All U.S. court systems have rules governing presumption and burden of proof in relation to a defense of insanity, and these rules declare whether a defendant will be presumed sane or insane. This presumption, in turn, determines whether sanity or insanity will have to be proved and by which side. The difficulty in this case developed because two different court systems were involved. Hinckley was charged in 3 counts of violating federal law, but he was also charged in 10 counts of violating laws of the District of Columbia. The problem was that the federal courts and District of Columbia courts have diametrically opposed rules of presumption and burden of proof on the subject of insanity.

Under District of Columbia law, if a defendant pleads insanity, the *defense* has the burden of proving by a preponderance of evidence that he was insane. Thus, the presumption is that a person charged with a criminal act is to be considered sane until proven insane. The burden is on the side that makes the claim of insanity. However, federal courts place the burden of proof on the prosecution. If a defendant claims insanity, the government *must* prove beyond a reasonable doubt that the defendant was sane when the crime was committed. So the presumption in federal courts is that a defendant who claims insanity is to be considered insane until proven sane—a rather remarkable idea. (How does one prove sanity?)

Clearly, it makes a great deal of difference which rules of presumption and burden of proof are used. Proving that a defendant was insane at the time a crime was committed certainly is not easy, but surely it is easier than proving that a person was or is sane. Neither sanity nor insanity are medical concepts. But at least we have some legal criteria for insanity, such as the rule that has the jury determine whether the accused could distinguish between right and wrong at the time of the crime. In any event, the government was unable to prove beyond a reasonable doubt that Hinckley was sane when he shot President Reagan and three others, as required by U.S. District Judge Barrington D. Parker.

Rules for Debate

Rules become increasingly important as we try to make sense of persuasive argument in its more formal manifestations, known as debate. The term *debate* refers to a fairly large range of argument processes. For example, we have legislative debate, courtroom debate, presidential debate, interscholastic debate, friendly and unfriendly debate, and we even speak of debating with ourselves. Clearly there are important differences among these activities, but are they all really *debate?* If they are, then what is it that all of them have in common? If they are not, then how do we distinguish genuine debate from the imposters?

Debates are human communication activities, or communication games of a certain sort, as we noted earlier, and we have some choices in the way we wish to construe them. However, if our definition of *debate* is so broad that it includes almost all communication processes, then it becomes uninformative. Likewise, a very narrow definition will arbitrarily restrict the concept to only some of the activities normally regarded as debates.

In his critique of the presidential debates between John Kennedy and Richard Nixon in 1960, J. Jeffery Auer presented an interesting argument in support of the position that they were merely "counterfeit" debates (not real) because they failed to meet the five criteria in his definition. A debate, according to Auer, "is (1) a confrontation, (2) in equal and adequate time, (3) of matched contestants, (4) on a stated proposition, (5) to gain an audience decision."[3]

Each of the five criteria is reasonable, and Auer's definition is helpful so long as we understand that its components are really desirable goals rather than absolute standards. Suppose someone were to say to Auer (in a paraphrase of Wittgenstein's famous argument), "You seem to have in mind *one* kind of debate, but there are others. Just as U.S. football is different from Canadian football, and both are different from British football, we can think of many legitimate debate activities (or games) that do not conform to your definition." The seven Lincoln-Douglas debates, for example, did not have a stated proposition (or single central question) and their audiences did not cast a decision at their conclusion. Yet the confrontations between Lincoln and Douglas in 1858 are considered a paradigm case of the very best of political campaign debating, and appropriately so.

Richard M. Nixon presents an argument in the first televised presidential debate with John F. Kennedy on September 26, 1990

Auer's definition seems to apply well to the intercollegiate debates of the 1930s, but its elements would exclude many contemporary debate activities, including most of the current interscholastic debate competition in the United States. If "to gain an audience decision" is a defining element, for example, what are we to make of the fact that interscholastic debate almost never has an audience, let alone an audience decision? Does it stretch the idea "of matched contestants" for us to speak of a debate with ourselves, considering reasons for and against a proposal in our own minds? And finally, if the "equal and adequate time" requirement is taken literally, what do we make of the fact that attorneys in courtroom debate frequently do not use equal amounts of time, perhaps on the theory that juries would rather hear a good argument than a lengthy one? Auer's definition of *debate* is interesting, but it should be viewed as simply a vehicle for pointing to what he saw as significant weaknesses in the design of presidential debate formats, and a kind of listing of criteria for designing more effective presidential debates.

I take the time to reject the imposition of only one constitutive rule because a broad concept like debate has a fairly large number

The ideal of political debates to guide a nation: Abraham Lincoln (left) and Stephen A. Douglas (right) in 1958

of useful applications and we need to make sense of a variety of debate activities. We will never make much sense of the variety of debate activities if we assume the attitude of the myopic individual who insists that the only *real* game of football is the U.S. game. At the same time, we want to avoid the trap of thinking that debate is whatever anyone wants to call by that name! In order to navigate between these extremes, we need to survey some of the generally accepted rules for debate, including rules for debate format.

Debate Should Provide Light Rather Than Merely Heat

One important purpose of debate is to test ideas and argument, providing listeners with a clearer grasp of the truth in a dispute and a better understanding of the issues. But we should not confuse the necessary clash of argument in debate with mere contentiousness— or the sort of pointless quarreling we associate with tiresome people, as depicted neatly by Foster: "It was said of one man, 'He is a born debater. There is nothing he likes better than argument. He will not even eat anything that agrees with him.'"[4] Debate rules and behavior should enhance the productive clash of argument and evidence in such a way that the advocates help us to see the truth or wisdom in a controversy and reveal weak evidence and reasoning.

Debate Should Focus Disagreement Over a Central Question

For some people, the word *debate* seems to evoke the same sort of negative feelings as the ideas of conflict, fighting, and unpleasant quarreling with other people. For others, debate is associated with the very foundations of democratic ideals, including our notions of free speech and the ideal of solving problems through reasoning and persuasion rather than force. These opposite connotations of debate are partly a result of the way debates are focused.

The Problem of Participant Focus
When debates focus primarily on the participants, they tend to degenerate into an unpleasant process of name-calling, and the advocates think of themselves as intellectual prizefighters. But when a debate is focused on the issues and arguments, advocates need not develop hostile feelings for each other. Ridicule of an argument can be entertaining as well as informative; ridicule of one's opponent is merely unpleasant.

However, we should not make the mistake of saying that argument should never be directed to the personalities of participants, even though generally that is undesirable. In political campaign debates, the candidates *are* the issues in one way or another, and their relative leadership skills and past behavior certainly are relevant topics. Nevertheless, arguments over such topics should be civil. There is considerable evidence that voters dislike an argument style they perceive to be angry or rude. There can be a fine line between being aggressive and being merely obnoxious.

The Problem of Ignored Arguments

Another sort of problem in debate focus occurs when advocates from the two sides ignore each other's arguments. Beginners in debate do this because they are afraid of coming to a classroom debate with something less than a fully prepared speech. More experienced advocates fail to clash with their opponents' arguments because they perceive their own responses to be weak and they hope that the audience or judge will forget the opposing argument or think it unimportant if they ignore it. But the clash of opposing arguments and evidence is the essence of debate. Thus, the only speech that may be prepared completely in advance of a debate is the opening speech of the affirmative side. Succeeding speeches should respond to arguments of the opposing side, either refuting these arguments or indicating where there is agreement.

This does not mean that the preparation for debate consists merely in the inspiration that occurs to us while we listen to the opposing speaker. Development of the brief enables the effective debater to prepare extensively for almost any opposing arguments in relation to each issue. When the preparation is effective, we can select from this prepared material whatever is needed to refute arguments presented by the opposing side.

Debate Rules Should Be Perceived as Fair

This principle is important as an end in itself, but it is also important as a means to ensure that debates will have a productive clash. Whenever advocates believe there is anything unfair about the rules governing a debate, the rules rather than the central question are what they talk about, and the debate process tends to degenerate into mere bickering between the two sides.

Fairness in Phrasing a Central Question

Perceived problems of fairness frequently are focused on the statement of the central question or resolution that is the topic of the debate. Advocates are almost certain to object if the wording of the central question seems to favor their opponents. In most cases, this problem can be solved by applying the principle of neutral terminology for the phrasing of a central question (discussed in Chapter 2).

Fairness in Argument Opportunity

Fairness problems also seem to focus on whether each side has an equal opportunity to present its case. Typically, this problem is resolved by providing each side with an equal amount of time to speak. Since there are usually two sides in a debate, it is a relatively simple matter to allocate one-half of the time to each side. But some legislative bodies, including the U.S. House of Representatives, can allow for more complex situations. The Rules Committee of the House decides how much time will be allotted for debate on each bill. If there are three distinct argument positions on a bill, the Rules Committee may allocate one-third of the time to the leader of each position. For example, if one hour for debate is allotted to a bill, the Rules Committee might specify that the hour be divided into three equal segments, with 20 minutes to be controlled by each faction.

Providing an equal opportunity to each side is one of the most important principles for any debate format, but it is not always essential that time allocation be equal. On the "MacNeil/Lehrer News Hour," for example, the moderator does not allocate a set amount of time to each side in debates. Rather, the moderator allows the pro side to present a major argument, and then the opposing side is allowed to respond to it. Then the pro side can answer the response, and so on until the topic has been reasonably covered in the view of the moderator. The emphasis is on providing an opportunity to argue and to respond rather than on providing advocates with a particular amount of time for speaking.

Time Available for Debate Is Always Limited

Advocates as well as critics of debate frequently are frustrated by the constraints of time limits. One of the perennial complaints about the presidential debates, for example, is that the questions posed to the candidates by the panel of journalists cannot be answered adequately in the 2 1/2 minutes typically allotted in the debate format. I sympathize with these complaints, but we need to understand that time is always limited—an advocate never has unlimited time to present an argument, or even an entire persuasive case. If there are not formal time limits placed on the length of speeches and questioning periods in a debate, there are always the more devastating informal time limits, imposed when the audience simply stops listening.

Presidential candidates doubtless could provide a much more complete discussion of the issues if presidential debates were expanded to, say, four hours, but such debates would have a tiny audience. It may be instructive to realize that congressional debate

Legislative debate in the U.S. Congress, 1861 (top) and in the British House of Commons, 1793 (bottom)

in the U.S. House of Representatives typically proceeds with alternating speeches of no more than five minutes' duration.

Rules for the Presentation of Evidence and Argument Should Be Adapted to the Purpose of the Debate

All rules must be understood in relation to the purposes of the activity they govern as well as the context in which they are applied. To subject a "bull session" debate to the straightjacket of courtroom rules of evidence and procedure would be to miss the whole point of bull sessions. Conversely, can you imagine what a mess a trial would become if attorneys were permitted to indulge in the antics and freedoms permitted by the rules for our informal arguments? The nature and purpose of procedural rules vary according to the debate situation.

We should have a rather strict adherence to rules of evidence in courtroom debate because this is consistent with its high purposes of revealing the truth and justice of cases before the court. Thus, it seems appropriate to exclude hearsay evidence and to permit extensive cross-examination of witnesses. Rules of procedure in our courts are intended to ensure that a jury will have access to all of the important evidence relating to a trial and will be protected from any erroneous or contaminating information. However, in legislative debate, there are few controls on the sorts of evidence advocates may present. Deliberative bodies seem to assume that individual legislators are capable of protecting themselves from faulty evidence or reasoning. They have many sources of information, and misinformation can be exposed if any is presented in debate.

In classroom debates, great emphasis is placed on rules for gathering evidence and on providing documentation of sources as evidence is presented. However, such evidence rules seldom seem to govern other debates on campus, partly because there is no one to enforce them. Students who have been exposed only to classroom debates are sometimes surprised by the failure of participants in campus debates, such as exchanges between U.S. and British debaters, to document their evidence or to provide dates for statistics or expert opinion.

In international debates with the British, the debaters' rationale for omitting documentation of sources is that it will consume time needed for presenting additional arguments, and audiences don't really care anyway. If this seems a rather convenient rationale, and a somewhat unflattering perception of the audience, it probably is both. I think that participants in campus international debates should present documentation for evidence cited, but omit it because they are not required to cite sources. Procedural rules have little impact unless they are enforced.

Debate Formats Should Foster a Productive Clash

By *debate format*, I mean such things as the order and number of pro and con speeches, the time limits for each speech, and the inclusion of cross-examination (or questioning of the advocates by opposing advocates or neutral third parties).

Formats used for competitive interscholastic debate are generally hybrids that blend features of courtroom debate with features of parliamentary or legislative debate. Although there are a variety of competitive formats, they always require the affirmative to give the opening speech and typically the affirmative gives the final closing speech as well. Consider, as an example, the following typical intercollegiate debate format, which provides a total of one hour of speaking time divided equally between an affirmative and negative team, with two debaters on each team.

First affirmative	8 minutes
cross-ex. by 2nd negative	3 minutes
First negative	8 minutes
cross-ex. by 1st affirmative	3 minutes
Second affirmative	8 minutes
cross-ex. by 1st negative	3 minutes
Second negative	8 minutes
cross-ex. by 2nd affirmative	3 minutes
Rebuttal from 1st negative	4 minutes
Rebuttal from 1st affirmative	4 minutes
Rebuttal from 2nd negative	4 minutes
Rebuttal from 2nd affirmative	4 minutes

An attractive feature of this format is that it permits each of the four speakers to participate in four different debate activities. Notice that each of the four speakers (1) presents an opening speech (called a *constructive* argument) of 8 minutes, (2) is questioned by an opposing speaker for 3 minutes, (3) asks questions of an opposing speaker for 3 minutes, and (4) presents a 4-minute rebuttal speech. However, this format requires a full hour of speaking time. When we add even minimal preparation time between speeches, this sort of format may require a minimum of an hour and a half for a debate—which presents a time problem for a normal 50-minute class. But there are a variety of ways to adjust a debate format to the time available.

An assumption of the intercollegiate debate format is that it is always clear which side is the affirmative or the advocate of change. But which side is the affirmative in a debate between political candidates? Not surprisingly, neither side wants to be identified as the negative. When there are only two candidates in a debate, as in the first Kennedy-Nixon debate in 1960, the candidates flipped a coin to determine speaking order for the opening speeches and reversed the order for the closing speeches. Thus, Kennedy gave the first opening speech, and Nixon gave the first closing speech.

When there are more than two candidates, which is frequently the case with debates among presidential candidates during the primaries, formats become somewhat more complex. However, the basis for designing formats is always the same: to provide a structure that gives no advantage or disadvantage to any of the participants but helps the advocates to focus the issues and to present and refute arguments.

In Appendix C you will find a detailed description of the modified debate format that may be used for classroom debates, as well as an explanation of the principles and rules for each speech. But it is important to understand the rationale behind the design of debate formats.

Summary

1. The structure of conflict requires an understanding of its parts and their relationships to each other. The process of argumentation is illuminated by three kinds of rules: (1) constitutive and regulative, (2) presumption and burden of proof, and (3) the general rules for debate.

2. Constitutive rules define elements of any "game" and provide a useful way of understanding how central concepts of rhetoric and argumentation are defined. Although there is always an arbitrary element in the definitions of concepts, there are good reasons for preferring one definition to another.

3. Regulative rules govern behavior. They rely on constitutive rules, but go beyond them to indicate whether the behaviors and moves defined are prohibited, required, or permitted. Regulative rules are also based in good reasons, and they are most easily comprehended within an institutional setting, such as a court. However, we also use regulative rules in everyday arguments with family and friends.

4. Presumption is an automatic decision rule that governs which beliefs or policies will be considered correct unless rejected by positive action. As a regulative rule, presumption tells us in any setting what will be decided if there is a tie in the persuasive arguments.

5. Burden of proof is a rule that stipulates and assigns requirements for overturning the presumption on a belief or policy. It tells the advocates what must be proven and who must do it.

    a. A persuasive case which, "on the face of it," would be considered sufficient to meet the burden of proof by any reasonable person is called a *prima facie case.*

    b. Other standards for determining when the burden of proof has been met are provided in our courts. In criminal cases, the prosecution is to establish its case *beyond reasonable doubt.* In civil cases, the plaintiff must establish a *preponderance of evidence.* Either standard must be applied by a jury.

6. Usually, existing beliefs and policies have the advantage of presumption, but this is more easily determined in formal institutions such as courts and legislatures. In less formal arguments with family or friends, it may be unclear what is an existing belief or policy. We need to be wary of unfair attempts to claim presumption and to shift the burden of proof.

7. Because the rules of presumption and burden of proof are socially determined, it is possible to presume guilt rather than innocence, or insanity rather than sanity in criminal trials. Like other regulative rules, presumption and burden of proof are framed according to the purposes of the society or the institutions within which they operate.

8. As we try to understand persuasive argumentation in more formal settings, it is important to grasp the constitutive and regulative rules of debate. There are many kinds of debate, but some general rules can be applied to them all:

    a. Debates should provide light rather than heat.

    b. Debates should focus argumentation on issues rather than participants.

    c. Debates should foster a sense of fairness in the phrasing of topics and the opportunity to present arguments.

    d. Debates should make effective use of limited time.

    e. Debate formats should foster a productive clash of arguments and reasoning.

9. A grasp of central rules enables us to make sense of the situations in which persuasive argument is used to manage and resolve conflict. A clear grasp of the constitutive rules clarifies the elements of argument games, such as debates. Regulative rules, like presumption, clarify strategy and action.

Exercises

1. Apply the concepts of presumption and burden of proof to the following:

   > Agnes and Mortimer, a rather contentious bore who likes to argue about everything, are winding down a dismal date when Mortimer asserts that public school teachers should be stripped of tenure in order to make it easier to get rid of incompetent teachers. For some reason Agnes bothers to disagree, and Mortimer huffs, "Listen, Aggie, everyone knows that the tenure system is the reason we have so many incompetent teachers in the public schools. If you want to argue that tenure is not the cause of incompetent teachers, you're going to have to prove it." I don't know why Aggie would want to continue this conversation, but how should she respond to this kind of statement?

2. Suppose that the Internal Revenue Service calls one of your classmates in for an audit of their tax return. If the tax return is challenged, what is the presumption? Who has the burden of proof?

3. Universities have a variety of policies in regard to student grade appeals. As a class discussion topic, if a student thinks that the grade she received in a history course was too low, what are the proper procedures for appealing it? When the student and professor disagree, what is the presumption? Who has the burden of proof? Would it be possible to reverse the presumption? Are there good reasons for the present assignment of the burden of proof?

Endnotes

1. Eric Berne, *Games People Play* (New York: Grove Press, 1964), pp. 19–20.
2. Lewis Coser, *Continuities in the Study of Social Conflict* (New York: The Free Press, 1967).
3. J. Jeffery Auer, "The Counterfeit Debates," *The Great Debates: Kennedy vs. Nixon, 1960*, ed. Sidney Krause (Bloomington: Indiana University Press, 1962), pp. 142–150.
4. William T. Foster, *Argumentation and Debating* (Boston: Houghton Mifflin, 1917), p. 275.

10

Building Affirmative Cases in Debate

Central Ideas in This Chapter

1. Case composition is the process of selecting and organizing materials from the analysis of a central question.

2. An affirmative case should meet the burden of proof, fit within the time limits, and persuade its audience.

3. One standard of proof is the prima facie case. Other standards are usually less formal but require proof that is sufficient to convince the audience.

4. Two useful case strategies for policy questions are traditional needs and comparative advantages.

5. Two of the more important cases for fact and value are the conjectural and definition, which correspond to the stasis categories discussed in Chapter 3.

6. Affirmative cases should always be based on audience values and beliefs. These determine what must be proved and guide argument strategy.

Building an affirmative case requires an ability to discern the available means of persuasion in a dispute. When we can see clearly the whole-part relationship between a central question and its principal components—the issues, arguments, evidence, and premises—we see as well the basis for the effective composition of a persuasive case for either the pro or con side.

In a sense, composition is merely the process of analysis in reverse. As the Port Royal logician, Antoine Arnauld, stated in his seventeenth-century *La Logique*, "Analysis and composition differ only as the road by which we ascend from a valley to a mountain differs from the road by which we descend from the mountain to the valley."[1] Viewed in this way, composition is a matter of communicating our analysis to others—a kind of retracing of our investigation of a central question. When a composition presents the entire product of analysis and investigation, it is called an *argument and evidence brief*, which we discussed and illustrated in Chapter 8. The brief clarifies the relationships of opposing arguments and evidence to the issues, and it enables us to see the entire substantive structure of a conflict, including all the persuasive materials. It is the primary source of substantive materials for either an affirmative or a negative case.

A completed brief provides us with the essential resources, but how do we approach the task of using these effectively? Before we begin the process of composition, it is helpful to have a clear idea of what we need to accomplish. Composition goals are most intelligible when we frame them as criteria for case construction.

Criteria for Affirmative Cases

A persuasive case for the affirmative position on a central question of fact, value, or policy should satisfy three criteria: (1) it should be persuasive to its audience; (2) it should be adapted to time limitations and any special features of the format for debate; and (3) it should meet the burden of proof. These three criteria overlap, of course, but each provides a useful way of thinking about affirmative case strategy.

Persuasion and Time Criteria

Ideally, an excellent brief will contain all of the possible arguments and evidence for each side. However, although completeness is a virtue in an argument brief, it can be deadly error in an affirmative case. The idea of an affirmative case in a debate is to persuade, and the first requisite of persuading others is to get them to listen. Audiences seldom have the time or the inclination to sit through a rehash of all of the arguments and evidence produced by an investigation. Moreover, as we observed in Chapter 9, there are usually formal time limits for speakers.

Consider the element of time in supporting a simple policy change—such as a proposal to ban the possession and use of alcoholic beverages on campus. Our analysis may discover a dozen or more arguments for each of the issues, but can anyone imagine that an audience would want us to present all of our arguments merely because we found them? Inevitably, some of the arguments would be stronger than others. Why should our audience listen to the weak arguments? Redundancy is tiresome, and a bored audience is likely to be finished with a speech long before the speaker is finished. Moreover, arguments that are interesting and persuasive to one audience may be tedious and unpersuasive to another audience. The skillful advocate selects arguments from the brief and adapts them to the interests, knowledge, and values of the audience. The idea is to be persuasive.

Burden of Proof and Persuasion

Burden of proof, as defined in Chapter 9, is a rule that stipulates and assigns requirements for overturning the presumption on a belief or policy. Thus, a burden of proof rule tells the advocates (1) what must be done and (2) who must do it. Ordinarily, as we have seen, the advocates of change are assigned the burden of proof, and the burden consists of a requirement to present arguments and evidence sufficient to support a response of yes for each of the issues. A case that meets this burden, at least initially, is called a *prima facie case*, as we noted in Chapter 9.

But how much support is required? This is where the persuasive standards of an audience become important. If the issues specify what must be proven, it is the audience that determines when or whether the proof offered is sufficient. For example, jurors will not want to convict a defendant unless they are persuaded that proof of guilt is sufficient. Thus, if persuasion is our goal, we need to adapt our arguments and evidence to the beliefs, values, interests, and needs of the audience that is to decide the matter. We will utilize the broad range of argument and evidence we have found in our research and analysis, but we will not try to use all of our ammunition with any audience. An effective case selects only those arguments that the audience will regard as good reasons in support of our position.

Guided by the twin concerns of adapting to an audience and meeting the burden of proof, advocates have a great deal of creative freedom to compose a persuasive case. When the discovery of arguments and evidence is reasonably complete, an advocate can choose a *case strategy*, or a general plan for selecting, organizing, and presenting the affirmative analysis. Therefore, our next topic is to explore the kinds of case strategies available to the affirmative, commencing with those for questions of policy.

Affirmative Cases for Policy Questions

The general notion of case strategies is more familiar in the formal, competitive debate arena than in many of the more informal settings of public debate. But all advocates need clear plans for organizing and presenting their arguments, and it is easier to devise a plan that uniquely fits your particular situation and topic if you are grounded in some standard models of case strategy that have been developed in competitive debate.

Over the years, intercollegiate debaters have evolved two very useful persuasive case strategies for meeting the affirmative burden on policy questions: (1) the traditional needs case and (2) the comparative advantages case. There are many other case types but these two enable us to see clearly what is most important about all of them—namely, that an overall plan can enhance our ability to meet the burden of proof in a persuasive way. Such standard case models also help us to adhere to both the formal and informal time limits in a debate.

Traditional Needs Case

An affirmative strategy that organizes arguments directly in relation to the stock issues categories is called a *traditional needs* case. Its name comes from its focus on a *need* to respond to a perceived problem. The affirmative justifies the need for change in the motive issue by arguing that there is a problem or harm that is so significant that it needs immediate solution.

Traditional needs cases are simple in structure because their main points respond directly to the issues of *motive*, *obstacle* (or *blame*), and *cure*. Consider, for example, the main points in the body of a traditional needs case for the following policy question:

> Should Colorado build a light-rail train system in order to reduce the problem of air pollution?

I. The problems of air pollution in Colorado are significant enough to warrant action. (motive)
   A. Present levels of air pollution are a serious threat to the health of residents.
   B. Visible air pollution in Denver and other major cities makes Colorado less attractive to tourists.
   C. Colorado is threatened with the loss of highway funds for persistent violation of federal air pollution standards.
II. The present system of north to south transportation, which relies primarily on private automobiles, is responsible for most of the air pollution. (blame)
   A. Most of the carbon monoxide and nitrous oxides comes from the exhaust of automobiles.
   B. There are, at present, no workable alternatives to the automobile for most people who must travel north or south in Colorado.
III. The proposed light-rail train system would significantly reduce the problem of air pollution in Colorado. (cure)
   A. Light-rail trains do not produce significant amounts of air pollution.
   B. Air pollution would diminish as travelers opt for trains in place of autos for traveling north or south in the state.
   C. Large numbers of travelers would ride the trains.

The above case structure is reasonably complete in providing a foundation of good reasons in support of each major claim. You should realize, of course, that each of the good reasons for the main points need supporting evidence. The evidence has been omitted in our example in order to focus attention on organization in the traditional needs case and to illustrate how the major responses to the issues of motive, blame, and cure provide a simple three-point structure for the body of an affirmative case.

Strategic Handling of the Cost Issue

At this point we need to digress just a bit. You may have noticed that the main points in the preceding example are, in one sense, incomplete: They do not respond to the *cost* issue. Why not? The answer to this question is rather complex for beginners in argumentation, but it goes to the core of composition principles. The principle is that advocates of change should not squander their available time by engaging in redundancy, by providing extensive development on issues that are not contested, or by developing the affirmative position on an issue at the wrong time. Typically, the cost issue is contested, but it usually makes more sense persuasively and strategically for the affirmative to force the negative to initiate any argument clash on the cost issue.

Consider two possible situations. First, if the negative chooses not to contest the cost issue, the assumption is that the con side must agree with the pro side that the benefits of solving the alleged problem (plus any additional advantages) justify whatever cost is involved in the proposed solution. The cost issue, like all issues, is potentially in dispute with all policy questions, but it is *always* the con side that determines whether a potential issue will be argued. Thus, if the negative does not contest the cost issue, our affirmative has saved whatever time and effort would have been required to develop affirmative arguments for it, and the time saved can be used to develop a stronger affirmative position on other issues.

Second, even if the negative chooses to argue the cost issue, the affirmative still is better off in most cases to force the negative to *begin* the argument. To understand this, consider the affirmative position on the components of the cost issue. Notice that the cost issue essentially has three components:

1. Benefits (or advantages) from solving the alleged problem, plus any secondary advantages of the new plan
2. The costs (or disadvantages) of the proposed solution
3. A comparison of benefits to costs

The first component—benefits from solving the problem—are established as we demonstrate the importance of a problem (focus of the motive issue) and then show that the problem will be solved by the proposed change (focus of the cure issue). Thus, the affirmative more or less simultaneously establishes benefits from solving an alleged problem—the first component of the cost issue—as the burden of proof is satisfied for the *motive* and *cure* issues. It would be merely redundant to establish benefits once again with separate arguments for the cost issue.

Of course, it may be possible that there are additional advantages of the proposed plan, in addition to the primary benefits of solving the problem. For example, in the illustrative case, the affirmative might find that in addition to the primary benefit of solving air pollution, a light-rail train would add to the aesthetic pleasures of life in Colorado, and that people would also like the convenience of not needing to worry about parking when they come to Denver. Whether these additional advantages should be included in the initial presentation of the case will depend on two considerations: Is there enough time to include them? and Are they important enough to warrant using time that could be devoted to strengthening other arguments that are crucial? Additional advantages of a proposed change are seldom crucial in the initial stages of deliberation.

What, then, of the other two elements—the alleged costs or disadvantages of the proposed policy or action and the relationship between benefits and cost? If the cost issue is contested (or argued) by the negative, the affirmative must be prepared to establish that the costs (or disadvantages) are insignificant or at least that they are outweighed by the benefits (or advantages). Notice, however, that it makes more sense for the affirmative to force the negative to bring up arguments on the alleged costs as well as the relationship between benefits and costs. It is usually much easier to answer cost arguments after they have been presented than it is to anticipate what your opponent will argue. Moreover, it can be persuasively better to bring up the additional advantages (aesthetic pleasures and convenience) when we are answering arguments about disadvantages to the proposal.

Strategy Is Based on Audience Beliefs

If it is clear to you, at this point, why it is strategically better for the affirmative to put the negative in the position of either conceding the cost issue or initiating argumentation on it, you may also realize that the same advantage could be available on the other principal issues of motive, obstacle, or cure. The dynamics of most policy disputes usually will force the affirmative to initiate argument on motive, obstacle, and cure, but in some cases, widespread agreement that a significant problem exists can minimize the affirmative's burden on motive, unless the negative chooses to deny that the problem is significant. For example, an affirmative would not ordinarily have to prove that such things as violent crime, unemployment, poverty, and illness are harmful per se. It is usually enough merely to quantify the existence of such problems.

This sort of belief is perhaps a kind of psychological presumption that favors the affirmative. If so, its analog on the cost issue is that we will, in normal disputes, be inclined to assume that the benefits of a proposed solution that has been shown to solve a significant problem will justify whatever it costs unless or until the opponents choose to argue that the cost is too high or that the benefits are not enough to justify the costs or disadvantages of the proposed change. Thus, in most policy disputes, the con side initiates arguments to show that any proposed change is too costly, or has significant disadvantages.

The practical considerations for handling the cost and the other issues in a traditional needs case are presented in Appendix C, which provides a detailed description of the typical content of the various speeches in one type of classroom debate format. There you will see that, in a debate consisting of a two-person affirmative and a two-person negative team, the cost issue is usually initiated by the second negative speaker.

The Comparative Advantages Case

For most policy questions, the traditional needs strategy is probably the best place to begin the process of composing a persuasive case. It has the advantages of simplicity and clarity, and most of the time it seems to spring naturally from the material generated by the analysis and research of a particular policy question. However, in many cases, advocates support a change in policy in order to gain an advantage rather than to solve a problem. The *comparative advantages* case provides a powerful alternative to the traditional needs approach, especially when the focus of the motive issue is either a goal, a desirable advantage, or a potential benefit rather than a problem or a harm.

Strictly speaking, there is no logical difference between a problem to be solved and an advantage to be gained, but there can be major psychological differences in the way we conceptualize and talk about these alternative sorts of motives. To clarify this distinction, first we need to understand the rational similarities between the terms *problems* and *advantages*.

Relationship Between Problem and Advantage

Most college students are concerned about the level of income they will earn in their first job after graduation, and salary is understood by most of us as an important potential motive. But what sort of motive? Should we think about that first salary as a problem to be solved or as an advantage to be gained? In objective terms, we are talking about the same thing—namely, our earnings from that first job. But whether we think about salary as a problem to be solved or an advantage to be gained seems to depend upon some not-so-objective matters that can vary considerably from one person or situation to another.

Most students approach graduation and the beginning of job interviews with a *level of expectation* for what they think they should earn in their first job after college. What level of expectation? Well, that seems to depend partly on what students know about the earnings of others in their line of work (the so-called market for people in their profession) and it also may depend on a highly personal sense of self-worth. Suppose that the level of expectation for Thomas—a student majoring in communication studies—is $45,000 per year for his first job out of college (perhaps a high sense of self-worth).

If Tom's job offers are, say, $15,000, we would at least understand why he might describe the difference between his level of expectation and the pay level from his job offers as a *problem to be solved*.

On the other hand, suppose Jennifer has a level of expectation for a $30,000 income, and she has found a job at precisely that salary. Then, one month later, she is offered a job at $45,000 by another employer. Certainly we can understand the $15,000 difference as a motive for change, but it makes more sense to call it *an advantage to be gained* than to call it a *problem to be solved*. Yet, in both cases, we are talking about a motive concerning the same thing—more money.

When we see clearly that an advantage to be gained and a problem to be solved are merely alternative ways of talking about the motive issue, it should also be apparent that the burden of proof for an advantages analysis is the same as for a traditional needs case. The burden, for both cases, is to justify a response of yes to the issues of motive, obstacle, cure, and cost. However, to keep the burden of proof in clear focus, it is helpful to rephrase the issues, beginning with the motive issue. When the focus of the motive is an *advantage*, such as an increase in salary, we would phrase the motive issue along these lines:

> Is the advantage of a salary increase of _____ significant enough to warrant action?

Most of us would grant that a $15,000 salary increase for Jennisfer is a significant motive for change, assuming salary is her chief concern, but that does not mean that *any* salary increase would be significant enough to warrant action. It is highly probable that Jennifer would reject an offer of, say, $15 more per year than her current job pays. But how about $500? Any salary increase is beneficial, but a benefit or advantage must pass the threshold of *significance* in order to warrant action. In this respect, once again, there is a functional identity between an advantage to be gained and a problem to be solved.

Burden of Proof for Comparative Advantages

When an advantage is clearly focused for the motive issue, students usually find it easy to see the affirmative burden of proof on the obstacle and cure issues. If the motive for Jennifer is a $15,000 salary increase, then the affirmative burden on the obstacle issue is to show that she cannot get that salary increase with her present employer. On the cure issue, the affirmative must show that Jennifer would indeed receive the promised $15,000 increase if she takes the new job. The increase might be merely possible if the job is in sales and the increase is to come from sales commissions.

Although a comparative advantages case has the same burden of proof as a traditional needs case in relation to the four principal issues, the burden sometimes seems to be more easily met. Comparative advantages cases narrow the focus of disagreement between affirmative and negative because they are based on goals or values of the present system. If both the present system and the new policy proposed by the affirmative are committed to the same goals, such as an expansion of the local economy or the saving of lives on the nation's highways, then it is unnecessary for the affirmative to prove that such goals are themselves desirable. Rather, the focus of proof for the affirmative is to establish, by means of a comparison, that the affirmative proposal would do a significantly better job of meeting the goals than the present system. Usually, the principal clash of argument will be on the issues of obstacle, cure, and cost.

Topics Suited to Comparative Advantages

A comparative advantages approach tends to work well when proposals for change are directed toward goals that are universally shared and uncontroversial. For example, few people in the United States would question Jennifer's goal of maximizing her income. Likewise, we would probably be surprised if anyone seriously questioned the goals of preventing the spread of a deadly disease or reducing the dropout rate of high school students. When the present system or policy is already committed to a goal, any new policy or action that is proposed as a way of moving us in the direction of the goal seems to conform naturally to the comparative advantages perspective. Let's consider an example of a comparative advantages case that is based upon a goal of the present system.

Comparative Advantages Illustration

The goal of preventing injuries and deaths on our highways is the basis for many of the laws governing the manufacture and sale of automobiles in the United States. Therefore, any proposed new policy that seeks to enhance this goal would lend itself to a comparative advantages case strategy. One such proposal, which was debated over a number of years, was for the federal government to mandate installation of air bags in all new autos in order to reduce highway deaths and injuries.

In the latter part of the 1980s, present policy (relative to this proposal) evolved incrementally as the federal government increased the number of safety devices over the years. Early on, for example, the government required the installation of seat belts in all autos. In later years, laws were passed in many states to mandate the use of seat belts, and automatic seat belts were installed in a number of car models. Therefore, in general terms, the comparison between present policy and the proposed policy might be characterized as *seat belts versus airbags.*

With this background in mind, observe how elements of the motive, obstacle, and cure issues are combined in the major lines of argument for the comparative advantages case that follows.

I. Airbags provide a significant increase in safety for all automobile passengers.
  A. Seat-belt protection is inherently limited.
    1. Many people do not wear seat belts, even when their use is mandated by law.
    2. Seat belts are designed for adults and provide inadequate protection for children.
    3. Seat belts have limited value in head-on collisions at speeds over 40 mph.
  B. Airbags make up for seat-belt deficiencies.
    1. Since airbags are a passive system, they provide some protection for those who fail to use seat belts.
    2. Airbags increase frontal collision protection for small children.
    3. Airbags provide superior protection from injury in head-on collisions.
  C. Airbags save lives and prevent injuries.
    1. A National Highway Traffic Safety Administration study estimates saving 8,900 lives and 500,000 injuries each year.
    2. The Insurance Institute study concludes that airbags reduce fatalities by 79 percent and injuries by 66 percent.
II. An airbag mandate by the federal government is better than the present approach.
  A. The present policy of continued testing and pilot programs is incapable of making airbags available on all new automobiles.
    1. Pilot programs make the airbags available only as an option that is expensive to consumers and manufacturers.
    2. There have been endless delays in implementation of pilot programs.
    3. More than a decade since the first pilot program, only some new automobiles have airbags available as an option.
  B. A mandate would make airbags available faster.
    1. Since the technology for airbag installation is currently available, auto manufacturers could begin installation with the next model year.
    2. A mandate would eliminate any hesitancy due to cost savings by manufacturers.
  C. A mandate would reduce the average cost of airbag installation and replacement.

Once again, each of the supporting reasons for the two major arguments would need to be supported with evidence, but this case outline illustrates the reasoning in a more or less complete affirmative justification for the proposed airbag mandate. Examine the issues for the proposed airbag mandate that follow and compare them to the two major arguments in the preceding case. Do you see how the motive element of decreased death and injury is combined with the obstacle and cure elements?

Motive: Is the advantage of saving 8,900 lives and preventing 500,000 injuries annually significant enough to warrant action?

Obstacle: Is the present system of reliance on seat-belt usage incapable of saving 8,900 lives and preventing 500,000 injuries per year?

Cure: Would the proposed airbag mandate produce the advantage of 8,900 lives saved and 500,000 injuries prevented each year?

Cost: Will the benefits of 8,900 lives saved and 500,000 injuries prevented justify the costs (or disadvantages) of an airbag mandate?

Notice that the comparative advantages case does not argue, in any direct way, that it is desirable to save lives and prevent injuries. That is an assumption of the case that is based on the prevailing values of our culture—an assumption that negative advocates would be unlikely to question. Probably the only element of the motive that the negative would question is the figures themselves: the 8,900 lives saved and the 500,000 injuries prevented, which are derived from studies of the National Highway Traffic Safety Administration and the Insurance Institute. But, of course, whether an airbag mandate would prevent that many deaths and injuries is precisely the focus of the cure issue. This means that elements of the motive are either (1) uncontroversial or (2) the same elements we find in the cure issue. So, the affirmative burden is effectively narrowed to cure, obstacle, and cost.

You should also see that our comparative advantages case does not argue directly that benefits will justify the costs of an airbag mandate. In this respect, the comparative advantages case is like the traditional needs case. It attempts to force the negative either to concede the cost issue or to initiate the argumentation on it. The only issues argued directly are the obstacle and cure issues—namely, that an airbag mandate would save lives and prevent injuries (cure), and the present system of reliance on seat belts is incapable of preventing the same numbers of injuries and deaths (obstacle).

The illustrations of the traditional needs and comparative advantages cases in this chapter should provide you with useful examples of two important strategies, but these examples are not intended as universal models to be mindlessly imitated. Every policy question has unique issues. The crucial standard for an affirmative case strategy is that it must justify the affirmative position on the issues—not that it conform to the pattern of a particular illustrative model. Mere imitation of affirmative models results in sterile and uninteresting cases that will probably not be persuasive. But if you use these models as a *way of seeing* the persuasive possibilities for arguing in favor of any particular policy proposal, the illustrations can be useful. In short, do not permit your creativity to be stifled. Develop an affirmative case that justifies the affirmative position on the issues, and make it as interesting and persuasive as possible for the audience you wish to convince.

Affirmative Cases for Fact and Value Questions

Just as the stock issues provide us with a direct approach for building an affirmative case on a policy question, the *stasis* categories suggest a useful starting point for building a case to justify the affirmative position on a central question of fact or value. The stasis model, as presented in Chapter 3, outlines four categories within which the issues for a question of fact or value will be found: (1) the conjectural, (2) the definitional, (3) the qualitative, and (4) the procedural. Thus, development of an affirmative case begins with the analysis of issues and a review of the pro and con arguments and evidence uncovered in the investigation of the central question. Here again, it is helpful to have the substance of affirmative arguments and evidence available in a brief.

Analysis of pro and con arguments in relation to the four potential issues from the stasis categories usually indicates where the principal clash with the negative will occur, thereby outlining what the pro side must prove in the affirmative case. However, even though the affirmative must be prepared to support a response of yes to issues from all of the stasis categories, it is rather unusual for negatives to contest all four of the potential issues. Usually, the focus of negative disagreement is either on the conjectural or the definitional issues, at least initially.

In a murder case, for example, the defense normally argues either the conjectural issue (so the jury is to decide who murdered the victim) or the definitional issue (the killing was not murder). It would certainly be tricky to argue both issues: (1) that the defendant did not kill her husband and (2) if she did, the killing was not murder. All of this means that, in most instances, an affirmative case on a question of fact or value will initially be focused either on the conjectural issue or on the definitional issue.

The Conjectural Case

When there is agreement on the meaning of critical terms in a dispute over a question of fact or value, but the two sides disagree on the facts alleged, an affirmative case is focused on the conjectural issue. Let's consider a simple case of this sort.

When a mother says to her son, "You lied to me about the missing cookies!" the definitional stasis alerts us to examine the meaning of the value term *lied*. Does the son understand what his mother means by the term *lie* and do the two of them agree on the criteria for lying as opposed to, say, creative fiction about events in one's life? If the mother and son agree (so there is no dispute) that the term lie means "to make a statement that one knows to be false, especially with intent to deceive," then the mother's affirmative case may be focused on the conjectural issues that derive from the definition of *lying*. These issues could be phrased as follows:

1. Did Herbie (her 2-year-old son) make a statement about the cookies that he knew was false?
2. Did Herbie make the false statement with intent to deceive?

In the improbable event that the mother would bother to present an affirmative case on this question, do you see how the two conjectural issues would provide a case structure with two major arguments? Of course, each of the two arguments would need supporting reasons and/or evidence, and might look something like the following:

I. Herbie made a statement about the cookies that he knew to be false.
   A. Herbie said the girl next door, Janie, climbed up to the cookie jar and ate the cookies.
   B. Herbie knows that Janie cannot walk yet, let alone climb on furniture.
II. Herbie made the false statement in order to deceive his mother.
   A. Herbie was told the morning of the theft that he was not to get any cookies.
   B. When his mother asked him why he had blamed Janie for the cookie theft, Herbie said, "Because I didn't want you to know that I did it."

Although the dispute here is hardly momentous, it provides a useful way of understanding the development of a conjectural case in more complex questions. The criminal cases in our courts are far more complex, yet their critical terms (*burglary, larceny, assault,* etc.) are defined in state laws. Statutory definitions, in turn, generally serve to obviate disputes over the meaning of critical terms in the questions of fact and value handled in our courts—at least in the initial stages of a dispute—thus enabling the prosecution to focus his or her case on factual or conjectural issues.

To see how this works, let's suppose that Harry Thug is accused of burglary in the state of Wonderland, which defines *burglary* as "the act of breaking into any building at any time to commit theft or other felony." Notice how the definition itemizes specific factual elements—namely, the actions and events that constitute burglary. This itemization, in turn, permits us to phrase the following factual issues:

1. Did Mr. Thug break into a building?
2. Did Mr. Thug intend to commit theft or other felony?

Initially, at least, the prosecution can assume that the definition of *burglary* is not itself in dispute, and will develop a case with two major arguments corresponding to the two issues, supporting each argument with the appropriate and available reasoning and evidence. Such a case might look something like the following:

I. Mr. Thug broke into Mary's Muffin Shop.
   A. Thug was arrested in the shop at 1:00 P.M. by Officer Jolly.
   B. The lock on the Muffin Shop door had been forced open.
   C. Thug had a crowbar in his possession that had paint on it matching the forced door.
II. Mr. Thug intended to commit theft.
   A. His pockets were stuffed with Mary's muffins.
   B. He admitted his intent to Officer Jolly.

The Definitional Case

Once the prosecution has presented a case based on the statutory definition of a crime, the defense has essentially two options: (1) the defense can choose to argue that the facts alleged are untrue or (2) that the alleged facts are insufficient to establish the crime as charged, for one of three kinds of reasons:

1. Because of unique circumstances that constitute an exception to the statutory definition

2. Because of a flaw in the definition
3. Because of universal principles of justice that override the statute or qualify its application in this case

The definitional stasis, as we noted earlier, alerts us to examine the *meaning* of critical terms. When the defense shifts the focus of a dispute from the conjectural to the definitional level, the dispute over the facts is sometimes dropped (although not always). A murder case may illuminate this sort of situation.

On January 16, 1987, Mrs. Kay Eichheim was acquitted of first-degree murder in the shooting death of her husband, Daniel, at their home. According to newspaper accounts, Mrs. Eichheim admitted that she shot her husband in the head while he slept. Further, after telling police that she shot her husband accidentally when she dropped his pistol, she changed her testimony and claimed that she shot him in self-defense, "moments after she tried to commit suicide—in terror that he had contracted AIDS in a homosexual encounter and would infect her."[2] In addition, Mrs. Eichheim testified that "she had suffered years of sexual, physical and emotional abuse from her husband, but was unable to walk out on their 27-year marriage."

According to statute, first-degree murder consists of three elements, giving rise to three factual issues: (1) Did Mrs. Eichheim kill her husband? (2) Did she intend to kill him? and (3) Did she premeditate the killing? However, state law also stipulates exceptions to the definition, or circumstances in which the definition will be set aside. One such exception is self-defense. But what is self-defense?

According to press accounts, much of the focus of this trial was on the definition of *self-defense*. Thus, if self-defense is "the right to preserve oneself with whatever force is reasonably necessary against actual violence or the threat of violence," the prosecution needed to establish that the definition excludes the idea of shooting one's husband in the head while he sleeps, providing it is possible for the defendant to escape from "actual violence or the threat of violence."[3]

A key element for the jurors apparently was the idea of what was "reasonably necessary" for Mrs. Eichheim to defend herself. If she could run away from the actual or threatened violence, then shooting her husband was not reasonably necessary. If she could not leave, and the violence from her husband was life threatening, then the shooting was reasonably necessary, at least in her frame of mind. One juror offered this explanation of why the jury accepted the explanation of self-defense: "I know a lot of people are asking, 'Why didn't Kay Eichheim just walk away from it instead of killing her husband?' That was discussed a lot by the jury, and I believe she didn't see that as an option . . . she ran away one night, but she came back, just as hundreds of battered women will run away to a shelter home, but then they come back again."[4]

The task of building an affirmative case for a question of fact or value is simplified if we begin by asking (1) What facts have been alleged in this dispute that support the affirmative side of the question? and (2) What are the standards or criteria for understanding the meaning of the critical terms in the fact or value question? Both approaches are helpful. By looking to the alleged facts, we get some sense about what criteria or standards will be useful for the critical terms in the question. At the same time, by defining the critical terms and arriving at standards, criteria, or defining elements, we can see more clearly which of the alleged facts are relevant in a dispute.

Using Audience Beliefs in Fact and Value Cases

Recall that a persuasive case should always be based on the beliefs and values of the audience to which it is addressed. When a dispute is focused on a central question of fact or value, audience beliefs may grant one or more of the issues to the affirmative, at least at the outset of argument. To see how this works, it is useful to consider how audience beliefs permit a prosecuting attorney to force the defense either to concede an issue or to initiate argument on it.

One of the issues in a first-degree murder charge, as we have seen, is concerned with the intentions of the defendant. It is not sufficient to establish merely that Jones killed Smith and that the killing was premeditated; the prosecution also has the burden of proving that Jones intended to kill Smith. Yet, prosecutors usually do not initiate argument in relation to the intent issue. The burden of proof rule requires the prosecution to establish intent, but it does not require the prosecution to initiate argument on this issue.

In our culture, we usually assume that people intend to do the things they have done—unless they can provide us with adequate reasons for believing they did not intend their actions. We infer intent from behavior. Thus, we usually believe that people intend to say what they have said, and if Harold strikes Mortimer, we will assume that Harold intended the action. Ordinarily, we would think it odd if someone asked for additional proof of intent—unless, of course, there is some reason for thinking the striking was accidental. (This is why we offer apologies. We want to prevent the automatic assumption that an action of ours was intentional when it was really accidental.)

The practical effect of such audience beliefs is that they help us to distinguish between a theoretical and a practical burden of proving a case satisfactorily to a particular audience. In other words, they tell us what we must establish with arguments and evidence, and they also tell us what issues the audience is likely to grant to the affirmative without further proof unless they are challenged by the negative side. They also enable the affirmative advocate to select what is likely to be the more persuasive criteria or standards when a fact or value question centers on definition.

Summary

1. Composing a persuasive case for the affirmative side of a central question is initially a matter of communicating our analysis to others. The most persuasive arguments and evidence are selected from the brief and organized in the most effective manner for presentation to an audience.

2. An effective affirmative case will satisfy three criteria: (a) it will meet the affirmative burden of proof, (b) it will be adapted to the time limitations and other features of the format for debate, and (c) it will be persuasive to its audience.

3. An affirmative case is called *prima facie* when it initially meets its burden of proof, but we need other standards for determining whether the case provides enough proof for its audience. We provide juries with standards such as "beyond reasonable doubt" for assessing sufficiency of proof in criminal cases. In other settings, advocates must be guided by the more general notion that a case must provide proof that is sufficient to satisfy the present audience.

4. A case strategy is a general plan for selecting, organizing, and presenting the affirmative analysis on a central question. Formal or prototypical cases derive from the more competitive arena of academic debate, but they can provide useful models to prompt the creative process for informal debates as well.

5. Two useful case models for policy questions are traditional needs and comparative advantages. The term *need* refers to an alleged problem or harm that serves as the focus of the motive issue. A traditional needs case usually presents a simple structure of three arguments that respond directly to the motive, obstacle, and cure issues. The affirmative usually finds it advantageous not to initiate argument on the cost issue. Typically, there are strategic advantages in forcing the negative either to initiate argument on the cost issue or to concede it.

6. A comparative advantages case has the same burden of proof as traditional needs, but it is a desirable option whenever both the present and the proposed policies have the same goals. Burden of proof can seem to be more easily met because the negative usually does not contest the motive issue. However, there is no logical difference between a problem to be solved and an advantage to be gained.

7. Affirmative cases for central questions of fact or value generally derive from the stasis model we examined in Chapter 3. Although we do not have prototype case strategies for fact and value questions, the focus of disagreement between affirmative and negative is usually on the conjectural or definitional stases. When the focus of dispute is conjectural, the case is organized along the lines of the factual issues in dispute. Definitional cases are focused on the meaning of critical terms in relation to the facts of the case.

8. Any affirmative case should be based on the beliefs and values of the audience to which it is presented. In some instances, audience beliefs grant one or more issues to the affirmative, at least initially. They are always critical in determining the real burden of proof.

Exercises

1. As a class discussion topic, examine the policy questions we considered in Chapters 2 and 3. Would it make more sense, with any of these, to construe the motive as an advantage to be gained? Can you identify policy questions, like our illustration on airbags, in which both the present policy and the proposed policy seem to have the same goals?

2. As a class discussion topic, outline a comparative advantages case for the following policy question:

Should the federal government establish a national system of examinations to measure the achievement of elementary and secondary students in the key subjects?

3. Select an editorial from your local newspaper or an article in an opinion magazine in which the author advocates a new policy or course of action. Outline the major reasons the author presents. Do you see either the traditional needs or the comparative advantages cases as the pattern of the case? If it is neither, does the case meet its burden of proof? (Or is it a prima facie case?)

4. As a class discussion exercise, develop a conjectural and a definitional case for the following central question of value:

Is the (fill in the name of your student paper) an excellent (or a lousy) newspaper?

Endnotes

1. Antoine Arnauld, *The Art of Thinking*, trans. James Dickoff and Patricia James (New York: Bobbs-Merrill, 1964), p. 307.
2. *Rocky Mountain News*, 17 January 1988, p. 6. Reprinted with permission of the *Rocky Mountain News*.
3. *Webster's New World Dictionary of the American Language* (New York: World Publishing, 1955), p. 1322.
4. *Rocky Mountain News*, 17 January 1988, p. 6. Reprinted with permission of the *Rocky Mountain News*.

11

Building Negative Cases in Debate

Central Ideas in This Chapter

1. Negative case strategies enable the advocate to provide a unified rationale for opposing a change in belief or policy.

2. Three principles guide negative case construction:
   - The advantage of presumption
   - The response to the affirmative
   - The ability to defeat change by winning one issue

3. There are four kinds of negative case strategies for debates over policy questions:
   - Defense of the present system
   - Repairs
   - Straight refutation
   - Counterproposal

4. The stasis model provides the basis for two common negative case strategies for questions of fact or value:
   - The conjectural case
   - The definitional case

Some years ago, I moderated a debate on the question: Should the Strategic Defense Initiative (so-called Star Wars) be abandoned by the United States? Almost immediately after the debate commenced, we hit the first snag. The opponents of this proposal—a professor of political science and a retired engineer for a nuclear weapons plant—objected that it was unfair to refer to their side as *negative*. They insisted that they should be called the *positive* position! The political science professor was especially insistent that there was nothing negative about their side of the question.

This incident illustrates one kind of confusion many people have about the negative side in a debate; it also reflects some of the confusion about the concept of the negative case. By this point, of course, all of us should know that the term *negative* merely refers to those who oppose the change that is proposed in the central question in dispute. Opposing advocates are called *negative* because they respond no to the central question. It does not mean that their arguments lack a positive view of the world. Indeed, there may be many positive and persuasive reasons for supporting a response of no.

As we have seen, by applying analytical formulas such as the stock issues model and the stasis system to the research process, even a relative beginner should be able to discern a substantial number of good reasons for rejecting most proposals for change. But how are all of these good reasons pulled together into a coherent and persuasive unit?

Up to this point, we have examined some of the ways a negative advocate can find flaws in affirmative arguments, evidence, and analysis of the issues. We have also explored the rules of burden of proof and presumption, along with their implications for affirmative and negative. All of this, combined with issues analysis and research, is quite useful in suggesting ways to attack particular evidence and arguments. But a negative advocate needs an overall strategy (a general plan that is organized around a central, compelling rationale for rejecting a proposed change). Thus, when we speak of a negative case, we do not mean a case lacking in positive qualities. Rather, we mean a coordinated strategy that presents a general, unified, persuasive case that makes it clear to the listener why a proposed change in belief or policy should be rejected.

Principles for Negative Case Construction

The composition of an effective negative case must be grounded in sound research and analysis, and the task is greatly simplified when all of the arguments and evidence are organized in a brief. However, a negative case is not the mere recitation of all the arguments from a brief. Rather, the brief serves as a kind of bank for argument resources. The negative advocate selects arguments for a case strategy that are based on three guiding principles:

1. The negative commences most debates with the advantage of presumption.
2. Negative argumentation is a response to an affirmative attack on present policy or belief.
3. The negative can defeat a proposed change by winning any one of the issues.

Let's examine these principles in order.

The Negative Has the Advantage of Presumption

What is the *advantage of presumption?* Recall that a rule of presumption provides an automatic decision about what beliefs or policies will be considered correct (or true) unless rejected. Clearly, it is an advantage to be considered correct at the outset of a debate and to have one's position prevail unless the opposition can overturn it with superior argument and reasoning. In most cases (but not all), rules of presumption give this advantage to existing beliefs or policies. Thus, in our courts, a defendant is "presumed innocent until proven guilty." In our legislative bodies, existing laws and policies are presumed to be correct until the legislators vote to change them. In our families, established rules of courtesy and behavior are presumed correct unless or until they are changed.

The most important practical consequence of this advantage is that it may be enough for the negative merely to show that the arguments and evidence presented by the two sides are inconclusive. Any tie in the arguments will be decided in favor of the belief or policy that has presumption—that is, the negative position. Thus, if the case of a prosecution is judged to be inconclusive, the court mandates a verdict of not guilty. Likewise, if a debate on a proposed new policy is inconclusive, the rule of presumption says that we reject the proposed change and stay with the present system, even if the present system is to do nothing.

The advantage of presumption means that the negative can win an issue merely by showing that the affirmative has not met its burden of proof. Thus, on the obstacle issue of a policy question, the negative does not actually have to prove that the present system can solve whatever problems the affirmative has developed on the motive (although the negative should do this if they can). Presumption means that we will assume the present system can solve whatever problems we may have until the affirmative proves that it cannot.

Negative Argumentation Is a Response to an Affirmative Attack

This is a very important principle that is sometimes troublesome to students, but it derives from the same rule of presumption that we have already considered. It makes sense that prosecuting attorneys must speak first, presenting the opening arguments and evidence in a criminal trial. After all, the prosecution initiates a dispute when it makes an accusation against a defendant, and most civilized nations subscribe to the presumption of innocence. So the burden of proof compels the prosecution to open a trial with a prima facie case, supporting its accusation with evidence and argument. In fact, if it were not for the prosecution's support for its assertion that the defendant committed a crime, the defense would not need to say anything, except perhaps to move for a dismissal of the charge.

Nevertheless, only an incompetent defense attorney would attempt to prepare a complete manuscript speech of defense arguments before hearing testimony and prosecution arguments. To be sure, the defense should plan general strategies and lines of argument in relation to each of the issues, but these must be adapted to what the witnesses actually say in their testimony. A competent attorney knows that the defense must respond to the arguments and evidence actually presented by the prosecution, or the negative case may be simply irrelevant in the trial.

The most immediate practical consequence of this principle is that we cannot assemble a complete negative speech until we know the essentials of the affirmative case. Why not? The simple reason is that we cannot oppose an argument effectively if we do not know what the argument is or what evidence supports it. Does this mean that a debater on the negative side must wait until the affirmative actually presents the opening argument before commencing preparation of the negative speech?

No, it does not mean that. As we have noted earlier, a thorough brief will include all of the most important lines of argument available to the affirmative and the negative. After all, the number of arguments in support of the affirmative position on each issue is limited. If your research and analysis is thorough, the affirmative should not be able to present an argument on any of the issues that would surprise you. With an effective brief, the negative can prepare to respond to affirmative evidence and arguments in relation to each of the issues.

So how should the negative side prepare its case? When we know what our opponent must argue, we can think through possible responses and arrange our evidence in support of them. Of course, until the affirmative presents the opening speech, the negative cannot know exactly which of the available arguments and evidence will be used by the affirmative or the exact order in which arguments will be presented. Thus, unlike the opening affirmative speech, which should be composed in advance, an effective negative speech is assembled as the affirmative speaks. Our negative speaker listens to what is said by the affirmative and decides what to say in response, selecting from the prepared arsenal of arguments and evidence. In this way, the negative speech responds precisely to the arguments presented by the affirmative.

The Negative Can Prevail by Winning One Issue

The affirmative must prevail on *all* of the issues (meaning that the decision makers must be persuaded that the best answer to all of the issues is yes). The corollary of this affirmative burden is that the negative defeats any proposed change in belief or policy if it wins any one of the issues.

The logic of our corollary follows directly from the definition of *issue* developed in Chapter 2, but students are sometimes surprised that winning one issue would be enough to defeat a proposed new policy or belief. The logic of this principle is vital for the negative, so let's review its support. Suppose, on a first-degree murder charge, that the prosecution loses the issue of premeditation while winning two issues—namely, that Jones killed Smith and that the killing was intended. In this case, the prosecution has established that Jones committed a crime (perhaps second-degree murder) but has not established first-degree murder. So the defense wins on that charge.

Similarly, on a policy question, if the negative wins only the cost issue, the proposed change logically has been defeated. Winning the cost issue means that the audience (or judge) has concluded that the costs (or disadvantages) of the proposed solution are greater than all of the benefits derived from solving the problem or eliminating the harm developed under motive, along with any additional advantages.

Since the negative needs to win only one issue, opponents of change can sometimes afford to ignore issues where the affirmative has overwhelming strength or to agree with the affirmative on those issues. It may be advantageous to concentrate the negative attack on the issues where negative arguments appear to be stronger. For example, suppose you were involved in a dispute with your significant other on the central question of whether you told a rotten lie when you said you had never dated a mutual acquaintance. The conjectural stasis, as we know, indicates that one issue is concerned with the facts in dispute. In this case, the facts consist of what you said to your significant other and your alleged behavior with the mutual acquaintance. If you decided to contest this issue, you might argue that your significant other's report of your statement is inaccurate, or that your alleged behavior with the acquaintance has been reported inaccurately. Or it might be more productive to concentrate your firepower on the definitional stasis, contesting the meaning of the term *rotten lie* or the term *date.*

Do you see the possible advantages of being able to focus defense where the negative is strongest? Your significant other may be willing to admit there is a difference between a rotten lie—which suggests evil intent—and a lie that has benevolent purpose, say to protect the feelings of your significant other. Moreover, he or she might be open to persuasion on the definition of *date* but never believe that reports of your being seen in a local pub with the mutual acquaintance are untrue.

The advantage to the negative of concentrating on issues where the affirmative is more vulnerable is often available on policy questions. Of course, the negative always has the option of attacking a proposed change in policy on all of the issues—motive, obstacle, cure, and cost—but it is sometimes more productive to agree on some of these, concentrating opposition on the issues where the negative appears to have the strongest arguments.

Suppose you are the negative on a policy question of this sort: Should the federal government adopt a national program of health insurance in order to guarantee medical care for all citizens? In past debates on this question, affirmatives always seem to be formidable on the motive and obstacle issues. This is not surprising if we think about it. U.S. citizens share a broad consensus on the value premise that it is deplorable for any human being to go without needed medical care, and certainly when the reason is an inability to pay for the care. Thus, when the facts reveal that many people in the United States suffer from a lack of medical care, the affirmative position on the motive issue is persuasively very strong.

This does not mean that the negative must give up on the motive issue. However, the negative may discover that it is more productive to concentrate opposition on the cure and cost issues instead of using valuable time to contest all four issues. Our national experience with Medicare and Medicaid over the past 20 years or so suggests that both programs have been vastly more expensive than any of their sponsors anticipated, and cost increases in the medical sector of the economy continue to outstrip the general rate of inflation. As a result, some of the most persuasive reasons against a major expansion of federal health insurance benefits are focused on cost, with opponents arguing that an expansion would outstrip even the federal government's resources.

So far, we have explored three principles for the negative case: (1) the negative has the advantage of presumption, (2) a negative case is always a response to an affirmative attack, and (3) the negative needs to win only one issue. As you deepen your understanding of these principles, you will find that it becomes easier to see how all of the negative arguments fit together into a persuasive whole. In addition, these three principles help us to understand the more useful negative case strategies that are available to anyone who is opposing change in relation to a question of fact, value, and policy.

Four Negative Case Strategies for Policy Questions

A negative case strategy on a policy question provides an overall rationale for opposing a proposed change. It presents a unified, persuasive view of why a proposed new policy should be rejected. A case strategy is like a blueprint for a house: It tells us where everything fits and it also indicates what arguments would be irrelevant to our persuasive position.

An important part of the negative case strategy is called the *negative philosophy* by some writers, which is perhaps a more grandiose term than is strictly required. However, the term *philosophy* may help us to understand that the negative side does not oppose change merely out of spite, contentiousness, or character defect. Rather, to say the negative has a philosophy is to say there is a set of values the negative seeks to promote and there is a view of the world that the negative believes to be true. Either the values or the beliefs about what is true rule out the proposed change.

The idea of a negative philosophy becomes somewhat clearer as we see its development in relation to the four basic negative case strategies: (1) defense of the present system, (2) repairs, (3) straight refutation, and (4) counterproposal.

Defense of the Present System

In many debates over policy questions, it is useful for the negative to construe the dispute as a choice between two ways of solving whatever problem is presented in the motive issue: We can choose either the proposed new policy or the present policy. In a *defense of the present system* strategy, the negative argues that the present system or policy is better than the proposed change, and that we should not adopt the proposed change because we are better off keeping our present system just as it is. When the motive issue is concerned with an alleged problem, the negative argues that the present policy provides a better solution to the problem than the proposed new policy. If the motive is a goal to be reached or an advantage to be gained, the negative argues that the present policy provides a better way to reach the goal or gain the advantage.

In many respects, defense of the present system (or policy, law, or solution) is the most positive of the negative case strategies. Its focus is not so much on the reasons for rejecting a proposed change as it is on reasons for preferring the present system. The negative argues that, in light of all the circumstances we face in the real world, the present policy is wisest, best, and certainly superior to the proposed policy.

A defense of the present system or policy means that the negative supports two separable dimensions of the present system or policy: (1) the basic principles of the present system and (2) the administration/implementation of the present system.

The Principles of Present Policy

Basic principles of present policy refer collectively to the goals of a policy, the values it seeks to promote, and its essential, defining features (i.e., those features that are essential to its identity as a particular policy, and especially the principles concerned with how the policy will achieve its goals). For example, in 1973 the United States Congress passed a law (which is the same as adopting a policy) that mandated a national speed limit of 55 mph. The initial goals of this policy were to conserve fuel and to reduce U.S. dependence on foreign oil. As the reduced speeds led to a decline in the number of fatalities and injuries on the highways, the goals of saving lives and preventing injuries were added. But notice also that the principles of (1) mandating a national speed limit and (2) slowing down the maximum speed to 55 mph are defining elements of the policy.

In 1987, when the U.S. Congress debated the proposal (now law) to allow the states to increase the speed limit to 65 mph on rural stretches of interstate highway, opponents argued that the principles and goals of the (then) present 55 mph speed limit were superior to those of the proposed increase. Opponents argued that the goals of saving lives, reducing the number and severity of injuries, and conserving fuel were manifestly superior to the relatively inconsequential goals of allowing people to travel 10 mph faster on sections of the interstate highways, and that reaching the more important goals required a mandated 55 mph speed limit—that is, the defining elements of present policy.

Administrative Elements of Present Policy

The administration or implementation of a policy is logically separable from its basic principles, though these elements are closely related. Many of the complaints about the 55 mph speed limit were directed to the very idea of mandating such a "slow" speed (that is, the basic principle of the policy), especially in the western states. But some of the complaints were concerned with various aspects of the administration (or enforcement) of the policy. For example, there were a number of complaints about inconsistent enforcement. Out-of-state motorists sometimes complained that local police picked on them, allowing in-state motorists to speed with impunity, and federal highway officials charged a number of states, such as Wyoming, with lax enforcement.

The distinction between basic principles of a policy and its administration also can be observed in such major public policies as the all volunteer force (AVF) policy for the military. Clearly there is difference between the goals and essential features of an all volunteer force on the one side, and its administration or implementation on the other. The basic principles, or defining elements, of an AVF are fairly clear when it is compared to the policy it replaced. Under the old policy, the compulsory draft, the federal government simply ordered young men to report for service in the Army, Navy, and Air Force whenever the forces needed them. In contrast, the new AVF policy abandons compulsion; it uses incentives, such as more generous pay and benefits, to entice sufficient numbers of young men to join the military forces. Thus, personal choice, use of incentives, and volunteerism are the defining elements or principles of the AVF policy.

These defining elements or principles could be administered or implemented in a variety of ways, however. Administrative elements include recruiting methods, pay and benefit levels, treatment of recruits, methods of advertising and persuasion, and so forth. These are but some of the items that could be administered in various ways, all within the general principles of an AVF policy.

The Defense Strategy: The Present System Is the Best Policy

A strategy of defending present policy means the negative supports both the defining principles and the administration or implementation of present policy. This strategy provides the most positive rationale for opposing a new policy. Its emphasis is on the superiority of the principles and administration of present policy rather than the inadequacies of the affirmative proposal. Moreover, this strategy provides a comprehensive, unified approach to all of the issues, and its use suggests some more or less standard, general lines of argument in relation to each of the principal issues:

Standard Lines of Argument for Defense of Present Policy

Motive:
1. The problem presented by the affirmative is insignificant. (application of the so what? or value application test, and comparison of the problem to standards or criteria for measuring significance)
2. The problem presented by the affirmative is declining over time, decreasing in significance.
3. Due to the nature of the real world, we must choose between two evils, and the problem presented by the affirmative is the lesser of the two evils. (the value comparison test)

Obstacle:
1. The present system *is* solving the problem.
2. The present system (policy) *can* solve the problem, given sufficient time.
3. Since we must choose between two evils, the present system is sound because it solves the most important problem.
4. The principles of present policy are philosophically sound.

Cure:
1. The present system provides a more effective remedy to the alleged problems than the proposed policy.
2. The proposed policy will not solve the alleged problem(s).

Cost:
1. The present policy has greater benefits than the proposed policy and fewer disadvantages.
2. The costs (or disadvantages) of the proposed policy are far greater than its benefits (or advantages).

The arguments listed above are not intended to be all-inclusive. Rather, they merely suggest some of the more standard lines of argument that can be adapted whenever the negative uses the defense of the present policy strategy. In addition to these arguments, you should consider how the negative can use tests of evidence and argument forms to refute the affirmative.

In order to defend a present policy as superior to a proposed new policy, we must know what it is. This means we must understand both the defining elements and the administrative elements of present policy. As a practical matter, the defining elements of present policy usually are identified in a process of comparing present policy to a proposed change in policy.

The process of comparison is especially important in those cases where it appears that present policy is essentially not to have a policy. For example, some states have repealed their laws mandating the use of motorcycle helmets. So a formal statement of present policy is that the law is silent on the subject of helmets. But it seems awkward and even misleading to say that present policy is not to mandate the use of helmets. The absence of a policy hardly seems intelligible as a policy. Yet, when there is a proposal to reinstitute the mandated use of helmets, it seems easier to see that the defining element of present policy is freedom of choice for each rider, and it is not so misleading to speak of a freedom of choice policy on the use of motorcycle helmets.

Repair of the Present System

To understand a *repairs strategy*, it is useful to commence with the two components of policy we identified earlier: principles and administration. In a repairs strategy, the negative supports the defining elements or principles of the present policy, and so it is the same as defense of present policy in this respect. However, the negative is not committed to the administration or implementation of present policy.

Persuasive Merits of Repairs

This strategy can be an attractive alternative to defense of the present system whenever it would be unpersuasive for the negative to argue that there is no problem. During the 1970s, for example, some members of congress advocated that we should abandon the all volunteer force (AVF) policy and return to the military draft—mainly because of three alleged problems:

1. Reduced birth rates in the 1960s and early 1970s indicated a smaller pool of young men available in the 1980s, suggesting the military would be unable to obtain the required number of volunteers.
2. Many of the volunteers were said to lack the level of education required to read army manuals or to operate sophisticated equipment.
3. Recruits seemed to come predominantly from minority and poverty groups, suggesting that the nation was exploiting its disadvantaged in providing for national defense.

Opponents argued that the problems were somewhat exaggerated, but found it difficult to deny them entirely. Instead, opponents argued that the essential features or inherent principles of the AVF were not flawed. Rather, the alleged problems simply indicated a need to *repair* some administrative features of the AVF, especially the incentives for volunteering. Opponents argued that you cannot make the manpower pool any larger with a compulsory draft, so the choice was either to (1) force young men into the military with a draft, which they thought was wrong; or (2) persuade young men to join by offering better incentives (i.e., higher pay, better benefits). Opponents argued that a minor repair of existing incentives would solve all of the alleged problems. If we need better educated young men or if we want a military that is more representative of the general population, better incentives will provide them.

Repairs Support Principles, Not Administration

Notice, in our AVF example, that all of the suggested repairs change only the administration or implementation of the AVF policy—not its defining elements or principles. Incentives for volunteering can be increased substantially without any alteration in the basic principles or philosophy of the AVF. Nevertheless, a *repairs strategy* is less committed to the present system than a *defense of the present system*, and the more extensive are the proposed repairs, the less the commitment to present policy.

One of the risks of this strategy is that, as the repairs become more extensive, the advantage of presumption is correspondingly weakened. The negative can continue to claim presumption for the principles/philosophy of the present policy because these are defended. But the advantage of presumption does not extend to the administrative features that are abandoned or proposed as repairs. In effect, the negative assumes a burden of proof for any repairs advocated, and the negative must be prepared to prove (on the cure issue) that the proposed repairs will solve the alleged problems better than the affirmative proposal and (on the cost issue) will provide much greater benefits in relation to costs.

On the obstacle issue, a repairs strategy usually means the negative disputes the affirmative analysis of the causes of the alleged problems. Thus, for example, on the controversy over the proposal to mandate the use of helmets for all motorcycle riders, the negative may admit that the number of deaths and injuries to riders is significant (motive) but deny that the cause of these injuries and deaths is the failure to wear helmets. Instead, opponents of a helmet law have argued that the real causes include inadequate instruction for beginning riders, careless riding, use of alcohol and drugs, careless automobile drivers, and the large increase in the number of motorcycle riders. The idea is to show that a law requiring the use of helmets will not significantly reduce injuries and deaths because it fails to get at their causes, and that repairs that specifically address the causes (namely, negative repairs) will reduce the problems.

Like the defense of present policy strategy, a repairs approach provides a unified way of responding to all of the issues in a policy debate. Once again, there are some standard lines of argument for repairs that can help us to think about ways of responding to affirmative arguments on each issue.

Standard Lines of Argument for Repairs

Motive:
1. We agree that there is a problem, but it is not as serious as the affirmative has claimed.
2. We agree with the affirmative on this issue.

Obstacle:
1. The affirmative has misanalyzed the causes of the problem.
2. The problem is not caused by the present policy.
3. The principles of present policy are correct; the problem can be solved merely by correcting some minor flaws in the administration of present policy.

Cure:
1. The present system, when it is repaired, provides a more effective remedy to the problem than the proposed policy.
2. The proposed policy will not solve the problem.

Cost:
1. The repaired present system provides greater benefits in relation to costs than the proposed policy.
2. Even if the proposed policy could solve the problem, its costs would be greater than its benefits.

The repairs position can be powerfully persuasive because it seems reasonable. It does not deny the existence of a problem that the audience may regard as serious, and it seems to profit from its positive approach of advocating an effective yet less costly solution to the alleged problems. Like the defense of present policy approach, it construes the dispute as a choice between two options: (1) the present policy, repaired so that it will work effectively; and (2) the proposed policy. The negative argues that a repaired present policy is superior, especially in relation to the cure and cost issues.

Straight Refutation

The term *straight refutation* means that the negative strategy is to defeat affirmative arguments and evidence or to weaken them to the point that they are unable to meet the burden of proof on the issues. Recall that the burden of proof rule ordinarily requires the affirmative to establish a response of yes to all of the issues. The negative generally is not required to prove that no is a correct response. This means that the negative does not actually have to prove the affirmative is wrong—a tie is sufficient for the negative to win an issue. If the negative can point to enough flaws in affirmative reasoning, arguments, or evidence on any one of the issues, the negative can defeat a proposed new policy.

Using the Advantage of Presumption

A straight refutation strategy depends on the advantage of presumption without actually arguing in support of either the principles or the administration of present policy. Rather than arguing that present policy is best, this strategy concentrates its attention on undermining the affirmative case, revealing its weaknesses. The idea is to show that the affirmative has not met its burden of proving that the present policy should be replaced with the new policy.

It may help you to see that the straight refutation strategy for policy debates has a direct analog in the courtroom. In our criminal courts, the defense is not required to take a positive position, vigorously arguing that the defendant is innocent (which is somewhat like arguing in the policy arena that the present policy is best). Rather, it may be sufficient for the defense merely to poke holes in the prosecution's case. If enough flaws can be found, the prosecution will have failed to meet its burden of proof, and the defendant must be acquitted—not because we believe the defendant truly is innocent but because guilt *has not been proven.*

A Unified Strategy of Denial

Despite its apparent nihilism, the straight refutation strategy also offers a unified way of thinking about the way to respond to an affirmative case. The idea is to assemble an arsenal for undermining affirmative arguments and evidence on each issue. This strategy provides an unlimited opportunity to apply the tests of reasoning and argument developed in Chapters 5 and 6, and the test of evidence and premises from Chapter 7. In addition, there are some useful standard lines of argument that may be adapted on the four principal issues.

Standard Lines of Argument for Straight Refutation

Motive:
1. The evidence in support of claims for significant problems is flawed or untrustworthy. It fails the tests of recency, relevancy, sufficiency, and so forth.
2. The affirmative fails to prove that there is anything really harmful in the situations they have described. (so what? test)

Obstacle:
1. The affirmative analysis is incomplete. It shows only that part of the present system cannot solve the problem, and it ignores other important parts of the present system.
2. The affirmative evidence fails to prove that present policy causes the problem or that it is incapable of removing the causes.
3. There are other causes of the problem than those identified by the affirmative. So present policy is not cause of the problem.

Cure:
1. The affirmative has not proven that its proposed policy will solve the problem or produce the advantage.
2. The affirmative has not proven that its proposal is workable (or enforceable).

Cost:
1. The affirmative has not proven that the advantages of its proposal will outweigh the disadvantages.
2. The affirmative evidence on benefits is flawed.

Persuasive Weakness of Straight Refutation

The major problem with a straight refutation strategy is that it tends to lack persuasive appeal. Juries are inclined to be suspicious of a defendant who chooses not to take the witness stand or in any way to mount a case in support of his or her innocence. It seems weak merely to poke holes in the case of the prosecution and to rely on the rule of presumption. People usually think that if the defendant really were innocent, he or she would at least say so, and support that position as well as possible. Similarly, it seems weak merely to point to flaws in affirmative arguments and evidence in relation to the four issues, and it seems especially weak when there is general agreement that a serious problem exists. People seem to prefer to try a new solution, even if advocates cannot prove conclusively that it will be successful (cure) or guarantee that benefits will outweigh costs. And as the perceived seriousness of a problem increases, people seem to be more inclined to "grasp at straws" and adopt solutions with very low probabilities of success.

Yet, despite its persuasive weakness, the straight refutation strategy is sometimes the best option for the negative. Suppose the negative agrees that there is a significant problem, such as the U.S. trade deficits of the 1980s, and concedes as well that present policy is unable to provide a remedy (ruling out a defense of present policy strategy). It may be that the negative does not see *any* solution to the trade deficit at present or see any way to repair present policy. Nevertheless, the negative may be convinced that a particular proposed solution will not solve the trade deficit (cure issue) and that its costs will outweigh any benefits (cost issue). In this sort of situation, a straight refutation strategy is the best choice. It makes sense for the negative to concentrate on the cure and cost issues, pointing to flaws in affirmative reasoning and evidence to show that it fails to meet the burden of proof. It can be far more sensible to do nothing than to waste limited resources on a solution that will not solve the problem but will be very costly and perhaps cause serious problems.

Counterproposal

The term *counterproposal,* or *counterplan,* means that the negative proposes its own solution to whatever problem is indicated in the motive issue, and argues that its solution is superior to the affirmative proposal. A counterplan is used only when the negative agrees with the affirmative that the problems identified in the motive issue are significant enough to warrant action, and agrees as well that present policy is incapable of solving the problem. However, like the defense of present policy and repairs strategies, a counterproposal strategy offers the audience a choice between two positions: the proposed affirmative solution and the proposed negative solution. The question for the audience, then, is which side has the best solution.

Competitiveness Standard
In order to qualify as a counterproposal, the negative solution must be substantially different from the affirmative proposal. A negative solution would not qualify as a legitimate counterproposal if it were more or less the same in principle, and different only in its details. In order for the negative counterplan to be a reason for rejecting the affirmative's plan, it must be directly competitive with the affirmative. This means the negative proposal must be a genuine alternative to the affirmative proposal, so that it would not be possible or make sense to adopt both.

To clarify the idea of competitiveness, let's look at a relatively straightforward example of a counterplan. A few years ago, the local sheriff closed one of the recreational rivers to "tubers" (people rafting the river on an innertube) because several people had drowned. He argued that the high cost of search and rescue efforts, not to mention body recovery, put a severe strain on his budget. He said it was not fair for local taxpayers to pay for this, especially since the people who drowned were mostly from out of state. However, to his surprise, he discovered that state law did not give him the authority to close the river. So he urged state legislators to propose legislation providing sheriffs with the authority to close rivers to tubing whenever they judged them to be sufficiently dangerous.

Opponents to this proposal held a variety of positions, of course, but one group opposed the sheriff's proposal by offering a counterplan. The group agreed with the sheriff that the high cost of search and recovery of drowned tubers was a significant problem and that present policy could not solve it. However, they argued, since the problem presented was only the cost to the sheriff and taxpayers, a better solution would be to require tubers to pay a permit fee to the county that would cover the cost of search, rescue, and even body recovery. The solution was better, they argued, because it solved the problem of cost to taxpayers without infringing on the rights of tubers to enjoy the thrills of white-water rafting.

You may or may not find this to be a sensible alternative to the sheriff's proposal, but do you see how it is competitive? If the counterplan were adopted, presumably there would be no need for the affirmative proposal granting sheriffs authority to close a river whenever they considered it dangerous.

Focus of Disagreement with Counterproposals

A common element in the use of counterproposal strategy is that the negative agrees with the affirmative on the motive issue. Thus, in our example, the negative agrees that the cost to the sheriff and the taxpayers is a significant problem. The negative also agrees on the obstacle issue that the present system is incapable of solving the problem, but disagrees on the reasons why the present system is unable to provide a solution. Thus, our affirmative advocate (the sheriff) argues that the present system cannot solve the problem because it fails to provide the sheriff with authority to close the river to tubing. However, the negative argues that the inability of present system to solve the cost problem has nothing to do with the sheriff's authority to close rivers; rather, the real defect of the present system is that it lacks a mechanism to ensure that tubers pay the cost of rescuc and body recovery. The focus of this disagreement can be seen more clearly by comparing the reasons each side provides for why the present policy cannot solve the problem.

Affirmative (Sheriff)	*Negative*
The present system fails to provide the sheriff with authority to close the river when it is dangerous.	The present system lacks a mechanism to ensure that tubers pay the cost of rescue and body recovery.

Do you see why this disagreement is crucial? It is because we generally think that the best solution to a problem is the one that directly solves the nature of the defect, or the causes of the problem, in present policy.

Focus on the Comparison Issue

A counterplan initially focuses debate on the subordinate issue of comparison, which would be phrased as follows for our tubing controversy: Is the proposal to grant the sheriff authority to close a "dangerous" river the best solution available for the problem of cost to the sheriff and taxpayers? The negative responds no to this question and supports its response by presenting a counterplan—namely, the proposal to assess tubers for whatever it costs the sheriff to search, rescue, and so on.

An interesting feature of the comparison issue is that it seems to serve primarily as a way of refocusing the cure and cost issues. After all, how do we go about supporting a claim that an alternative solution is better? Better in relation to what? In general, we argue that our solution (whatever it is) is better because it is a more complete solution to the problem (the cure issue) or that it has a superior ratio of benefits to costs, or advantages to disadvantages (the cost issue). Thus, when the negative presents a counterplan, the audience is asked to choose between two competing solutions, and the choice is to be based on a comparison of the alternatives in relation to two criteria:

> *Criterion #1 (Cure)*: Which plan will ensure the most complete solution to the problem?
>
> *Criterion #2 (Cost)*: Which solution provides the best cost/ benefit ratio?

The focus on cure and cost can be helpful initially in sorting out the arguments for a counterplan strategy. However, the apparent simplicity of this focus can be misleading unless we realize that both sides will be basing their arguments for these issues on their opposing analysis of the causes of the problem, or the reasons why the present system is unable to solve the problem, as we noted in relation to the obstacle issue.

Relationship Between Counterproposals and Repairs

Students are sometimes confused about the differences between a counterproposal and a repair of the present system. After all, as students correctly observe, both strategies have the negative agreeing that a problem exists and both propose new remedies for it. However, these apparent similarities are both superficial and misleading.

On the motive issue, it is true that a repair strategy admits that the world is not as perfect as it could be, but it does not agree that the problems we have are significant enough to warrant major change. Rather, a repairs strategy argues that a minor adjustment here and there is more than sufficient. In contrast, the counterplan strategy has the negative agreeing on the significance of the problem without reserve. If there is any disagreement with the affirmative here, it would be on the precise definition or description of the problem rather than its significance. Admittedly, this difference may seem small, but it becomes very important when we look at how the two strategies part company on the obstacle or blame issue.

On the obstacle issue, a repair strategy supports the principles, philosophy, and defining elements of present policy without reserve, and argues that there is no flaw in the inherent features of present policy. However, even though the problems identified in the motive issue are not really important enough to justify major change, they do warrant minor repairs in the administration or implementation of present policy. Thus, in relation to our AVF (all volunteer force) policy, a repairs strategy would argue that its principles are absolutely correct, but it may be desirable to adjust some of the ways the policy is administered, such as increasing efforts to recruit women.

In contrast, a counterproposal strategy does not support anything about present policy. Rather, it agrees with the affirmative that everything about present policy—its principles and its administration—are hopelessly flawed, and only a new policy will solve the major problems we have. So, if the affirmative is advocating a return to the military draft as a solution to the problem of an insufficient quality or quantity of volunteers for military forces at present, a counterplan would not offer repairs for the AVF. Rather, a counterplan might propose something like a major reduction in U.S. military commitments around the world, arguing that quality and quantity problems can be solved easily if the required size of the military can be reduced.

Although the use of counterplans is not rare in public policy debate, there are at least two reasons why negative advocates should be cautious about selecting this strategy. First, when a counterplan is offered, the negative simultaneously abandons the advantage of presumption and acquires a burden of proof that is more or less as onerous as the affirmative burden. The advantage of presumption extends only to the present system. When the negative agrees that the present system is hopelessly flawed and incapable of solving the problem, the advantage is abandoned. Moreover, since the negative counterplan is a new policy as much as the affirmative proposal, the negative must meet a burden of proving that its counterproposal will solve the problem (cure issue) and that its benefits will justify whatever it costs (cost issue).

A second reason for caution is that use of counterplans typically increases the complexity of a debate, with the attendant problems of confusion for members of the audience. In a sense, the audience finds itself trying to decide between two affirmatives since both sides are advocating change from the present system. And it is not always easy to sort through advantages and disadvantages of two proposals in addition to the competing analysis of which plan solves more of the alleged problem.

Despite the grounds for caution, however, the counterproposal is an important strategy to have available in the negative arsenal, and it is used in the legislative arena more frequently than many people realize. Whenever an advocate in the legislature or Congress offers an amendment that proposes to substitute an alternative policy for the one contained in an original bill, the counterplan strategy is being used.

Negative Case Strategies for Questions of Fact and Value

In one of the happier instances of symmetry in rhetoric and argumentation, it turns out that negative case strategies for questions of fact and value more or less parallel the affirmative focus on the stasis categories: conjecture, definition, quality, and procedure. However, while the affirmative must be prepared, at least in theory, to support a response of yes to the issues in all four categories, the negative has a range of choices.

The negative can choose to develop a case strategy that concentrates on only one of the four issue categories or just about any combination of the four. A negative case that addresses all four of the stasis categories is possible but rare. More typically, advocates seem to focus negative strategy on one or two of the *stases*, with most cases focused either on the conjectural issue (the facts or who killed the victim) or the definitional issue (the killing was not a murder).

The Conjectural Case Strategy

In a conjectural strategy, the negative can pursue either or both of two goals:

1. To weaken or destroy the evidence and reasoning upon which the affirmative factual or value claim is based
2. To support a contradictory claim

Suppose Jim's spouse (or significant other), Judy, says to him, "You lied to me when you said you liked my new hairdo." Now, of course, a term such as *lie* can be defined in several ways. But, for now, let's assume that Jim elects to defend himself with a conjectural case strategy. His first move should be to learn why Judy thinks he has lied—that is, what evidence led her to that conclusion.

After her evidence is presented, the first goal of a conjectural strategy is to point to its flaws. This is primarily a matter of applying the tests of evidence we examined in Chapter 7. The mere question— What evidence supports the claim that Jim lied?—leads simply and efficiently to the four tests of the evidence-claim relationship: (1) assertion, (2) relevance, (3) recency, and (4) sufficiency.

If Judy says, "Well, I really don't have any evidence, but I feel like you weren't telling me the truth," then Jim should explain the assertion test and the difference between an assertion and an argument claim. If she says, "I heard you say you like Amy's hair, and it is much longer than mine," then Jim might apply the test of relevance, pointing out that a person certainly can like hair of different lengths on different people. He might also use the test of sufficiency and gently observe that this sort of "evidence" is awfully flimsy as a basis for accusing a person of lying. In a similar way, the three tests of the evidence source and the four tests of evidence substance provide additional tools for discovering and exploiting weaknesses in an opponent's evidence and reasoning.

In some cases, as we noted earlier in our discussion of the straight refutation case strategy, it may be sufficient merely to poke holes in the evidence and reasoning of the affirmative and rely on the rules of presumption and burden of proof. But as we have seen, this approach tends to be unsatisfying and unpersuasive to an audience that wants to decide in favor of what is true. Claiming victory by merely poking holes in an opponent's case also seems to resemble the *argument from ignorance* fallacy—that is, "You can't prove your position, so therefore I'm right." However, a negative advocate seldom needs to confine his or her efforts merely to attacking an opponent's case. So, if he can, Jim should not content himself merely with refuting the evidence Judy uses. Rather, he should try to support the contradictory position, that he told the truth when he said he liked her hair, and he should offer whatever evidence he has in order to overcome her feeling or intuition that he does not mean it.

A conjectural strategy always pursues one or both of the goals we have examined: namely, (1) to weaken or destroy the evidence upon which the affirmative value or factual claim is based and (2) to support a contradictory claim.

The Definitional Case Strategy

In some disputes over questions of fact or value, the focus of disagreement is not so much on what the facts are (what actions a defendant performed and in what circumstances, etc.) but on what the facts mean or what the actions constitute. When a negative advocate elects to use a definitional case strategy, the idea, once again, is to reach at least one of two goals:

1. To refute the affirmative definition of the critical term in a dispute by showing that it doesn't apply to the facts
2. To replace it with a negative definition

When he was accused of lying to Judy, Jim could have maintained that the facts, as she put them, were essentially accurate but that they did not constitute *lying*. To initiate the first part of the definitional strategy, Jim might ask Judy what she means by *lying*. She might respond that lying, to her, is "making a statement that one knows to be false, especially with the intent to deceive." This definition seems straightforward and honest enough, and this should not be surprising. In fact, generally we should expect that our opponents will define terms in an honest, straightforward way. But these qualities do not mean a definition is above refutation or that it is appropriate in this case.

One useful way to think about refutation of this definition of *lying* is to ask whether it would be reasonable in all cases. Isn't there a difference between lying and, say, creative fiction? After all, a storyteller makes statements that he or she knows to be false, and sometimes with an intent to deceive listeners—at least for a little while—in order for the story to have its proper, dramatic effect. To place a storyteller in the same definitional category as a liar is not merely an injustice, it is also to deprive the word *lying* of its utility.

Thus, Jim might argue that Judy's definition of lying is clearly too broad, according to this example. But, more to the point of this case, shouldn't we admit that there is a difference between lying and making statements that are intended to make Judy feel good about herself? Clearly, a person can have radically different reasons for making false statements with an intent to deceive, and that is why Judy's definition is flawed. Not all deceptions are malevolent.

To summarize, the refutational strategy of Jim's case has two elements: (1) he admits that he said he liked Judy's hairdo when he really did not, and intended to deceive her, but that (2) his actions do not constitute *lying* because they were intended to make her feel good about herself, and there was no evil intent on his part.

You may notice that Jim's argument seems to assume a competing definition of *lying*, which adds qualifying conditions—namely, that an untrue statement, even if it is deliberate and meant to deceive, is not a lie unless it is intended to harm its victim or bring unwarranted profit or advantage to the one who makes the statement. Or perhaps Jim might say that when Judy asked him if he liked her hairdo, he was afraid of the consequences of a truthful answer, and that there is a difference between lying and making untrue statements in order to save a life—namely, his own!

In summary, a definitional case strategy always pursues one or both of two goals: (1) to refute the definition used by the affirmative by showing that it is too broad or at least that it is inappropriate for the facts of this case and (2) that there is a better (negative) definition of the critical term in dispute.

Admittedly, our example of Jim and Judy is somewhat contrived, and it could hardly be considered as one of the more momentous controversies of our time. But the situations of ordinary life are an important argument arena for us to understand. And if this sort of case is clear to us, we will understand how to apply the conjectural and the definitional negative case strategies to more complex disputes. Even the most complex fact and value disputes in science, education, law, foreign policy, and so on involve the same elements as our illustrative case. As an example, let's examine a current dispute in the field of public education.

In a speech to educators, Mary Krugman, an expert in the field of child abuse, contended that teachers "who rule their classrooms through fear and intimidation commit the kind of psychological abuse of children that one day will be punished by the courts."[1] As reported, Krugman defined *psychological maltreatment* as "acts of rejecting, terrorizing, isolating, and exploiting children." Now suppose an elementary school teacher, Mr. Meany, is accused of psychologically abusing two third-graders, Billy Whine and Mary Brat. Specifically, it is alleged that Mr. Meany yelled at the children, told them in front of the class that he was disgusted with their constant disruption of the class, and made them sit in a corner for 30 minutes. An attorney for the parents of Whine and Brat argues that these actions constitute psychological abuse because they surely rejected, terrorized, isolated, and exploited the children. How can Mr. Meany respond?

Let's assume that the dispute is before the school board, acting in a quasi-judicial capacity, and that the school board understands the rule of presumption. Using the conjectural strategy, Mr. Meany could deny that he did any of those things or deny that he did some of them. He might admit that he told Whine and Brat that he was disgusted with their behavior, for example, but deny that he yelled. He might admit that he made them sit in the corner, but maintain that it was for 5 minutes rather than 30. In supporting his position, he could (1) attack the evidence against him as certainly biased, especially if it consists of testimony from Whine and Brat; and (2) support a contradictory version of the facts by providing evidence from the testimony of other children.

Alternatively, Mr. Meany might admit that he performed all of the actions as charged, but argue that they do not constitute psychological abuse. Here, as we noted, the idea is to refute the definition of the affirmative and, whenever possible, provide an alternative definition from the negative. The point of either or both approaches is to show that the facts of this case do not constitute psychological abuse, or at least that Mr. Meany's actions should not be considered criminal.

Mr. Meany might argue that a definition of a crime should differentiate clearly between desirable and prohibited behavior. Yet, Krugman's definition of *psychological abuse* is so general as to include almost anything a teacher might do in trying to maintain discipline in the classroom. Moreover, the criteria in her definition—acts of "rejecting, terrorizing, isolating, and exploiting"—are themselves so abstract as to be meaningless. After all, a teacher's act that is rejecting or terrorizing to one child could easily be considered mild or merely strict to another. Does yelling really terrorize a child in a harmful way? If so, what are we to make of the yelling by parents? And is it necessarily a bad thing for some children to feel terrorized and/or rejected at times? How does Krugman's definition allow us to distinguish between psychological abuse and ordinary discipline? What could a teacher do to establish order and respect for authority that would not be considered psychological abuse according to this definition?

Mr. Meany might offer an alternative definition for *psychological abuse*, but he could also maintain that the concept is simply too vague for precise definition at present. The definitional case strategy does not require the negative to provide a counterdefinition. Rather, that is merely one option. The idea is to prevail with the overall position that the admitted facts to not constitute psychological abuse or any other crime or blameworthy action.

Summary

1. The purpose of case strategies is to unify the argument position of the negative and to maximize the persuasive rationale for opposing an affirmative position on a question of fact, value, or policy. The primary value of case strategies outlined here is not that they provide simple formulas for success. Rather, they should enable us to see some of the possibilities.

2. Three principles guide negative case construction: (a) the negative commences a debate with the advantage of presumption, (b) the negative argumentation is a response to an affirmative attack, and (c) the negative can defeat a proposed change by winning one issue.

3. Negative case strategies provide a unified rationale for why the audience should reject a proposed change in belief or policy. They help to clarify the relationships between all of the negative arguments and evidence, and they provide a kind of checklist of the possible ways to refute a proposed change.

4. There are four case strategies for policy questions: (a) defense of present policy, (b) repairs, (c) straight refutation, and (d) counterproposal. The first three strategies can be used alone or in combination, and you may see other variations as you work with a particular policy dispute.

5. A defense of present policy strategy is committed to both the basic principles as well as the administrative elements of the present system. A negative advocate argues that present policy is the best available in relation to the problems alleged in the motive issue.

6. A repairs strategy is committed to the principles of the present policy but not to its administrative elements or implementation. The negative acknowledges that some problems exist but argues that the present system can provide an effective response to the problems if a few, minor administrative defects are repaired.

7. Straight refutation does not indicate positive support for present policy. Rather, it rests on the advantage of presumption and argues that the affirmative case does not meet its burden of proof on the issues. Its approach is to provide a unified attack on affirmative arguments and evidence, pointing to any flaws or weaknesses.

8. A counterproposal strategy completely abandons the present policy. The negative agrees with the affirmative on the need for a change by conceding the motive and obstacle issues but disagrees on cure and cost. The negative proposes its own policy that is different in principle from either the affirmative proposal or the present system, and argues that its policy provides a superior solution to the problem.

9. The stasis categories suggest a range of options for negative cases on questions of fact and value. A conjectural case may try to weaken or destroy the evidence and reasoning of the affirmative case or actively support a contradictory position on the question in dispute. A definitional case may accept the facts presented by the affirmative but deny the affirmative's interpretation of their meaning.

Exercises

1. As a class exercise, apply the strategies for policy disputes to the following question and outline a negative case for each of the four strategies:

   > Should the federal government establish a national system of examinations to measure the achievement of elementary and secondary students in the key subjects?

2. As a class discussion exercise, develop a negative case based on the conjectural and definitional strategies in response to the following question:

   > Is the (fill in the name of your student paper) an excellent (or lousy) newspaper?

3. Select an editorial from your local newspaper in which the writer argues against a proposed change in belief or policy. Outline the major lines of argument presented and identify the kind of case strategy they represent.

Endnote

1. *Rocky Mountain News*, 8 August 1988, p. 6. Reprinted with permission of *The Rocky Mountain News*.

12

Rhetoric and Argumentation in Social Conflict

Central Ideas in This Chapter

1. The principles of rhetoric and argumentation enable us to make sense of social conflict and to see clearly its major kinds as well as the methods for terminating it.

2. There are two major kinds of conflict. Issue conflict is focused on central questions. Hostility conflict is focused on an antagonistic relationship and such feelings as aggression, competition, and anger.

3. Issue and hostility conflict differ in relation to the purpose of conflict behavior and their termination potential.

4. Six methods of conflict termination enable us to deepen our understanding of the uses and limitations of argumentation:
   - Avoidance
   - Conquest
   - Reconciliation
   - Compromise
   - Award
   - Chance mechanisms

5. All six methods of termination can be applied to issue conflict. Only avoidance, conquest, and reconciliation are applicable to hostility conflict.

6. Award is the only method of conflict termination that requires debate.

One evening in late October of 1973, I received a telephone call from an administrator in my college. He felt troubled, he said, by the lack of responsible dialogue on campus in response to the so-called Yom Kippur War then in progress between Israel and its Islamic neighbors. He thought I should correct this oversight by organizing a debate, featuring students on campus from Israel and various Arab nations as the principal advocates. Such a debate, he said, could foster dialogue between these students and also test the merits of conflicting claims about the war.

I said it would be a serious mistake to attempt a debate on the war in progress, and especially if it included students from the nations involved. When asked why, I explained that the "debate" would begin as a shouting match and might very well escalate into a riot. Emotions on the war among Islamic and Israeli students at the university were understandably intense, and many of our American Jewish students had family members in Israel or felt a strong sense of kinship with the Israeli people. A debate, I explained, is *not* a method for promoting understanding or building goodwill between students when their respective friends and family members are killing each other on battlefields thousands of miles away, and we certainly wouldn't want to bring that war to our campus. People could be hurt. "Oh, I see your point," he said, and quickly changed the subject.

Most of us hate to confront our own ignorance, so it was not surprising that this administrator was embarrassed when the folly of his suggestion was made clear to him. He probably realized that his enthusiasm for the debate process was somewhat like the small boy with a new hammer, who seems to think that everything needs pounding. No sane person wants to start a riot by supposing, mistakenly, that a debate between hostile factions of foreign students will somehow promote understanding. But his response—"I see"—illustrates a fundamental theme of this book. All arts enhance our abilities to *see* things that are functionally invisible to a person who is ignorant of them. And the art of rhetoric, as Aristotle conceived it, is especially a faculty of discerning—an ability to see and to make sense of the vital elements of persuasion in any situation where there is conflict.

But what enables us to "see" when debate is useful and when it is not? In a way, the simplicity of this question is deceptive, as you may have guessed. It is a way of getting at a more fundamental question: How do we use the principles of rhetoric and argumentation to make sense of the larger range of persuasion and conflict? Our response to this question should enable you to assess the limitations of debate as well as its uses, but our more basic goal is to integrate the principles and skills of rhetoric and argumentation so that they are useful to you in any situation where it is important to make sense of argument and conflict.

To understand the larger range of social conflict and the uses of argumentation principles for purposes other than formal debate, we need two kinds of conceptual tools. First, we need a conceptual basis for seeing the nature and the major kinds of conflict. Second, we need a way of analyzing conflict in relation to methods for its termination, or ending.

The Nature of Conflict

Traditionally, rhetoric and argumentation have been limited to rational disputes that can be framed as central questions of fact, value, or policy. But thoughtful students might ask: Are conflicts always rational? Is it possible to frame all conflicts as central questions? The short answer to both questions, as you might have guessed, is no. And we can readily see evidence for such an answer by looking to our own experiences. All of us have had conflicts (fights) with parents, brothers or sisters, friends, or co-workers that certainly did not seem rational. And if we can analyze such conflicts, we may realize that they cannot be focused by one or even several central questions. How do we make sense of conflicts that cannot be framed as central questions?

Jessie Bernard, a sociologist, argues that the focus of such conflicts is hostility. She suggests that we can make a useful distinction between *issue conflict* and *hostility conflict*.[1]

Issue Conflict

Bernard's concept of issue conflict is instantly intelligible to us because she is talking about the familiar struggles or disagreements over central questions of fact, value, or policy. You are well able to recognize and to phrase questions for such conflicts by now, of course, but it will assist our effort to make sense of hostility conflicts if we examine a range of some reasonably current societal and interpersonal arguments that belong to the *issue* category.

When bus drivers went on strike against Greyhound in 1990, their stated rationale was an inability to settle differences with management over wages and work rules. The drivers said they wanted a 5 percent pay increase, and management did not want to pay that much. In addition, the drivers were opposed to changes demanded by management in some of the work rules. Like most labor-management disputes, this one was complicated by the number and variety of demands from each side. But what is important for us is to see that disputes over wages and work rules each can be framed as a policy question to which one side says yes and the other side says no. When all of the demands are phrased in this way, we can say in more or less precise terms what the conflict is about.

Issue conflicts in the scientific or academic arenas frequently center on questions of fact. Thus, for example, when some astronomers reported their findings of huge galactic clusters that appear to be organized into "walls" of galaxies, evenly distributed throughout the universe, it provoked a major argument among astronomers over the accuracy of the generally accepted *big bang theory* on the origin of the universe. Whether the big bang theory is correct or not is, of course, a central question of fact. Here again, if the central question for this sort of issue conflict is correctly phrased, it will indicate exactly what astronomers are arguing about.

Probably most conflicts on an interpersonal level are mixed; not all of them are issue conflicts. But the mixture should not be troubling if we grasp the essential criterion: Interpersonal arguments are to be construed as issue conflicts insofar as the opposition of the participants can be expressed or contained within a central question of fact, value, or policy. A central question focuses or contains a conflict in the sense that if the question were decided, there would be no more conflict. At least, conflict on that matter would have been terminated.

Let's consider a reasonably typical interpersonal argument. Suppose Tom and Warren are arguing over the correctness of the Supreme Court decision that held that burning the U.S. flag is a form of expression that is protected by the First Amendment to the Constitution. Even if they never reach agreement over the underlying value question, notice that their argument consists of their disagreement over the correctness of the Court's decision. If the central question on flag burning were resolved, their conflict would be terminated.

Regardless of the arena of dispute, the focus of issue conflicts is on opposing responses to central questions of fact, value, or policy: One side says yes and the other says no, and the central question thus contains the dispute.

Hostility Conflict

Hostility conflicts cannot be expressed or contained by central questions. Moreover, such questions are usually of little help in getting at the focus of hostility conflict. Rather, the focus of hostility conflict is on two more or less inextricable elements:

1. An antagonistic relationship exists with another person or group.

2. The parties are typically preoccupied with such feelings as aggression, competition, frustration, alienation, revenge, and anger.

In a pure hostility conflict, these feelings and the relationship of participants are both the focus of conflict behavior and, in a sense, its cause. Hostility relationships typically foster aggression and intensify feelings of alienation, and these are manifested when a person or group lashes out at another.

Hostility from Internal Problems

Jessie Bernard suggests that some hostility conflict is essentially pathological, deriving from internal problems of individuals and groups that cause them to lash out at others. The conflict "drama, ostensibly between or among people, is really internal; the outside world merely furnishes props."[2] Thus, a woman who has had a miserable day at the office may vent her frustration on her husband when she comes home. The husband, in turn, lashes out at one of his children, and the child kicks the dog. Notice that such conflict behavior is not focused on any disagreement over a matter of fact, value, or policy. Moreover, the target of the behavior may have done nothing to provoke it. In some cases, as Bernard puts it, "the accumulated frustration-generated aggression wreaks itself on any accessible, convenient, or safe object," and it is merely unfortunate if husband, child, or dog satisfy these criteria.

Mutual Hostility and Pseudoissues

All of us have observed the more standard behaviors of hostility conflict in our daily lives. The general behavior of lashing out that I referred to earlier can be readily observed in what we call personality conflicts. When we say that people rub each other the wrong way or there is bad chemistry between them, we usually mean that one or both are predisposed to take offense and to attack the other, or that they seem to look for suitable opportunities, which we may call pseudoissues, to start a fight with each other. A pseudoissue merely appears, on superficial analysis, to be a struggle over a central question of fact, value, or policy, but it is not really the focus of the conflict. Thus, for example, if Esther and Thelma despise each other, they may fight over any number of trivial matters that neither of them really cares about.

Focus on Revenge for Atrocities Suffered

The absence of any real central question does not mean that Thelma and Esther are unable to explain or justify their mutual hostility. Parties in a hostility conflict frequently explain it by referring to atrocities they have suffered at the hands or mouth of their enemy. Thus, Esther explains her conflict with Thelma by reciting insults and bad treatment she has received from Thelma, going all the way back to when they were children, if she is pressed. Thelma in turn itemizes the insults and evil deeds she has suffered from Esther.

Curiously, both women may admit or even boast of the insults and other atrocities committed on the other, so that there is no question, central or otherwise, about what each has said or done. Their conflict is not about a difference of opinion on a matter of fact, value, or policy. Rather, it is about their relationship. They fight now for the reason they have always fought: because they are sisters who have always had a competitive and aggressive relationship. Their conflicts reflect their mutual feelings, and they can be understood only in the context of their sibling rivalry.

Group Focus of Hostility Relationships

When groups or even nations engage in hostility conflict, we can usually find the familiar combination of a competitive relationship plus a history of traded atrocities. Many of the troublesome conflicts around the globe feature a sense of group rivalry or enmity. For instance, the conflict between English and French Canadians has some issue dimensions, but it seems to center on group identity and antagonisms that go back to events of early Canadian history when the British defeated the French. Similarly, group identity and antagonisms characterize the conflicts between Israel and its Islamic neighbors, Bulgarians and the Turkish minority in Bulgaria, Romanians and ethnic Hungarians residing in Romania, Zulu and Xhosa tribal members in South Africa, blacks and whites in the United States, English and Irish in the United Kingdom, Bengalis and Biharis in Bangladesh—and the list could go on. Although there are undoubtedly issue dimensions involved in these examples, the competition, rivalry, and enmity between the groups seem to dominate their struggles.

Many of the more troublesome and intractable conflicts around the world seem to be primarily hostility. In Northern Ireland, the bloody conflict between Protestants and Catholics appears to be fundamentally a hostility conflict, even though it has important issue elements. Competition between Catholics and Protestants seems to dwarf even the major question of Northern Ireland's future within the United Kingdom. Much of the discourse of the two sides focuses on atrocities rather than issues, and there is much to talk about. The history of traded atrocities dates back at least to the seventeenth century when Cromwell conquered Ireland.

Similarly, many of the conflicts between ethnic groups in the former Soviet Union are focused on the long-term relationships of competition and hostility. In 1989 and 1990, as the central government of the former Soviet Union initiated dramatic reforms in its processes of *perestroika* and *glasnost* (restructuring and openness), the more tolerant political climate seemed to allow the surfacing of long-simmering feuds between Moslem Azerbaijanis and Christian Armenians, and what began as an issue conflict (over political control of Nagorno-Karabak, a disputed territory) was transformed into a full-scale hostility conflict with random killings of innocent Armenians and Azerbaijanis, adding mutual atrocities to the centuries of enmity between the two groups.

Competition Is a Catalyst for Hostility

Competition between groups fosters hostility conflict; cooperative relationships seem to inhibit it. In India, Hindus and Sikhs have maintained a generally cooperative and friendly relationship since the founding of the Sikh religion in the thirteenth century. However, especially in the decade of the 1980s, a nationalistic movement among Sikh militants aimed at creating an independent state in the Punjab has shifted the relationship between Sikhs and Hindus from cooperation to competition and conflict.

The demand for an independent nation is, of course, an issue conflict, and there is an important insight here: The real world is seldom so neat and tidy that a conflict will be solely issue or hostility. Issue conflicts can provoke hostility conflicts, and hostility conflicts frequently spawn issue disputes. The behaviors of antagonists in an issue conflict can easily be perceived by opponents as atrocities, and the trading of atrocities is a primary feature of hostility conflict. Conversely, when people or groups do not like each other, they tend to generate disputes over issues.

Two Differences Between Issue and Hostility Conflict

To this point, our exploration of issue conflict and hostility conflict has been concentrated primarily on the focus of each: Issue conflict is focused on central questions; hostility conflict is focused on the feelings of an individual or group, especially as these are directed toward another person or group. We are now ready to examine two other major points of difference between issue and hostility conflict: (1) the purpose of conflict behavior and (2) resolution/termination potential (see Figure 12.1).

Purpose of Conflict Behavior

In an issue conflict, the purpose of conflict behavior is *means to end.* Participants view their own behavior in a conflict as a way of prevail-

FIGURE 12.1 *Features of Issue and Hostility Conflict*

	Issue	Hostility
Focus	Central question	Relationship of parties and feelings
Purpose of conflict behavior	Means to ends	End in itself
Termination potential	Can be resolved or decided	Cannot be resolved, but can be treated

ing on the question in dispute. This is true even when the participants engage in violence. If the participants engage in violent behavior, they see this behavior as a means of reaching the desired end. Such behavior is not an end in itself. For example, in a labor-management dispute, a labor union may engage in a strike if that seems necessary in order to gain its objectives. Likewise, management may decide to close a plant or try to bust a union. However, the use of such means by either labor or management is potentially quite costly. If they are used in an issue conflict, it is because they are perceived to be necessary means to the desired end. A strike, in an issue conflict, is certainly not an end in itself.

In a hostility conflict, behavior directed toward the opponent tends to be an *end in itself.* If one side hurts or insults the other, it is because that is the goal. The following excerpt from Victoria Graham's report on Sikh-Hindu violence in India provides a dramatic illustration of the way behaviors in a hostility conflict are perceived as atrocities, and revenge acts are reciprocal, ends in themselves. See if you can identify the atrocity elements.

> *The anti-Sikh revenge riots this week are the latest explosion in the mounting sectarian violence that threatens the country's secular foundations and non-violent traditions.*
>
> *The cycle of violence began two years ago when Indira Gandhi was assassinated by Sikh guards who the government said were seeking revenge for the army attack on Sikhdom's holiest shrine, the Golden Temple, to rout terrorists. Her slaying led to riots in which vengeful Hindus slaughtered nearly 2,000 Sikhs.*
>
> *The violence is an ominous sign of estrangement between two communities which lived as brothers for centuries, worshipped together, intermarried and used to describe themselves fondly as "fingers of the same hand."*

> *India is predominantly Hindu, but its population of 780 million includes 13 million Sikhs, as well as people of many other faiths. Sikhs form a majority in Punjab, a rich farming state, and militants demand an independent Sikh nation there. More than 600 people, most of them Hindus or moderate Sikhs, have been killed in that state this year.*
>
> *The riots Tuesday were the biggest since four days of anti-Sikh carnage in New Delhi and north India following the slaying of Prime Minister Indira Gandhi by two Sikh guards Oct. 31, 1984. At least 2,700 people, mostly Sikhs, died before her son and successor called out the Army. Several thousand Hindus rioted in the capital and clashed with Sikhs and police July 27 after terrorists massacred 14 Hindu bus passengers in Punjab.*[3]

It is not solely the violence that makes the conflict between Sikhs and Hindus a hostility conflict. Participants in an issue conflict sometimes decide to use violence as a means to their ends. In a hostility conflict, however, violence does not display this means to ends function. Rather, violence seems to be viewed as an end in itself; its purpose is to hurt the enemy. Thus, in Graham's report, Sikh guards killed Indira Gandhi in revenge for her ordering troops to rout militants from the Golden Temple, Sikhdom's holiest shrine (an atrocity in the eyes of Sikhs), and Hindus in turn killed ordinary Sikh residents in New Delhi in revenge for the slaying of the prime minister. And the trading of atrocities and seeking of revenge continues.

News accounts suggest that it did not matter to Hindus whether the Sikhs they killed had anything to do with the assassination of Indira Gandhi. As we have observed, when people are engaged in hostility conflict, they tend to lash out, and revenge is frequently taken on people merely because they are handy. Notice, also, that the violence is not a means selected to achieve any end that could be framed in a question of fact, value, or policy. The violence is an end in itself. Its point is to hurt the other side.

What is so difficult about any attempt to manage or treat hostility conflict is that it tends to escalate as its participants trade atrocities. Each side seeks revenge for atrocities committed by the other, and so it goes. If the conflict does not escalate, it at least continues. Even when overt behaviors in a hostility conflict have been absent for years, individuals and groups can retain memories of past atrocities for a long, long time—and the desire for revenge may persist until a new opportunity arises.

Resolution/Termination Potential

Another major difference between the two kinds of conflict is that issue conflicts can be *decided* or resolved. Hostility conflicts can be *treated*, but they cannot be decided or resolved. This is a troublesome distinction for most people, so it is essential to commence with a clear notion of what it means to decide or resolve a conflict.

In theory at least, all questions of fact, value, and policy can be decided or resolved because they permit a judgment of yes or no. Notice that the idea of deciding or resolving a dispute does not necessarily mean that everyone is happy with a decision or agrees with it. To resolve an issue conflict simply means to decide it by making a judgment that has some degree of finality or authority to make it stick. In the flag burning case, the Supreme Court did in fact decide the matter, and its decision is now the law, even though many people continue to disagree with the Court's decision.

To understand the ideas of deciding or resolving a central question, we must be clear about the *arena* of decision as well as the *power* to decide. Within our own minds, at least, all of us can have the power to decide for ourselves questions of fact, value, and policy. And, if we have sufficient power of decision, we may be able to decide such questions for others as well. Within the home, for example, parents can make decisions for their children, even when the children do not like or agree with the decisions. Likewise, courts can make decisions on the cases before them, providing they have jurisdiction, and it does not matter, in a sense, whether litigants before a court agree with its decisions.

When there is no direct power of decision within an arena of dispute, it may yet be possible to resolve a central question by mutual assent of the disputants. For example, neither Tom nor Warren has the power to decide the flag burning question for the other, but it may be possible for Tom to persuade Warren that his position is correct. Or, if the nature of the central question permits, it may be possible to resolve or decide it with some sort of compromise. Thus, if the argument were on a policy question of who should pick up the check for their dinner, the two might resolve the matter with a compromise: Tom pays this time and Warren pays the next.

Unlike issue conflicts, hostility conflicts *cannot* be decided or resolved. It is possible to decide a central question—the focus of issue conflict—because it makes sense to respond yes or no. But the focus of hostility conflict is a relationship between people and their respective *feelings*, and there is no way for an outside agency to decide feelings of other people. We may even have difficulty trying to alter our own. A judge in a courtroom may render a decision in favor of one side or the other on a civil lawsuit, and have the power to make it stick. But the same judge would think we were talking nonsense if we suggested that she or he could decide the feelings of the participants, making the losing side happy with the decision.

Hostility conflicts cannot be decided or resolved; however, Bernard indicates that they may be *treated*. Parents, for example, have no powers to decide the feelings of their children toward each other, but they are not helpless. Children, like adults, respond to their environments, and parents can at least try to make sure that the environment does not provoke negative hostility conflict. Competition between children may be guided so that, if it does no particular good, at least it does no significant harm.

Kinds of Conflict versus Harmfulness of Conflict

We should not make the mistake of thinking that all hostility conflicts are bad, or that issue conflicts are the more desirable kind. These are merely the kinds of conflicts we have. Although either hostility or issue conflicts can be harmful or unproductive for their participants, whether individuals or groups, some hostility conflicts are beneficial.

Competitive relationships and the feelings that are the focus of hostility conflict are probably universal among human beings. All of us can have hostile feelings of aggression, frustration, envy, competition, or anger in relation to other people and groups. It may be enough merely to be aware that our group is not identical to another group in order to awaken such feelings.[4] But aggression or even anger is not always undesirable or negative. When hostility conflict is properly channeled, it can be positive and rewarding.

Perhaps the clearest examples of (generally) positive hostility conflicts are the contests (or battles) between athletic teams. College and professional sports provide an extensive, socially sanctioned arena for hostility conflicts, and large numbers of fans and players seem to enjoy the feelings of competition, aggression, and even anger they direct toward the enemies of the opposing teams. Notice, especially, how it is the big rivalries that draw the greatest attention from fans and media. Have you ever thought about the opposing schools you love to hate? Many college students continue to relish the rivalries of their high school days, recalling fondly the times when they "destroyed" the football or basketball team of their arch rival.

People seem to think it is enjoyable to express aggression toward athletic opponents. Evidently, we agree with the idea that there is a healthy catharsis, as a psychologist might say, when we vent our rage against opposing teams or officials during a game, purging ourselves of aggression and anger in a socially acceptable way. Even the idea of atrocity is not clearly negative in the athletic arena, and the notion of revenge also needs to be recast. Consider how players and coaches seem almost to treasure atrocities suffered in past games or unkind statements of opponents as they are trying to get "up" for a coming game.

Even our nonviolent elderly seem to relish the potential carnage their favorite football team may visit upon a despised rival. I was fascinated, and charmed, listening to a gentle lady in her eighties express outrage at the evil Los Angeles Raiders who had insulted *her* quarterback on the Denver Broncos. In rather precise and colorful terms, she encouraged her Broncos to exact a bloody revenge on the offenders. Such enthusiasms add spice to life, and allegiances to athletic teams seem to help groups achieve a sense of community as well.

There are probably many other cases of positive or at least socially acceptable forms of hostility conflict. In fact, although they might deny it, I rather suspect that Thelma and Esther have always enjoyed the competition of some of their ongoing hostility conflicts. Their quarrels and fights provide a certain excitement, allowing them to conjure up an element of drama to offset the tedium of everyday life. Their fights are noisy but not dangerous. They appear to abide by a set of rules that keep their conflicts within bounds, preventing them from going too far. Moreover, their rules of engagement bear an interesting resemblance to the rules that govern combative athletic contests, such as discouraging players on football teams from using unnecessary roughness.

Methods of Conflict Termination

An understanding of argumentation principles helps us to make sense of the variety of issue and hostility conflicts, as well as their principal features. But we also need to have some sense of where a conflict is going. We use persuasive argument in conflict as a means to an end. But what sorts of ends are possible? When we find ourselves in a conflict, when is it advisable to try to use a kind of debate process to reach a decision? When would debate be rather pointless or unprofitable? If debate is not a good option, what other sorts of options are there for ending a conflict? Which of these use the principles of argumentation that we have developed throughout this book?

A comprehensive response to these questions requires us to grasp the general methods of conflict termination. When we can see clearly the possible ways of ending a conflict, we see as well the appropriate uses of debate as well as its limitations. Moreover, we can gain an understanding of how to adapt the concepts of rhetoric and argumentation to the larger arena of social conflict. In the next pages, we shall survey six methods of conflict termination that are based on the seminal work of Kenneth Boulding: (1) avoidance, (2) conquest, (3) reconciliation, (4) compromise, (5) award, and (6) chance mechanisms[5] (see Figure 12.2).

Avoidance

The first method of conflict termination is both simple and pervasive. Its simplicity springs from the fact that conflict requires interaction. Mike and Harry cannot fight unless they are in contact with each other. So a conflict will be terminated if contact is ended or made impossible. A conflict is terminated by avoidance, according to Boulding, when the parties "increase the distance between them to the point where the conflict ceases from sheer lack of contact."[6] A

FIGURE 12.2 *Methods of Conflict Termination*

Method	Features
Avoidance	Terminates conflict by either physical or cognitive separation.
Conquest	Terminates conflict when participant with superior power overwhelms the participant with inferior power. Conquest can be physical or symbolic.
Reconciliation	Ends conflict by eliminating misunderstanding or producing convergence in the choices of participants in a process of deepening communication.
Compromise	Terminates conflict over real issues when parties decide to settle for less than they want rather than risk the costs of continued or escalated conflict.
Award	Terminates conflict over issues with mutually exclusive choices. A third party awards the decision to one side or the other on merit.
Chance mechanisms	Terminates conflict when parties agree to use a nonrational, automatic device such as flipping a coin to determine the decision.

fight between two small boys on a playground is terminated when they are separated by a teacher, holding each out of range of the other. A husband and wife who cannot get along separate or divorce. People who quarrel incessantly with their extended families move to another state. Nations, such as North Korea and South Korea, maintain a demilitarized zone between their two armies.

Physical Avoidance

To this point, our examples illustrate physical avoidance, or putting some kind of physical separation or distance between the participants. Little boys on the playground cannot hit each other if the space between them exceeds their reach. Likewise, the demilitarized zone on the Golan Heights between Israel and Syria, controlled by United Nations forces, imposes a separation between the opposing armies that exceeds the range of their rifles and mortars.

Cognitive Avoidance

Physical separation between antagonists is one way of stopping the contact that is essential for conflict behavior. Another common method is cognitive avoidance, which means the parties either ignore each other or they avoid topics that provoke unwanted dispute. Friends and family members frequently use cognitive avoidance when an argument has become so heated that it cannot continue without permanent damage to their relationship. The parties stop speaking to each other for a time, the duration of which varies according to individual needs and the seriousness of the quarrel. The passage of time allows both sides to cool down, regroup, and save face—resuming their relationship after a day or two (or a week or two) as if there had never been an argument.

An alternative form of cognitive avoidance is an agreement, often unspoken, not to discuss topics that lead to unproductive, harmful, or unwanted disputes. Thus, a daughter and her Jewish parents avoid discussions about religion after she has converted to Catholicism. A husband and wife choose not to talk about her driving and his snoring. Democrats avoid discussing political topics at work with their Republican employers. More generally, people decide not to express their opinions whenever they seem to be at odds with those of the group they find themselves in, even if they are not a member of the group. Thus, a male chauvinist may keep silent in a group that dislikes chauvinism.

Societies also use cognitive avoidance when social classes, ethnic groups, and religious organizations cultivate ignorance of each other and avoid direct communication. Thus, while Catholics and Protestants have been the focus of conflict in Northern Ireland, in the United States these groups have a kind of entente to preserve peace: They generally ignore each other.

One-Party Initiatives

An interesting and important feature of both physical and cognitive avoidance is that it is possible for one party in a conflict to engage them. As my mother used to put it, "It takes at least two people to argue or to fight." A man can decline to argue with his father-in-law or even to respond to any of his insane opinions on political matters. Conflict ceases in a marriage if one person leaves it. In fact, as Boulding points out, the most likely form of avoidance is for only one of the parties to separate, either physically or cognitively. "Both parties may remove themselves, though this is less likely, as once one party begins to remove himself, there is little incentive for the other to move."[7] Thus, it is more typical for either Thelma or Esther to stop speaking, not both. The first party to stop speaking seems to have preempted the move, making it more or less redundant or spiteful for the other to engage it.

Argumentation and Avoidance

The avoidance mechanism does not terminate conflict with a process of argumentation or debate, but it is nevertheless a potent method for ending arguments that cause harm if they continue or escalate. Moreover, we can use the principles of argumentation in two ways: (1) to determine whether the conflict is issue or hostility and (2) to assess the potential for terminating a conflict on the basis of good reasons. Avoidance is an especially useful way to terminate hostility conflicts because they are generally unresponsive to argument or good reasons. But it is also useful for terminating issue conflicts that are either too complex, intense, or otherwise beyond the abilities of the participants.

Conquest

The key element in conquest is power. Conflict is terminated when a superior power overwhelms an inferior and has its way. Boulding says conquest is the most extreme form of avoidance in the sense that it terminates conflict because the inferior has been removed, leaving the victor in sole possession of the field. When the victorious army annihilates its opponent, conflict ends because there is no one to fight.

Physical Conquest

The idea of conquest is perhaps most commonly understood in its physical manifestation. Physical conquest is the "extreme case of forcible removal, in which the removed party is removed completely. In a quarrel, one man kills another. In a war, one nation exterminates another."[8] Physical conquest is perhaps most easily understood when the mechanism of removal is killing, but there are other ways of removing one party more or less completely. When a rebellious 2-year-old child refuses to go to bed, the parent simply carries the little toddler to his crib. When there is a struggle in a trade union, the group with superior power expels a quarrelsome faction.

Symbolic Conquest

Whenever a superior enforces its will on an inferior by communicating the fact of its superior power and a willingness to use it, the mode of conquest is symbolic. Thus, prior to the breakup of the former Soviet Union, the relatively weak nation of Lithuania found itself forced to rescind its March 1990 declaration of independence from Moscow. However, most of the force used was symbolic. Gorbachev did not use any significant military forces, or even arrest members of the Lithuanian government. Instead, he cut off oil and natural gas supplies to Lithuania and established an economic blockade. These economic pressures communicated the power relationship of superior to inferior, and the Lithuanians yielded (at least for the moment) when they became convinced that Gorbachev's power could not be resisted effectively.

Boulding suggests that symbolic conquest is really an extreme form of avoidance because the weaker party *decides* to leave the field of struggle or just give up. Thus, when a boss indicates, directly or indirectly, that an employee is risking his or her future with the firm by discussing controversial topics, the employee clearly has the ability to decide whether to terminate the conflict by avoiding the topics. Likewise, a victim has an element of choice in deciding what to do when a robber says, "Your money or your life!" In both instances, the inferior power has a choice, albeit not a very attractive one. So, in this sense, giving in to the demands of the superior power is a kind of avoidance that is elected by the party with inferior power. For Boulding, pure conquest is when the boss simply fires the employee or the robber kills the victim, thereby eliminating participation of the weaker party.

Authority in Symbolic Conquest

Symbolic conquest is the method of conflict termination whenever authority is invoked. An authority figure can dictate to a subordinate, and has legitimate power to terminate conflict within a particular arena. Parents, for example, normally have legitimate power to decide whether to participate in an argument with their child and for how long. If the argument becomes tiresome or pointless, it may be terminated by parental edict: "My decision is final and this argument is ended. Not another word!" And the use of authority in this way is quite common in our experience. As Cialdini observes, "We are trained from birth to believe that obedience to proper authority is right and disobedience is wrong."[9] The authority figures of our childhood—parents and teachers—are generally supplanted for adults by employers, judges, physicians, police, and government leaders.

An interesting feature of symbolic conquest is that it is the weaker party who decides whether its use will terminate the conflict. As Coser observes:

> *Termination involves a reciprocal activity and cannot be understood simply as an unilateral imposition of the will of the stronger on the weaker. Therefore, contrary to what common sense might suggest, not only the potential victor but also the potential vanquished makes crucial contributions to the termination. As a military commentator has pointed out, "war is pressed by the victor, but peace is made by the vanquished. Therefore, to determine the causes of peace, it is always necessary to take the vanquished's point of view. Until the vanquished quits, the war goes on." Victory, in other words, involves the yielding of the vanquished.*[10]

When conquest is the only method of termination, what will happen if the weaker party refuses to yield? Total annihilation or extermination, fortunately, is quite rare. But even powerful nations are sometimes frustrated when weaker opponents refuse to yield, despite great losses and an objectively weaker position. Over a period of several years, for example, the Israeli government had formidable military power in relation to the Palestinian civilians in the occupied West Bank and Gaza, but found it very difficult to put down the *intifada* (uprising) among the Palestinians. However, it is unusual for the weaker party to refuse to yield. "Resistance to the last man," as Coser observes, "is almost always a phrase."[11]

Argumentation Principles and Conquest

Physical or cognitive conquest can terminate conflict, but it does not resolve a conflict when a superior party simply enforces its will on a weaker party. Physical conquest ends or terminates conflict behavior, but it decides nothing. Symbolic conquest of superior over inferior provides the appearance of a decision because the victor gets his or her way, but it is not a resolution process. To resolve a conflict is to decide it on the basis of its rational elements—namely, its issues, arguments, evidence, rules, and premises. The term *rational* means based on reasons. The conquest of one participant over another does not evaluate; it ignores issues, reasons, and evidence.

However, it is a very different matter if the superior power is possessed by a judging authority rather than the participants. Symbolic conquest can be both rational and evaluative if the superior power is vested by society in a judge, for instance, who will decide a dispute on the basis of arguments and evidence. The judge has the power to impose his or her decision on the participants, but the basis of termination in this case is a decision on the merits of the arguments presented. Similarly, a parent may impose a decision after listening to the arguments of two children. An employer may decide a dispute between two employees. An arbitrator can issue a decision to settle a dispute between labor and management. In these cases, the process of symbolic conquest is rational, and it involves the process of persuasive argument and debate.

Reconciliation

Reconciliation can take many forms, but it is always a method of resolving conflict by deepening the communication between contending parties, leading to a convergence of their positions. If the reconciling communication is successful, the antagonists come to see their interests, values, goals, and beliefs as either identical or at least compatible. As Boulding put it, "They now have common preferences in their joint field: they both want the same state of affairs . . . and so conflict is eliminated."[12]

Reconciliation and Pseudoissues

The communication process of reconciliation has many faces. Marriage counseling, family therapy, and labor mediation are some of its more clinical forms in our culture, but all of us use reconciliation whenever we try to get beyond what seems to be a pseudoissue, or to arrive at a consensus decision in a conflict that is resolvable if the two sides are sufficiently flexible.

Reconciliation seems to be especially useful for two kinds of issue conflict. In the first, the conflict is caused by some kind of mistake or flaw in communication: The conflict is the result of a misunderstanding, a lack of information or communication on the part of one or all of the parties. For example, a mother is angry with her son when he asks for the source of information she has presented during their discussion. The mother is deeply insulted because she thinks her son is questioning her honesty, perhaps even implying that she has fabricated the information she has presented. But the son merely wanted to compliment his mother and to learn the source of her superior knowledge. Reconciliation, for this kind of conflict, is a matter of eliminating the misunderstanding.

The second kind of conflict consists of a real clash between the value positions, goals, beliefs, or interests of the participants—as these are initially defined. Suppose Sam, a teenager of 16 years, is in conflict with his parents because he disagrees with their rule that he should be home by midnight. The clash between the positions of the two sides is real in this case, so the conflict does not stem from a misunderstanding or lack of information. But it may be possible to resolve this dispute with a reconciliation process that deepens the communication—getting beyond the surface disagreement—and allowing both sides to redefine their positions, leading to a convergence. The potential for reconciliation depends on the relative rigidity or flexibility of the participants in relation to their value positions.

Convergence by Deepening Communication

In this case, to *deepen* the communication is to identify and assess the reasons behind the positions of the two sides. Sam disagrees with his parents' rule that he must be in by midnight, but he agrees with their reasons for the rule—their desires for him to be alert in school and to keep safe. For their part, Sam's parents see the midnight rule merely as a means to the desired ends, and they do not want to be arbitrary with their son or to prevent him from the normal and healthy fun of his teen years. So it may be possible for both sides to be flexible and to redefine their positions, ensuring that both sides can get what they really want. They may find a consensus position with a rule that allows Sam to stay out after midnight on Friday and Saturday if he makes sure his parents know where he is and what he is doing.

Notice, in Sam's case, that the reconciliation process works by enabling each side to see their initial conflict as a clash over relatively superficial value positions. If reconciliation is successful, both Sam and his parents come to see their more basic interests either as identical (Sam and his parents really want the same thing) or as compatible (Sam and his parents can both get what they want without sacrificing anything of importance). "A prerequisite to reconciliation," Boulding observes, "is flexibility . . . in the value images of the parties concerned. If the images of the two parties are completely rigid, it is clear that no process of convergence can take place."[13]

Values of Reconciliation

One of the chief values of reconciliation is that there are no losers. Everyone can claim victory because the consensus position is chosen by all participants. Moreover, this value is sometimes crucial in permitting dramatic resolutions of conflict, even on the international level. In what is probably the most dramatic reconciliation process of our century, Gorbachev and the leadership of the former Soviet Union swept aside an amazing range of their value positions in 1989–90 in a dazzling process of redefinition: the Berlin wall, a seemingly permanent symbol of East-West hostility, was suddenly unnecessary; Eastern European nations, tightly controlled as an essential component of Soviet defense for more than 40 years, were suddenly free to determine their own political systems; and heretofore rigid opposition to capitalistic market forces was reversed. In 1990, the Soviets seemingly abandoned the aggressive features of Marxist-Leninist doctrine, with its goal of world communism, and embraced many of the western values of human rights, market economics, and pluralistic democracy. Likewise, the United States and Western European nations, displaying a reciprocal flexibility, redefined their positions in 1990, shifting from the hostility reflected in former President Reagan's early characterization of the Soviets as "the evil empire" to an attitude of mutual cooperation.

Argumentation Principles and Reconciliation

Reconciliation resolves conflict by eliminating it. One or both sides change their perceptions of what is important or real, and they choose the same position. If the conflict is caused by misunderstanding, the parties eliminate it by coming to a consensus position on what is real (what really happened, was said, was meant, etc.). If the conflict is caused by a clash in value positions, the parties reconcile by redefining their positions to eliminate the clash.

The process of reconciliation does not and cannot involve debate. The process of debate tends to freeze its advocates into an inflexible posture as each side marshals arguments and evidence to attack and defend. However, the analytical principles of argumentation are essential in reconciliation. We discover that a dispute is a pseudoissue or that convergence is possible by determining the nature of the dispute, identifying the important values, assessing evidence, and weighing the general reasons for the choices of each side.

Compromise

Unfortunately, some conflicts involve issues that are real: The clash between the interests of the parties cannot be defined out of existence, and problems of communication play no important part in the dispute. What if one party's gain is the other's loss? What can we do with conflicts when the difference in interests are real?

Compromise When the Issues Are Real

The process of compromise through bargaining is an essential method of conflict resolution whenever the issues in dispute are not the result of misperceptions or arbitrary positions. Some disputes, by their very nature, involve a clash of interests in which at least part of the conflict involves a "zero-sum" game: One party's gain is the other party's loss.

Labor-management disputes frequently involve a real clash of interests that are not amenable to reconciliation. Suppose labor wants a $5.00 per hour increase in wages and the owners do not want to pay it. The conflict represents a real clash of interests; labor's gain is the owner's loss, and and there is no misunderstanding between the two sides. Labor really does want the increase, and management truly does not want to pay it. If one side or the other held overwhelming power, they would probably be inclined to use conquest, simply forcing the other to go along with their position, and this is exactly what happens in some labor-management disputes. Labor strikes to force management to yield to its demands, or management closes a plant to force concessions from labor. However, if the power relationship between the two sides is perceived to be more or less equal, then they will be inclined to seek a compromise settlement. The Reverend Brazier, former president of a civil rights group in Chicago, stated, "Superiors *discuss* things with inferiors; equals *negotiate!*"[14]

Preconditions for Compromise

Compromise is a possible method of resolution for an issue conflict if two conditions are met. First, both sides must come to believe that they will be better off by settling for less than they really want rather than to accept the risks of continuing the conflict. Labor really does want the $5.00 increase but might be willing to settle for, say, a $2.50 per hour increase rather than risk the costs of a continued or escalated conflict with management. Likewise, management would prefer not to pay any increase in wages but may be willing to pay the $2.50 increase rather than continue the conflict.

Why? What sort of risks would each be concerned about? If the conflict continues, it may escalate by labor going on strike or the company closing its doors, perhaps even going out of business. If labor strikes, the owners may fear that business losses to competitors will be much greater than their loss from a $2.50 pay increase. For its part, labor may worry that wages lost while their members were out of work may be greater than the gains from any increase in pay after a strike is settled. And what if the owners shut down the business or relocate?

A second condition is that the issue in dispute must permit some sort of middle ground, allowing each side to have at least part of what they want. In our example, the opening positions of the two sides—a $5.00 increase and a zero increase—provide the bargainers with 499 possible compromise positions, and $2.50 may be the most salient choice.

Argumentation and Compromise

The processes of bargaining and negotiation necessarily rely on argument as each side tries to marshal good reasons for its position or demands. This means that all of the analytical principles of argumentation are essential as each side tests the reasoning and evidence of the other. But debate processes, as such, are not used. The unique feature of compromise is that the two sides must cooperate at the same time that they are competing. Without cooperation, an agreement would be impossible. Each side must be able to persuade the other at the same time that they are locked in competition over their opposed interests. All in all, it is a tricky business that requires the willingness to concede an argument or to back off on a demand. Debate processes, on the other hand, tend to freeze the advocates into a position by virtue of their emphasis on an unchanging central question.

Compromise shares the value of reconciliation in permitting each side to define the settlement as a victory, so there are no losers. If neither side got exactly or entirely what it wanted, there is at least the satisfaction of gaining something, or losing less than what could have been lost in the absence of compromise. But what if the positions of the two sides are mutually exclusive?

Usually, positions are mutually exclusive only when one side or the other chooses to define them in this way. Labor, for example, could say "We demand $5.00 and we will settle for nothing less." Probably in most cases this would be merely a ploy to gain a superior position in the bargaining to follow, with labor hoping that its tough opening will yield a compromise settlement closer to $5.00 than to the salient $2.50. But in some cases, the nature of the issue, or the lack of flexibility of one or both sides, results in mutually exclusive choices, and a compromise resolution is unavailable.

Award

An award is a decision by an outside person or agency that grants victory, or awards the decision, to one side or the other. A jury decides whether the defendant is guilty or not guilty of tax fraud. A legislature either passes or defeats a proposed bill to restrict abortions. Voters say either yes or no to an ordinance that grants collective bargaining rights to local police. An arbitrator either upholds or overturns the firing of an employee who was dismissed for tardiness.

Award and Mutually Exclusive Issues

Notice that in each of these examples the choices between the two sides are mutually exclusive, from the very nature of the issue in dispute. Compromise may have been possible at an earlier stage, but at this stage the choice is either yes or no; there is no middle ground to permit a compromise. Attorneys for prosecution and defense may have considerable latitude for compromise (plea bargaining) in early stages, but when a defendant goes to trial on a charge, the question to the jury is guilty or not guilty. Similarly, in the legislative arena, the process of compromise and negotiation dominates in the drafting of a bill, but if conflict persists, as it has over the abortion bills debated in various state legislatures, the final process will be an award, with a bill either passed or defeated.

Award by Third-Party Agencies

We use a variety of outside agencies, or third parties, for the award process in our society. Juries and/or judges decide disputes in our courts; arbitrators decide labor-management disputes; legislators rule collectively, by majority vote; voters accept or reject ballot initiatives or candidates; and parents preside over the disputes of their children. Despite this variety, however, there are important similarities among the range of outside agencies.

In each case, the award process is likely to break down unless the third-party agency is impartial or beyond the control of either side. To protect the sense of impartiality, usually there is a sharp distinction between the roles of third-party agencies and participants in a dispute. In our courts, attorneys for prosecution and defense are permitted to argue the case, but they are excluded from the process of deciding guilt or innocence. Juries and judges have decision powers, but they are prohibited from acting as advocates for one side or the other. In the legislature, the situation is more complex because advocates and opponents of a bill are also allowed to vote for or against it. But the awarding mechanism of the legislature is majority rule. If either the advocates or opponents of a bill own the majority, then the process of termination would be conquest, not award. It is an award process when advocates and opponents must convince the uncommited legislators that their position is the right one.

Value of Award

An important value of the award process is that it is an attempt to resolve issue conflicts on their merits. The award process almost always involves debate, with the advocates from each side free to present their strongest arguments and evidence and to reveal weaknesses in the case of their opponents. An underlying assumption is that the clash of arguments will reveal the truth, wisdom, or justice of the issue in dispute to the uncommited third party who will decide. Competent attorneys, for example, will point out any weakness in the evidence or reasoning presented by each side, and a jury should have a better idea of the truth and justice of a case than would otherwise be available.

Disadvantages of Award

To award a decision to only one side, and on the basis of superior merit, also has some disadvantages as a method of conflict resolution. Unlike reconciliation and compromise, there are losers as well as winners in the award process. There is no easy way for the prosecution to put a happy face on a not guilty verdict from a jury. The loss here is complete, and because the award process is an effort to decide on the basis of superior merit (i.e., truth, justice, wisdom) it seems that the loser is wrong rather than merely unsuccessful. If the verdict is correct, then the prosecution would seem to have been wrong in bringing the case to trial. At the very least, the verdict means the prosecution has struggled in vain.

Argumentation Principles and Award

All of the concepts and principles of rhetoric and argumentation apply to any award process in which the decision is based on the merits of the cases presented by each side. The award method of conflict termination almost always involves debate as its basic process of setting forth the grounds for decision by the third-party awarding agency.

Chance Mechanisms

Some issue disputes are relatively trivial in themselves, but the method selected for deciding them can have significant harmful or beneficial effects on the relationship of the parties involved. Suppose that Susan and Fred, for their first date, have decided to see a film at one of the two theaters in their town. Fred wants to catch the last showing of *Bambi* at one theater, but Susan wants to see an R-rated film at the other. Which methods of conflict termination could be used for this sort of disagreement?

Susan or Fred could elect to use some form of physical *avoidance* and merely separate, with each going to see their preferred film. The separation might be temporary, only for that evening, or permanent, if they decide that such differences in taste for films means they have little in common. But if they are attracted to each other, a disadvantage to the use of avoidance is that Fred and Susan do not have their first date.

Alternatively, one or the other might try to use symbolic *conquest*. For example, Fred might say that he should choose where they are going since he is paying. Some people in our culture believe in the legitimacy of claiming superior power from a version of the golden rule: He or she who has the gold gets to rule. However, in order for symbolic conquest to be successful, the party with inferior power must decide to yield. Susan may reject Fred's symbolic conquest and go her own way, opting for avoidance. Worse still, she might yield to it and then find herself so irritated that she does not enjoy the evening or comes to despise Fred.

Reconciliation is worth trying, but it is unlikely to work if both Susan and Fred really want to see the film each selected initially. Few of us have doubts about our taste in films. But it may be possible for them to decide that a conflict over film taste is unimportant, especially in light of their mutual attraction. They could perhaps achieve consensus if both decide they would rather go dancing.

Compromise is not available if the dispute is limited to the different film preferences. There are only two choices, and no apparent way for each to get part of what he or she wants. It is even more obvious that an *award* process is out of the question. Although the choices are mutually exclusive, neither Susan nor Fred would be inclined to submit her or his dispute to an outside agency. Can anyone think that they would want to debate their preferences and have a third party decide which film would be the superior choice? A debate might take up the whole evening. And who could decide for them? His mother?

Our sixth method of termination, *chance mechanisms*, includes such devices as flipping a coin, drawing straws, or picking numbers from 1 to 10. These mechanisms are ideal for this sort of conflict. Unlike the award process, flipping a coin is fast and it allows Fred and Susan to save face. Most people do not feel defeated if they lose with a chance mechanism. After all, a coin is not our opponent and it certainly does not say that either side was right or wrong. Chance mechanisms are nonrational because they provide a decision that is not based on reasons, and the flip of a coin does not convey superiority or inferiority. It provides a decision without hurting the relationship between the parties.

People are remarkably inventive in crafting chance mechanisms for deciding issues that are trivial in themselves but troublesome in their capacity for generating harmful conflict. Which of us should do the dishes? Take out the garbage? Walk the dog? Mow the lawn? Go for groceries? When we have disputes over such matters, we are usually more concerned with the way they are decided than with the decisions themselves.

Termination Methods and Kinds of Conflict

Our rather extended analysis of Fred and Susan's date shows that we must understand the nature of a conflict before we can say very much about the best approach to termination. Now that we have examined the major kinds of conflict and methods of termination, we can summarize our findings in relation to two application questions: Which methods of termination can be used to end issue conflict and hostility conflict? Which methods of termination should use debate?

Useful Termination Methods for Issue Conflict

Because an issue conflict consists of disagreement over a central question, *all* of the six termination methods are potentially useful. Clearly, it is possible to avoid a disagreement, either for a time or permanently. Central questions in dispute do not always need to be resolved. If two brothers cannot agree on the issue of flag burning, and arguing about it merely upsets them, causing potential harm to their relationship, they may simply put the topic aside and forget about it.

If one side has superior power to force either a yes or no decision on a central question, conquest may be possible. Reconciliation is feasible when a central question derives from a problem in communication or where the two sides may eliminate conflict with a consensus position. Compromise may be used if the central question permits middle ground, enabling each side to gain more than it would lose by continuing conflict. An award is possible if the two sides are either willing or compelled to settle their dispute by accepting the verdict of an outside person or agency. And finally, chance mechanisms can be used to decide an issue conflict, especially when it is more important to have a quick decision that allows the parties to avoid the appearance of personal defeat.

Useful Termination Methods for Hostility Conflict

Although all of the termination methods can be useful for issue conflict, only three of the six methods are available for hostility conflict: avoidance, conquest, and reconciliation. Compromise, award, and chance mechanisms are unavailable. To see how the first three methods work, let's examine each in turn.

Since the focus of a hostility conflict is on the relationship between persons or groups and their feelings of competition, anger, and so forth, it is clearly possible to use *avoidance* mechanisms to terminate or to treat a hostility conflict and its participants. In order to engage in any kind of conflict behavior, people have to be in physical range and to have contact. Hostility conflict, in particular, tends to feed on itself as the moves and countermoves of the parties are perceived as atrocities, needing revenge. A physical separation at least stops the conflict behavior and provides a kind of treatment since both sides have an opportunity to cool down. Intense hostility is difficult to sustain when the enemy is absent.

If one side has superior power, *conquest* is a feasible method of termination. In a personal hostility conflict, one gunslinger kills the other. In warfare, one tribe exterminates the other. In the less extreme symbolic conquest, a superior power may subjugate an inferior, terminating hostility conflict behavior, at least for a time. Moslems in Azerbaijan may have despised Mikhail Gorbachev as a result of their conflicts with Moscow in 1990, for example, but they felt powerless to engage in overt conflict against the overwhelming power of the Soviet government.

Hostility conflict cannot be resolved, but sometimes it can be treated in a process of *reconciliation*. When people or groups are in a competitive relationship, it is easy for them to misunderstand each other and to hear insults where none were intended. In many business organizations, for example, the competitive relationship between departments is an ideal environment for hostility conflict. A simple request for information may be construed as criticism or sarcasm, prompting a reply in kind. Reconciliation can be used to de-escalate a hostility conflict that has been caused or intensified by misunderstanding. It is a process of deepening communication between parties in conflict, perhaps helping members of different departments to see each other in another light.

Uses and Limitations of Debate in Terminating Conflict

Some issue conflicts can be managed or resolved with debate, and the process need not be unpleasant. Because the focus of debate is a central question, the relationship of advocates can be civil and even cordial, with the clash of argument and refutation directed toward the issues. Debate over an issue conflict need not be taken as personal attack. But debate is clearly not a useful activity with hostility conflict. Since central questions are generally irrelevant or merely sham in hostility conflict, there is nothing for the advocates to support or defend.

A debate does not foster helpful dialogue when the focus of conflict is hostility between individuals or groups. Rather, the clash and competition is almost bound to be directed to the participants, thereby leading to additional verbal atrocities and revenge seeking. That is why I advised against a debate over the war between Israel and its Arab neighbors, and especially if its participants were students from the very countries whose armies were killing each other on battlefields. Debates can degenerate into ugly events when the focus is on mutual feelings of hostility between the participants rather than on a central question in dispute.

Of the six methods of conflict termination we have examined, debate is useful and appropriate only in an *award* process. People are sometimes confused by this limitation. It is easy to see why debate processes could not be used in termination by avoidance or chance mechanisms, but what about conquest, reconciliation, and compromise?

Debate Is Not a Method of Conquest

Some students mistakenly view debate as a kind of conquest process, primarily because they are beguiled by images of competition between intellectual gladiators. It is at least an intelligent mistake and worth examining. Although it is true that debaters sometimes like the sense of trouncing their opponents, and there is a kind of intellectual combat in constructive argument and refutation, there are at least two major differences between conquest and a debate process. First, the focus of debate is on the rational bases for decision—the issues, arguments, and evidence—whereas the focus of conquest is, at best, nonrational.

Conquest operates on power, not argument. Even when conquest is symbolic, and the weaker participant yields in the face of overwhelming strength, as when Lithuania suspended its March 11, 1990, declaration of independence in the face of overwhelming Soviet power, the process of conquest does not resemble debate. Overwhelming military might has nothing to do with justice, wisdom, or rationality—and Gorbachev did not prevail over the Lithuanians because anyone thought his arguments against independence were superior.

Second, a debate features argument and refutation by the advocates for each side—but we do not let the advocates decide the matter. Whenever debate is used as a process of decision making, the role of the advocates is restricted. Prosecuting and defense attorneys can argue vigorously and do their best to persuade, but it is the jury or judge who decides. Compare this with any process of conquest. In even the most benign, such as a parent exercising authority over a child, there is no third party. In a conquest, it is the stronger side that calls the tune and simply decides the matter.

Debate Is Not a Method of
Reconciliation or Compromise

A second, though less common, mistake is to confuse debate with the processes of reconciliation and compromise. Once again, the mistake is intelligent or at least understandable. People do, in fact, use arguments and evidence when they try to achieve consensus in reconciliation or to settle a dispute with a compromise, and a kind of refutation is used as participants test reasoning and evidence.

But debate is a zero-sum game of pure conflict over a central question, with each side advocating its position (yes or no) until the end of the debate, when the matter will be decided by an outside agency. In contrast, reconciliation terminates conflict by eliminating it, and the participants must emphasize cooperation rather than competition in order to achieve consensus. Similarly, compromise involves "a curious mixture of cooperation and conflict," as Boulding observes.[15] The interests of the two sides are in conflict, but they must cooperate in order to arrive at a mutually satisfactory compromise. If they become locked into yes and no positions on a central question, then negotiations will break down and a compromise becomes impossible.

Debate Is the Method for Award

Debate is useful and appropriate in an award process because its essential conditions are provided. First, the focus of conflict in an award process is always a central question, not the hostility between participants. Second, the central question presents choices that are mutually exclusive—yes or no, guilty or not guilty—enabling the advocates to prepare their cases and to argue consistently for their respective positions. Third, an award process provides an institutionalized setting with a third-party decision maker and rules for the advocates. And finally, when an award process is functioning properly, the clash of arguments in a debate helps a jury or a legislature to make good judgments about what is true, just, and wise in the central question in dispute.

Summary

1. Two central ideas have guided the development of this book. The first, which has a way of intruding itself throughout, is Aristotle's position that rhetoric is a faculty of discerning, or a power of seeing the rational elements of persuasion in any situation where there is both conflict and a perception of choice. The second idea is that all students—indeed, all citizens—need to grasp the elementary principles of rhetoric and argumentation. A citizen should be able to draw on his or her education and argue persuasively, make sense of public controversies, and distinguish sound from unsound arguments and evidence.

2. To understand the larger field of application for rhetoric and argumentation, we need first a conceptual basis for understanding the nature of social conflict and its major kinds: issue and hostility. The focus of issue conflict is a central question of fact, value, or policy. The focus of hostility conflict is an antagonistic relationship in which the parties are preoccupied with feelings of aggression, competition, anger, and so on.

3. The focus of hostility conflict can be examined in relation to internal problems, pseudoissues, atrocities, group rivalries, and competition.

4. Issue and hostility conflict also differ in relation to the purpose of conflict behavior and termination potential. In an issue conflict, behavior is viewed as a means to an end. In a hostility conflict, the behavior tends to be viewed as an end in itself. Issue conflicts can be resolved because it is possible to respond yes or no to a central question. Hostility conflicts may be treated, but not resolved or decided.

5. The distinction between issue and hostility is not a distinction between good and bad conflict. Some issue conflicts are harmful, and some hostility conflicts, such as athletic rivalries, can be enjoyable and apparently beneficial.

6. To understand the uses and limitations of argumentation principles and the process of debate, we need to understand six methods of conflict termination: (a) avoidance, (b) conquest, (c) reconciliation, (d) compromise, (e) award, and (f) chance mechanisms.

Avoidance terminates conflict by separating the participants either physically or cognitively. Conquest ends conflict as the superior power overwhelms the inferior either physically or symbolically. Reconciliation ends conflict by eliminating misunderstanding or by producing convergence in the choices of the participants through a process of deepening communication. Compromise involves disputes over real issues in which it is possible for each side to get part of what it wants. Compromise terminates disputes when each side concludes it is better off to settle for less than it wants in order to avoid the risks of continued conflict. Award involves issues in which the choices are mutually exclusive. A third-party agency awards the decision to one side or the other on the basis of superior merit in the good reasons presented. Chance mechanisms involve methods such as flipping a coin to produce a quick decision that allows each side to save face.

7. All six of the methods of termination can be used with issue conflict, but only avoidance, conquest, and reconciliation are applicable to hostility conflict. We cannot compromise on feelings nor make an award that can terminate an antagonistic relationship. Likewise, chance mechanisms of flipping coins are generally irrelevant to hostility conflict.

8. Principles of rhetoric and argumentation enable us to distinguish issue and hostility conflict and to discern the possibilities for intelligent uses of argument in the alternative methods of conflict termination. Debate, however, has limited uses in managing or resolving conflict. It is an essential method for the award process, but it can be damaging in reconciliation or compromise, and dangerous if it is applied to a hostility conflict.

9. Perhaps every age has thought itself complex, or certainly more complex than its predecessors. But probably none of our ancestors were challenged by anything like the range of conflicts and controversies we must understand. To be unable to make sense of conflict is to be intellectually unprepared to respond to the world as we must face it. We should not be so presumptuous and simple as to think than any single course of study will provide everything that we need, but I agree wholeheartedly with the dean of my school, that "every student needs a good course in argumentation."

Exercises

1. As a class discussion exercise, examine the stories in one issue of your local newspaper that seem to have an element of conflict in them. On the basis of the facts provided in the news account, determine whether the conflicts are focused on issues or hostility. If they are mixed, try to sort out the issue elements. Bring your newspaper to class and be prepared to share two or three of your conflicts for class analysis.

2. As a class discussion exercise, examine the events leading up to the war with Iraq. What were the principal issue elements of this conflict? Were there any hostility elements? If so, can you identify perceived atrocities that seem to lead one side or the other to seek revenge?

3. As a class discussion exercise, apply Boulding's methods of conflict termination to the situation faced by the United States in the fall of 1990, prior to the war with Iraq. The war actions were clearly an example of the physical conquest method of termination. What other methods of termination were attempted by the United States or other nations to terminate the conflict with Iraq? Which of the six methods of termination would not apply to this case?

4. On a more personal level, try to identify at least four instances of serious conflict with your friends, family members, roommates, or co-workers in recent years. Which of the four are issue conflicts, if any? Which were hostility conflicts? If they were mixed (issue and hostility elements), can you sort out the elements of each? If the conflicts were terminated, which of the six methods examined in this chapter best fit the method used in your conflicts? If none of the six methods seem to fit the process of termination you or the other participants used, try to identify what was different about your method.

5. Suppose that Joe, a newlywed, finds himself in a heated argument with his new father-in-law at a family gathering at Thanksgiving over the topic of a proposed welfare bill in Congress. Which of Boulding's methods of conflict termination should Joe try to use? Would your answer be different if the topic of argument concerned the father-in-law's sudden refusal to continue paying for his daughter's tuition, as he had promised to do? What method would you advise in the latter case?

Endnotes

1. Jessie Bernard, "Parties and Issues in Conflict," *Journal of Conflict Resolution, 1* (June 1957), pp. 111–121.
2. Ibid, p. 119.
3. Victoria Graham, "Sikh-Hindu Violence Splits India," *The Coloradoan,* 3 December 1986, p. A9. Reprinted with permission from the Fort Collins *Coloradoan.*
4. See, for example, Muzafer Sherif and Caroline Sherif, *Groups in Harmony and Tension* (New York: Octagon Books, 1966).
5. Kenneth E. Boulding, *Conflict and Defense: A General Theory* (New York: Harper & Row, 1962). See especially Chapter 15.
6. Ibid, p. 308.
7. Ibid, p. 309.
8. Ibid, p. 309.
9. Robert B. Cialdini, *Influence: Science and Practice* (Glenview, IL: Scott, Foresman, 1988), p. 206.

10. Lewis A. Coser, *Continuities in the Study of Social Conflict* (New York: The Free Press, 1967), p. 42.
11. Ibid, p. 41.
12. Boulding, *Conflict and Defense*, p. 310.
13. Ibid, p. 311.
14. Unpublished speech presented at YMCA-YWCA Faculty Forum at University of Illinois, Urbana, March 1968.
15. Boulding, *Conflict and Defense*, p. 314.

Appendix A ━━━━━━━━━━━
Sample Bibliography

Carson, Rachel. *Silent Spring.* Boston: Houghton Mifflin, 1962.

Doe, John. Colorado State University, Fort Collins Interview, 11 November 1991.*

Ehrlich, Paul R. *The Population Bomb.* New York: Ballantine, 1968.

Laws, E. R., Jr. "Evidence of Antitumorigenic Effects of DDT." *Archives of Environmental Health, 34* (Fall 1971): 46–60.

McNulty, Faith. "The Silent Shore." *Audubon Magazine,* November 1971, pp. 5–11.

Poorbird, Robin. "Agricultural Study Favors DDT." *New York Times,* 3 December 1982, sec. 4, p. E12.*

Quincy, Robert E., and Richards, Peter. *Chemical Constraints for a Small Planet.* Fort Collins, CO: Arete Books, 1990.*

U.S. Congress, House. Committee on Agriculture. *Federal Pesticide Control Act of 1971.* Hearings before a Subcommittee of the House Committee on Agriculture, 92nd Cong., 1st sess., 1972.

Woodwell, George M.; Craig, Paul P.; and Johnson, Horton A. "DDT in the Biosphere: Where Does It Go?" *Science,* 10 December 1971, pp. 1101–1107.

*Denotes fictional sources included above to illustrate correct bibliographic format. See the bibliography at the end of Appendix E for additional examples.

Appendix B ——————————

Correct Rebuttal Form

Perhaps the most important single skill needed for effective refutation of opposing arguments is organization. To refute an argument is to attack its support, the reasoning it employs, or its importance in relation to the issue. The idea is to persuade our listeners that the arguments presented by our opponents in debate are either untrustworthy, untrue, or unimportant, and we cannot do this unless our refutation is clearly communicated. Our listener must at least know *what* we are refuting and be able to grasp the essential points of our attack. Thus, we need an organized method of attacking our opponent's arguments. This method is called *correct rebuttal form.*

The organization pattern for correct rebuttal form varies with each speech following the first affirmative, but it always consists of four essential steps: (1) name it, (2) explain it, (3) prove it, and (4) conclude it. Let's begin with an examination of the four steps for the negative speakers.

Rebuttal Form for the Negative

1. *Name It.* This step is merely a kind of verbal pointing to the argument to be refuted. The audience should always know which argument is being discussed. The negative begins by pointing to the affirmative argument to be refuted (usually by restating it briefly). The negative speaker then names his or her objection or response to the affirmative argument. For example, the negative speaker might say "the evidence used the affirmative to support this claim is biased." The idea is that the audience should, in a sense, see the affirmative point and the negative objection to it side by side.

2. *Explain It.* Unless the negative objection is immediately clear to the audience, it should then be explained. It is better to be almost painfully concise in stating the objection because brevity helps the listener to understand the essential point, and a brief statement is easier to remember. A concise objection can always be amplified or

explained after it has been stated. You should be sure your objection is understood before going on to the next step. In relation to our preceding example, you would explain what you meant by saying the affirmative evidence is biased. You might explain that the evidence comes from a group that has a conflict of interest. Thus, for example, we have reason to be doubtful if the evidence that suggests a link between an artificial sweetener and cancer comes from research sponsored by the American sugar industry.

3. *Prove It.* The term prove it may be a bit strong in relation to what the negative realistically can expect to do, but it is easier to remember than *support it* or some such phrase. The idea here is to support the negative objection to the affirmative argument by presenting evidence, or reasoning, or both. Note, however, that the negative claim is presented before any evidence is read, and this is always the correct order. Never read evidence and then try to explain what it means. Present the claim first.

4. *Conclude It.* Listeners become completely lost when speakers drift from one point to the next. So this step means that you want to inform the audience that you are finished with one point and are ready to go on. Sometimes, however, this step involves a bit of additional explanation of the importance of the refutation just presented. For example, a negative speaker might point out that the entire affirmative case hinges on the point just refuted, and if that point falls, everything falls.

Rebuttal Form for the Affirmative

In general, the second affirmative follows the organizational pattern of the first affirmative speaker. An essential goal is to defend each first affirmative argument, and usually the best plan is to defend them in the same order they were presented. Like the first negative, the second affirmative also uses correct rebuttal form in defending affirmative arguments against negative attack, but the pattern is slightly altered. We want to keep the debate focused on the affirmative analysis rather than the negative.

1. *Name It.* For this step, the second affirmative should always begin with a brief restatement of the first affirmative argument. Then the second affirmative should briefly refer to the negative refutation of the affirmative argument. In other words, never begin with the negative arguments. The idea is to keep the argument focused on affirmative ground rather than negative. This is very important, so pay special attention to the difference between the "right" and "wrong" illustrations below.

> *Wrong:* "On the motive issue, the first negative speaker said . . ."

> *Right:* "On the motive issue, our first argument was that the number of functional illiterates graduating from high school is a national disgrace. Now what did the negative say about that?"

When the affirmative and negative claims are properly focused for the audience, the second affirmative then names the affirmative response to the negative refutation. That is, the affirmative provides the audience with a short (two- or three- word) phrase encapsulating what is wrong with the negative objection to the original affirmative argument.

2. *Explain It.* This step is essentially the same as for the first negative. In order to keep the *name it* step concise, the affirmative response to negative refutation may not be entirely clear to the audience. For example, suppose our affirmative names his or her response by saying that the negative argument is "true but irrelevant to the issue." The response is concise but would probably be unclear to a listener without additional explanation. What does the affirmative mean by "irrelevant to the issue"? The affirmative speaker should be sure that the nature of the response is clear, and this may need to be done before supporting the response with evidence. However, if the this step is clear, the *explain it* step may be omitted.

3. *Prove It.* The second affirmative should present evidence or some sort of support for the response to the negative argument. This step is really the same for affirmative and negative. However, second affirmative should realize that the first affirmative has already provided evidence for each affirmative argument, and it may be possible to use this to refute the negative attack. This is especially important when the negative has not really denied first affirmative evidence or has simply ignored it. But it may also be important for the second affirmative to build on the original support, making it more important or stronger than it was initially.

4. *Conclude It.* The argument should be concluded before going on to the next point. The best concluding remarks are those that make it clear why the negative refutation has been refuted and the original affirmative argument still stands, stronger than ever.

The four-step pattern of correct rebuttal form should be used for each argument, in turn. For beginners, correct rebuttal form sometimes seems rather complex or overly formal. But it is neither. It is, in fact, a simple and natural method for developing the analysis in the debate, as the arguments from each side build upon each other. Without some such method, debates degenerate into a confusing jumble, with each side resorting to vehemence rather than reason and evidence. When correct rebuttal form is used well and fairly, the debate process becomes pleasurable and enlightening. Consider the following example of correct rebuttal form in one of the fine columns from James Kilpatrick:

> *The American Medical Association kicked up a nice, diverting hullabaloo last week with its recommendation that boxing be banned. Nothing will come of the proposal, but for the record this should be said: The AMA is right. Of course boxing should be banned.*
>
> *My brother columnist Carl Rowan, a dedicated sports enthusiast, recently devoted his column to making a case in favor of boxing. Let me respond by offering a case against it.*
>
> *Carl's first point is that boxing offers poor kids "an exit visa from their world of violence, crime, drugs, vice." He might have mentioned the examples of Joe Louis and Sugar Ray Leonard in addition to the story of Cassius Clay. But the problem with this argument is that it falls of its own infinitesimal weight. For every poor kid who gains a measure of fame and fortune in the prize ring, there must be a hundred—more likely 500—who never get beyond preliminary bouts in second-rate clubs. Many of these wind up as punch-drunk stumblebums, their occasional purses diverted by promoters and managers. The prize ring may offer riches for a few; it offers less than a minimum wage to the many.*
>
> *Carl's second point is that many professions and many sports contain elements of risk that are well-known to those who enter these fields. Coal mining is dangerous; being a foreign envoy is dangerous; playing football is dangerous. Carl dwelled especially on the broken bones that go with football.*
>
> *The point is interesting; it is also irrelevant. Injuries occur in every sport. Jockeys get hurt; race drivers are killed. But boxing is fundamentally different from these other sports. The object of racing is to get a horse or a car first across the finish line. The object of football is to score touchdowns. The object of hockey is to get a puck in the net.*
>
> *The object of boxing is to batter one's opponent into unconsciousness. The whole purpose of boxing is to inflict pain.*
>
> *For me that is the crucial point. The injuries that occur on a football field are incurred accidentally. They may be unavoidable, but they are not intentional. We have referees to impose penalties for personal fouls and unnecessary roughness. In the prize ring, by contrast, knockouts are the name of the game.[1]*

Notice the excruciating care that Kilpatrick takes to provide an accurate statement of Carl Rowan's argument claims as well as a summary of Rowan's supporting evidence. To be fair, Kilpatrick even offers to provide additional support so the audience can see that his refutation does not depend on some oversight or ineptitude on the part of Rowan. Kilpatrick wants his readers to see that the arguments presented by Rowan are unsound, even if we grant their support. But the most important feature of this extended example is the superb usage of all four steps of correct rebuttal form. Notice, for both arguments refuted, the careful *naming* of the opponent's argument as well as Kilpatrick's objection to the argument. The objection is then *explained, supported,* and *concluded.*

Kilpatrick's use of correct rebuttal form has only one flaw from our perspective: It begins with Rowan's negative argument rather than the first affirmative argument that we might assume was presented by the American Medical Association—the group which proposed (and presumably supported) banning the sport of boxing. Generally it is undesirable to debate on negative ground; the affirmative wants to keep the debate focused on affirmative arguments.

Endnote

1. Taken from *A Conservative View* column by James J. Kilpatrick. Copyright 1984. Reprinted with permission of Universal Press Syndicate.

Appendix C ━━━━━━━━━━━━━━━━━━

Debate Format and Speaker Responsibilities

As we noted in Chapter 9, debates can have a wide range of formats, depending on such factors as (1) the purpose of the debate, (2) the number of participants, and (3) the time available. For example, one purpose of the epic political debates between Lincoln and Douglas in 1858 was their contest for the U.S. Senate seat, but they also wanted to promote their ideas on the problems of slavery and national unity. With only two participants and an audience willing to sit through three hours of debate, the candidates agreed on a fairly simple format for their debates. When Douglas spoke first, the format looked like this:

> Douglas: 1 hour
> Lincoln: 1 1/2 hours
> Douglas: 1/2 hour

Few modern audiences would be willing to listen to a 3-hour debate, and I do not know of any format for a modern political debate that would permit one candidate to speak for an hour or more. More typically, an entire debate will take only an hour, and the time allotted for any one speech is no more than 5 to 10 minutes. Thus, in the first televised presidential debate between John Kennedy and Richard Nixon in 1960, the format allowed each candidate to make an opening speech of 8 minutes and a closing speech of 3 minutes.

In between these speeches, the candidates responded to questions from a panel of four correspondents and commented on answers made by their opponent. The format was as follows:

Opening speech by Kennedy:	8 minutes
Opening speech by Nixon:	8 minutes
Questions from correspondents:	38 minutes total
question to Kennedy	
Kennedy response (2-1/2 minutes)	
Nixon comment (1 minute)	
question to Nixon	
Nixon response (2-1/2 minutes)	
Kennedy comment (1 minute)	
(the pattern continues)	
Closing speech by Nixon	3 minutes
Closing speech by Kennedy	3 minutes
Total time for the debate	60 minutes

The typical format for a competitive, intercollegiate debate involves four debaters (two affirmative and two negative speakers) and it requires one hour. Each speaker delivers one constructive speech and one rebuttal speech, and each asks questions of a speaker for the opposing side. Thus, the one hour is allotted as:

First affirmative speech	8 minutes
questions from 2nd negative	3 minutes
First negative speech	8 minutes
questions from 1st affirmative	3 minutes
Second affirmative speech	8 minutes
questions from 1st negative	3 minutes
Second negative speech	8 minutes
questions from 2nd affirmative	3 minutes
Rebuttal—1st negative	4 minutes
Rebuttal—1st affirmative	4 minutes
Rebuttal—2nd negative	4 minutes
Rebuttal—2nd affirmative	4 minutes

This format allows each speaker to participate in a range of activities, presenting constructive arguments, refuting opposing arguments, and asking and answering questions. However, many university classes have only 50 minutes or less, and not all of that can be allotted to the speakers. Moreover, many of the settings for debate outside of the university may have even less time available. The "MacNeil/Lehrer News Hour," for example, frequently has only 10 or 20 minutes available for debate on a topic. Although these shorter time periods pose difficulties, informative and interesting debates are possible if the format is properly designed and advocates have the skills to present their arguments concisely.

Debate formats should promote an enlightening clash of arguments and reasoning, and a format for classroom debates should also provide students with the maximum range of argument experiences for the available time. The following format is designed for a 40-minute debate for four speakers:

First affirmative speech	7 minutes
questions from 2nd negative	2 minutes
First negative speech	7 minutes
Second affirmative speech	7 minutes
Second negative speech	7 minutes
questions from 2nd affirmative	2 minutes
Affirmative Summary/Rebuttal	4 minutes
Negative Summary/Rebuttal	4 minutes
Total speaking time	40 minutes

In the following section, we will outline the general responsibilities of each speaker in relation to the above format. You should realize, of course, that no list of general duties can substitute for the creative use of the artistic principles of rhetoric and argumentation; however, such outlines can be helpful in the initial stages of preparation.

First Affirmative Speech—7 Minutes

Introduction

1. The opening sentences generally serve the functions of gaining attention and orienting the audience to the contents of the affirmative case. Useful attention devices include startling statistics, interesting facts, and examples of the problem. Sometimes it is helpful to indicate how the problem affects the immediate audience.

2. The first affirmative should present the policy question and the affirmative response to it. It may also be useful to define any unclear terms at this point; however, it is sometimes better to present definitions at a later point, where they may be more informative.

3. The first speaker should partition the case and/or explain the affirmative approach for justifying the proposed change.

Body

1. Major argument claims generally will be presented in relation to each of the issues of motive, obstacle, and cure. These argument

claims will be worded as declarative sentences. For example, if the motive issue is: Are there significant problems of incompetent teaching in U.S. elementary and secondary schools?—the affirmative argument claim would be: There are significant problems of incompetent teaching in U.S. elementary and secondary schools.

2. Each of the major argument claims will, in turn, be supported by "good reasons," and these good reasons will be supported with evidence.

3. Development of the major claim on the cure issue should first explain the proposed solution. For example, if the affirmative were advocating a common market for North America as a solution for the economic problems of the United States and other nations, the affirmative should explain the major features of the common market as the first step in developing the cure issue. Be careful that you do not take too much time for this (1 to 2 minutes is usually about all you can afford). Next, the speaker should present reasons and evidence to show that the common market would solve the economic problems developed in the motive issue.

Conclusion

The speaker should summarize briefly the major reasons for the proposed change. If there is time, the speaker may wish to close with an appropriate quotation or statement that focuses the affirmative case for the audience.

Questions from the Second Negative—2 Minutes

1. The second negative speaker has two minutes to question the first affirmative speaker. Effective use of this time can make the debate more interesting and clear to the audience, and the questioner may find the responses useful in clarifying areas of agreement between the two sides as well as differences.

2. The best cross-examination results from careful advance planning of lines of questions on a single topic or two. Think of the cross-examination as an opportunity to get additional information on assumptions of the affirmative, their sources of evidence, or details of how their proposal would be administered. If the affirmative were advocating, say, a policy of comparable worth for the determination of wage levels in the United States, it could be useful to present

them with troublesome examples and ask how their proposal would handle them.

3. The affirmative speaker should answer questions in a fair and conscientious manner, but the negative questioner must understand that asking questions is not a license to be abusive or rude. If the negative asks an open-ended question, such as: What do you think should be done about problems of enforcing a mandatory seat-belt law?—the affirmative has the right to a reasonable amount of time to answer, and 2 minutes can evaporate with the answer to one such question. Thus, the negative should frame some lines of questions in advance of the debate that can be answered with short responses. It is not necessary to frame all questions to elicit a response of yes or no, but you should always try to phrase questions so that a long answer would be inappropriate.

First Negative Speech—7 Minutes

Introduction

1. Explain the basic position of the negative and indicate areas of disagreement or agreement with the affirmative. On a policy question, the basic position of the negative is one of the four negative strategies discussed in Chapter 11, or possibly a combination of these. The negative team should decide in advance of the debate which strategy will be used, and usually it is a good idea to convey this to your audience. The strategy includes your "positive" reasons for rejecting the affirmative proposal.

2. After explanation of the negative approach to the policy question, the first negative speaker will normally follow the same pattern of organization used by the first affirmative, responding to the affirmative arguments in the order in which they were presented. If, for any reason, you wish to deviate from the affirmative organization and respond to the arguments out of the original order, you need to make sure that you inform the audience of your plan in advance, and you should explain your purpose briefly.

Body

1. Systematically respond to the arguments of the first affirmative speech, one at a time. Much of your response will be an effort to refute the affirmative arguments by presenting counterclaims (with evidence to support them), undermining the credibility of affirmative evidence by using the tests of evidence discussed in Chapter 7, or indicating flaws in the affirmative reasoning.

2. If some of the arguments you wish to present do not seem to fit as responses to affirmative arguments, you should first refute the affirmative arguments and then present your arguments. The idea is to keep your organization simple for the audience to follow.

3. The first negative speech responds to the arguments presented by the first affirmative; therefore, this speech may not be written in advance of the debate. However, this does not mean the first negative is unprepared. Your own research and analysis of the policy question should reveal all of the important arguments and evidence in relation to each issue, so you can anticipate what the affirmative must argue.

Since you know what must be argued, you can make general plans about how you want to respond to each potential affirmative argument, including a general plan about what evidence you can use to refute the affirmative argument. Such advance preparations can be organized on cards, called *rebuttal blocs*. A rebuttal bloc is a card that phrases a generalized affirmative argument at its top, and lists below the affirmative argument a number of potential negative responses, along with references to evidence that can be used to support the negative responses. Then, as you hear an argument from the affirmative, you can use your rebuttal bloc as a kind of weapons cache, and draw forth a quick and effective response. Once again, organization is the key, as well as effective preparation.

4. You may, in consultation with your teammate, decide to concentrate your speech on the motive and obstacle issues, leaving the cure and cost issues for second negative. The point of this sort of strategy is for each person on the team to specialize a bit and to maximize the value of the total time available to the negative side.

Conclusion

The conclusion for the first negative should summarize the major arguments presented and should attempt to put the debate in perspective for the audience in relation to the issues contested.

Second Affirmative Speech—7 Minutes

Introduction

The introduction for this speech is usually brief since the debate topic and issues have already been introduced by the two preceding speakers. Ordinarily, the second affirmative should begin by indicating what will be covered in this speech along with whatever explanation will be needed for the audience to follow the speaker's organizational pattern.

Body

1. If any additional explanation or evidence is needed to make the affirmative proposal (or plan) clear or to show how it will solve the alleged problems, this should be handled first. The audience should know precisely what actions are being proposed, and this may include the topic of enforcement. For instance, if the affirmative were advocating a law to mandate the use of seat belts with shoulder straps by all rear-seat auto passengers, the affirmative should explain how such a law would be enforced.

2. The major duty of this speech is to reestablish the arguments of the first affirmative speech—that is, to defend or rebuild the first affirmative arguments by responding to the refutation from the first negative speaker. This means that the second affirmative speaker must be thoroughly familiar with the arguments to be presented in first affirmative, and the second affirmative must be organized to extend and develop the first affirmative arguments.

3. This speech responds to what has been said in the previous two speeches. Therefore, it may not be written as a manuscript in advance of the debate. Yet, like the first negative, the second affirmative should prepare rebuttal blocs for all of the major lines of argument. For each argument to be presented by the first affirmative, the second affirmative should have a rebuttal bloc that lists the various negative objections or refutation for that argument, and then lists the kinds of response the second affirmative can make to each negative objection. Once again, the idea is to anticipate by using the fruits of your own analysis and research to determine the potential arguments for the negative side, and then to use these same skills to develop a response to negative arguments.

All of this may seem terribly complex to the beginner, but students who are prepared tend to do very well.

Conclusion

The major purpose of the conclusion for the second affirmative is to help the audience understand the development of arguments on the major issues, chiefly by summarizing them. However, whenever possible the second affirmative should also try to show the audience how the affirmative arguments prevail on each issue. In most debates, the second affirmative will not have much time for the conclusion; this tends to be a busy speech. But keep your listeners in mind. Listening to the development of complex arguments can be difficult. You can help them here.

Second Negative Speech—7 Minutes

Introduction

The introduction for this speech also tends to be brief. Its function is to provide the audience with an organization plan for what is to be developed and to clarify the relationship of first and second negative refutation.

Body

1. Usually it is most effective for the second negative to concentrate 4 to 5 minutes on the cure and cost issues. The idea is to focus most of the time in this speech on the issues that concern the proposed change, to demonstrate that the specific affirmative proposal presented in this debate will not solve the problems initially developed in the first affirmative speech, and to show that the disadvantages or costs of the proposal will greatly outweigh any alleged advantages or benefits.

2. Many of the cure and cost arguments can be prepared in advance of the debate, but do not be misled into attempting to prepare a manuscript for this speech. In order for this focus on cure and cost to be effective, the second negative must be able to respond to the specific details of the proposal presented by the immediate affirmative opponents. Negative advocates sometimes make the mistake of thinking that all affirmatives have exactly the same proposal in mind simply because the general wording of the policy question is the same. However, there is substantial opportunity for variation in the details of a proposed policy change.

Consider the proposals for mandating the usage of seat belts for all automobile passengers. What does it mean to "mandate usage"? Clearly, the idea of a mandate permits considerable latitude in enforcement, at the very least. A fine of $5.00 might constitute a kind of mandate but probably not an effective one. Alternatively, revocation of a driver's license when either a driver or one of the passengers is without a seat belt might be substantially more effective as enforcement but would probably create substantially more disadvantages or costs.

3. The second negative has the opportunity to ask questions of the first affirmative. This questioning is an opportunity to elicit details about how a plan might work or be enforced. The answers should be used in the second negative speech. In addition, the second negative should listen to the arguments on the motive and obstacle issues. At times, the affirmative analysis on why the present policy cannot solve the alleged problems, if it were accepted as correct, would also mean that the affirmative proposal could not solve the problems. Picking up on this can be the difference between a mediocre and an excellent speech.

4. In some cases, the second negative speaker may wish to extend the negative refutation of arguments on the motive and obstacle issues. Whether this option is desirable will depend somewhat on the nature of the policy question. There is no value in merely repeating arguments already presented by the first negative speaker.

Conclusion

The conclusion of the second negative speech should summarize the major arguments presented and should attempt to provide an overall perspective for the audience on the development of the issues to this point.

Questions from the Second Affirmative—2 Minutes

1. The second affirmative speaker has 2 minutes to question the second negative. Review the discussion on questions from the second negative. In general, the same basic principles we discussed earlier apply to this questioning period.

2. The primary focus for the cross–examination here should be on the new arguments presented by the second negative on the cure and cost issues. The purpose of the questioning is to weaken the arguments presented by the second negative, either by revealing flaws in the evidence or in the reasoning. Second negative speakers sometimes fall victim to the mistake of itemizing flaws of the affirmative proposal that are also problems of the present policy or system. For instance, when the proposal to raise the drinking age to 21 was debated, negative speakers sometimes argued that underage youth would obtain alcoholic beverages illegally. But, of course, the problem of underage youth obtaining beer illegally was a problem in the present system as much as it would be a problem under the proposed higher drinking age.

3. There is not enough time in 2 minutes to ask questions in relation to all of the cure and cost arguments that have been presented by the second negative. Therefore, the best approach is to pick arguments that can be undermined effectively by questioning that reveals flaws or inconsistencies in the reasoning of the negative.

Affirmative Summary/Rebuttal—4 Minutes

1. Ordinarily, in competitive debate, the rebuttals commence with the first negative rebuttal, and the affirmative presents the final rebuttal. In this abbreviated format, however, it is more desirable to have an affirmative response to new arguments presented in the second negative speech than it is to adhere to the traditional competitive format. Also, with only one rebuttal for the affirmative, it is desirable for the first affirmative speaker to present this speech, thus affording all speakers an opportunity to refute arguments presented by the other side.

2. The primary purpose of this speech is to extend the debate in relation to the most important contested arguments and issues and to help the audience to see that the affirmative side has met its burden of proof and has carried all of the issues.

3. Since this speech is limited to 4 minutes, obviously the speaker cannot be expected to respond to everything that has been said in the debate. Yet, the audience should have the sense that everything of importance has been covered and that the final speaker has provided a useful summary of the affirmative analysis that does more than merely repeat what has been said in previous speeches. The audience's unspoken question for this speech is: What does this all mean?

4. Neither the affirmative nor the negative summary/rebuttal speeches may introduce new arguments. All of the argument claims in relation to the four issues should have been presented in the four constructive speeches. New or additional evidence, however, is permitted in relation to arguments that have been presented in the constructive speeches. The rationale for these rules is somewhat a matter of debate tradition, but they also derive from a concern that each side should have an opportunity to confront and refute the arguments from the opposition, and the only way to make sure of that opportunity is to limit new arguments to constructive speeches.

Negative Summary/Rebuttal—4 Minutes

1. This speech may be presented by either of the negative speakers, but the participation time for the negative speakers is more equal if the first negative speaker presents the rebuttal speech.

2. The general goals for this speech are essentially the same as those for the affirmative summary/rebuttal, except that the speaker wants to show the audience that the negative has won at least one issue. Sometimes the negative side may choose to focus the 4 minutes of this speech on some rather than all of the issues, especially if the negative position is stronger on some the issues. The strategy derives from the principle that the negative only needs to win one issue in order to win the decision, and the negative position may be strengthened if more time can be devoted to the issues most vulnerable to negative refutation. However, this strategy can be persuasively risky, suggesting a retreat in the face of strong affirmative refutation. In any event, the final speech should attempt to put all of the issues in perspective for the audience.

Appendix D ⸻

A Public Policy Debate: Should the Equal Rights Amendment Be Ratified?*

The public controversy over equal rights for women and men has a long history in the United States, and its arguments and issues have a rather timeless quality. The debate presented here is an unedited transcript from "The Advocates," a series of broadcast debates produced by WGBH Boston. This debate was recorded live at Faneuil Hall, Boston, and broadcast on PBS July 6, 1978. In addition to the arguments and issues, one of the interesting features of this debate is its unique, quasi-judicial format and its use of expert witnesses.

> *Moderator:* Marilyn Berger
> *Pro:* ADVOCATE Laurence H. Tribe
> Professor of Constitutional Law, Harvard University
> WITNESS Barbara Babcock
> Assistant United States Attorney General, Civil Division
> WITNESS Eleanor Smeal
> President, National Organization for Women
> *Con:* ADVOCATE Jules Gerard
> Professor of Constitutional Law
> Washington University Law School
> WITNESS Phyllis Schlafly
> President, Stop ERA
> WITNESS Senator Sam Ervin
> Former United States Senator, North Carolina

* From "The Advocates," copyright 1978, WGBH Educational Foundation.

ANNOUNCER: From Faneuil Hall in Boston, "The Advocates." Tonight's question: *Should the Equal Rights Amendment Be Ratified?* Arguing in favor is Laurence Tribe, Constitutional Lawyer and Professor of Law at Harvard University. Appearing as witnesses for Mr. Tribe are Barbara Babcock, Assistant United States Attorney General in Charge of the Civil Division; and Eleanor Smeal, President of the National Organization for Women. Arguing against the proposal is Jules Gerard, Professor of Constitutional Law at Washington University in St. Louis, Missouri. Appearing as witnesses for Professor Gerard are Phyllis Schlafly, President of Stop ERA; and Senator Sam Ervin, Jr., former United States Senator from North Carolina.

BERGER: Good evening, and welcome to "The Advocates." The Equal Rights Amendment—the subject of tonight's debate—is probably the most controversial change that has been proposed for the American Constitution in recent years. Never, in fact, in the history of constitutional debate have so many people been so passionately involved on both sides. And never has a proposed amendment had a potential impact on so many people—virtually the entire population of the United States. The question tonight is whether the proposed 27th amendment to the Constitution— the Equal Rights Amendment—should be ratified. Advocate Laurence Tribe says yes.

TRIBE: Two hundred years ago we declared our independence with the ringing words, "all men are created equal." Today most of us know better than that. We're here tonight because the elected representatives of 70 percent of the people of this country in 35 states across the nation have voted to broaden that to "all people are created equal," and but for a handful of votes that basic principle would now be the fundamental law of this land. With me tonight to help explain why we should ratify the Equal Rights Amendment are Barbara Babcock, Assistant Attorney General of the United States, and Eleanor Smeal, President of the National Organization for Women.

BERGER: Thank you. Thank you. Advocate Jules Gerard says no.

GERARD: Tonight's issue is not, as the proponents would have you believe, whether you are for or against discrimination against women. No sensible person favors making women second-class citizens. The issue is whether the ERA is needed to protect women, or whether instead, it would be harmful to them. With me tonight to alert you to the dangers of ERA, and to speak in favor of women's rights, are Mrs. Phyllis Schlafly and Senator Sam Ervin.

BERGER: Thank you. Although we've been hearing a lot about it recently, the Equal Rights Amendment is not a new idea. It's been around for more than 50 years. It was first introduced 55 years ago—in 1923—three years after women won the right to vote. It's come up in every Congress since then. But it wasn't until 1972 that it was passed by both houses of Congress—and that's the first step toward ratification. A requirement was set then that the states must ratify within seven years. The deadline is next March—that's 1979. Thirty-five states have already ratified—three more are needed. Many supporters of the amendment want the deadline extended. Opponents, of course, do not. But that's not the subject of tonight's debate. What we want to look at tonight is whether the amendment itself—the ERA as it's called—ought to be added to the Constitution. The questions you might want to consider are these: Do you believe that women are treated fairly, or unfairly, under existing law? Does the Constitution as it now stands go far enough to ensure equality of women—or do we need a principle written into it that as the amendment states "Equality of rights under the law shall not be denied or abridged by the United States or by any state on account of sex"? Or do you think that amendment could serve to diminish rights that women now enjoy? And there's another question I've been wondering about. Has American society developed to the point that we don't need the Equal Rights Amendment? Or, now that it has been proposed, will failure to ratify it mean a real setback for women in America? Now, let's go to the cases. Mr. Tribe, why do you say we should have an ERA?

TRIBE: Equality of rights under the law shall not be denied or abridged on account of sex. It's hard to think of a clearer or a more compelling statement of our fundamental national beliefs that all people, and not just all men, are created equal. For most purposes it shouldn't matter what sex you are—to drive a truck, go to school, to run a computer, to raise a child—and we want the law to reflect the fact that sex should be irrelevant to those things.

Sure there are a few cases, a very few, where gender specifically makes a difference. For example, I guess we'd want all male guards at an institution for violent male sex offenders, and the ERA would allow that. But for a long time sex stereotypes have been used. They have been used to rationalize unequal pay and unequal opportunities, and that is exactly what the Equal Rights Amendment would stop.

And to answer Marilyn Berger's question: If the ERA is defeated, we would not simply be where we are today, we'd be telling courts and bureaucrats throughout this country that it's all right to discriminate on grounds of sex. We'd be turning back the clock. That's not what we want. We want people to be treated not just as men and women; we want everyone treated as a human being.

I call as my first witness, Barbara Babcock. Miss Babcock is the author of the leading text on sex discrimination, she is a Professor of Law at Stanford and she is currently (the) Assistant Attorney General of the United States. In a word, why do we need the ERA?

BABCOCK: We need, I think, at this point, a statement in our fundamental document of government that everyone believes in, the statement that men and women are equal. And at this point we have really reached the stage where it is a glaring omission, that in the constitution itself, we do not make this statement which is part of our history and part of the beliefs of most of the people.

TRIBE: What would it mean to defeat the Equal Rights Amendment? What would that do?

BABCOCK: I think that would be a very clear message to the courts, that the courts—the lower courts particularly—are going all different ways, with very unclear directions from the Supreme Court as to the standards to be applied.

TRIBE: And this would be a message to the courts to approve discrimination?

BABCOCK: It would be a message to the courts that they can continue doing as they are now, which is muddling through.

TRIBE: Now, apart from that—what about the muddling through approach? Right now we're relying on the 5th and 14th amendments to combat sex discrimination. Why isn't that enough?

BABCOCK: It hasn't been enough because the courts have really— the Supreme Court particularly—has taken one step forward and two steps back along the road in determining these cases of sex discrimination—which have just become prominent in the last decade.

TRIBE: What are some examples?

BABCOCK: Well, for instance, just last week, in passing the Bakke Case, the court very clearly said, in Justice Powell's opinion, that sex discrimination under the 14th amendment would not be given as careful scrutiny as other kinds of discrimination, racial discrimination for instance. And gratuitously, the court added that sex discrimination has not had a long and tragic history and that history should be recognized and spoken against at this point.

TRIBE: Now, has that included some particular Supreme Court decisions upholding gender discrimination that you think are, ought to be called to our attention?

BABCOCK: Well, I think that a case that comes to mind that shows the ambivalence of the Supreme Court, which is very quickly translated to the lower courts, is the case in which there was a special property tax exemption for widows but not for widowers.

TRIBE: No matter how poor the widowers were, they couldn't get a benefit, because they were males?

BABCOCK: That's right, and that case would not be decided the same way under the Equal Rights Amendment because that is clearly not equality of rights . . .

TRIBE: And that that's the way it comes out now under current law?

BABCOCK: It certainly can come out that way. Under current law, because there's no clear message, it comes out every which way. You cannot walk into court and know what is going to happen.

BERGER: Can I interrupt there you mean to say though, would a woman not get those special benefits if there were an Equal Rights Amendment. You say a man doesn't now, but would a woman not get them?

BABCOCK: The whole decision on whether special benefits on the basis of past discrimination would be made upon an individual basis and upon the background and history . . .

TRIBE: . . . If there was an economic need, the benefit would be given. Not that it would be taken away from the woman, it's that it would be given to those that needed it. Is that right?

BABCOCK: And it would be tied to the factors that went into it, rather than some notion that all widows are poor, especially all widows in Florida are poor and need a property tax exemption because they are women.

TRIBE: I see. Now what about—some people say that ERA is great for women who, like, want new roles, but wouldn't it push women away from traditional roles, those who want to stay where they are?

BABCOCK: The ERA does not take anything away from anybody that they have now, whatsoever. What the ERA does is establish a principle of equality and a principle of choice for women.

TRIBE: And why do you think it's fair to ask the country for more time to establish that principle? Some say an extension is unfair.

BERGER: We'll need a quick answer to that.

BABCOCK: The whole purpose—let's look at the purpose of the seven-year limit, which was not in the statute itself, it's not in the amendment itself. The purpose is to allow the debate to be

current, and the debate is very current at this moment. Why end it before the end has come? Right now the issues are hot and
. . .

TRIBE: . . . it would send a negative message.

BERGER: Let's go to Mr. Gerard now for some cross-examination of Miss Babcock, please.

GERARD: Miss Babcock, Powell's opinion in Bakke was for himself only. No other justice joined in that opinion, isn't that correct?

BABCOCK: It was the opinion of the court. It's the only opinion in Bakke that can be called the opinion of the court.

GERARD: I asked whether any other Justice joined in Powell's opinion. You should know the answer to that.

BABCOCK: Well, I certainly do, as do you. But, but nevertheless . . .

GERARD: . . . The answer is "no," is it not?

BABCOCK: He was expressing what the court has expressed in other opinions, which is that a lesser standard is going to be applied to sex discrimination cases than are applied to other discrimination cases that he expressed at this time—very, very clearly.

GERARD: The State of Florida gave widows a property tax exemption because it believed that the widows as a class deserved a little extra help. You say Kahn against Shevin, the case that sustained that law, was wrong. If the ERA is ratified it will prevent society from enacting similar remedial laws to help women to catch up with men economically, will it not?

BABCOCK: No, it will not, but it will require that those laws be based upon the actual needs of women or the actual needs of men and not some notion that all widows in Florida need a property tax exemption. There may be men in Florida, widowers, who need a property tax exemption. But if we require that you look at the needs of the individual and tailor the legislation. . .

GERARD: You testified that a woman who chose a traditional role will not lose any rights. Isn't it a fact that she will lose at least three rights that traditionally were hers? The right to be supported by her husband, the right that her husband bear primary responsibility for supporting any children, and the traditional law that makes the husband liable for the debts incurred by the wife in buying food, clothing and other necessities?

BABCOCK: Well, we have to look first at what the actual situation is today. The notion that women are very well off today in terms of support . . .

GERARD: The question was, they would lose those rights. That's what the question was.

BABCOCK: Not at all. I think that within marriage, under the Equal Rights Law . . .

GERARD: . . . Those laws would be unconstitutional under the Equal Rights Amendment, would they not?

BABCOCK: Which, the support laws?

GERARD: Yes.

BABCOCK: Not at all. No, in terms of, it would involve . . .

GERARD: . . . The law that imposes the primary duty of support on the husband would not be unconstitutional under the Equal Rights Amendment?

BABCOCK: It would involve—the Equal Rights Amendment, I think, would involve, say, reworking as they always have, as they already have started to do and as many states have done very progressively, reworking their domestic relations laws in order to fairly allocate the benefits within a marriage.

GERARD: Nevertheless, the law would be unconstitutional.

BABCOCK: That requires . . .

GERARD: That requires a husband to support a wife.

BABCOCK: Not necessarily. The law would be that the, that one partner . . .

GERARD: Oh, really? Tell me, tell me, what part of the language under Section 1 of the Equal Rights Amendment supports that conclusion?

BABCOCK: The, the law, the Equal Rights Amendment would require that states look at their domestic relations laws which are full of anachronisms. For instance, in Pennsylvania, under the state Equal Rights Amendment there, the courts just struck down a law which is very typical of domestic relations laws in which a wife did not own her household goods unless she could prove that she had actually given money to buy them, and so the fact that she had contributed unremunerative services to the household gave her no right to the household goods. Under the state Equal Rights Amendment that law was struck down. And that's what would happen across the board in terms of the unfairnesses under the present domestic relations laws. They need to be reworked and they are discriminatory against women as they presently stand.

BERGER: All right, Mr. Tribe.

TRIBE: As Assistant Attorney General you must get quite a broad overview of what the lower courts are doing, both under current law and under the new Equal Rights Amendments that have been passed in some 16 states. Could you quickly summarize what the difference is in the approach between what courts do under their current law and what they appear to do under equal-rights type amendments?

BABCOCK: As far as I can see, in the thousands of cases involving sex discrimination charges now, the law is completely helter skelter. You cannot tell as you go into court as a litigator what the mandate is, and that's the great value of the Equal Rights Amendment. It would be in our fundamental documents, a statement that the courts are to look at this in a certain way. Certainly as a litigator I would very much prefer to have the constitution behind me and I think that most people who litigate these issues would feel the same way.

BERGER: Mr. Gerard, a final question for Miss Babcock.

GERARD: About those messages that you say would result from failure to ratify ERA, ah, let me pose this: Perhaps the reason ratification has been stalled is because people have taken a second look and have decided that the harms that will result from ERA, which include a total reconstructuring in society in ways that are not foreseeable at the moment, outweigh whatever slight benefits it could bring, and the message isn't at all that it's okay to discriminate against women. Now isn't that possible?

BABCOCK: Well, I have trouble with that question—isn't what possible?—isn't it possible that society would be totally . . .

GERARD: . . . Isn't it possible that the message is that we don't want to restructure our society, not that it's all right to discriminate against women.

BABCOCK: Well the message that is coming across is that, that a vast majority of states, with 70 percent of the population, have passed the Equal Rights Amendment, and I think that is the message that the country wants to express as principle, and that it is only a very, very few people who are standing against it.

BERGER: Thank you. Thank you, Miss Babcock, for joining us on "The Advocates." Mr. Tribe. Your next witness, Mr. Tribe.

TRIBE: I call as my second witness, Eleanor Smeal.

BERGER: Mrs. Smeal, welcome to "The Advocates."

TRIBE: Mrs. Smeal is a housewife, a mother of two, and the President of the National Organization for Women, the largest women's rights organization in the country. Why have you worked so hard and for so long, Mrs. Smeal, to see the ERA passed?

SMEAL: Because I believe in justice for all, and I don't believe that that justice for all has an exemption, and that women should be exempted from justice. Rather, I believe that we should be included, and in so being included, I think that the most discriminated person in our society right now is the housewife, and I think she will be benefited.

TRIBE: How does it affect housewives?

SMEAL: Well, today the opposition asserts that we have a right to support. The reality is that we have a right to whatever our husband chooses to give us under the current law.

TRIBE: Under current law . . .

BERGER: Oh, let's let the questioning go on.

TRIBE: Under the current law, the woman has no actual claim to anything more than mere maintenance and whatever the husband chooses to give while married, right?

SMEAL: That's absolutely right. We have a claim to maintenance. But the reality is, in court case after court case, maintenance could mean no indoor plumbing, it could mean one dress in seven years, it has no standard, it is what the husband chooses to give.

TRIBE: Suppose a woman, to escape that plight, decides to go to work. Isn't she then protected under current law against sex discrimination?

SMEAL: No, unfortunately there are loopholes in the current laws, and that is one of the reasons why today, the average woman working outside the home for pay gets approximately half as much in pay as the average man.

TRIBE: So that the promise of equal pay for equal work remains really an illusion?

SMEAL: That's correct, and we believe that the weight of the constitution behind the statutes that exist, which do have loopholes, will help to plug those loopholes but they'll do something even more important. They will put the presumption, ah, that the state will have to prove if there is a law why it is, why sex is permissible as discriminatory.

TRIBE: So women will not then have to go in and bear all of the burden themselves.

SMEAL: That's right. Right now the burden is on the women to prove that the law is unreasonable rather that the state to have to prove that a sex classification is unreasonable.

TRIBE: Now opponents say the ERA would somehow lead to abortion on demand, unisex marriage, unisex toilets. What do you make of all that?

SMEAL: They're simply red herrings, and you don't have to believe me as a proponent of the ERA, you can look at the 16 states where there are ERAs and in all of those states there are no uni-sex toilets and in none of those states are homosexual marriages permissible. So the reality of the situation is that these distortions are advocated and put forth to take our mind out of, off of the real merit of the ERA.

TRIBE: And what about the military? It is said that women are going to be subject to the draft and to combat. What do you think about the implications of the ERA to the military?

SMEAL: Well, this is a case where there is some substance, but the opponents have turned everything inside out because in reality the military situation discriminates against women today. Today women are denied job opportunities, denied an education, because indeed the military is still the number one educator of men in this society.

TRIBE: Does the military impose higher requirements for women than for men to enter voluntarily right now?

SMEAL: Absolutely. For a woman you must have a high school education, for a man you can have less than that, and what is happening is more qualified women are turned away, thousands are turned away from allowing to serve in the armed forces while less qualified men are accepted. It does two things: it denies women job opportunities in training and it provides for our armed services less qualified personnel.

TRIBE: Well, given all this—why do you think the ERA has bogged down—why hasn't it prevailed if all of this is right?

SMEAL: Well one of the reasons is the distortion, they have sort of clouded the issue. But the more important reason is that an organized minority has succeeded in blocking it in just a few states. There are just, we have won in the bulk of states.

TRIBE: Do people stand to profit . . .

BERGER: I'm sorry. Mr. Gerard, it's your turn for cross-examination now of Mrs. Smeal.

GERARD: Thank you. Miss Smeal, I'm sorry, you have stated that the specter of unisex toilets, unisex prisons and homosexual marriages are red herrings. Yet Professor Paul Freund of Harvard, and Professor Phillip Kurland of Chicago, two of the most highly respected constitutional lawyers in the nation, both testified before Congress that they thought those things would inevitably come about if ERA is ratified, or at least, that it was likely to happen. Is it your testimony that Professors Freund and Kurland were engaged in red herring tactics when they testified before Congress?

SMEAL: Well obviously they were wrong, and that's the important point.

GERARD: Why? Obviously?

SMEAL: Because today we have the experience . . .

BERGER: Ladies and gentlemen, let's have Mr. Gerard go on with his questioning, please.

SMEAL: We have the experience of 16 states and in some of that experience, for example, I am a resident of the State of Pennsylvania, and they have had, we have had an Equal Rights Amendment since May of 1971 and that Equal Rights Amendment has the exact same wording as the proposed Equal Rights Amendment and you can come visit our bathrooms—they are some of the finest in the nation.

GERARD: State court decisions are not binding on the Supreme Court of the United States though, are they?

SMEAL: Well, I think that . . .

GERARD: . . . The state experience in Pennsylvania . . .

SMEAL: One of the beauties of a state experience is that we are not entering unknown territory. The state constitutions have been interpreted by state courts to mean that they are not binding. Incidentally, if anything, there is probably a stronger position under the Federal law, the presumption, for example, against unisex toilets, because of the present belief that there is a privacy clause under the 14th amendment. So if anything, the case under the Federal clauses will be stronger, and I do think one should use experience as a better track record than some professor's opinion.

GERARD: I'll overlook the insult that's implicit in that question, in that answer. Um, when the Equal Rights Amendment was in the Senate, Senator Ervin introduced this amendment, proposed amendment: "This article shall not impair the validity, however, of any laws of the United States or of any state which secure privacy to men or women, boys or girls." That amendment was defeated by an overwhelming vote of 80, 79 votes nay, 11 votes aye. That is part of the legislative history of the Equal Rights Amendment, is it not?

SMEAL: Yes, part of the history is that there were several amendments offered and each one of those were an attempt to restrict the principle, and the principle is one of equality towards men and women, boys and girls, and there was not to be any excuse used to deny that kind of principle.

GERARD: Precisely. The principle that was attempted to be restricted in this case was the principle of privacy.

SMEAL: Well, I would like to hear the entire context of the debate, because I believe that in reality it had nothing to do with bathrooms and I, you know as a chief advocator of Equal Rights, as one of the proponents of Equal Rights, you will see no movement right now, or I have known of no one advocating of the integration of bathrooms. This is a very important issue, we're talking about jobs, we're talking about poverty, we're talking about employment.

GERARD: Well, let's, let's, well we would move on to more things . . .

BERGER: Please go on, Mr. Gerard.

GERARD: Well, let's move on to something else and maybe we can get a shorter answer. You talked about the equal pay opportunities for women in big business, yet we both know and if you don't you can see by turning and looking over your left shoulder, that the Equal Rights Amendment doesn't say "shall not be denied or abridged by big business or by private enterprise," it says "denied or abridged by the United States or any state." Only 20 percent of the women in the work force . . .

BERGER: . . . We're going to have to get in a quick question and a quick answer. I'm sorry.

GERARD: All right—only 20 percent of the female work force is employed by government and it is only that 20 percent that would be protected by Section 1 of the Equal Rights Amendment. Now that's correct, is it not?

SMEAL: The Federal government is the largest employer of women and I think it's a disgrace that right now Congress does not protect its own employees against sex discrimination. It's those kind of abuses that the ERA will eliminate.

BERGER: Thank you. Mr. Tribe—one more question please. No, no, please stay with us.

TRIBE: Among the many people who voted against that privacy amendment on the grounds that it was obviously redundant, there were a number of men. Why do you think men, in addition to women, tend to favor the ERA?

SMEAL: Because there are some real benefits for men as well as women behind the ERA. There are discriminatory clauses, for example, widowers are treated in discriminatory fashions and thereby denied benefits that would be just for them. Not only that, the ERA benefits all people because it benefits families. If a woman is underpaid, it is the entire family that suffers. If a woman who is the head of a household is discriminated against, her children indeed receive less benefits, and of course most of us are related to men and so, thereby, if we are treated less and our worth is considered less, the entire family's worth is considered less.

BERGER: Thank you. Mr. Gerard, you have another chance to get an answer, if you want one, to your question.

GERARD: You have conceded that if ERA is ratified, women will be drafted and sent to combat units on the same basis as men. If people vote for ERA they are voting, in other words, that our society should not have the option to exempt all women from combat because that would be unconstitutionally impermissible. That's what they would be voting for, is that not correct?

SMEAL: What they'd be voting for is to judge people on their individual merits and their individual abilities and what they would be voting for really is to judge their sons as their daughters and their daughters as their sons, and I really believe it would be spreading experience to everybody. Incidentally . . .

BERGER: . . . We're going to have to cut in on that. Thank you, Mrs. Smeal, thank you for joining us on "The Advocates." Mr. Tribe?

TRIBE: You've heard what I think is some pretty conclusive testimony for the ERA, not that it would revolutionize everything, but that it would help fight a legal system in which all are equal but some are just a little more equal than others. You are now going to hear the case on the other side, or rather I should say, the two cases on the other side—because I think if you'll listen you will hear two different ideas: (1) that the ERA will really make no difference at all because we already have all that it provides, and (2) that it will make such a terrific difference that it'll wreck our society. Now as you listen I think you'll know that both of those things cannot be true. And I think you'll figure out that both of them are false.

BERGER: I thank you. For those of you—thank you—for those of you who may have joined us late, tonight's debate asks whether the Equal Rights Amendment should be ratified. Advocate Laurence Tribe and his two witnesses, Barbara Babcock and Eleanor Smeal, have just presented their side for ratification. Advocate Jules Gerard and his two witnesses will now take the side against ratification. Mr. Gerard, you now have the floor.

GERARD: Ladies and gentlemen, one impression I would like to correct to begin with is the one that Professor Tribe created in his opening remark. The question is not whether we are going to amend the Declaration of Independence. The Declaration of Independence is not law. The Constitution is. The question is, are we going to amend the Constitution? And amending the Constitution is the most important of all the political acts in our democracy. It should be done carefully, it should be done cautiously, and with a clear national consensus for the consequences. It should not be done as an experiment in the hope that it will turn out all right. The burden of proof lies with the proponents to persuade you—not by a little, but overwhelmingly—that the ERA is needed and that it will have no harmful effects.

Why don't the proponents give you any significant examples of discrimination against women? Because there are none. They don't cite any new rights or benefits ERA will give women that they don't already have. In one breath they say that ERA will give us a gender-free and unisex society, but in the next breath, in the next breath they tell us we must rely upon the Supreme Court to tell us what ERA means after it is ratified. The real issue in ERA is this: whether we want to give the Federal government and the Supreme Court the power to restructure our society on terms that can be decided only after the ERA is ratified. I call as my first witness, Mrs. Phyllis Schlafly.

BERGER: Mrs. Schlafly, welcome to "The Advocates."

GERARD: Mrs. Schlafly is the President of Stop ERA, a homemaker, mother of six children and the author of several books. Mrs. Schlafly, are you opposed to women's rights?

SCHLAFLY: Absolutely not. I'm for women's rights and that's why I am opposed to the Equal Rights Amendment, because it would be a take-away of the rights and benefits that women now enjoy.

GERARD: What kinds of rights will the ERA take away?

SCHLAFLY: Well, the most obvious example of a law that would be changed by ERA is the Draft Act. For 33 years the Draft Act always said male citizens must register. Obviously, under ERA you could not have a draft act that applied only to men and it would have to say persons. Furthermore, the Equal Rights Amendment will wipe out the existing laws which give women the wonderful exemption from military combat duty. As the House Judiciary Committee clearly said in its report, not only would mothers, women including mothers, be subject to the draft, but the military would be compelled to place them in combat units alongside of men. Now, Mrs. Smeal said she wants to extend these privileges to her daughters, but I think you have to be kidding to call this an advance for women to say we would be subject to the draft and to military combat duty.

GERARD: Underlying the dispute about ERA seems to be a dispute about social values. Does ERA take away social options or other rights and benefits that women now have?

SCHLAFLY: Well it's a big take-away of the rights of the homemaker because obviously a law that says the husband must support his wife is a sex-discriminatory law. It imposes an obligation on a husband who is by definition a man, and it would be unconstitutional under ERA. Likewise, the law that says the primary obligation for the support of minor children should be on the father is a sex discriminatory law and it's unconstitutional under ERA. Now in the educational field we have a certain minority of our people who like certain single sex schools or colleges, or activities or sports, such as fraternities or sororities, or football or wrestling or Girl Scouts and Boy Scouts or mother/daughter school events, but the Equal Rights Amendment as the supreme law of the land would wipe out all of these exceptions in the present law and deprive them of their rights.

GERARD: Does ERA mandate all this unisex nonsense?

SCHLAFLY: Well, sure, the language of it is strict, rigid, and inflexible, and of course if you don't accept that strict language of it, then you have to go with the idea that we're giving a blank check to the Supreme Court to write its own terms after it's ratified.

GERARD: What new power would Section 2 of ERA give to the Federal government that it doesn't have at the present time?

SCHLAFLY: Well, it would give the Federal government power over any type of laws that have traditionally made a difference between men and women—such as marriage, divorce, child custody, prison regulations, homosexual laws, the insurance rates, any type of legislation that makes any difference—and it would give to the Federal government all this new power that they have never before had.

GERARD: Why do you think the ERA proponents are asking Congress to change the rules and give seven more years to ratify the amendment?

SCHLAFLY: Because they can't persuade enough people by living by the rules. The seven year limit was clearly stated in the original resolution passed by Congress and it's contained in the state ratification of 28 states, and it is an arrogant piece of Federal mischief to have the idea that the Congress can come along and change the terms of those state ratifications.

BERGER: Thank you. Mr. Tribe, it's your turn for cross-examination of Mrs. Schlafly please.

TRIBE: Mrs. Schlafly, your 1977 book suggests some rather sweeping male/female differences. On page 19, for example, you say that men may philosophize while women are concerned about feeding the kids, and on page 50 you praise laws that make the husband the ultimate decision maker in matters like where the couple should live. You attack the ERA for ending the husband's legal right to force his wife to move where he wants the family to be. Now, is that what you mean when you say you are for women's rights? That you want to preserve that kind, that kind of law?

BERGER: Would you please let Mrs. Schlafly answer the question?

SCHLAFLY: I thought we were talking about what's going into the Constitution, and I do support the laws that say the husband must support his wife.

TRIBE: I didn't ask you that. I asked you about the husband forcing his wife . . .

SCHLAFLY: . . . Oh I know, you're asking me about my social philosophy, but is that really relevant? We're talking about what's going into the Constitution and it would be a unisex rule that would deprive our right to have such a law as the husband must support his wife.

TRIBE: And it deprives us of our right to have such a law as the husband may force the wife to move wherever he pleases, right?

SCHLAFLY: The husband must establish the domicile because how are you going to keep the family together if the wife can establish a separate domicile?

TRIBE: I understand. Let me, are you suggesting . . .

SCHLAFLY: That's only showing the anti-family nature of the ERA proponents who want to have the wife establish a separate domicile . . .

TRIBE: . . . I think you have answered the question. You seem to be concerned that ERA either mandates identical treatment of the sexes or is a blank check. Let's just take one example: pregnancy. You've argued, if I'm correct, that the ERA would forbid any special benefits for pregnant women . . .

SCHLAFLY: I didn't argue that at all . . .

TRIBE: Well, it's in your book. Do you believe it or do you take it back?

SCHLAFLY: No, I didn't argue that at all.

TRIBE: Oh, okay. So the ERA . . .

SCHLAFLY: . . . Why don't we talk, why don't we talk about the effect that ERA would have?

TRIBE: Well, would it be possible after the ERA to give special benefits to pregnant women?

SCHLAFLY: Ah, not, probably, well, who knows?

TRIBE: Would it or wouldn't it?

SCHLAFLY: Who knows? The Supreme Court will tell us after it's ratified.

TRIBE: Well the Supreme Court has told us. I wonder if you've read the Court's statement that because only women, as it happens, can get pregnant—a rule for pregnant women is not a case of sex discrimination.

SCHLAFLY: Mr. Tribe, you know perfectly well that the Gilbert Case held that that was not a case of sex discrimination.

TRIBE: That's my point—not the sex discrimination.

SCHLAFLY: And if we had ERA that decision would not have been any different.

TRIBE: That's exactly my point, Ms. Schlafly. If we had ERA it would still be possible to give special benefits when sex is really relevant, like pregnancy—right? Let me pursue—let me ask you . . .

SCHLAFLY: It would not be possible to have anything except the unisex rule.

TRIBE: Well you say that, but look at what it says—"Equality of rights." Does it say unisex? Where do you find that in the Equal Rights Amendment?

SCHLAFLY: Well, I think you're the one who doesn't know what the amendment says because you misquoted it in your opening statement, and when you quoted it you dropped out the words "by the United States or by any state."

TRIBE: I'm sorry, there they are, there they are. Ms. Schlafly, it's been said that the ERA represents a kind of elitist movement of wealthy women, but I'm curious whether it isn't to some extent the other way around. You've talked, for example, about how women don't need the ERA for equal pay, or for child care or family support, and in your book you say that women can just charge everything to their husband's bank account. This is the right to support that you have mentioned. Don't you think those views apply rather better to women with money and servants and so on rather than to poor women or working class women?

SCHLAFLY: Well, this is just another example of the type of personal attack. The reason women don't need ERA in the field of employment is because of the Equal Employment Opportunity Act of 1972.

TRIBE: . . . But what about the loopholes?

SCHLAFLY: There are no loopholes in it.

TRIBE: No loopholes? Congress isn't covered, is it?

SCHLAFLY: As a matter of fact it is being enforced by EEOC with affirmative action, and the Equal Pay Act, and all of these acts which give women all that they would want.

TRIBE: But it's your position . . .

BERGER: Now, Mr. Tribe, excuse me, Mr. Tribe we're going to go. . .

SCHLAFLY: . . . There are not only no loopholes, the government is supporting it with affirmative action.

BERGER: Mr. Gerard.

GERARD: Ms. Schlafly, the proponents made some issue of the experience in state ERAs. Why can't we rely upon that experience?

SCHLAFLY: Well, of course, there's no state that has the same language as the Federal ERA that we are discussing here tonight because no state has a Section 2 which gives the grant of power to the Federal government. But even in the only six states that have the unisex language of Section 1, first of all the states are not interpreted in the Federal courts, they are interpreted in the state court, and secondly, those state amendments don't have the kind of legislative history you have on ERA, where the Senate specifically voted down all the exceptions—the exceptions for the draft, for military combat, with the support of the wives and widows and all of those exceptions—and the legislative history of the Federal ERA is entirely different from that of any state ERA.

BERGER: Thank you, Ms. Schlafly. Mr. Tribe, one last question—a quick one please.

TRIBE: There's one thing, one thing that genuinely confuses me. Do you believe that equality of rights under the law should be denied or abridged on account of sex?

SCHLAFLY: I do believe that women should be exempt from the draft, as women . . .

TRIBE: . . . But should equality be denied?

SCHLAFLY: I do not believe in equality in fighting in Vietnam, in drafting women, in the support of children in the marriage relationship where it requires the financial support of the children. No. That puts a double burden on the wife. It is grievously unfair and shows why we believe the Equal Rights Amendment is a big take-away of rights that women now have.

BERGER: Thank you, Mrs. Schlafly. Thank you very much for joining us on "The Advocates." Mr. Gerard, your next witness, please.

GERARD: I call as my next witness, Senator Sam Ervin.

BERGER: Senator Ervin, welcome to "The Advocates."

GERARD: Senator Ervin, of course, is the former senator from North Carolina and noted constitutional scholar and was, as I hope you will have the opportunity to learn, a major participant in the debates on the Equal Rights Amendment when it was in the Senate. Senator Ervin, are you opposed to discrimination against women?

ERVIN: I'm not opposed to discrimination against women. In certain cases I'm in favor of discrimination in their favor—especially if they are pregnant wives, if they are mothers and if they happen to be widows.

GERARD: All right. What, why then are you opposed to the Equal Rights Amendment?

ERVIN: I'm opposed to the Equal Rights Amendment for four reasons. First, it's unnecessary, second, it's unrealistic, third, it's irrational and fourth, it will be highly destructive on the system of government we now enjoy under the constitution.

GERARD: Why is it unnecessary?

BERGER: Ladies and gentlemen, we'll be able to get to these cases much better if you'll bear with us, please.

GERARD: Why is it unnecessary, Senator?

ERVIN: It's unnecessary because all of the old decisions and all of the old laws that the advocates of ERA invoked to show that it is necessary—the decisions have been overruled and the laws have been repealed and we have laws today like the Title 7, the Equal Rights Amendment of 1964 that prohibits discrimination on the basis of sex in hiring, firing, pay, promotion, or any term or condition of employment.

GERARD: Why is it unrealistic, Senator?

ERVIN: It's unrealistic because it tries to convert the two sexes God created into identical legal beings of a neuter gender without sex. And furthermore, it's irrational because it's just like old

Procrustes. Procrustes used to entertain the guests, the travelers who came his way. He had a bed for them to sleep in. He made all of the guests fit the length of his bed. If the legs were too long, he'd cut them off. If they were too short, he stretched them so they'd be long enough, and that's exactly what ERA would do. It would destroy or make an effort to destroy, maybe a half dozen unjust laws, it would destroy hundreds and hundreds of just laws, fair laws, reasonable laws, and rational laws.

GERARD: Now you said it was irrational. Elaborate on that for us.

ERVIN: Well, it's irrational to try to convert men and women into identical legal beings. That's exactly what it would do. In other words, it would say to Congress and the legislatures of the 50 states, you must pretend that sex does not exist when you make laws to regulate the rights of men and women and children.

GERARD: Well, Senator, we're running short of time. Let me skip one question and take this one: you proposed amendments which would temper the harsh interpretation of the ERA. For example, you proposed one amendment that would preserve benefits for widows, wives and mothers, another that would protect privacy, another that would exempt women from combat. They were all defeated. And this means that they became part of the legislative history of that amendment and means . . .

BERGER: Mr. Gerard, we're going to have to have a quick question—I'm sorry—and a quick answer.

GERARD: Okay. Senator, take it from there, please.

ERVIN: This history of the legislature—in the first place the amendment itself makes no exceptions to anything. It applies for everything just exactly alike, no matter whether it is wise or foolish. In the second place, the history of it shows, and this was shown by a vote of 82 to 9, it shows that the amendment will impair the validity of any laws of the United States or any state which exempts women from compulsive military service or from service in combat units of the armed forces, that it will invalidate any law which extends protections or exemptions to wives, widows or mothers.

BERGER: Senator, thank you. Mr. Tribe also has some questions for you. We're going to have to go to him.

TRIBE: Senator, you've made quite a bit out of the support that women supposedly get. Were you aware that less than 14 percent get alimony and that less than half of the divorce cases actually get, under our wonderful current laws, the child support to which they are supposedly entitled?

ERVIN: I didn't understand—I think you made a statement instead of asking a question.

TRIBE: Well, were you aware of the correctness of those facts? That is, I take it you are suggesting that the present situation is really rather desirable in terms of the economic support women get. I'm asking you whether you are aware of statistics suggesting that the truth is quite the opposite?

ERVIN: The truth is that most husbands support their wives—and you ask the question about pregnancy, a woman who is pregnant. . .

TRIBE: . . . No, no, no—I'm not asking you about pregnancy. I was satisfied with the answer on that one.

ERVIN: Well, I wish you would.

TRIBE: Let me get, let me get to the heart of it. You've called the ERA in one of your statements, the most destructive piece of legislation to ever pass Congress. Now back in the 1950s and 60s a great many people were saying exactly that about Civil Rights legislation, as you probably recall. You'd agree that that didn't turn out to be true, wouldn't you?

ERVIN: Well, let's stick to the ERA. We haven't got much time to talk about it. I'm not going off after red herring. . .

TRIBE: . . . No, I'm trying to figure out how we can assess the validity of all these predictions of doom. Another rather related one is that the 14th amendment solves the problem, the current laws solve the problem, and again it was argued back in the 50s and 60s that we didn't need Civil Rights laws.

ERVIN: I would say that since 1973, beginning with Reed against Reed, the Supreme Court of the United States has handed down 14 decisions in which they hold that any law which makes any distinctions between the legal rights of men and women is unconstitutional unless it is based on reasonable grounds and is designed to protect women in some role they play in life.

TRIBE: But when the Assistant Attorney General says that the thousands of lower courts are going every which way and that women are not assured protection, what do you think of that?

ERVIN: I'm like the Assistant Attorney General, I read a lot of lower court decisions and haven't been reading any of that kind.

TRIBE: You haven't?

ERVIN: I've been reading ones that harmonize with these 14 decisions I've mentioned.

TRIBE: And do the 14 include the one that says that you can deny widowers any benefit, no matter how poor they are? Is that part of your count?

ERVIN: I favored that because the Supreme Court was intelligent enough to know that there are more men working than there are women. . .

TRIBE: (inaudible)

ERVIN: Well wait a minute. Let me answer the question. That women who are housewives and mothers do not have much opportunity to accumulate money and therefore they said it was all right to give a widow a tax exemption of $500, because of the fact, and I think that's a very reasonable fact, and if you had the ERA you couldn't give a woman anything, unless you gave it to a widower, too.

TRIBE: If you had the ERA wouldn't you have to look at who needs money, and then decide, rather than generalizing?

ERVIN: Not unless you rewrite the laws. That's one of the troubles with ERA.

TRIBE: That's, as Miss Babcock pointed out, the laws are being rewritten to come into compliance with that.

ERVIN: Or you've got to rewrite the laws and use gender. You've got to pretend that in the laws there are no men and no women and no sexes. That's what you've got to do.

TRIBE: You worried about Section 2. You indicated that Congress would go too far.

ERVIN: Yes.

TRIBE: But of course you say that sex discrimination is already banned under the 14th Amendment, right? So Congress under the 14th Amendment can already do what you're afraid of?

ERVIN: No doubt that discrimination is banned by the 14th Amendment. It was on the basis of race 'til they handed down the Bakke Case the other day, and it changed that.

BERGER: Ah, Mr. Gerard, one more question for Senator Ervin.

GERARD: Yes. Senator Ervin, I didn't give you a chance to tell us why you thought ERA was disruptive of states' rights.

ERVIN: Because it has a second clause that's like the 5th clause of the 14th Amendment, which is exactly like the same words. The Supreme Court held in Katzenbach against Morgan that under that clause, the power of enforcement of the 14th Amendment, that the Federal government could pass a law nullifying the state law which the Supreme Court itself had unanimously held was perfectly constitutional and could, ah, which the state was authorized to pass by three separate provisions of the constitution and not only could nullify the state law, but could substitute for it a Federal law which the Congress was forbidden to pass by three separate provisions of the Constitution.

BERGER: Mr. Tribe, one last question for Senator Ervin, please.

TRIBE: I would like to ask you the same question that I asked Miss Schlafly since I must admit I couldn't follow her answer. Do you believe that equality of rights under the law should be denied or abridged on account of sex, or not?

ERVIN: I believe that equality of the law should be guaranteed to every person in a similar situation. But I think there's a lot of difference between a pregnant wife who needs somebody's support and a single woman, a business or professional woman, a single woman or her husband.

TRIBE: So, equality of rights. . .

BERGER: No. Thank you, Mr. Tribe. Senator Ervin, thank you very much for joining us on "The Advocates." And now, let's go to the closing arguments. Mr. Tribe?

TRIBE: You know, I've been trying this evening to get both of these advocates to answer a rather simple question. Do they agree with what Section 1 says, that equality of rights under the law shall not be denied or abridged on account of sex. And at one point Miss Schlafly actually said "No, I don't believe that," and I think that's the whole point. Either we agree with that principle or we don't. I agree with it—and I do not agree that current law, including the 14th Amendment, just does the whole job as it was argued long ago earlier laws did the job before people proposed the Civil Rights legislation.

The fact is that as we have shown, there are loopholes in those laws—the federal government, for example, being exempted—loopholes big enough to drive a truck through. And Miss Schlafly says there are no loopholes. Lower courts every day are ruling in favor of treating men and women differently even when, unlike a case of pregnancy, there are no real differences. I say that in that situation all of you who believe that all people are created equal, should vote, yes, on the Equal Rights Amendment.

BERGER: Thank you. Mr. Gerard, Mr. Gerard, please.

GERARD: Ladies and gentlemen, what are those overwhelming reasons the proponents have offered in support of ERA? Well, let me review the ones that they have offered: to eliminate tax benefits for widows; to eliminate single sex schools; to allow divorced husbands to collect alimony; and to require women to be drafted and sent into combat on the same terms as men. All of this, mind you, in the name of eliminating discrimination against women. Why haven't they given you any of those real horror stories that we keep hearing about? The answer is simple. There are none.

The Constitution and the statutes already protect women without risking the dangers that are inherent in the Equal Rights Amendment. The proponents refused to trust the Supreme Court to interpret the 14th Amendment, yet they rely upon that same court to make sense out of the ERA by reading it to mean exactly, exactly the opposite of what it says, to save us from unisex toilets, unisex prisons and homosexual marriages. Ladies and gentlemen, these arguments don't come close to meeting the overwhelming burden of persuasion that the proponents should be required to bear on this issue.

BERGER: Thank you, Mr. Gerard. Thank you, Mr. Gerard. Now, you've heard the arguments on both sides, ladies and gentlemen —now that you've heard the arguments, why don't you let us know what you think about the questions raised in tonight's debate: *Should the Equal Rights Amendment be Ratified?* Send us your vote on a postcard to: The Advocates, Box 1978, Boston, MA 02134. And if you would like a transcript of tonight's debate, or of any of our previous debates, please send a check or money order for $2 to that same address: The Advocates, Box 1978, Boston, MA 02134. In our last debate on "The Advocates" we discussed a Federal Trade Commission proposal to limit advertising on children's television. There was an exceptionally light response on this question from our audience: 707 for bans and other limits on advertising; 440 against. And now, with thanks to our advocates and their distinguished witnesses, we conclude tonight's debate.

Appendix E

Argument and Evidence Brief
by James H. Joy, III*

Policy Question: Should the United States phase in a total ban on the use of chlorofluorocarbons (CFCs) in order to protect the ozone layer in the atmosphere?

I. Are the problems of a depleting ozone layer significant enough to warrant action?
   A. Advocates of a ban on CFCs argue that the emission of CFCs is causing a significant problem of depletion of the ozone layer.
      1. A "hole" in the ozone layer over Antarctica is an indication of what can happen over the rest of the globe.
         a. Representative James Scheuer, Chairman of the U.S. House Committee on Science, Space, and Technology: "In 1985, British scientists discovered that during every spring over one-half of the ozone over Antarctica mysteriously disappeared. Since the hole was not predicted there is concern that this may be a harbinger of future ozone depletion over other more populated areas of the ozone . . . of the globe" (*Stratospheric Ozone Depletion*, 1987, p. 1).
         b. Richard Kerr, in reference to a report by NASA's Ozone Trends Panel: "The weight of evidence strongly indicates that man-made chlorine species are primarily responsible for the observed decrease within the polar hole" (Kerr, 25 March 1988, p. 1489).
         c. John Gribbon, journalist for *New Scientist:* "The discovery of a 'hole' in the ozone over Antarctica shows that the atmosphere may respond in a 'nonlinear' way to this kind of disturbance (CFCs). The buildup of chlo-

* Reprinted with permission of James H. Joy, III.

rine had very little effect on the ozone layer until some critical threshold was reached. Then, a very small increase in the amount of chlorine caused a big change in the chemistry of the stratosphere. . . . There is now concern that some separate nonlinear effects may be at work in other parts of the world, and that other holes in the ozone layer might appear" (Gribbon, 5 May 1988, p. 4).

2. Large depletions of global ozone have already occurred.

   a. Clive Rodgers, member of NASA's Ozone Trends Panel: "TOMS (Total Ozone Mapping Spectrometer on NASA's Nimbus 7) data show a global decrease of 2.6 percent from November 1978 to October 1985" (Rodgers, 17 March 1988, p. 201).

   b. David Lindley, citing NASA's Ozone Trends Panel: "Atmospheric ozone levels at middle and low latitudes decreased by 2.5 percent between 1978 and 1985, and some part of the depletion has been caused by CFCs, according to the Ozone Trends Panel" (Lindley, 24 March 1988, p. 293).

   c. Robert Watson, chairman of NASA's Ozone Trends Panel: "I am more convinced that CFCs have a role. The indicators are bad. Everything points more and more to their being involved" (Kerr, 25 March 1988, p. 1489).

3. We do not know the full extent of the damage that will be caused by CFCs that have already been produced.

   a. Cass Peterson, citing the work of chemist Sherwood Rowland: "Chlorofluorocarbons never break down on the surface of the planet. They rise slowly, over a period of 50 to 100 years, into the stratosphere" (Peterson, January/February 1988, p. 36).

   b. John Gribbon: "CFCs pose a potential threat to the ozone layer because the ones widely used today are long lived (some longer than 100 years)" (Gribbon, 5 May 1988, p. 4).

   c. Cass Peterson, journalist for *Sierra:* "The stratosphere has not yet received the full load of CFCs produced in the last 50 years; millions of tons have yet to be released" (Peterson, January/February 1988, p. 39).

4. A decrease in ozone results in an increase in the amount of ultraviolet rays that reach the earth's surface.

   a. Joseph Steed, environmental manager for DuPont: "For every 1% change in ozone, an additional 2% of ultraviolet radiation is allowed to penetrate the earth's atmosphere" (MacKerron, 6 April 1988, p. 7).

5. Increased ultraviolet radiation will be hazardous to human health.
   a. Cass Peterson: "Ultraviolet rays can cause skin cancer and cataracts and weaken the body's ability to fight disease" (Peterson, January/February 1988, p. 36).
   b. Senator Albert Gore, before the U.S. Senate Committee on Commerce, Science, and Transportation: "The EPA has recently projected that with present growth rates in the emissions of CFCs, there will be an additional 40 million skin cancer cases and an additional 800,000 deaths for Americans who are alive today and those born within the next 88 years" (*Global Environmental Change*, 1987, p. 5).
   c. John Gribbon: "UV-C does not reach the ground at all today. We cannot be certain, though, that under different circumstances it might not reach the ground. In the laboratory, UV-C destroys nucleic acids (RNA and DNA) and protein . . . the basic molecules of life" (Gribbon, 5 May 1988, p. 4).

6. Increased ultraviolet radiation will be hazardous to the ecosystem.
   a. Cass Peterson: "Studies indicate that increased ultraviolet radiation would exacerbate smog, adversely affect aquatic organisms, and possibly influence the climate" (Peterson, January/February 1988, p. 38).
   b. John Gribbon: "Soybean, a key crop in modern agriculture, suffers a 25 percent decrease in yield when UV-B is increased by 2 percent. Cattle, like people, are afflicted by eye complaints if UV-B is increased, including cancer eye and pink eye" (Gribbon, 5 May 1988, p. 4).
   c. Thomas Coohill, president of the American Society of Photobiology: "The entire food chain is potentially at risk. A 5% increase in ultraviolet light can cut the life of some microorganisms in half" (Mahoney, 28 March 1988, p. 22).

B. Opponents argue that the effects of CFCs on the ozone have been exaggerated.
   1. The depletion of the ozone over Antarctica is not indicative of what will happen over the rest of the world.
      a. Mack McFarland, member of the Fluorocarbon Program Panel, before the U.S. Senate Committee on Environment and Public Works: "The Antarctic phenomenon is highly unlikely to have global significance. The prelimi-

nary findings indicate that both unique climate conditions, meteorology, and unusual atmospheric chemistry contribute to the recently observed seasonal ozone decreases over Antarctica" (*Ozone Hole*, 1987, p. 15).

    b. John Gribbon: "The unique meteorology of the Antarctic means there is little prospect that the hole in the sky there will spread to cover the rest of the world" (Gribbon, 5 May 1988, p. 4).

  2. The data relating to worldwide depletion are not conclusive and, therefore, do not prove a negative correlation between CFCs emissions and ozone depletion.

  3. Other factors are accelerating the production of ozone and canceling out the effects of CFCs.

    a. Quotation from *The Economist*: "Emissions from carbon dioxide (from deforestation and the burning of fossil fuels) and methane (from paddy fields and farting livestock, among other things) are accelerating the production of ozone and canceling out the effect of CFCs" ("Can the Air Absolve," 19 September 1987, p. 97).

II. Are the present policies regarding ozone emission—the Montreal Protocol—incapable of solving the problems of depleting ozone?

  A. Advocates of a ban argue that the Montreal Protocol is not capable of sufficiently reducing the levels of chlorine in the atmosphere.

    1. With present restrictions, chlorine levels will continue to rise.

      a. Thomas Mahoney, journalist for *Air Conditioning, Heating and Refrigeration News*: "Even if CFC emissions are cut in half in the 1990's, the levels of chlorine gases in the atmosphere will continue to rise" (Mahoney, 28 March 1988, p. 22).

      b. Conrad MacKerron, journalist for *Chemical Week*: "DuPont notes that the Protocol now allows a nearly 100% increase in chlorine levels by 2050" (MacKerron, 6 April 1988, p. 7).

    2. The Montreal Protocol is not as strong as its proponents would have us believe.

      a. David Doniger, attorney for The Natural Resources Defense Council: "In Europe and Japan, ratification still meets resistance. Only Mexico and the U.S. have taken action" (MacKerron, 6 April 1988, p. 7).

      b. Conrad MacKerron: "An EPA staffer says provisions exempting the Soviet Union and allowing for continued growth of CFCs for 10 years in developing countries means the Protocol will result in a 40%, rather than a 50% cut" (MacKerron, 6 April 1988, p. 7).

3. The data used for determining control measures are poor.

a. Richard Kerr, in reference to a report by NASA's Ozone Trends Panel: "The models predict only small changes in ozone if the global production rate of CFCs were frozen. However, those same models did not predict the ozone decrease that has happened over the Northern Hemisphere during the past seventeen years" (Kerr, 25 March 1988, p. 1489).

b. Conrad MacKerron: "Chemist Sherwood Rowland states that his and later predictive models did not foresee the Antarctic ozone effect, so predictions remain risky" (MacKerron, 6 April 1988, p. 8).

4. CFCs must be eliminated in order to ensure safe ozone attainment levels.

a. Lee M. Thomas, EPA administrator: "The depletion that has already occurred calls into question our earlier projections of future damage. Regretfully, our *new* analysis predicts an even worse scenario than anticipated" (Associated Press, 27 September 1988, p. A1).

b. Conrad MacKerron: "DuPont is now urging that the 50% cut in CFC consumption agreed to in the Montreal Protocol be extended to 100%. The reason for the change in position is new evidence that the earth's ozone layer is being eroded up to four times more rapidly than had been previously thought" (MacKerron, 6 April 1988, p. 7).

c. Daniel Hall, journalist for *Supermarket News*: "DuPont, maker of about 25% of the world's CFCs, announced on April 10 that it planned to phase out production of CFCs over a ten year period" (Hall, 30 May 1988, p. 38).

d. "The major trade association of producers and users of CFCs said for the *first* time the world should aim at 'phasing out' CFCs to the maximum extent feasible" (Associated Press, 27 September 1988, p. A1).

B. Opponents argue that the Montreal Protocol is fully capable of eliminating the possible ozone depletion due to CFCs.

1. Present standards are sufficient in controlling the depletion due to CFC emissions.

a. Mack McFarland, member of the Fluorocarbon Program Panel, before the U.S. Senate Committee on Environment and Public Works: "Recent computer modeling studies of the impact of the Protocol show that, between now and 2060, calculated future reductions of stratospheric ozone will be less than natural fluctuations that have occurred over the past 30 years" (*Ozone Hole*, 1987, p. 16).

2. There are mechanisms built into the Montreal Protocol to allow for review of standards in light of scientific developments.

   a. John Negroponte, Assistant Secretary for Oceans and International Environmental and Scientific Affairs: "It sets out a schedule for controls based on current knowledge. But it also specifically provides for periodic assessment of scientific, environmental, technical, and economic developments, and for review of the protocol provisions on the basis of developing knowledge" (U.S. Dept. of State, December 1987, p. 61).

   b. Montreal Protocol, Article 6 and Article 2, sec. 9, a, ii: "The parties shall assess the control measures on the basis of available scientific, environmental, technical and economic information. . . . Based on the assessments, the parties may decide whether further reductions of production or consumption of the controlled substances should be undertaken" (UNEP, 1987, pp. 5, 8).

3. There are mechanisms built into the Montreal Protocol to ensure international cooperation.

   a. Montreal Protocol, Article 4, sec. 1 and sec. 7: "Each Party shall ban the import of controlled substances from any State not party to this Protocol . . . Each Party shall discourage the export, to any State not party to this Protocol, of technology for producing and for utilizing controlled substances" (UNEP, 1987, pp. 6, 7).

   b. Montreal Protocol, Article 8: "The Parties shall consider and approve procedures and institutional mechanisms for determining noncompliance with the provisions of this protocol and for treatment of Parties found to be in noncompliance" (UNEP, 1987, p. 8).

III. Will a ban on CFCs solve the problems of a depleting ozone layer?

A. Advocates of a ban argue that it would eventually reverse the effects of CFC use.

1. Elimination of CFC emissions would restore the ozone to its normal level.

   a. Conrad MacKerron: "DuPont notes that the Protocol now allows a nearly 100% increase in chlorine levels by 2050. The company says that tightening the Protocol to require a 95% cut would decrease chlorine levels by 75%" (MacKerron, 6 April 1988, p. 7).

    b. Chemist Sherwood Rowland: "The only way to repair the damage done to the ozone layer is to enact a total ban on CFC emissions and wait 200 years . . . the time needed to replenish the ozone" (MacKerron, 6 April 1988, p. 8).

2. The international community will be willing to cooperate in a ban.

    a. John Negroponte: "A consensus has emerged both in the U.S. and in the international community that the risks are sufficiently serious to warrant cooperative control measures" (U.S. Dept. of State, December 1987, p. 61).

    b. Mark Crawford, journalist for *Science:* "EPA analysts reveal that a U.S. ban on CFC compounds would impose steep cutbacks and force Western countries to develop CFC substitutes anyway" (Crawford, 28 November 1986, p. 929).

3. Replacement development, which would be a necessary result of a U.S. ban, will solve the problem of worldwide need for harmful CFCs.

    a. Premise: With good replacements available for the United States, other countries would be pressured by environmental groups, etc., to impose a ban also.

    b. The development of CFC replacements is making great progress (see IV, A, 2).

B. Opponents argue that a ban would be incapable of solving the problems of a depleting ozone layer.

1. Other producing countries would not participate in a ban.

    a. Cass Peterson: "Only a few nations took a cue from the United States and banned CFCs in aerosols" (Peterson, January/February 1988, p. 38).

2. A U.S. ban might escalate worldwide production of CFCs.

    a. Representative James Scheuer, before the U.S. House Committee on Science, Space, and Technology: "Even if we prohibited their use, the Europeans and Japanese might well step in and increase their production CFCs" (*Stratospheric Ozone Depletion,* 1987, p. 2).

3. The data used to determine the results of a total ban are poor.

    a. Kevin Fay, director of the CFC Alliance: "The NASA report shows that the scientific models remain unreliable. So it is not clear whether faster cuts in ozone consumption will have a significant effect" (MacKerron, 6 April 1988, p. 8).

IV. Will the benefits of protecting the ozone layer from CFCs justify the costs of a ban?

    A. Advocates of a ban argue that the benefits of the elimination of harmful CFCs would far outweigh any costs of a ban.

        1. The costs incurred by a ban will be insignificant compared to the benefits that will be afforded to our environment due to a ban.

        2. The related industries would still prosper due to CFC replacements that are presently being developed.

           a. Joani Nelson-Horchler, journalist for *Industry Week*: "DuPont says substitutes will become commercially available in five to seven years" (Nelson-Horchler, 15 February 1988, p. 21).

           b. David Lee, program analyst for the EPA: "R-134A, an alternative to R-12, has been developed by DuPont Co." (Hall, 30 May 1988, p. 38).

           c. Richard Koenig, journalist for the *Wall Street Journal*: "HCFC 22 contains little chlorine and is regarded as less of an environmental threat than the CFC it would replace. HCFC 22, already in refrigerants for residential air conditioners, is now finding a new use in foam-plastic packaging" (Koenig, 28 March 1988, p. 6).

           d. Richard Koenig: "Petroferm Inc., a specialty chemicals company in Fernandina Beach, Florida, is finding a market for cleaning solvents it derives from several natural sources, including orange rinds" (Koenig, 28 March 1988, p. 6).

           e. Richard Koenig: "Cryodyamics Inc., a small company in Mountainside, N.J., has been trying to find new uses for cooling devices that make use of helium. They have already been used in cooling aircraft" (Koenig, 28 March 1988, p. 6).

    B. Opponents argue that the problems created by a ban would far outweigh any alleged benefits.

        1. The cost to the "user" sector of the industry would be great.

           a. Joani Nelson-Horchler: "Replacing CFCs in kind will be very difficult since they are nonflammable, noncorrosive, low in toxicity, chemically inert and very stable" (Nelson-Horchler, 15 February 1988, p. 21).

           b. Laurie Hays, journalist for the *Wall Street Journal*: "It will cost hundreds of millions of dollars in research and plant construction" (Hays, 28 March 1988, p. 6).

    c. David Lee: "When the alternative refrigerant becomes available (R-134A), its price may be three to five times the present cost of R-12" (Hall, 30 May 1988, p. 38).

    d. Russ Griffith, manager of application engineering for Copeland Corporation: "Refrigeration systems used now are highly engineered for specific purposes and are designed to run using one refrigerant. Switching refrigerants should not be taken lightly since it can lead to costly equipment changes" (Hall, 30 May 1988, p. 38).

    e. Laurie Hays: "Under the worst circumstances, producers would stop making CFCs before substitutes are available. Shortages would develop, prices would skyrocket and manufacturers of appliances such as refrigerators would go bankrupt" (Hays, 28 March 1988, p. 6).

    f. Laurie Hays: "If DuPont says we choose to get out of this, DuPont goes on. But GE can't just say we won't make refrigerators. It's a much tougher position for user industries" (Hays, 28 March 1988, p. 6).

2. U.S. producers would lose business on the international market because of "inferior replacements."

3. A ban without sufficient alternatives would cause health risks.

    a. Joseph Steed, DuPont: "Severe CFC cuts before alternatives are available could threaten human health. For example, restrictions on refrigeration would make food preservation difficult. Also, air tight buildings would have to be redesigned if air conditioning is curtailed" (MacKerron, 6 April 1988, p. 7).

Bibliography

Associated Press. "EPA Urges More Action to Protect Ozone Layer." *The Coloradoan,* 27 September 1988, p. A1.

Can the Air Absolve Man's Sins of Emission?" *The Economist,* 304 (19 September 1987): 97.

Crawford, Mark. "U.S. Floats Proposal to Help Prevent Global Ozone Depletion." *Science,* 234 (28 November 1986): 927–29.

Gribbon, John. "The Ozone Layer." *New Scientist,* 118 (5 May 1988): 1–4.

Hall, Daniel. "Replacing CFC Refrigerant Seen Exacting a High Price." *Supermarket News,* 38 (30 May 1988): 38–41.

Hays, Laurie. "CFC Curb to Save Ozone Will Be Costly." *Wall Street Journal,* 28 March 1988, p. 6.

Kerr, Richard A. "Stratospheric Ozone Is Decreasing." *Science,* 239 (25 March 1988): 1489–1491.

Koenig, Richard. "Search for Substitutes for Refrigerants Shows Some Progress But Has Far to Go." *Wall Street Journal,* 28 March 1988, p. 6.

Lindley, David. "CFCs Cause Part of Global Ozone Decline." *Nature,* 332 (24 March 1988): 201–203.

MacKerron, Conrad B. "How Long a Farewell to CFC Production?" *Chemical Week,* 142 (6 April 1988): 7–8

Mahoney, Thomas A. "Evidence of Ozone Loss Deepens Urgency of New CFC Substitutes." *Air Conditioning, Heating and Refrigeration News,* 173 (28 March 1988): 22.

Nelson–Horchler, Joani. "Ozone's Price Tag." *Industry Week,* 236 (15 February 1988): 21.

Peterson, Cass. "High Anxiety: Ozone." *Sierra,* 73 (January/February 1988): 34–39.

Rodgers, Clive. "Global Ozone Trends Reassessed." *Nature,* 332 (17 March 1988): 293–294.

United Nations Environment Programme. *Montreal Protocol on Substances That Deplete the Ozone Layer: Final Act.* 16 September 1987. UNEP, 1987.

U.S. Department of State. "Montreal Protocol." *Department of State Bulletin,* 87 (December 1987): 60–63.

United States House. Committee on Science, Space, and Technology. Subcommittee on Natural Resources, Agricultural Research, and Environment. *Stratospheric Ozone Depletion: Hearing, March 10 and 12, 1987.* 100th Congress, 1st Session, 1987.

United States Senate. Committee on Commerce, Science, and Transportation. Subcommittee on Science, Technology, and Space and The National Ocean Policy Study. *Global Environment Change Research: Hearing July 16, 1987.* 100th Congress, 1st Session, 1987.

United States Senate. Committee on Environment and Public Works. Subcommittee on Environmental Protection and Hazardous Waste and Toxic Substances. *Implication of the Findings of the Expedition to Investigate the Ozone Hole over the Antarctic: Joint Hearing, October, 27, 1987.* 100th Congress, 1st Session, 1987.

Index ―――――――――――――

Acceptance of applied
   generalization, 161
Admitted issues, 69–70
Advocacy, procedural rules,
   224–250
Affirmative cases in debate,
   252–270
   criteria, 252–254
   fact and value questions, 263–268
   policy questions, 254–263
Agreement, method of causation,
   146–147
Alleged facts, 60
Ambiguous terms, 82–83
Analogy as an argument form,
   138–143, 162
   tests, 141–143, 163
Analysis, definition of, 25
Anger, 14–15
Applied generalization as an
   argument form, 158–161, 162
   tests, 160–161, 163
Appropriateness of statistical unit,
   198–199
Arbitrary constitutive rules, 225
Argument, 41–45. *See also*
   Rhetorical argument
   adapting to audience, 44–45
   from ignorance, 291–292
   patterns of, 54–55
   rhetorical definition of, 43–44
   tests of, 102–104
Argument brief. *See* Briefs
Argument forms, analysis of,
   132–167
   analogy 138–143
   applied generalization, 158–161

causal application, 154–158
causal correlation, 143–149
example, 133–138
sign, 149–154
summary analysis, 162
and tests, 163
Argumentation:
   and avoidance, 311
   and award, 320
   and compromise, 318
   and conquest, 313–314
   definition of, 19
   and reconciliation, 316
Aristotle, 2, 8, 10, 12, 13, 14, 15,
   17, 19, 55, 58, 73, 117, 123,
   133, 151, 188
Arnauld, Antoine, 252
Assertion:
   definition of, 44
   test of, 179–180, 202
Assumption of uniformity, 107–108
Audience:
   adapting to in argument, 44–45
   beliefs and case strategy,
      257–258, 267–268
   proof based on, 13–16
Auer, J. Jeffery, 239
Author of source, 185–186
Authoritative testimony, 117
Avoidance as conflict termination
   method, 309–311
Award as conflict termination
   method, 309, 318–320

Backing, definition of, 122
Behavior and regulative rules, 227
Bernard, Jessie, 299

Berne, Eric, 224
Bias of source, test of, 190–191, 202
Bibliographic sources, 88–90
Bibliography, sample of, 331
Bitzer, Loyd, 129
Boulding, Kenneth, 309
Briefs, 208–221
　constructing, 211–213
　definition of, 208
　developing, 208–210
　example of, 371–380
　illustrative, 214–221, 371–380
Bullying tactic, 179–180
Burden of proof, 229–230, 232–235, 253
　for comparative advantages, 259–260
　definition of, 232–233
　rules of, 235–239
Business Periodicals Index, 89

Card catalog, 88
Case strategies, affirmative, 254–268
　fact and value questions, 263–268
　policy questions, 254–263
Case strategies, negative, 277–294
　fact and value questions, 290–294
　policy questions, 277–290
Categorical syllogism, 116
Causal application as an argument form, 154–158, 162
　tests, 157–158, 163
Causal correlation as an argument form, 143–149, 162
　tests, 147–149, 163
Causation, methods for discovering, 146–147
Cause-effect relationships. *See* Causal application as an argument form; Causal correlation as an argument form
Central questions, 25–38
　expressing, 34–35
　fact, 26–30
　and issues, 38, 39
　phrasing, 34–38, 243
　policy, 33–34

value, 30–32
Chance mechanisms as conflict termination method, 309, 320–321
Cicero, 55
CIS Index, 89
Claims, 98–99. *See also* Supporting claims
　definition of, 98
Classical probability, 108–109
Cognitive avoidance as conflict termination method, 310–311
Coherence in causal correlation, 149
Common ground, definition of, 86
Comparative advantages case, 258–263
　illustration, 260–263
Comparison in analogy, 141–142
Comparison issue, 68
　in counterproposal, 288
Competitiveness:
　of counterproposal, 286–287
　and hostility, 303
Compromise as conflict termination method, 309, 316–318
Conclusion, definition of, 42
Concomitant variation, method of causation, 146
Conflict, 2–5, 299–308
　avoiding, 2–3, 4
　behavior, purpose of, 303–305
　hostility, 300–307
　issue, 299–300, 303–307
　responses to, 4–5
　using force, 4–5
Conflict termination, methods of, 308–321
　avoidance, 309–311
　award, 309, 318–320
　chance mechanisms, 309, 320–321
　compromise, 309, 316–318
　conquest, 309, 311–314
　reconciliation, 309, 314–316
Congressional Digest, 90
Congressional Quarterly Weekly Report, 90
Conjecture, stasis of, 56, 60, 61

Conjectural case, 264–265, 291–292
Conjectural issue, 56, 73
Conquest as conflict termination
method, 309, 311–314, 323
Consistency:
in causal correlation, 148–149
test of, 193–195, 202
Constitutive rules, 224–226
Containment principle, 113–114
Contested issues, 69–70
Context:
definition of, 193
test of, 193, 202
Contradiction:
of examples, 138
of signs in argument, 154
Controversy:
analyzing issues, 38–41, 54–55
analyzing stasis model, 55–62
central questions, 25–38
causes of, 83–84
key elements in, 82–86
overview, 24–51
participants in, 84
stock issues model, 62–73
Corax, 7, 17, 55
Corporate expertise, 189–190
Coser, Lewis, 3, 230
Cost issue, 66–67
Counterarguments, 173. *See also*
Counterproposal
Counterplan. *See* Counterproposal
Counterproposal, 286–290
and repairs, relationship,
289–290
Critical characteristics of statistical
sample, 197
Cure issue, 66

Debate:
affirmative cases. *See* Affirmative
cases in debate
definition of, 239
illustration of, 348–370
negative cases. *See* Negative
cases in debate
rules for, 239–248
uses and limitations in
terminating conflict, 323–324

Debate formats, 247–248
and speaker responsibilities,
337–347
Deductive arguments, 151–152
Deductive reasoning, 112–120
enthymeme, 116–117
necessity of, 114–115
principle of containment, 113–114
syllogism, 114, 116
truth vs. acceptance, 118–120
validity, 115
Defense of present system, 277–281
Defining terms, 82–83, 118–119
Definition, stasis of, 56
Definitional case, 265–267, 292–294
Definitional issue, 56–57, 59, 74
Degree of belief, definition of, 111
Degrees of confirmation probability,
110–111
Deliberative persuasion, 17
Denial, strategy of, 284
Description in analogy, 142–143
Descriptive statistics, 195–196
Difference, method of causation, 147
Discerning, 43
definition of, 9
power of, 7–9
Discovering issues, 54–55
Distortion of comparison, 199–200

Education Index, 89
Egos and argument, 230
Emotional appeals, 13–14
Enthymeme, 116–118
definition of, 116
Epideictic persuasion, 18
Ethos, 9–13
Evidence, 41–42, 48
card, 92, 93
definition of, 48, 177
and factual premises, 177–178,
202
incomplete, 105–106, 134
source, 184–191, 202
substance, 192–201, 202
testing. *See* Testing evidence and
premises
Evidence-claim relationship,
178–184, 202

Example as an argument form,
133–138, 162
tests, 136–138, 163
Exceptions in applied
generalizations, 161
Experienced vs. inexperienced
individuals, 11
Expert opinion, 182–183, 186,
187–190
Expertise:
of audience, 188
of source, test of, 187–190, 202
External consistency, 193–195

Fact, questions of, 26–30
Fact and value questions:
affirmative, 263–268
negative, 290–294
Factual evidence, 177–178
Factual premises, 45–47
Faculty, definition of, 9
Fairness, rule of, 37
Field standards for argument,
124–125
Figurative analogy, definition of,
140
Foster, William, 242
Frequency probability, 109–110
Future facts, 29–30

Good moral character, definition of,
12–13
Good reasons, 43, 44, 99–101
and definitions, 225–226
vs. ordinary reasons, 99–100
and regulative rules, 227–228
relevance of, 103–104
sufficiency of, 104
truth or acceptance, 103
Good sense, definition of, 10–11
Goodwill, definition of, 11–12
Grounds, definition of, 120–122

Hearsay evidence, 185, 189
Hermagorus, 55
Homer, 7
Honesty of evidence, 192–193
Hostility conflict, 300–303

and issue conflict, 303–307
positive, 307–308
and termination methods,
322–323
Humanities Index, 89

Identification of source, test of,
185–187, 202
Ignorance, argument from, 291–292
Illustrative brief, 214–221, 371–380
Immediate causes, 83–84
Incomplete evidence, 134
Incompleteness, 105–106
Index Medicus, 90
Index to Legal Periodicals, 89–90
*Index to U. S. Government
Periodicals*, 89
Inductive arguments, 151–152
Inductive reasoning, 104–112, 134,
138, 143
assumption of uniformity,
107–108
patterns of, 106–107
probability, 108–112
Inferences, known to unknown,
106, 135
Inferential statistics, 195–196
Informal settings and rules,
228–229
Infotrak database, 88
Inherent, definition of, 39, 68
Institutionalized settings and rules,
228
Integrity, test of, 192–193, 202
Internal Conflict. *See* Conflict
Internal consistency, 193–195
Intervention and causal application,
158
Issue conflict, 299–300
and hostility conflict, 303–307
and termination methods, 322
Issues, 38–41. *See also* Discovering
issues
admitted, 69–70
and central questions, 38, 39
contested, 69–70
focus research, 81–82
potential, 69–70

Karnap, Rudolph, 108, 110–111
Key terms, identification of, 87

Literal analogy, definition of, 140
Locke, John, 132
Logic, 18–19, 42–43, 103–104, 125
Logos, 16–19
  and argument form, 18–19
  and argumentation, 19
  relationship to ethos and pathos,
    9–16

Manipulation of statistics, 199–200
Manipulative persuasion, 24
Message, proof based on, 16–19
Mill, John Stuart, 146
Monthly Catalog of U.S. Govern-
  ment Publications, 89
Motive issue, 64–65, 73

Necessity in sign argument,
  152–153
Necessity of deductive conclusions,
  114–115
Negative cases in debate, 272–296
  fact and value questions, 290–294
  policy questions, 277–290
  principles for construction,
    272–277
New York Times Index, 88–89
Number of examples, 137
Number of signs of argument, 153

Obstacle issue, 65–66
Opinion evidence, 178

Participants in a controversy, 84
Past facts, 27–28
Pathos, 13–16
Patterns of arguments, 54–55
Perelman, Chaim, 97
Persuasion, study of, 7
Persuasiveness of case, 252–253
Phrasing central questions, 34–38,
  243
Physical avoidance as conflict
  termination method, 310
Physical conquest as conflict
  termination method, 311–312

Place of publication of evidence, 187
Policy questions, 33–34
  affirmative, 254–263
  negative, 277–290
Post hoc fallacy, 148
Potential issues, 69–70
Premises, 41–42, 45–48
  definition of, 42, 45
  factual and value, 45–48,
    170–177, 201
  testing. *See* Testing evidence and
    premises
Present belief or policy, 84–85
  administrative elements, 279
  principles of, 278, 280–281
Present facts, 28–29
Presumption, 229–232
  advantage of, 273–274, 284
  definition of, 230–231
  rules of, 235–239
Prima facie case, 234, 253
Primary source of evidence,
  186–187
Principal stock issues, 62, 63–64
Probability, 104, 135
  concepts of, 108–112
  definition of, 108
Problem and advantage,
  relationship, 258–259
Procedural issue, 56, 58–59, 69
Procedural rules in advocacy,
  224–250
Procedure, stasis of, 56
Proof:
  based on audience, 13–16
  based on message, 16–19
  based on speaker, 9–13
  burden of. *See* Burden of proof
  modes of, 9–19
Proposed belief of policy, 85
Public Affairs Information Service
  (PAIS), 88
Public polls, 135

Qualifiers, definition of, 122
Qualitative issue, 56, 57–58
Quality:
  issue, 74
  stasis of, 56, 60, 61

Questions:
  of fact, 26–30
  of policy, 33–34
  of value, 30–32

*Reader's Guide to Periodical
    Literature*, 88
Reading research materials, 90–91
Reasoning, 106
Rebuttal, definition of, 122
Rebuttal form, 332–336
Recency, test of, 182–183, 202
Reconciliation as conflict termination
    method, 309, 314–316, 323
Recording evidence, 91–92
Refutation, 173. *See also* Straight
    refutation
Regulative rules, 224–225, 227–229
Reichenbach, Hans, 109
Relevance, test of, 180–182, 202
Repairs strategy, 281–283
Representativeness:
  of examples, 137–138
  of statistical sample, 196–198
Research process, 80–94
  focus of, 80–86
  locating materials, 86–90
  reading and writing materials,
    90–92
Resolution/termination potential,
    305–307
Resolutions, 34–35
Revenge, 301–302
Rhetoric:
  definition of, 9, 19
  nature of, 5–9
Rhetoric and argumentation:
  conflict termination, 308–321
  constitutive rules, 226
  nature of social conflict, 299–308
  overview, 2–22
  relationship to logic, 43
  in social conflict, 298–329
  termination methods in social
    conflict, 322–325
Rhetorical argument:
  argument field, 124–125
  deductive reasoning, 112–120
  and good reasons, 96–129

inductive reasoning, 104–112
nature of, 97–101
structure of, 101–125
tests of argument, 102–104
Toulmin model of argument,
    120–124
Rhetorical syllogism, 116–118
Rule of fairness, 37, 69
Rules. *See* Procedural rules in
    advocacy

Salmon, Wesley, 103
Sample selection (statistical),
    method of, 197
Secondary source of evidence,
    186–187
Self-selecting statistical sample,
    197–198
Sign as an argument form,
    149–154, 162
  tests, 152–154, 163
Size of statistical sample, 197
Slighting, 15
So what? test, 171–174, 201
Social Sciences Index, 89
Social conflict. *See* Rhetoric and
    argumentation, in social conflict
Speaker, proof based on, 9–13
  good sense, 10–11
  goodwill, 11–12
  moral character, 12–13
Stasis:
  definition of, 55, 60, 61
  and value comparisons, 60–62
Stasis model, 55–62
  application of, 59–62
  in relation to stock issues model,
    73–74
Statistics:
  appropriateness of, 198–199
  as evidence, 195–201, 202
  manipulation of, 199–200
Status quo, 232
Stock issues:
  definition of, 62
  using, 70–73
Stock issues model, 62–73
  analysis of, 70–72
  logos of, 64–67

phrasing of, 62
principal issues, 62, 63–64
in relation to stasis model, 73–74
subordinate issues, 62–63,
    67–68
Straight refutation, 284–286
Strength in causal correlation, 148
Subordinate stock issues, 62–63,
    67–68
Suetonius, 59
Sufficiency of causal application,
    157–158
Sufficiency:
    of causal application, 157–158
    test of, 183–184, 202
Supporting claims, 96, 100–101,
    104, 134, 139–140, 144–145,
    150–151, 155–157, 158–160,
    183
Syllogism, definition of, 116
Syllogism model, 114
Symbolic conquest as conflict
    termination method, 312–313

Termination potential, 311
Tests of:
    argument, 102–104
    assertion, 179–180, 202
    bias of source, 190–191, 202
    consistency, 193–195, 202
    context, 193, 202
    expertise of source, 187–190,
        202
    identification of source, 185–187,
        202
    integrity, 192–193, 202
    recency, 182–183, 202
    relevance, 180–182, 202
    statistical evidence, 195–201, 202
    sufficiency, 183–189, 202
Testing evidence and premises,
    170–206

evidence source, 184–191
evidence substance, 192–201
evidence-claim relationship,
    178–184
factual, 177–178
value premises, 170–177
Third-party agencies, 319
Time in causal correlation, 148–149
Time in relationship between
    evidence and claim, 182–183
Topics suited to comparative
    advantages, 260
Toulmin, Stephen, 129
    model of argument, 120–124
Traditional needs case, 254–258
Truth:
    in causal application, 157
    and deductive premises, 118–120

Uniformity:
    assumption of, 107–108
    of nature principle, 135

Validity, 115
Value application or interpretation
    test, 176–177, 201
Value comparisons:
    and stasis, 60–62
    test, 174–176, 201
Value disputes and stasis, 60
Value premises, 47–48, 170–177,
    201
    definition of, 170
    tests of, 201
Value questions, 30–32
Value term, definition of, 31

Wallace, Karl, 97
Warrant, definition of, 122
Weary listeners, 46–47
White lies, 12
Willard, Charles, 103

LEWIS AND CLARK COLLEGE LI
PORTLAND, OREGON 972

Lewis and Clark College - Watzek Library
PN4181 .V36 1993   wmain
Vancil, David L./Rhetoric and argumentat

3 5209 00460 8861